AF847364

MYSTERIES OF THE WORLD

MYSTERIES OF THE WORLD

UNEXPLAINED WONDERS AND MYSTERIOUS PHENOMENA

Parragon

Bath • New York • Cologne • Melbourne • Delhi
Hong Kong • Shenzhen • Singapore • Amsterdam

Contents

Myth or Reality? 92

Contemporary Mysteries

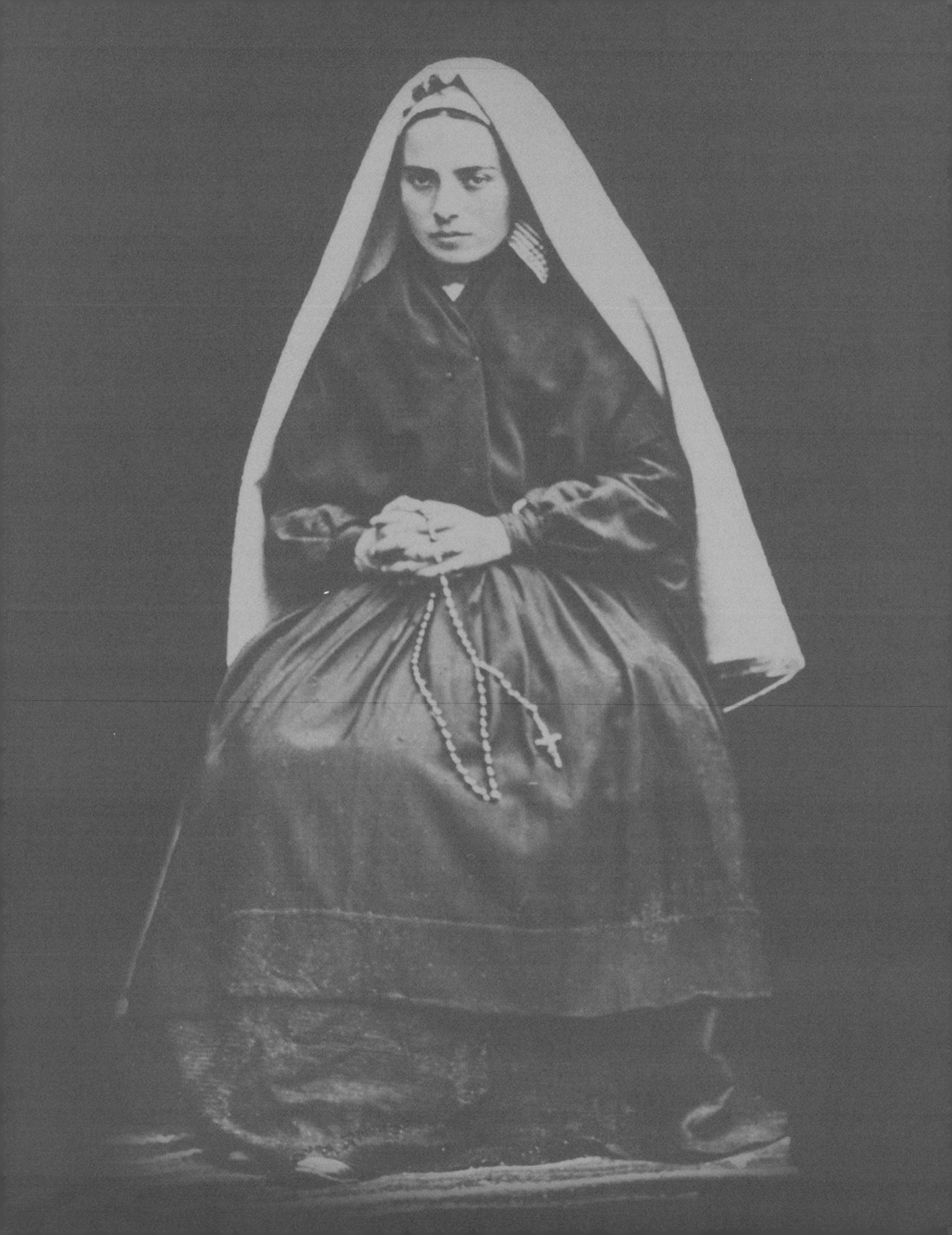

Foreword

We live in a highly developed, technologically advanced society, but there are nevertheless a great many mysteries all around us. Ancient places and mysterious beings, sunken worlds and cultures, landscapes imbued with symbolism, unexplained apparitions and unbelievable finds from ancient times – all of these remain mysteries for humankind, despite intense investigation.

While many mysteries have been partially or completely solved, their grip upon our imagination is rarely broken. Atlantis, for instance, the legendary island empire lost beneath the sea, has been the subject of speculation for over two thousand years. Although many investigators are convinced that the island never existed, there are nonetheless individuals today who set off in search of it in the firm belief that sunken Atlantis is more than a myth. The pyramids of the Egyptian pharaohs continue to fascinate us as much as they ever have, as does the curse of Tutankhamun, which is believed by some to have caused the death of many people associated with the excavation. Are these tales mere superstition – or reality?

This book explores mysteries that continue to intrigue us. Among these are holy places and ancient sites located at power vortices, about whose builders we know very little. Topics also include legendary civilizations and their lost cultures, about which so little information was left behind. Who were these people exactly, and how did they acquire their secret knowledge? Did they receive assistance from alien life forms, as several respected researchers have concluded? Are there people who are genuinely in contact with ghosts and the walking dead? We will also look at more recent mysteries, such as UFO sightings and the ever-puzzling phenomenon of crop circles. Finally, we will consider subjects that fall under the heading of parascience because, at least in part, they challenge and cast doubt on the canon of "serious" science.

One thing is certain: legend and myth overlap with archaeology and the natural sciences in a number of different areas. Full of fascinating questions about the mysteries of the world, this book presents a variety of interpretations, all the while on the track of those enigmatic forces that surround us all....

Saint Bernadette Soubirous died in 1879 at the age of 35. When her grave was opened forty years later in 1919, her body showed no sign of decay – an unexplained mystery. Overlaid with a coat of wax, today her body lies in a shrine in the convent chapel of Nevers, France.

Puzzling Remains of Earlier Cultures

Mysterious Places

Legendary ancient places tell stories that provide archaeologists and historians with information that is essential for the study of culture. In the past, we have often been less than careful with old buildings and religious sites, many of which were left to fall into decay after their abandonment. Lack of repair and natural forces took care of the rest, leaving the larger part of most ancient sites in ruins.

These ruins can still yield a lot of information about the production, form and quality of building materials. They can also tell us what led to their destruction. The location and function of the structures can be used to help interpret past cults and cultures.

The following chapter presents cultural remains that have become woven into numerous myths and legends, and at the same time continue to present what seem to be insoluble riddles to both scholars and the general public. Many of these mysterious places are said to be located in so-called power vortices, locations where the strong powers of the earth are concentrated. Earlier cultures recognized these places, and knew how to use them.

For centuries, the famous circle of stones at Stonehenge has raised questions for scholars that haven't been satisfactorily answered even today. No one knows who erected this monumental work, when, or why.

With an oval plan and five terraced levels, the so-called Magician's Pyramid, located in the Mayan city of Uxmal, is one of the world's most unusual pyramids.

Pyramids

Pyramids are found not only in the Egyptian Valley of the Kings, but exist throughout the entire world. They stand in Sudan and Iraq, in Mexico, Chile, Guatemala and were even part of Ancient Rome. We find them in the Philippines just as we find them in Austria. Not long ago, a pyramid was even discovered underwater off the south coast of Japan. Many of these structures were only partially investigated until quite recently, and some remain unexplored to this day due to their inaccessibility.

Are pyramids burial monuments?

We may well think that, in most cases, pyramids are burial monuments. However, there is also evidence that there were other reasons for their construction. The pharaoh Snofru, father of the famed Cheops, for example, built five pyramids during his reign, which began in 2575 BC and continued an estimated forty-eight years. Among these are the Bent Pyramid (see box on page 16) and the Red Pyramid located in Dashur, Lower Egypt.

One theory is that the pharaohs used these imposing structures to demonstrate their strength and power. Other researchers maintain that the pyramids were erected to facilitate astronomical observations. The plans of many of the pyramids are clearly oriented according to the four cardinal points of the compass, and we now know that Egyptian astronomy was a very highly developed science. This provides some support for the astronomical theory, although direct evidence is lacking.

> **European pyramids**
> The first pyramids in Europe are fairly recent in date, though they were inspired by the ancient pyramids. Built in 1989, the glass pyramid standing in front of the Louvre in Paris is an example. Similarly modern is the pyramid of the Euromed Klinik in Furth, Germany. In contrast, the Karlsruhe pyramid that has become a symbol of the city goes back to the nineteenth century (1823), as do the two pyramids in the park and castle of Branitz in Cottbus (1856/57). In the Neuer Garten in Potsdam there is a pyramid built in the Classical style (1791/92).
>
> One in Rome, dating to approximately 20 BC, was named after its patron, Gaius Cestius. What is probably the oldest known European pyramid lies in the Austrian forest between Zwettl and Gross-Gerungs. It is thought to be over two thousand years old.

Naturally, there are also pyramids that quite clearly did serve as burial monuments. Taking into account the fact that robbers plundered nearly all of the graves in the Valley of the Kings, with Tutankhamun's tomb the only exception, we can assume that over the course of the millennia these highly visible superstructures also attracted thieves. In fact, nearly every pyramid known shows traces of break-ins. This would explain why there are rarely any burial gifts or mummies found.

Building a pyramid

It is still not entirely clear how the ancients went about building a pyramid. These structures would be difficult to realize even with the modern construction methods available to us today. Given that so many pyramids have been built by such a wide variety of cultures, it is probable that more than one construction method was used.

At the end of the 1980s, a French chemist named Joseph Davidovits published a theory stating that the stones of one of these pyramids – in this case, an Egyptian pyramid – had been manufactured on location using a mixture of crushed limestone and other materials that were combined with water. This sludge would then be poured into a form made of wood, clay, or brick that was set in the desired spot, where it would slowly harden into a block. For general application, however, this theory is easily disproved. Egyptian pyramids, in particular, show many examples of irregularly fitted, poorly laid stones. Nevertheless, it is certainly possible that this perfectly straightforward method was in use in other places.

Most scholars accept the theory that the stones were transported from a quarry to the desired building site, where workers pushed or pulled the stones to their ultimate locations using a ramp that grew taller as the pyramid increased in height. Some interpretations go further, arguing that the ramp itself would later become part of the pyramid. Voids would be left during the construction phase that would later be closed by the ramp stones. Although some recent evidence supports the use of a ramp, definitive proof is still lacking; and in some cases a ramp can be completely excluded because there simply is not enough space available at the site.

It is assumed that the underwater pyramid found in the Sea of Japan was originally built directly on the coast. The structure is now underwater because sea level has risen nearly 100 feet (30 m) over the last millennium.

The Step Pyramid of Djoser in Sakkara is one of Egypt's first monumental stone structures. It was built around 2700 BC.

Rumours and riddles

Even pyramids that have been thoroughly investigated can still continue to harbour secrets. While there have always been rumours about the valuable treasures that might be found inside certain secret hallways and chambers, scholarship and excavations have at times contributed to the mystery, rather than clearing it up. Their discoveries continually reaffirm suspicions that there is still more to be found within.

While working within the Bent Pyramid in 1839, for example, the British archaeologists John Shae Perring and Howard Vyse reported that the wind rushing through the passageways inside the pyramid was so strong and so cold at times that it was necessary to stop the excavation. Yet there was no connection between the interior of the pyramid and the outside world except for the passage through which the archaeologists had entered. In the 1950s, the Egyptian researcher Ahmed Fakhry mentioned sounds that could be heard inside the pyramid on windy days. The cause of both of these phenomena has not yet been explained. It is possible that other openings and additional rooms are allowing air to enter, which then circulates within the pyramid's interior, causing draughts and noise.

The Bent Pyramid

The Bent Pyramid of Dashur was built in the Fourth Dynasty (2639–2504 BC) under the pharaoh Snofru. Its name comes from the reduction of the angle of its slope during construction, which left it with a distinct bend halfway to the top. This alteration was apparently necessary to ensure the stability of the pyramid. The poor quality soils beneath the structure were subsiding and could have led to its collapse. Reducing the angle of the slope, along with some additional modifications, ensured that the pyramid could at least be completed.

The Bent Pyramid was the first Egyptian pyramid not designed to be a step pyramid.

According to a rumour that has been in circulation for centuries, the builders of the pyramids left behind signs or numerical puzzles as messages for their descendents, or the gods. There are also claims that all the pyramids throughout the world are oriented to the north, and that this implies they were all erected according to a global plan. This particularly persistent rumour is nevertheless very easily explained. Nearly all the Egyptian pyramids are oriented according to the cardinal points of the compass because of the long-standing Egyptian interest in astronomy. All other pyramids from more recent centuries that follow the Egyptian model were probably not consciously oriented in this fashion.

The claim that the pyramids were built to serve as oversized sundials is also without merit. After all, some pyramids have shadows that fall on ravines or rivers. In addition, because of their base width, the shadows cast by pyramids are not particularly well suited to defining a single point on a solar clock.

Finally, it is claimed that the pyramids were constructed according to a strict formula, whereby the base area would permit the calculation of the pyramid's height. The example of the Bent Pyramid proves this false (*see* box above). It is not the area of the base that is crucial for the pyramid's height, but the angle of its outer walls – and this depended both on the personal taste of the builder and the technical skills of his workers. This false assumption was the undoing number of scholars in the past, including Charles Piazzi Smyth (1819–1900), who, standing close to the top of a buried pyramid, wanted to calculate how long one would have to dig to reach the bottom.

Naturally, there are a great many additional riddles and rumours surrounding the pyramids. Most of these refer back to still older tales, which in general suggest that their truth content is rather low.

The glass pyramid erected in the courtyard of the Louvre in 1989 is the work of the Chinese-American architect I.M. Pei.

The pyramids were the symbol of the ancient Mayan city of Tikal, located in present day Guatemala. With a height of 235 feet (72 m), this is the tallest known Mayan pyramid.

The Pyramids of Giza

The most famous pyramids in the world are found in the Egyptian city of Giza, near Cairo. Already described by Herodotus, they are the only one of his Seven Wonders of the World that has survived into the present-day. Their history and function have attracted more interest than any other ancient remains. Rather than recount the numerous rumours and mysteries surrounding these structures, two new theories based on recently acquired data are presented below.

Herodotus and the slaves

When the historian Herodotus (ca. 484–420 BC) presented his list of the Seven Wonders of the World around 450 BC, he promulgated the image of hardworking slaves, forced to move heavy blocks of stone all year long to construct the pyramids. In the last few years it has become increasingly clear that his impression was false and that the pyramids were, in fact, built by free workers.

The starting point for this new theory is the Nile River, which in antiquity was the life-blood of the fertile Nile delta, and also torrential – overrunning its banks every year between June and October, flooding large areas of land. The Nile silt that was deposited into the fields and fertilized the soil was one of the main reasons Egyptian civilization was able to develop in such a magnificent fashion. The annual flooding, therefore, was not perceived as a catastrophe, but just the opposite, as a blessing.

In order to celebrate this event appropriately, and presumably to keep the population busy during the flood season, the pharaoh had his subjects work on the pyramids every year during those four months. This resulted in a closer bond between the ruler and his people and provided the basis for an expansion of knowledge in a number of different fields. This, in turn, contributed to the development of the society as a whole. We now know that new professions came into existence and developed right on the building site. Doctors cared for the injured; bones found show that breaks were well healed, indicating the presence of good medical care at the site. Bakers supplying the workers with food exchanged ideas and acquired experience. There were even administrators who, by means of writing found on stone tablets, kept track of how long individual workers were employed.

The pyramids of Giza were built some 4500 years ago on a plateau near the present-day metropolis of Cairo. They were originally clad in white limestone.

In the depths of the pyramid

It is often said that many pyramids hide exceptional treasures. For the Great Pyramid of Giza, this statement has practically been accepted as fact. According to legend, in fact, there is a chamber underneath the pyramid that contains a library in which all the wisdom of Ancient Egypt is yet preserved.

When it became evident at the end of the 1980s that some of the stones of the Great Pyramid were becoming mouldy due to their exposure to human perspiration, a climate-control system was installed there. After work in the King's Chamber was successfully carried out, the Queen's Chamber proved to be more problematic. Unlike the King's Chamber, the shafts leading to the Queen's Chamber did not connect to the outside, but to dead ends. A robot was sent into the passageways to investigate. In the south shaft the robot unexpectedly ran into stones, decorated with two linear markings, that blocked its path. The press immediately jumped on the story of the Chamber of Knowledge and a research team began to make plans for the removal of the blockade.

In 2002, a more sophisticated new robot fitted with both a drill and a camera was sent into the shaft. Due to the intense interest from the international press, it was decided that the process of boring through the stones blocking the passageway would be broadcast live on television. After drilling through the stone, the robot's arm extended a camera into the hole it had made, transmitting images of the shaft on the other side.

The disappointment was great as it became clear that behind the blockade there was nothing but a further continuation of the empty passage, approximately 18 inches (45 cm) long, which again ended in a stone that apparently belonged to the outer wall.

The Sphinx also plays a role in some of the legends surrounding the Giza pyramids. According to one story, there is still an immense treasure hidden in an underground passageway leading from one of the pyramids to this guardian figure.

Nevertheless, this stone must be moved aside as well in order to be sure that no additional chamber is hidden behind it. Time will tell whether or not there really is a Chamber of Knowledge, either here or in some other location inside the Great Pyramid of Giza. Science, in general, responds to this supposition with scepticism.

The robot "Pyramid Rover" attracted great media interest when it was readied for a reconnaissance of the interior of a shaft in the Great Pyramid of Giza.

Teotihuacan: A City Modelled on the Cosmos

The impressive pyramids of Teotihuacan rise above the Mexican plateau not far from Mexico City. For a long time thought to be the work of the Aztecs, the pyramids are in fact the product of an unknown people who built them centuries earlier, before the Aztecs arrived in the region. The pyramids are but one part of an expansive city designed to be a perfect reflection of heaven.

The history of the city

Teotihuacan means "place of the gods" in Nahuatl, the language of the Aztecs. Because the Aztecs had given it its only known name, it was long thought that they were the Native Americans who had built this oldest city on the North American continent. But the Aztecs only entered the Mexican highlands from the north in the fourteenth century, later building their capital city of Tenochtitlan on the site of present-day Mexico City. We now know that Teotihuacan is much older. Eventually discovered by the Aztecs and used as a religious site, Teotihuacan had been abandoned for centuries by then. Its residential areas were destroyed; only the magnificent pyramids still stood tall.

The Pyramid of the Sun is the tallest structure in Teotihuacan. Its dimensions are comparable to the Giza pyramids.

The golden age of Teotihuacan was very likely between 150 and 600 AD. At that time the city was enormously wealthy and, with a population of 200,000 inhabitants, it was the sixth largest city in the world. Just like its beginnings, the end of Teotihuacan also remains unexplained. No one knows exactly when and how the city came to be abandoned. Perhaps a drought reduced the harvests to a point where survival in Teotihuacan was no longer guaranteed. Religious considerations may have played a role, as well. In the end, the city was probably destroyed around 700 AD, burned to the ground by barbarians.

The Pyramid of the Moon has a flattened top, like all the Teotihuacan pyramids. This suggests that the pyramids were cult sites where human sacrifice was practiced.

A city modelled on the cosmos

Even today there are many unanswered questions: we know neither Teotihacan's original name, nor who built the city, nor what inspired the phenomenal pyramids. All that is certain is that the city's builders were master architects and craftsmen with precise knowledge of the heavenly bodies, for Teotihuacan is indeed a faithful reproduction of the heavens. In the 1970s, American engineer Hugh Harleston Jr. studied the measurements of the buildings and their relationships to one other, and concluded that the dimensions for the orbits of Mercury, Venus, Earth, Mars, Jupiter, Saturn, Uranus and even for Neptune and Pluto – planets that were only discovered in 1846 and 1930 – were reproduced exactly within the city plan. Teotihuacan is a perfect model of our solar system.

The Temple of Quetzalcoatl, with its sculpted heads of the feathered serpent, is further evidence of the preoccupation of the city's builders with the heavens. The number of statues on the temple facade corresponds to a 366-day leap year, the number of steps (13) on each facade refers to the number of months within a transit of the moon, and the sum of all the steps (4 x 13 = 52) equals the number of weeks in a year.

Key facts

Area of the city: 9.3 square miles (24 square km)
The Pyramid of the Sun, built in the first century AD:
Area – 745 x 745 ft (227 x 227 m); height – 220 ft (67m)
The Pyramid of the Moon:
Area – 492 x 656 ft (150 x 200 m); height – 157 ft (48 m)
The Quetzalcoatl Pyramid:
Overbuilt with a pyramid, the original temple has been partially uncovered. It is named for the feathered serpent (Quetzalcoatl) sculpted on its facade, which symbolizes the connection between heaven and earth.

Numerous warriors' skeletons were buried along the Street of the Dead. Once identified as part of the original population of the city, this is no longer thought to be true. It is now known that the early inhabitants cremated their dead.

Construction of the city

The Sun, Moon and Quetzalcoatl Pyramids dominated the layout of Teotihuacan. It is thought that more than 3,000 people laboured daily for thirty years in order to build the Sun Pyramid alone. An approximately 1.9-mile-long (3-km) boulevard, the Street of the Dead, serves as a north-south axis running through the city. Smaller pyramids line both sides of it, followed by a row of closed courtyards that were once thought to be graves, giving the street its name. We know now that this was a false assumption, and that the original inhabitants of the city burned their dead instead of burying them.

There are a number of theories regarding the function of this street. The American engineer Alfred Schlemmer proposed that the courtyards were really basins that would be filled with water, reflecting the sky and stars above. Swiss author Erich von Daniken saw the street as a mighty landing strip for aliens, gods from outer space who inspired the pyramids and cosmic city plan. Other scholars see the street as the symbolic connection between heaven and earth, joining the sacred pyramids with the living city of its inhabitants.

The mica chambers

The most recent Teotihuacan mystery has to do with the mica chambers. In 1983, archaeologists came across cellar rooms with ceilings that are insulated by a layer of mica sandwiched in layers (stone-mica-stone) to a thickness of about 6 inches (15 cm). It is still not clear what purpose these rooms served. One theory suggests that sensitive materials were stored here for protection against extreme external heat, for example. Other theories suggest the heat was generated inside the chambers, and that the rooms may have served as smelting ovens. In the view of quarrelsome American author and self-described antiquarian Zecharia Stichens, these are locations for refining and purifying mineral substances.

More puzzling still is the fact that there is hardly any mica to be found in Mexico. Mica is found primarily in South Africa, Brazil, the USA and Russia. Where did the mica in Teotihuacan come from? Why was the underground room insulated in this manner, and who ordered that it be done? A pipe insulated with mica runs out of one of the rooms, raising further intriguing questions. No one knows its function.

Mica

Mica, also known as muscovite ("Moscow glass") is a component of granite. It is a colourless mineral that glimmers like mother of pearl. Chemically calcium silicate, it possesses very special properties. It is highly elastic, heat-resistant up to 1470 °F (800 °C) and resistant to both sudden temperature changes (heat/cold) and organic acids. Mica was first recorded in 1546, long after its use in Teotihuacan.

Alien masters?

Like Erich von Daniken, Stichens believed the pre-Columbian cultures came into being with the help of gods called the Anuaki ("they who came from the sky"). This parallels the pyramids of Giza, which are also often said to have been been built by "gods". Stichens concludes that the builders of the Sun and Moon Pyramids knew of Giza and built their own pyramids in imitation, but added stairs and a platform. They have the same proportions, though the Great Pyramid at Giza, at 479 feet (146 m), is more than twice as high. In certain borderline-science circles, it is believed that the Giza pyramids were already standing at the end of the ice age, some 8500 years before the first pharaohs. This theory raises a number of unanswerable questions. What Stone Age men would have been capable of such a feat? Are the pyramids of Teotihuacan also from that time period?

These death masks are among the many traces left behind by the Aztecs at Teotihuacan and one of the reasons they were originally thought to be the founders of the city.

While many scholars and scientists assume that we are not the only intelligent beings in the universe, was there ever a time in which the gods – aliens – came to us as masters? Is there any evidence to support this? There is, of course, according to the borderline-scientists. "The earth is full of evidence", says Erich von Daniken, "and it is always right in front of our eyes. We see it in museums, but fail to recognize it."

Erich von Daniken believes that the Street of the Dead was originally a landing strip for the aliens who inspired the city's builders.

The Ruins of Puma Puncu

The ruins of the former Indian village of Tiauanaco, lying on the high plateau of Bolivia, came to the attention of science at the beginning of the twentieth century. The so-called Sun Gate, with its relief sculptures and complex notches, is by far the most intriguing find. Its prominence in early investigations led scholars to overlook yet another mysterious place lying only a few hundred yards away.

The Sun Gate, the pyramids and the ruins

Early in the twentieth century, the German engineer Arthur Posnansky (1873–1946) thoroughly investigated the ruins of Tiauanaco over the course of many years. Using the sections of the masonry walls that were still preserved, he was able to determine the extent of the village and its buildings. He paid particular attention to the settlement area, known in the native Indian language of Aymara as Kalasasaya, or "Standing Stones". Based on the position of the stones and their orientation, he concluded that a pyramid or astronomical observatory had stood on the site thousands of years ago, an interpretation that was later confirmed by German architect Edmund Kiss. Posnansky attempted to date the pyramid according to the height of the entire area and the direction in which he assumed it was oriented. As a result, he concluded that it must have been laid out around 15,000 BC.

From the point of view of archaeological scholars, this estimated date was to be treated with great scepticism. At the same time, however, Posnansky's work did inspire several research teams to assemble additional data during the 1920s. Several investigators, including Posnansky himself, re-dated the foundation taking into account additional factors. The most recently published work describes a formative period between 10,150 and 4050 BC. In 1981, a radiocarbon sample dated to 1580 BC. It probably came from a more recent building phase and is therefore unlikely to be representative for the entire settlement complex.

At this point, the ruins of Puma Puncum which lay some 330 feet (100 m) away from Tiahuanacu, were finally included in the investigation.

One of the regularly shaped stones from the ruins of Puma Puncu, showing incised decoration.

It is still not clear whether the ruins are the result of a natural catastrophe or of stone robbing by a nearby settlement.

It is thought that the Sun Gate collapsed during an earthquake that caused it to break. The gate was only recently re-erected.

The ancient modular construction system

The ruins of Puma Puncu contain nearly 1000 tons of stone blocks. They seem to represent the remains of many buildings. The form of the stones is unusual. They are so precisely worked that they could be fitted to each other in a variety of ways, comparable to a modern modular system employing a uniform construction unit. Metal clamps held the stones in place, a method familiar to archaeologists from the site of Delphi, thousands of kilometres away.

It is still not clear what destroyed Puma Puncu and Tiauanaco. Although a comparison based on masonry styles shows that the sites were not founded at the same time, their proximity to each other would make an exchange of technology unavoidable. In the case of Puma Puncu, the destruction was much more complete. The nature of the structures is nearly unrecognizable, and there are very few places where one stone stands next to another.

In Tiauanaco, however, occasional walls are still standing. If one assumes that an earthquake destroyed Puma Puncu, as is probable given the condition of the site, then it should have been so devastating that Tiauanaco would have sustained heavy damage, too. Since this is not the case, say some scholars, it suggests that Puma Puncu is much older than Tiauanaco.

This poses a problem. The natives who lived nearby in that period were not familiar with either writing or metal technology, and therefore could not be responsible for the metal clamps used in the construction. It is also questionable whether they would have had the technical ability to work stone so precisely. The natives who live in the Altiplano area today do not claim that their ancestors built these structures. According to their legends, the gods or giants who lived there built both sites. From their point of view, this explains the origins and remains of these places very satisfactorily.

The Sun Gate

In contrast to the "modular" building principle that characterizes the stones from Puma Puncu, the Sun Gate of Tiauanco was cut from a single stone. It is decorated with relief sculpture and some incisions, most of them found on the lintel area over the gate opening, which is 4.6 feet (1.4 m) high. The central relief shows a figure armed with two spears, or snake sceptres, flanked by forty-eight winged observers. Of these, thirty-two have human faces, while the other sixteen have condor heads. It is thought that the central figure represents the creator god Viracocha.

The Sun Gate is so named because if an observer stands directly in front of it, the sun rises exactly over the midpoint of the gate on the first day of spring. One theory suggests that the forty-eight sculpted figures represent a basic calendar. This would serve as an additional prehistoric connection with astronomy.

Tiermes, the Stone City

The northern Spanish city of Tiermes is remarkable because a large part of its architecture isn't built, but cut into the bedrock. The stone is so cleverly and unusually worked that there are questions as to whether or not they were built by the cultures most commonly associated with the region. Archaeologists have been investigating the city since the end of the nineteenth century.

THE HISTORY OF THE STONE CITY...

Exactly who built Tiermes, and when, remain unknown. Located in the old Castilian province of Soria, the first recorded mention of the city is in documents by the Greek mathematician and geographer Ptolemy (ca. 100–175 BC), who called it Arevacos and described its inhabitants as Iberian-Celtic people.

What is certain is that the settlement came under Roman control in 98 BC. In the course of the first century of the Common Era it even became the capital of a Roman administrative sector. This marked the start of an economic upswing that triggered a building program that included a marketplace and a system of running water. Tiermes was overtaken by the Western Goths in the sixth or seventh century, and then later, around the beginning of the eighth century, by the Moors.

In the course of the following decades, the city's location on the border between Christian and Muslim regions led to the decline of the local culture. By the twelfth century, Tiermes no longer played a significant role.

After visiting the city in 1888, local historian Nicolas Rabal began the first scientific study of the structures, which, then as now, were well preserved due to the mild climate.

The Bazar of Tiermes is a typical section of the city. Walls, passageways and architectural structures, much like those found in any other city, are located next to the houses that have been cut out of the bedrock.

... AND ITS RESIDENTS

Many aspects of the remains found in Tiermes are highly atypical for the constructions of that time period or culture. The pipe system, which was used either to supply fresh water or drain away waste water, is one example. A pump-like machine would have been required for the system to function, but as yet we have no idea what this pump might have looked like. The walls and roofs of many of the structures are uncommonly thick, with widths between 5 and 10 feet (1.5 to 3 m) not at all uncommon.

In addition, many of the buildings and open spaces have ramps that seem to be connected to a track system with a span of 4.5 feet (1.4 m). Narrow, grooved tracks run over the entire plateau, some of which lead down into underground passageways.

In the 1960s, several investigators proposed that these features were more in line with what one would expect from a modern air defence system, one that would let the civilians retreat to bunkers while the defenders moved heavy weapons around on the tracks.

In the course of further excavation, additional evidence was uncovered that was also out of line with our understandings of an ancient fortification. No one could explain, for example, the rectilinear cuttings that resembled the trenches used in World War I. It was also not considered possible that the people who had lived in Tiermes since the Roman conquest had created them. It seemed more likely that the constructions were even older than originally thought, and were utilized by a people for whom these peculiar arrangements fulfilled a specific purpose.

In the 1980s and 1990s there was considerable speculation that these were evidence of prehistoric aliens, whose weapons would have been raised and pointed toward the sky to ward off attacks from outer space. When confronted with these theories, serious scholars happily point out that similar proposals are usually disproved.

Traces of the track system are still clearly recognizable everywhere in Tiermes. Nothing is known about its purpose.

It is not clear if Ptolemy visited the city of Tiermes himself, or relied upon travellers tales in his description.

The simple houses along the main street could accommodate some 30,000 people. An earthquake destroyed part of the residential quarters in 363 AD.

The Rock City of Petra

On a journey through the Orient in August 1812, the Swiss traveller Johann Ludwig Burckhardt (1784–1817) heard from a pilgrim that there was a rock city nearby. In disguise, he had himself led there by the bedouins. Inside a gorge nearly 4000 feet (1200 m) long and up to 330 feet (100 m) deep, he discovered the city of Petra, which most Europeans at that time had assumed was imaginary.

The city in the stone

The oldest evidence indicates that this gorge, the Siq (Arabic *siq* = gorge), had already been settled during the Neolithic period. The origins of the city of Petra, which today lies within Jordan, go back as far as the Edomites, the traditional enemies of Israel, who originally settled there. After they fell, the Nabateans settled on this site in the third century BC. Under their control, Petra (or Sela) became one of the most important trade centres in the Near East. The majority of the buildings cut directly into the cliffs were built by the Nabateans, or were at least brought into their present form by them. Among these are the Treasury (Khazne al-Firaun), which was originally a rock-cut tomb, the Roman Theatre, which seated 5000, and the city centre with its colonnaded street. There are additional rock-cut tombs, as well, leading some to suggest that Petra was initially founded as a dedicated burial place and was only later expanded into a city.

Myths and legends

The news of the rediscovery of the city of Petra during the nineteenth century, although only Muslims were permitted to visit, gave rise to somewhat macabre rumours. It was said that one might find the remains of Crusaders inside the stone houses, as they were the last ones to report of the city. Going even further were tales that portrayed the city in light of its supposed biblical origins, which tell of Moses arriving here and striking a well out of stone to provide water for the people of Israel following behind him. One nineteenth century rumour claimed that this water was now poisoned, which of course only the Muslims could know in the nineteenth century. Petra's reputation as an eerie but fascinating city was enhanced by the stories told of atrocities visited upon Christians in the isolated rock city, along with other tales of living and dead creatures. Interest was raised most of all by accounts of the treasures said to be lying deep in the silent underground passageways.

In the year 106 AD the Nabateans were defeated by the Romans. The city lost its former importance when the region, with its new capital city of Bostra, became part of the Roman Empire. After large sections of Petra were destroyed by earthquakes in 363 AD and 551 AD, more and more inhabitants moved away from the rock city. It is fairly certain that by the time of the Arab conquest of the region in 663 AD, the city was barely occupied.

Following the Crusades of the Middle Ages, Petra fell into oblivion from a European perspective, becoming less real and more and more of a legend, until it was finally rediscovered. Excavations have taken place in Petra since the 1920s, and it has been open to tourists of all faiths since that time.

Mysterious or reasonable?

For reasons that were certainly strategic, the city of Petra was built inside a long, narrow gorge. Enemy forces that wanted to conquer the city in the gorge could do so easily if they succeeded in controlling the surrounding cliffs, provided that the buildings were in the gorge itself. The builders of Petra went a step further, however, cutting their dwellings directly into the cliffs. This gave them a tremendous advantage, because it was no longer possible for the enemy to attack directly, let alone to estimate the fighting strength and stamina of the inhabitants. While there were also buildings standing in the gorge, these were for the most part commercial structures. If enemies wanted to take Petra, they knew that they had to leave any kind of cover behind and storm the gorge without protection, without much of an idea of what they faced. For most opponents, this was too great a risk.

Whether or not the structure called the Treasury was actually used to store treasure is still not clear. It is usually thought to have been built as a monumental grave.

Due to the almost mythical status that Petra had long held in Europe, it was natural that during the nineteenth century, when non-Muslim were still not permitted to visit, legends and special attributes were associated with the place. Many of these are still maintained today. In fact, Petra is neither an unimaginably ancient city, nor was it built in a mysterious manner.

Over 165 feet (50 m) wide, the Cloister is the largest facade in the city. Its name comes from the many crosses found inside. Whether it was really used for religious services is uncertain.

The Great Enclosure was presumably the first and, for its time, largest, trade centre in Africa. The prosperity of Great Zimbabwe was directly related to its position in world commerce.

Great Zimbabwe

There is a ruined city in southeast Zimbabwe between the Zambesi and Orange Rivers that has been shrouded in mystery for centuries. Again and again, traders and sailors would tell of a place known in the language of the Shona as *dzimba dza mabwe*, or "great houses made of stone". According to legend, this was the capital city of the Queen of Sheba.

A GREAT CITY BUILT ENTIRELY OF STONE

The first Europeans to stumble upon the ruins of Great Zimbabwe were the Portuguese in the sixteenth century. They spread the tale that this was the home of the legendary Queen of Sheba. In 1871, German researcher Karl Gottlieb Mauch (1837–1875) succeeded in locating Great Zimbabwe. The many secrets that the ruins have since revealed came to light between 1890 and 1910 through the work of the very treasure hunters and amateur archaeologists who, in fact, destroyed many of the historic traces.

The ruined city consists of three sectors, the Hill Complex, the Valley Complex and, within that area, the elliptical complex known as the Great Enclosure. The Enclosure consists of a wall 830 feet (253 m) long made of brick-sized stones laid without mortar. It stands between 16 and 35 feet (4.9–10.7 m) tall. The interior of the ring wall is subdivided into numerous small buildings and courtyards, all of unknown function. Its most puzzling element is the conical tower that adjoins the outer wall. Having no visible function and possessing neither doors, windows nor stairs, the tower has naturally inspired the imagination of researchers since its discovery. Some scholars interpret the tower as a religious phallic symbol, related to the fertility of the region. Others argue that the tower served as some kind of signal post or observatory.

King Solomon's gold

For centuries people have searched for the fabled mines of Ofir, the source of King Solomon's treasures. In 1522, the Portuguese historian Joao de Barros described a fortification in Sofala with an indecipherable inscription over its gate. The local inhabitants were called the Symbaoe, which sounds a lot like Zimbabwe.

The earliest finds from the site date back to the fourth century BC. As the centre of the Munhumutapa empire, which included both present-day Zimbabwe and Mozambique, the site experienced a golden age between the tenth and fifteenth centuries. This period is divided into three phases. During the first, beginning in the eleventh century, there was already strong centralized rule. Then, around 1000 AD, gold was discovered here. Indian influence is suspected because similar mining techniques are known from India. Systematic excavation in 1932 produced finds that mark the thirteenth century as a second period of wide-

A conical tower with no visible function, no doors, no windows and no steps adjoins the outer wall. Is it an observatory, or a phallic symbol promoting the fertility of the land?

The outer wall of the Great Enclosure rises as high as 33 feet (10 m). The stones are cut in the form of bricks and laid without mortar.

ranging long-distance trade, including imported pottery from the Ming Dynasty (1384–1644) and the Persian empire of the thirteenth and fifteenth centuries. Flourishing trade and the riches that resulted from it contributed to the monumental architecture, the ruins of which amaze us today. In the fifteenth century, which is transitional to the third occupation phase, Great Zimbabwe fell. The reasons for the end of this sophisticated African culture, the only one, with the exception of Egypt, known to exist prior to the Arab invasion and European colonization, remains unexplained. The end or interruption of long distance trade is a likely factor.

The market centre of Great Zimbabwe

Archaeologist Wilfried Mallows advanced that theory that Great Zimbabwe had been a great market centre later used by the Arabs as a central slave market. The unique character of the ruined city and its fascinating connection with Arabia, India and the Far East continues to inspire scholars and visitors alike, making Great Zimbabwe one of the most magnificent and mysterious monuments in the world.

Underground Cities

In addition to the city of Petra, dug almost completely into the surrounding cliffs, there are other cities that have been founded in equally unusual places. Cities that are located almost entirely beneath the earth's surface have been discovered primarily in Turkey.

The deep hole

In 1963, approximately 50 miles (30 km) south of Nevsehir in Turkey, Omer Demir stumbled across a deep hole (in Turkish, *derinkuyu*). According to local legend, he became aware of the place when one of his hens suddenly disappeared though a crack in the earth. He began to dig and came across a steep path leading deeper down. Taking a torch he climbed down and encountered steps, narrow passages, niches and shafts dug into the bedrock. Although some of the passages had collapsed over time and others were blocked off, it was obvious that what was buried here was much more than a simple underground cave.

In fact, as became clear after intensive excavation, there was an entire city built in that deep hole beneath the surface. Occupying multiple levels, shafts and passageways that led ever deeper into the earth were found, many of which could be shut off by large, millstone-sized, rounded stones. This led at first to the conclusion that Derinkuyu was a kind of emergency housing or refugee shelter. Yet the longer the investigation continued, the clearer it became that much more was involved. The dimensions of the complex were simply too vast for a shelter or hiding spot.

In the course of the excavation, houses, storage rooms, wine cellars and shops were discovered, as well as hall-like rooms in which school was presumably held. The city included an underground church some 215 feet (65 m) long, as well as spaces that could have been used as stables. Altogether, the area of the underground city was approximately 1.5 square miles (4 square km), with thirteen stories excavated so far. Additional levels are expected to be found as work continues.

The lowest floor lies at a depth of 290 feet (85 m) below the earth. According to estimates, more than 20,000 people

A complex system of shafts brought fresh air into the underground passageways of Derinkuyu.

could live here comfortably. The planning and construction of the hidden exits and thousands of air shafts were so well thought out, and the passageways so extensive, that it can hardly be considered a hurried, temporary solution. On the other hand, the arrangement that permitted the passages to be shut off by large rocks, along with the common rooms and complex ventilation system – the latter also potentially useful as a communication system – has led some to conclude that the people of Derinkuyu feared persecution.

Is this city unique?

After the sensational discovery of Derinkuyu, additional underground cities were sought out, with considerable success, in this Turkish region of Cappadocia. With thirty cities of this type now identified, it would seem to follow that there are more that still exist, or did exist at one time. This theory is supported by the fact that some of the passageways lead out of the underground city zone, perhaps as part of a network connecting with other cities. Most of the complexes are now either filled with fallen debris or are impassable for other reasons. Derinkuyu, Kaymakli and Ozkonak are the three sites where excavations have made the most progress. Some sections of the underground passageways and spaces are now open to tourists.

Many of the far-ranging passageways and rooms in Kaymakli are now open for tourists. Nevertheless, the excavation is not yet complete.

But Cappadocia is not the only place where underground cities exist. Settlements beneath the surface of the earth have been found world wide. It is estimated that there either were or still are between 300 and 500 of these cities all over the world.

The secret tunnel system of Kaymakli passes through numerous levels.

The origins of the underground city

Some archaeologists believe that with its church and baptismal basin, Derinkuyu must have been a city whose inhabitants were persecuted because of their Christian faith. Other theories exist, most of which are questionable for various reasons. The suggestion that the people living underground were seeking protection from invaders during wartime or were fleeing from the lava flow of an erupting volcano is greatly weakened by the existence of the air shafts, which almost certainly would have been blocked by enemies or filled in with the lava, bringing certain death to everyone below.

A further point offers strong support for the persecuted Christians theory, namely, that every single one of the underground cities investigated thus far has included churches.

We now know that underground cities first appeared with the Phrygians approximately 3000 years ago. Whether they are also responsible for the construction of these underground complexes is not yet clear. There is some evidence that the Hittites were the original master builders. While the surrounding cities of Bogazkoy and Alaca Hoyuk fell in fiery conflagration, no such evidence is found in Derinkuyu. It is therefore possible that the Hittites, fleeing before the Phrygians, retreated into the tunnels. Given the lack of evidence for destruction along with the fact that no Phrygian remains have been found in Derinkuyu, scholars and popular authors alike conclude that their escape was successful.

The city later fell to the Byzantine Empire, which apparently continued to enlarge it until the sixth century AD, when the Arabs invaded the region and Derinkuyu was repeatedly attacked. After this, Derinkuyu lost its significance. None of this history, however, provides an explanation for the existence of the underground churches, for neither the original Phrygians nor the Hittites professed Christianity. One theory, still not entirely ruled out, is that the churches date to a much later time, although the layout of the passageways, which circumvent the church areas, makes this proposition unlikely.

Sand in the passageways, Cattle in the meadows

Derinkuyu and many of the other underground cities remained undiscovered for such a long time in part because after they were abandoned, their shafts and passageways were purposely filled in with sand and rubble. Why this was done has remained unexplained because there are no records at all of these operations, although one would think, under normal circumstance, that accounts of such extensive work within a very large complex would have been written down somewhere.

There are parallels between the aboveground city of Uchisar and the underground cities. Here, too, the living spaces could be closed off with large rocks.

The Hittites

According to contemporary understanding, the Hittites originally came from the Caucasus. From there they immigrated to Anatolia in the third millenium BC, today the Asian portion of Turkey, and mingled with the Hatti people who already lived there. For reasons we don't understand, they managed to become the rulers of the land and built up an empire which even included a large portion of what is now Syria. For almost a thousand years, the Hittites lived as an equal power alongside the Egyptians and the Babylonians.

The demise of the Hittite empire was sealed in the early twelfth century BC, after most of the Hittite cities had been detroyed by fire or invasions. For a few centuries, several tribes continued to live in the southern and eastern reaches of the former empire, but all trace of them was eventually lost. It is assumed that the remaining groups fell under Assyrian rule.

One suggestion is that the city was abandoned and filled in with debris in order to permit surface cities to be built above them on solid ground, without the danger of cave-ins. This idea would make sense because, as is clear from the existence of underground animal stalls, if those living below the surface wanted to survive, some above ground activity was required. While cattle could be kept underground, it would nevertheless still be necessary to bring them to the surface to graze.

This brings us back to the question of why a population made such an effort to build their city underground at all. What was their motivation for such extensive underground construction? Who were the people who built the intricate passageways and galleries? And, finally, how did they dig and carry away stone rubble and earth to create passageways extending nearly twenty stories deep into the earth? All these questions remain unanswered.

In Cappadocia there are numerous houses and apartments cut into the cliffs aboveground.

The ruins of Bogazkoy, about 120 miles (200 km) from Ankara, have been identified with Hatusa, the former capital city of the Hittite empire.

The Megalithic Temples of Malta

The temple complexes of Malta are almost as old as the Irish Newgrange, but much more extensive. Built with megalithic stones between approximately 7000 and 2500 BC, seven of the twenty-three temples identified so far are still preserved today.

Stone temples

We know very little about how the ancient inhabitants of Malta worshipped their gods. Occasional bone finds suggest that animal sacrifices were offered in the temples found there, and their existence demonstrates that religion must have played an important role in this civilization. The stone temple complexes are constructed with great care and inventiveness. The plan of the Gantija Temple, for example, resembles the form of a cloverleaf.

Some calculate that several successive generations must have worked on the construction of each temple. Given the dimensions of the structures and the approximately 50-ton weight of the stones, a 500-year-long construction period would be required.

Remains of an unknown people

The stone temples of Malta are remains of a sophisticated culture that continues to pose riddles today. Apart from the existing structures, along with individual underground graves or temple complexes and a few art objects, nothing

The Hagar Qim ("standing stone") temple complex incorporates unusual rock formations that are probably meant to represent ghosts or spirits.

The available evidence suggests that women played an important role in this society, or at least in the religion. Many of the preserved artefacts are female figures, often with unnaturally small heads, hands and feet. These representations lead some scholars to conclude that Malta was the home of a fertility goddess. Others interpret the common occurrence of female figures in the temples as evidence for the existence of a matriarchy, that is, a society ruled by women.

It is questionable whether the future will provide additional information about this culture that has long since disappeared. The salty air that surrounds Malta has already inflicted great damage on the ruins, and it is certainly possible that other relics have already suffered this fate long ago. Ideally, however, one can still hope to find additional underground temples containing objects that would provide further leads for investigation.

Many representations of women, sculpted and incised on stone blocks, were found during excavations and investigations.

else from this civilization seems to have survived. Nothing has been discovered so far that would divulge any information as to the origins, identity, or later whereabouts of this culture.

What the remains do tell us is that these builders possessed an extraordinary knowledge of astronomy. Most of the temples were laid out according to the paths of heavenly bodies, perhaps allowing the buildings to be impressively illuminated on specific days. One stone fragment was found incised with a pattern that can be interpreted as a map of the stars. Some parts of the temples have stones or walls cut through with an unusual number of holes. While these are usually interpreted as having a purely decorative function, the pattern could also represent the stars or plant life.

Some of the temples incorporate megalithic stone formations with unusual, irregularly fissured upper ends. In many cases the blocks are laid next to each other in such a way that the structures resemble faces. One theory proposes that these stones served as representations of certain creatures, such as ghosts or gods.

The temple complexes were typically open to the sky. Only a few places, like this entranceway, were roofed.

Newgrange

Newgrange (called *An Liamh Greine* in Irish, meaning cave of the sun) is a grave complex in the Irish county of Meath. Built during the Bronze Age some 5000 years ago, it is older than the pyramids of Giza and even Stonehenge. Newgrange is one of the earliest structures that proves prehistoric cultures had sophisticated knowledge of astronomy.

An astrological cult site

Newgrange is constructed of both megaliths and individual unworked stones. Taken together, these roughly form a circle with a diameter of almost 225 feet (70 m). It is thought that it must have taken twenty years to erect the stone circle alone, and that perhaps 300 men were involved in building this monumental grave. The outer wall was finished with a cladding of quartzite, a medium-grained stone. This quartzite was heavily damaged over the course of the millennia, but it was restored following the excavation of the gravesite.

Newgrange had an entryway 56 feet (17 m) long with a narrow, 33-foot- (10-m-) high shaft at one end. For approximately a week before and following the winter solstice, which occurs on 21 December, sunlight enters this shaft, travels along the passageway, and terminates at a stone block decorated with spirals. Given the size of the stone and earlier finds of bone at the site, it has long been assumed that this stone was originally an altar used for human sacrifice. It is now known that the dead were burned outside the monument, after which their remains were laid to rest within Newgrange.

Are the spirals divine symbols?

Spirals are found on many stones at Newgrange that do not belong directly to the outer wall. Their exact meaning is not understood, although some people surmise that they symbolize a deity. This would explain their frequent appearance and also give the passage of the sun, which terminates at a spiral-decorated stone, increased meaning. It may be that the people who founded Newgrange worshipped the sun as a god, as was the case in many other earlier civilizations. This proposal is supported by the orientation of the complex as a whole, which itself presupposes astronomical knowledge.

There are other monumental graves dating from approximately the same time period in Scotland and Ireland,

This long passageway directs the rays of the sun into the grave chamber at winter solstice.

Megaliths

The megalithic monuments were erected primarily during the Neolithic period and the Bronze Age, which dates them to between 5000 and 1000 BC. In addition to individual stones, relatively simple structures such as Stonehenge and even complete buildings have been preserved.

Although megaliths are most common in Europe, the phenomenon is not limited to that continent. They are also found in North Africa, South America and on Easter Island, as well as in some Asian countries. The reason why these enormous stones and buildings were erected during this time all over the world is still unknown.

Between 1962 and 1975, Newgrange was partially reconstructed by archaeologists, who repaired the outer wall.

including some that are architecturally more noteworthy than Newgrange. But only here is the entire complex laid out so exactly in line with the sun's rays and their movement that the phenomenon of the wandering sunbeam is possible. This suggests that the sun had a very special meaning for the builders, perhaps even taking on the rank of a deity.

Even after the age of Newgrange was established, conjecture and speculation remained. Nothing is known regarding which culture of that time period could possibly have been responsible for its construction. Few useful traces of art or other remains of this civilization have been found either inside the grave complex or elsewhere. Today Newgrange is open to tourists, for whom the path of the sun at winter solstice is artificially recreated.

Incised spirals decorate many stones at Newgrange. It is thought that these are symbols of the divinity to which the complex is dedicated.

The megalithic monument of Stonehenge in Salisbury, England was begun during the Neolithic period.

Stonehenge

The megalithic monument of Stonehenge, located in Salisbury, in the English county of Wiltshire, has puzzled scholars for a long time. Begun during the Neolithic period, it was probably in constant use far into the Bronze Age. It is thought that the complex facilitated observation of the sun and moon. The construction of such a complex, however, presupposes sophisticated astronomical knowledge that should not have existed in that time period or even much later. How, therefore, did the builders gain this knowledge?

The "hanging stones" of Stonehenge

The name Stonehenge is derived from the old English *stanhen gist*, which means something like "gallows stones". Stonehenge consists of multiple groupings of enormous stones, all set inside a banked ditch. The outermost stone circle includes a row of stone posts that are as much as 13 feet (4 m) high, which are linked together by lintel stones laid across them. Inside the outer circle, ten blocks are set up in the shape of a horseshoe, and some of these are again joined by means of lintels. Additional structures made of smaller stones and a series of pits are found between these two areas.

Cultural periods
Paleolithic – Old Stone Age, 2 million to 10th millenium BC
Mesolithic – Middle Stone Age, approx. 8th to 5th millennia BC
Neolithic – New Stone Age, 6500 to 4000 BC
Copper Age – 4th millennium to 18th century BC
Bronze Age – 18th century to 8th century BC

* The chronological divisions do not follow directly one after the other because various regions developed differently.

Stonehenge was constructed in stages over a period of several thousand years, which can be roughly subdivided into three phases. The earliest phase included the bank and

The mighty standing stones of Stonehenge were cut from the hill and quarry of Carnmerion in Wales. They were transported over a distance of some 480 miles (300 km).

ditch complex, and dates from around 3100 BC. The conspicuous megalith structure was erected during the second phase, dating from between 2500 and 2000 BC. Finally, two rings of pits were dug around the exterior of the circle of stones around 1700 BC. The circles enclose an additional thirty holes that were dug, but never occupied by stones. These holes were gradually filled in, in some periods with graves.

Historical descriptions of Stonehenge

The oldest surviving record of Stonehenge is a description by the Welsh historian Nennius, in the ninth century AD. He reported that it was a monument erected for 400 nobles who were slaughtered in 472 AD near Hengist. In 1615, the English architect Inigo Jones speculated that the site was a Roman temple sacred to the pagan god Caelus. Later historians though it might have been built by the Danes. In the ensuing years, Stonehenge was ascribed to the Saxons, an idea that persisted into the late nineteenth century. In 1740, religious scholar William Stukeley (1687–1765) was the first to complete accurate drawings of the site, showing the significance of the astronomical and/or calendar related positioning of the stones. Finally, in 1900, it was conclusively demonstrated that Stonehenge was in use well into the Bronze Age.

The transport of the stone blocks

Not only the meaning of Stonehenge puzzles scholars all over the world, but also the origin of the stones used to build it. Thus far, only the source of the blocks that make up the inner stone circle has been explained. These come from a small quarry in the southwest of Wales. This means that they had to be brought in from a distance of some 480 miles (300 km). But how could that be possible using the means of transportation available at the time?

In 2001, as part of an experiment, an attempt was made to transport a stone the size of one of the blocks used at Stonehenge along the purported route from Wales to the site. Volunteers pulled the stone overland using a wooden sledge. This did in fact work, and no one doubted that there were methods for moving enormous blocks of rock with ropes and wood. But afterwards, when the block was loaded onto a reproduction of an ancient ship, a method that might also have been employed at that time, the ship – with the stone – sank in rough seas. English archaeologist Aubrey Burl proposed an alternative theory. He was of the opinion that the stones might have been brought to their destination by glacial action.

Modern Druids with burning torches celebrate the summer solstice. Today the area of the monument is closed to all events.

The construction of Stonehenge

Archaeologists have calculated how many workers and how much labour would have been required to build Stonehenge. The estimate runs to several million man hours, including all three phases. The first phase required some 11,000 hours of labour, the second 360,000 and the various sections of the final phase around 1.7 million hours total. Preparation of the stones required approximately 20 million hours, taking into account the kinds of tools that were used. It follows that the desire to build Stonehenge must have been enormous indeed. Its construction required magnificent organization skills, and the builders must have been wealthy as well, for they had to feed thousands of workers who could not provide for themselves while engaged in the task. Who was in a position to do all of this?

The astronomical orientation of Stonehenge

The stones of Stonehenge are laid out according to the sun's position at solstice and at equinox, making the important seasonal turning points predictable. Did priest-kings use this knowledge for the benefit of their farming populations? Sowing and reaping are, after all, dependant on these dates. In order to ascertain the astronomical values, there would have to be some means for obtaining the necessary information. In the case of Stonehenge, this might mean that the complex was originally a prehistoric observatory. Although the manner and significance of the site's use is still not completely clear, it is highly unlikely that the arrangement of the stones is simply random. They are set out too precisely to be arbitrary. The northernmost position of the sun in the sky is dependent on its angle of ascent with respect to the earth. At Stonehenge this figure is 5 degrees and 11 minutes longitude, a figure that would have to have been either calculated or observed very exactly. Precise measurement was therefore extraordinarily important for the placement of the stones, which could only function if they were set just so. This would make Stonehenge a kind of calendar for predicting the seasons.

Stonehenge in mythology

Mythology frequently draws connections between Stonehenge and the Arthurian saga. Geoffrey of Monmouth, the archbishop of the Welsh diocese of Saint Asaph, wrote that the Druid Merlin led settlers from Ireland to the region near

How was it possible to move the enormous blocks in those days? In 2001, an experiment moved a block to Salisbury using a wooden sledge, ropes and timbers. The transport took months.

In 1893, English art nouveau artist Aubrey Beardsley produced this print of the Celtic magician Merlin and the Lady of the Lake in his series "The Death of Arthur". Many investigators believe that Merlin directed the construction of Stonehenge.

Stonehenge. On Mount Killarney in Ireland there is a standing stone monument that was reputedly built by giants, who are said to have brought the stones all the way from Africa. In the seventeenth century, English scholar John Aubrey wrote that the stone circle is a temple of the Druids, whom he viewed as the builders and users of Stonehenge. Since then, this theory has been overturned. By the time of the Druids, the monument had already been standing for 2000 years.

The choice of this place for the construction of the Stonehenge complex is also of interest. The light phenomenon called "earthshine" can be observed near numerous megalithic monuments in England and Wales. Was it understood to assist prophecy or serve as a marker for the gateway to the underworld? Professor Michael Persinger of Ontario, Canada describes earthshine as the product of strong electromagnetic fields capable of producing consciousness-altering effects. Would this make Stonehenge a religious centre instead?

Megalithic tombs
Megalithic tombs from the Neolithic and Early Bronze Age are found in the Mediterranean and coastal regions of western Europe. The different grave types include dolmen, consisting of three or more standing stones supporting a capstone, and passage graves, in which the burial chamber is approached through a long passage. Megalithic tombs were often used for collective burials.

A crane lifts the final lintel back into its original position, from which it fell in the year 1797. With its resetting, the stone circle of Stonehenge once again resumed its original form.

Constructed around 2500 BC, the large outer circle of the Avebury complex has a circumference of approximately 4000 feet (1200 m) and a diameter of 1400 feet (427 m).

The Stone Circle of Avebury

The Avebury stone circles in the county of Wiltshire, England are among the largest and oldest in the British Isles. Their importance is comparable to that of Stonehenge and Silbury Hill.

The Avebury complex

The wall surrounding Avebury encloses an area of some 37 acres (15 hectares). The complex itself consists of a large outer circle dating to 2500 BC, 4000 feet (1200 m) in circumference with a diameter of 1400 feet (427 m). Originally, ninety-eight stones stood atop an earthen bank 20 feet (6 m) high; twenty-seven of them are still preserved. Within the outer ring are two additional circles. The small north circle from 2600 BC has a diameter of 320 feet (98 m); four of its twenty-seven stones remain. The south circle, of the same age, has a diameter of 340 feet (104 m) and originally had twenty-nine stones, of which five still stand today.

Unlike Stonehenge, the sandstones of Avebury come from nearby and could therefore be transported more easily. They are 7 to 18 feet (2.1–5.5 m) high and weigh up to 40 tons. To keep them from tumbling, their foundations are sunk between 6 inches and nearly 2 feet (15–60 cm) into the earth. The obelisk, the largest stone at the site, was reportedly once 18 feet (5.5 m) high before it fell and was destroyed in the eighteenth century. Two stone-lined alleys lead away from the outer circle.

The monument must have remained relatively intact until the fourteenth century, when, on orders from the Christian church, destruction of the "heathen" cult site began.

During the seventeenth and eighteenth centuries, stones were moved to make room for agriculture or reused to build houses. Numerous monuments have suffered similar fates throughout history, including the Coliseum in Rome and the city wall of Tarragona, Spain, which was destroyed for similar purposes.

The discovery and interpretation of the stone circles

In 1648, the antiquarian John Aubrey recognized the great stones in the village and fields as prehistoric stone circles, which, like Stonehenge, he ascribed to the Druids. In 1720 the scholar William Stukeley also described the stone circle as a Druid sanctuary. The National Trust re-erected many of the stones in 1930. Of the original 154 megaliths, just thirty-six are preserved today. Together with the stones lining the alleys, the number was once 600.

William Stukeley was the first to notice that the overall design of Avebury resembles a serpent winding through a circle, which is a traditional alchemist's symbol. The two broad stone-lined alleys, nearly 56 feet (17 m) wide, wind 1.5 miles (2.5 km) through the landscape, forming the head and tail of the giant snake. One of these alleys, West Kennet Avenue, terminates in another stone circle, known as the Sanctuary.

Earthshine is commonly observed nearby and crop circles are often found in surrounding fields.

The sandstone blocks, which come from nearby hills, are from 7 to 16.5 feet (2.1–5 m) high and weigh up to 40 tons. To keep them from tumbling, their foundations are sunken 6 inches to nearly 2 feet (15–60 cm) into the earth.

Avebury as a pagan fertility temple

Author Terence Meaden offered an interpretation for both of the inner stone circles. He proposed that Avebury was a sanctuary for the moon and the sun, as symbolized by the two circles. The moon would represent the female gender or the earth goddess *Tara*; while the sun would be the masculine principle and the sky god *Taran*. The earth goddess and sky god meld together on midsummer's eve, as a sign of the renewal of the world. Meaden argues that just as the circle is a symbol of femininity within fertility rituals and religions, the snake represents masculinity. According to this theory, Avebury would thus have been a pagan fertility temple.

Names of the earth goddess and sky god

Tara was the Indo-European name for the earth goddess, *Tara* in India, *Turan* for the Etruscans, and *Terra Mater* in Rome. Similarly for the Hebrews, the goddess was *Terak*.
The male equivalent was *Taran*, the thunder-and-rain fertility god. The Hittites called him *Taru* and the Andaman Islanders knew him as *Tarai*. In Scandinavia he is *Thor*, and in Germany he is *Thunar* or *Donar*. In German the "day of thunder", *Donnerstag*, is the day of the god *Donar*. The Anglo Saxons said *Thunaer*. The English Thursday is "Thor's day". The Celts called him *Taran* in Wales, and *Torann* in Ireland.

Silbury Hill

The original significance of Silbury Hill, which was established more than 4500 years ago, is unknown. Theories propose it was a solar observatory of an earth sculpture for the earth goddess. Geomancers recognize the powerful energy field that surrounds the mysterious spot.

The structure of Silbury Hill

The enormous, artificially constructed Silbury Hill, just south of Avebury, rises 130 feet (40 m) into the air and has a flattened top. It consists of approximately 444,000 cubic yards (339,600 cubic m) of re-deposited earth. It was apparently built in three phases, the first dating to around 2660 BC. In the second phase, a chalk hill was built spiralling upward in six steps. The final phase filled in these spiralling steps with gravel and earth, giving the hill its characteristic conical form.

The Celtic harvest festival

Not surprisingly, there are many tales surrounding the impressive mound. According to one legend, this place is the grave of the Celtic king Sil. In other stories a knight in golden armor and a massive golden horse are buried here. Another tale says that the Devil wanted to tip a sack of earth over the city of Marlborough, but the mighty priest of nearby Avebury was able to make him to empty his sack here instead.

In 1723, the scholar William Stukeley wrote of excavations at the top of the hill, where bones and an ancient bridle were found. Additional excavation took place in the years 1776, 1849 and 1967. No graves or any other evidence that might elucidate the purpose of the hill have ever been found. The archaeologist Richard Atkinson, using radiocarbon dating and an analysis of ancient insects found buried in the chalk, was able to date the start of con-

Some researchers think that Silbury Hill is a solar observatory, while others see it as a sculpture of the earth goddess. Geomancers sense a powerful energy field surrounding this mysterious place.

The famous grave mound of West Kennet Long Barrow lies atop a ley line running from Avebury to Silbury Hill. First excavated in 1859, the grave complex was completely exposed in 1955/1956.

struction to midsummer, sometime around 2660 BC. Midsummer is the time of the Lugnasad Festival, also known as the Celtic harvest festival, a shamanic ritual celebrating the feminine abundance of nature.

Earth sculpture or UFO meeting place?

There are always new theories about the function of Silbury. The researcher Michael Darnes conjectured that, like Glastonbury Tor, it was a sculpture of the pregnant earth mother, Tara. Another theory interprets Silbury as a solar observatory based on the shadows it throws on the plain. Geomancers point out that Silbury sits atop the same ley line as the Neolithic West Kennet Long Barrow and Avebury obelisk. They claim that this same meridian runs through Glastonbury, Avebury Church, Stonehenge and the stone circle of Winterbourne Abbas. The Roman road that leads between Marlborough and Bath runs directly up to and around Silbury. It is possible that the Romans were aware of the ley line when planning their road. The author John Mitchel has written:

"If we recall that there are similar hills in China sitting on the *lung-mei*, the Dragon Path, we have some basis for proposing that Silbury was laid out atop the Dragon line by pre-Celtic Druids with help of geomantic compasses. It stands to reason that the Chinese *lung-mei* extends over the entire globe." (1)

Healing power and the energy field around Silbury

It is said that the energy fields around Silbury have the power to heal. Diviners have determined that the ley line upon which the hill is sited possesses feminine attributes, and that earthshine is frequently observed nearby. Crop circles are also found relatively often in the surrounding fields. Unsurprisingly, UFO researchers see evidence of alien activities here.

Many years will pass before all of the secrets of Silbury and its neighboring sites are brought to light. Since the 1980s, scientists and spiritualists have been working together using archaeology and intuition to solve the riddles of this mysterious place.

Consisting of 444,000 cubic yards (339,600 cubic m) of re-deposited earth, the artificially constructed Silbury Hill rises some 130 feet (40 m) high.

Glastonbury: A Heavenly, Holy Place on Earth

Glastonbury Tor, a hill some 525 feet (160 m) high, looms over the Somerset Levels like a mighty ancient beast. The ruins of a legendary church stand atop it, making it one of the most mysterious places in England. Was the Tor the centre of a fertility cult based on an earth goddess myth? Or is it the legendary island of Avalon and the grave of King Arthur?

Avalon, place of the dead

A system of terraces encircles Glastonbury Tor (*tor* is a word of Celtic origin meaning "hill" or "mountain"), which bears structural similarities to those at Silbury Hill. Weathered and broken down by forces of nature over time, the terraces can still be easily identified. This has long been thought of as a giant labyrinth following an ancient, magical pattern. Were this true, this would have to have been a ritual site laid out 4000 or 5000 years ago, like Stonehenge. Two thousand years ago, wetlands came up to the foot of the Tor, closing off the hill and turning it into an island during periods of flooding. The water drained into an enormous lake. At that time the Tor was known as Tor Ynys-witrin, or Island of Glass. The name Avalon comes from the semi-divine Avalloc or Avallach of Celtic legends, according to which he is the ruler of the underworld. For the Celts, Avalon was a bewitched – though pagan – place. It therefore makes sense that the church atop the hill is named for the Archangel Michael, a warrior against powers of darkness. Avalon, where land and sea met, was a place of the dead; here they moved between one world and another.

Glastonbury Tor, topped by the ruins of the legendary church of Saint Michael, looms like an ancient beast over the landscape.

The ruins of Glastonbury Abbey rise above holy ground. Joseph of Arimathia is said to have erected the first church here.

The history of the abbey

In the seventh century, Somerset was conquered by Saxons, who had converted to Christianity under their king, Ine of Wessex, an important figure in the abbey's history. It was reportedly he who erected the original stone church, and its foundations still lie under the western end of the nave. The church was enlarged in the tenth century by the Abbot of Glastonbury, Saint Dunstan, who was later named Archbishop of Canterbury in 960. After the Norman Conquest in 1066, Turstin, the first Norman abbot, extended the abbey from the cemetery to the site of the Saxon church.

By 1086, Glastonbury was the richest abbey in the land, yet just 100 years later, it lay in ruins, destroyed by fire, along with all its valuable treasures. The new church would not be consecrated until Christmas Day of the year 1213. Glastonbury was then the second wealthiest monastery in England, after Westminster Abbey, well into the fourteenth century, and its abbot was a powerful man. In 1536, during the reign of Henry VIII, there were more than 800 monasteries in England. But when Rome denied him a divorce from Catherine of Aragon, he made himself supreme head of the new Anglican Church and dissolved them all. Monks and nuns were driven off, the crown seized the treasures, and Glastonbury fell into ruins.

The grave of King Arthur

One of the greatest mysteries surrounding Glastonbury is whether or not King Arthur is buried here. In 1190, monks recorded that his mortal remains were placed in a grave underneath the abbey together with those of his wife, Guinevere. Inscribed in Latin on a lead cross standing atop a coffin cut out of a tree trunk were the words: *Hic iacet sepultus inclitus rex arturius in insula avalonia* ("Here lies King Arthur, buried on the island of Avalon"). In 1278, in honour of a visit by King Edward I, the bones were laid in a black marble sarcophagus in front of the abbey's main altar. And there, it is said, they remained until the monastery was destroyed in 1536. Since then, every trace of them has been

The official name of the Glastonbury Festival, which has been celebrated annually at Worthy Farm near the ruins since 1970, is the Festival of Contemporary Performing Arts.

The ruins of Glastonbury Abbey stand on consecrated ground. It was once one of the greatest sanctuaries in England.

lost. Stories tell of a black knight with glowing red eyes seeking out the abbey and erasing all traces of the legendary king.

The Holy Grail

There is an old well at the foot of the Tor where the water, blood red from the iron oxide in the surrounding bedrock, bubbles up with a sound like the beat of a heart. It is known as the Chalice Well. According to legend, the well was built by the Druids to hide the cup used during the Last Supper, the Holy Grail, which was filled with the blood of the crucified Christ and brought to England by Joseph of Arimathea. In Glastonbury and Somerset lore, Jesus visited Glastonbury with his uncle Joseph and built the first church on the site out of wattle and daub. This is why Joseph returned here to hide the Grail. It is said that he buried the chalice within the Tor, not far from the entrance to the underworld. The Chalice Well sprang from the spot, with waters that bestow eternal youth. This was the Grail that Arthur and the Knights of the Round Table brought to Avalon.

The Tor goddess

Author Kathy Jones interpreted the Tor as a ritual site associated with the earth goddess, claiming that the Tor itself was a mighty sculpture raised in her honour. The Tor would then be a hollow hill, cut through with grottos in which trolls and elves live to honour the earth and fertility goddess known variously as Rhiannon, Venus, Aphrodite, Morning and Evening Star. Jones believes that the Tor, together with its surrounding terraces, is laid out like a seven circuit labyrinth resembling the one pictured on coins from Crete and on the rocks of Tintagel in Cornwall. It is also a powerful symbol of the earth mother honoured by the North American Hopi Indians. An image of the fertility goddess is also found within the dolmen Luffang-en-Crach in Carnac. The entrance to the labyrinth is said to be at the western end of the Tor, running over the hill and into the heart of the goddess.

The Glastonbury temple of the stars

The Glastonbury Zodiac, identified in natural features that include forests, rivers, springs, paths and meadows, has been identified within a radius of 10 miles (16 km) around the Tor. A veritable "nature park" of astrological signs, this mighty natural temple of the stars connects the Arthur saga with astrology and New Age. Since the park is based more on geographical names and legends than historical fact, recognizing the signs requires a great deal of fantasy. Arthur was the Archer (Sagittarius), Guinevere the Maiden (Virgo), Merlin the Ram (Capricorn) and Lancelot the Lion (Leo). Glastonbury lies within the Waterman (Aquarius), identifiable as a Phoenix. The Chalice Well is the beak of the phoenix, the Bull (Taurus) is its head and the monastery is the Grail castle. Katherine Maltwood, a sculptor, discovered the nature zodiac in 1929 and art professor Mary Caine, filming from an aeroplane, drew the first map. In her opinion, the star signs form a gigantic image of the messiah.

No one doubts that Glastonbury is a magical place; its energy is palpable. As historian William de Malmesbury (ca. 1080–1143) wrote in the twelfth century, Glastonbury is "a heavenly, holy place on earth".

The Chalice Well. Built by the Druids, according to legend, its red waters later became the hiding place of the Holy Grail.

Julian's Bower, an earthen labyrinth in the county of Humberside, in England. In nearly all cultures, labyrinths symbolize enlightenment.

Labyrinths, symbols of the soul

Impenetrably laid out, with winding, crisscrossing paths that visitors must negotiate to find a way out, labyrinths have long been understood in nearly every culture around the world as paths to enlightenment. The seven circuits or rings of most labyrinths are analogous to the seven chakras (human energy centres) and are viewed as representing physical, mental, psychological, or spiritual stages along a path.

A darker interpretation became associated with the three-dimensional labyrinth of Knossos, where the semi-divine man-beast known as the Minotaur lurked. With its construction, according to Kathy Jones, the fertile, feminine symbolic power of the labyrinth as a path to self-knowledge came to an end, replaced by a threatening, patriarchal system. The labyrinth stands for the established pattern of our fate. We can't change it, but can now and then vary our path and learn to live with it.

The Megalithic Alleys of Carnac

Beginning around 3000 BC, an unknown people erected enormous stone blocks on coastlines ranging from the Orkney Islands to Jordan. The greatest number of these are in Brittany, France, where the most mysterious are found in Carnac. These seemingly endless megalithic alleys, once sacred to a vanished population, have long had a magical effect on the viewer.

A prehistoric monument consisting of more than 3000 megaliths

A prehistoric monument consisting of over 3000 colossal stone blocks – up to 13 feet (4 m) in height – the site of Carnac still covers nearly 2 miles (3 km) of the French North Atlantic coast, and originally stretched along 5 miles (8 km) of it. The stone rows, circles and graves date to somewhere between the third millennium and 1800 BC. The granite menhires (from the Breton *ar-men-hir*, "long stone") stand individually, forming alleys or as part of megalithic grave structures.

Later generations carved their own symbols on the sacred stones of a vanished people.

It is fairly certain that neither the Romans nor the Gauls nor the Celts set up these stones. They are related to an unknown people who, toward the end of the Neolithic period, expended unimaginable effort to erect these monuments. They have become immortal through their work, even if we don't know who they were. Due to the fact that nearly all the stones stand near the sea, researchers assume that the instigators of the project were seafaring people.

The Menher-H-roek at Locmariaquer

Individual, large menhires standing some 65 feet (20 m) tall and weighing 350 tons can often be seen near long barrows and post-and-lintel passage graves. One of these is the Mener-H-roek at Locmariaquer. It stood as tall as a six-storey house. How the builders quarried such a stone, brought it to the site and set it in place remains a mystery. For comparison, in 1556 it took 800 men with seventy horses to set up the obelisk in Saint Peter's Square in Rome, although the Roman stile "only" weighed half as much.

The builders of Carnac must have had a highly developed social structure; the stones bear witness to high levels of technical and organizational achievement. In 1700, the menhire of Locmariaquer was struck by lightning and now lies broken on the ground. It had been a landmark for sailors for centuries.

Observatory or fertility symbol?

The Bretons worshipped the stones as cult objects well into modern times. In earlier periods they served religious purposes. The Roman army noticed them while on campaign, and covered them with chiselled images of their own gods. In the Middle Ages, Christians added crosses and other symbols of Christ.

Countless legends are woven around the Carnac stones. Saint Cornelius, martyred in the year 235, is said to have fled to Brittany from the persecution of the Romans. The emperor sent his legionnaires after Cornelius, but the successor of Peter, with the help of fervent prayer, turned the army into stone.

Questions abound. What purpose did these enormous rows and circles serve? Why were they set up at that time? Many investigators are of the opinion that they are cemeteries. Others believe that the stones have something to do with astronomy. It is certain that the stones were sacred to those who erected them, and that their presence continues to keep pagan and Druid customs alive today. Thus, some stones are thought to promote fertility, in particular the menhir of Saint Cado, which is thought to make women fertile. Couples who want children embrace at night under its magical influence. Countless marvellous and terrible legends swirl around the stones of Carnac. But they must forever be legends, because the truth about the stones remains shrouded in darkness.

Some investigators think Carnac is an enormous cemetery. Passage graves are found here, as they are in many other places. Other researchers believe that the graves are all of a more recent date than the menhirs.

Rows of more than 3000 stone colossi up to 13 feet (4 m) in height form this prehistoric monument extending nearly 2 miles (3 km).

The Externstones of Teutoberg Forest

The Externstones are a freestanding rock group within an otherwise stone-free landscape. These strange stones have been the location of human activity dating back to the Middle Ages, but the mystery is whether or not they may have been used during prehistoric times.

A natural and cultural monument

The rocks, which stand 130 feet (40 m) high, are certainly a natural wonder, but also a mysterious cultural monument. Again and again the stones have been interpreted as a Stone Age cult site. According to an inscription, in the twelfth century the Bishop of Paderborn consecrated a grotto within the western rocks as a church. To the left of its entrance is the oldest preserved stone image in Germany, a relief sculpture showing Jesus' descent from the cross. This is the only verifiable date for the use of the site. New Age and Spiritualist groups have triggered a great interest in the Externstones, which have also attracted modern day witches, Druids and Celtic religious groups.

Nationalist and racist interest in Germanic cult sites

The place attracted particular interest from the Nazis, who offered it as proof of the hegemony of Nordic high civilization over those of the Mediterranean. Thus, in 1935, amateur archaeologist Wilhelm Teudt claimed the Externstones were the remains of the Saxon Irminsul, dedicated to the god Irmin. In neo-pagan and neo-fascist circles, Irminsul is the symbol of the resistance of Germanic religion against Christianity. Charlemagne is said to have destroyed the Externstone cult site, and thereby Irminsul, in 722 AD during the war against the Saxons. This is why neo-Nazi groups meet here for solstice festivals and to reinvigorate the worship of Germanic deities like Wotan and Freya. Here they revive nationalist and racist mottos that were laid to rest in 1945. Many (pre)-Germanic interpretations of the Externstones invariably overlap with fascist ideology.

Reachable only by an arched bridge, a chamber is located high above the ground at the top of the rocky outcrop. It has long been in use as a chapel.

Jesus's descent from the cross is depicted on one of the Externstones. It has been suggested that this was an initiation image associated with the Knights Templar.

Stone Age finds

Stone projectile points and flakes that have been dated to the late Paleolithic period (ca. 10,000 BC) were found near the stones. However, this only proves that people lived in the area. It does not in any way provide evidence of the cultic activity that so many would be happy to ascribe to the site. Archaeological excavation uncovered no notable finds proving cult activity for the periods prior to the tenth or eleventh century.

The question as to the pre-Christian function of the Externstones remains obscure, and the list of possible theories is long. Was it the site of a Germanic religious observatory, the power source and cult site of the Germanic gods, or, as the anthroposophist Rolf Speckner suggested, was it the seat of an oracle? Do the rocks really display traces of ancient stone working, as proposed by the mason and author Ulrich Niedhorn? The questions remain.

Traces of fire in the rock grotto

Some time ago, Ulrich Niedhorn discovered traces of fire inside the rock grotto. Since the grottoes are artificially constructed and fire is a sign of human intervention, perhaps these serve as evidence that the stones were finished using fire-cracking, a method in which stone is split by the deliberate application of concentrated heat. But the question remains: what is the date of these traces of fire?

Thermoluminescence dating is the only method available that is capable of dating burn marks like these. It can determine when the quartz and feldspar were last exposed to heat. In this case, however, tests have produced no results, as though the stones are unwilling to divulge their secrets.

On the right, Nicodemus leans on the bowed Irminsul symbol; underneath, the Midgard serpent is shown, itself a symbol of the Externstones' telluric ("earth") power. More than one artist worked on this piece. A stylistic analysis shows that the serpent is the work of an Anglo-Saxon.

The Easter Island Giants

On Easter Sunday in the year 1722, a ship captained by the Dutch sailor Jacob Roggeveen (1659–1729) landed on an unknown island. The native people possessed only primitive stone tools and weapons, and a few canoes. The sailors were impressed, and terrified, by the over 1000 colossal and mysterious stone statues that they found there.

The Polynesians: A People of Many Islands

Jacob Roggeveen named the isle of the stony colossi "Easter Island". Its discovery began a long tale of woe for the islanders that only came to an end in the mid-twentieth century.

Sailors from New Guinea had already reached Fiji around 1000 BC, from there navigating to Samoa and Tahiti. 400 years later this restless folk were again underway, searching for further islands, as their legends say, "above the wind". In powerful catamarans they took long journeys and became the people of the many islands, the Polynesians. One story claims that around 380 AD, Polynesians from Tuatomu set off in search of new land. They reached an island where, for over 1000 years, they lived without contact with other peoples. They named their world "Rapa Nui", the navel of the world.

Norwegian researcher Thor Heyerdahl proposed an alternative view, in which the original inhabitants of Easter Island came the South American mainland. Only this, he said, could explain their magnificent achievements in stone sculpture. The inhabitants of Rapa Nui were the best stonemasons in the entire Pacific. At the same time, the Easter Island culture was the only one in the Pacific to develop its own written language, the Rongorongo script.

Rongorongo writing
Rongorongo is a phonetic pictorial script depicting people, animals, body parts and tools used in daily life. It is thought that it served as a kind of memory aid for Easter Island's original inhabitants. It records essential terminology, expanding upon memorized words and sentences. The inscribed boards that have survived are found in a number of museums around the world.

The sculptures do not look out to sea, but turn their backs to it. They gaze instead on the land and clan members.

Geographical location
The South Pacific Easter Island belongs to Chile and is located south of the Tropic of Capricorn at 27 degrees latitude and 109 degrees longitude. It lies isolated nearly 2300 miles (3700 km) from the Chilean coast and over 2500 miles (4000 km) from Tahiti. In 2002, 3791 people were living on Easter Island.

The figures are cut out of volcanic stone; the whites of their eyes are made of shell. Many statues wore hats, symbols of the particular worthiness of their clans.

Figures with stylized heads and long ear lobes

The construction of massive stone platforms called *ahu* was already underway in the year 400 AD. These were open-air burial sites. The corpse would be exposed atop the *ahu* until the birds and insects in conjunction with the wind had completely removed the flesh, leaving only bones behind. Afterwards the bones would be buried inside the *ahu*, a festival in honour of the dead would be celebrated, and an enormous statue carved from the soft stone of the volcano Ranu Raraku would be set atop the stone platform in order to bear witness to the wealth and power of the clan. After 1000 AD, the dominating figure was that of a man with a stylized head, extended ear lobes and, frequently, decorations on the body that can be interpreted as tattoos. The sculptures gaze over the land and people of the clans, with their backs to the ocean. The size and decoration of the statues became prestige symbols.

The decline of the Easter Island population

Perhaps an enemy attacked at some time after 1400, although this cannot be proven. It is certain, however, that wood was in short supply and that the transport and setting up of the statues, as well as the more practical construction of houses and ships, had decimated the island's forests. Without trees, life was wretched. The earth could no longer retain moisture and lost its fertility. Cannibalism began, often involving the consumption of an enemy's wife and children. The *ahus* were destroyed and the statues knocked down. Then came the worst enemies of all – land hungry Europeans. Anyone who could exploit the island did so, with devastating effects. As late as 1862, the Peruvians carried off all the men and women capable of working in their mines as slaves. The few who returned brought epidemics to the land. By this time only a few statues still stood. Christians stepped in to continue the destruction of the "heathen works". By 1877, the island had only 110 inhabitants. Annexed by Chile in 1888, it became an enormous livestock pasture for European businesses, as well as a leper colony. Democratic political structures only came to the island in the late 1960s, but the mystery of the stone colossi lives on.

The size and decoration of the statues became symbols of the clans' status. Construction and transport of the statues decimated the island's forests.

Rapa Nui
Rapa Nui is today the official language of Easter Island. Approximately 200-300 people who speak it currently live in Chile, Tahiti and the United States.

The Australian natives, especially the Anangu, named the dramatic red cliffs of Ayers Rock Uluru, their greatest sanctuary.

Ayers Rock

The Australian natives, the Anangu, named the red cliffs of Ayers Rock Uluru, their greatest sanctuary. According to Aboriginal mythological tradition, two young men playing in the mud after a rain created Uluru during Dreamtime. The mythical beings who inhabit the monolith remain a mystery.

Uluru: "Seat of the Ancestors" and Aboriginal Sanctuary

The engineer William Gosse, while exploring the northern territories of Australia in 1873, became the first white man to come upon the monolith. He named it after Sir Henry Ayers, who was the prime minister of Australia at the time. Discovery of the dramatic rock contributed to what had been the fate of the continent since its "discovery" by Europeans: banishment of the natives from their hunting grounds, and destruction of their sacred sites. Life became unbearable for the Aborigines. Their present day population has been reduced to around 50,000.

In the Anangu language, *Uluru* means "seat of the ancestors". Except for ceremonial reasons, they are forbidden to set foot upon the rock. Nevertheless, ever since its discovery, hundreds of curious tourists climb the sanctuary of Uluru every day. Many stumble, suffer heat stroke, or injure themselves in some other way. A hospital with helicopters has been built near the site to help them. The Aborigines can only stand by and watch.

Crossroads of the Paths of Dreamtime

Uluru is the second largest monolith on the earth. It is sandstone, more precisely arkosic sandstone. It has a circumference of 5.8 miles (9.4 km), is 1.5 miles (2.4 km) wide and 2.3 miles (3.6 km) long. Standing 1150 feet (348 m) high, it covers an area of some 1.25 square miles (3.3 square km). The cliff, which is estimated to be six million years old, has lost small portions of its total surface to erosion, but has maintained its original form.

Every crack, every protuberance, every rise in the rock's surface, no matter how small, is meaningful to the Aborigines. The drops of condensation on its walls are the blood flecks of the poisonous snake-man, who was killed in a famous Dreamtime battle. Every cave at the foot of Uluru has a specific meaning tied to their rituals. The caves are decorated with a multitude of drawings, some more than 3000 years old. The many images of Dreamtime events have yet to be successfully deciphered. Dreamtime contains the Aborigines' creation story and mythology. It isn't written down, and is only passed on orally. When the natives are threatened with extinction, so are their rituals and traditions.

The revenge of the spirits

Time and again visitors have reported, entranced, how the Uluru radiates a magical energy field. In the same breath, as an explanation for the countless falls and injuries, they speak of revenge taken on the white invaders by the spirits of the Aborigines. One woman was threatened with death because she had come too close to a spot that was taboo for females. The baby Azaria is perhaps the most famous case. The Chamberlain family lost their two-month-old baby on the mountain, testifying in court that dingoes, wild dogs, had stolen the child from their tent. Lindy Chamberlain was nevertheless tried for murder and condemned to life in prison, until, after six years in prison, she was freed when a bloody baby jacket was found in dingo territory. Naturally, the case revived the mythology. It was said that deadly beasts straight out of Dreamtime had killed the baby. Revenge against invaders again became a subject of conversation.

Hidden streams run through and under Uluru, most of them known only by the Aborigines.

The Aborigines call the tourists "ants" because when they climb holding onto a steel rope, they look like a line of ants.

Taishan, the Holy Mountain

"Not far from the birthplace of Confucius is the holy mountain Taishan, the Chinese Olympus. Since the earliest days of Chinese history the mountain has soared high from the middle of an extensive massif. It reclines in majestic silence with streams converging from all directions at its base. Clouds wreathe its peak, dispensing rain and sunshine to all." (2)

Inscribed with characters, holy places for prayer line the Path to Heaven. Symbolic banknotes are still burned here today to ensure wealth and prosperity.

The harmony of Heaven and Earth

In the Yellow River valley, in the province of Shandong, cradle of Chinese culture, Taishan soars nearly 5000 feet (1524 m) high, the third highest peak of the massif known as the Five Holy Mountains. Although it isn't the highest mountain, it is considered the greatest sanctuary in China, a centre of Taoist belief. In the early days of Chinese culture it marked the boundary between the known world and the unknown. Many magicians lived in Shandong, who traditionally devoted themselves to the study of eternal life in close conjunction with immortals. Chinese emperors offered sacrifices on Taishan from 2000 BC onward. A total of seventy-two emperors made pilgrimages here, bringing offerings for

A pilgrim carries his bundle up the Steps to Heaven.

the Heavens and Earth. Still, Taishan was never really bound to the teachings of Confucius, which were the basis of the political philosophy of the Chinese throne. Instead, it was magicians who reigned here, along with alchemists and rebels.

The massif of the Five Holy Mountains is wreathed in thick clouds. In early Chinese culture the mountains were considered the boundary between the known world and the unknown.

The religion of rebellion

The rebel was Lao Tsu, the founder of Taoism and author of *Tao Te Ching*, also known as *The Book of the Way and its Virtues*. Little is known about this mystical master, a contemporary of Confucius, who was born here in 604 BC. He taught the path of least resistance and living in harmony with nature, rather than fighting against it. Taoism is at the same time the strictest and the worldliest religion. Born in an era of constant war, Lao Tsu preached peace and harmony through improved understanding of the inner and outer world. All confrontation arises out of the inability to be in accord with the true nature of reality, the Tao.

Taoists disavow any differentiation between superiority and inferiority in the human and animal worlds, preferring to promulgate harmony between all beings. As a result, they became masters of alchemy and predicting the future. Taoism views the earth as a living organism full of vital energy. They created feng shui, literally "the teaching of the wind and water", in order to determine in which places and with what arrangement of buildings the highest level of harmony could be createed. All centres of Taosim were chosen because they housed a great deal of vital energy, the greatest source of which was centred on Taishan, the most mysterious and holiest place of all.

The way is the destination

Precisely 6293 steps lead from the lowest temple on the summit, which is consecrated to the mountain god, up to the Jade Emperor Temple, with a difference in elevation of almost 4500 feet (1350 m) between the two. Before reaching the heights one steps through the southern Heaven Gate. Yu Huang, the Jade Emperor, is Taoism's highest deity, the lord of the present. But along the path leading upward there are smaller temples, wells, cypress groves, waterfalls and lakes, all places for reflection, prayer and offering. In earlier times up 10,000 people made the pilgrimage up to the sanctuary daily; but, following Taoist teachings, each of the countless deities can also be encountered along the way, and thus prayers and sacrifices are offered everywhere. In Taoism, the path is the destination.

Chartres

The early Gothic Cathedral of Chartres, 426 feet (130 m) long, 150 feet (46 m) wide, and crowned by a tower more than 325 feet (100 m) high, is one of the largest and most impressive structures on earth. Thirty years were devoted just to the creation of the 173 windows that translate the Bible into stained glass images. Although the name of the architect is forgotten, he was a master of his craft. Instead of using weight-bearing walls, he designed a magnificent construction that rests entirely on Gothic arches.

The miracle of the Marian statue

Chartres lies only 56 miles (90 km) from Paris in a fertile plain on the River Eure, a landscape that has long been an agricultural centre. On a hill rising in the middle of the plain, there has always been a church, perching like a brood hen, for over 1500 years. Even earlier, there was already a dolmen on the site, dating to the period of the construction of Stonehenge. It is thought that it marks one of the most important energy points on earth. The dolmen, together with a nearby grotto, has long been recognized as a holy place. According to legend, around 100 years before the birth of Christ, a Druid prophesied that a virgin would bear a child. This led, in pre-Christian times, to the dedication of the site to that virgin. She was perceived as a black Madonna because the Celtic Druids had carved an image of mother and child out of the trunk of a pear tree. She was known as the Underground Virgin, because her image was kept in the grotto.

Notre Dame de Chartres, built in perfect harmony with the golden ratio.

Even since the days of the Druids, who conducted a school on this site, Chartres has been a centre of the Marian cult.

Early Christians discovered the place with its statue of the virgin in the third century AD. They founded the first church, constructing the first ecclesiastical building at Chartres, and dedicated it to Mary. What we admire today is the sixth house of God called Notre Dame de Chartres on the site – all of its predecessors were destroyed by fire. The duke of Aquitaine burned the first church in 743 AD and the Danes incinerated the second in 858. The third and fourth churches fell victim to flames in 962 and 1020. The first cathedral on the site, the fifth structure, was also lost to an inferno. A mysterious story is associated with this last fire, which destroyed the entire area, not just the cathedral. Chroniclers record that every attempt at extinguishing the flames failed, and that one could see the glow of the fire as far away as Paris. Days later, after the village and church had been reduced to their foundations, Mary's cloak, a relic donated to the cathedral by Charlemagne's grandson in 876, remained in the crypt, under the rubble, completely unharmed. This encouraged the rapid construction of a new cathedral, the one we know today, which rose like a phoenix from the ashes barely thirty years later.

Ease for the spirit, stimulation for the mind

Gothic architecture began to bloom in Europe at the onset of the twelfth century, though no one is sure who planted the first seed. Chartres is the most impressive of more than eighty cathedrals built in France during this time. Had the Knights Templar discovered secrets in the Holy Land that, with the help of the Cistercians, they now put into practice in Europe? It has been suggested that they had found the Wheel of Moses in Jerusalem, a legendary object that incorporated sacred measurements, numbers and weights. The Cistercians may have decoded its mysteries and used them for the first time in the construction of the new Chartres Cathedral, making it a building planned and executed according to divine rule. All the proportions, alignments and architectural systems are designed to soothe the spirit and stimulate the mind. Collectively, the proportions follow the basic relationship contained in the golden ratio, known since antiquity: 1.618 to 1. The distances between the columns, and the length of the nave from transept to choir, are all factors of the golden number. The floor level of the crypt lies 120 feet (37 m) beneath the altar, with the Gothic roof built exactly the same distance above. The buttresses are so perfectly proportioned that they do not appear to bear any weight at all.

Like the cloak of Mary donated to the cathedral by Charlemagne's grandson in 876 AD, this stained glass window from the twelfth century survived a devastating conflagration.

After the French Revolution, the cathedral, with its long history, was converted into a wine depot. Robespierre saved it from destruction, dedicating it as a temple to "highest reason".

Notre Dame de Paris

The mother of all Gothic cathedrals stands in Paris: Notre Dame, Our (Dear) Lady, as Mary is known in France. It forms the centre of Paris, and is thereby the focal point for all of France. The cathedral square is the location of France's "point zero", the point from which all distances are measured, for example along highways leading to Paris. Notre Dame is where Napoleon Bonaparte crowned himself and his wife Josephine emperor and empress of France in the presence of Pope Pius VII on 2 December 1804.

The twelfth-century building craze in France

Notre Dame is the name of countless cathedrals and churches in the French-speaking world, and thus this Gothic house of worship is known as Notre Dame de Paris. Its construction, begun in 1163 under bishop Maurice de Sully, was completed only in 1345. During those 182 years every Gothic stylistic phase, many adopted from other great French cathedrals, flowed into the architecture of Notre Dame. But the place was already marked by a special energy in prehistoric times, when it was a cult site. A Gallo-Roman temple stood here before the birth of Christ, followed by an early Christian basilica and, finally, by a Romanesque church. When de Sully commissioned his cathedral, he had the basilica, which had been restored shortly before, torn down. This was due to the building craze that had gripped all of France, an expression of their desire for the new: not the heavy Romanesque style, but the weightless architecture of the Gothic. The Knights Templar had brought this desire for a new transcendence to Europe.

The central nave of Notre Dame is 426 feet (130 m) long, 157 feet (48 m) wide, 115 feet (35 m) high and seats 9000 people. The northern rose window, with eighty scenes from the Old Testament, is particularly beautiful. Nearly all the stained glass in the cathedral dates from the thirteenth century.

The enigma of the cult of Mary

As already mentioned, there are a great many Gothic cathedrals in northern France alone. Notre Dame de Paris was the first; in 1176 came Strasbourg, Bourges in 1185, Chartres in 1194, Rouen in 1200, Reims in 1211, Amiens in 1220, Beauvais in 1247, and still others at Bayeux, Laon, L'Epine and Evreux. If one connects all of these places on a map, the lines depict the constellation Virgo, the Virgin. It has been said that, like the legends surrounding Chartres, this proves that worship of a childbearing Virgin must have roots in pre-Christian times. When Caesar's legions marched through, before the birth of Christ, all of these cities were Celtic settlements, as shown by the existence of dolmen and cult sites. Who was it that gave the Gothic building masters their knowledge? The oldest written accounts of the Celtic Virgin are too late to provide confirmation one way or another. They are from the fourteenth century, a time when the cathedrals were already in existence.

The sacred geometry of the Gothic

Philip the Fair disbanded the Templar order at the beginning of the fourteenth century, burning the knights as heretics. Along with them, the pure Gothic building style also disappeared as suddenly as it had come into existence some 200 years earlier. Churches were still built in the Gothic style, with its characteristic high vaults and pointed arches, but they were visually cluttered. The sacred geometry of the Gothic had come to an end, much like those who had orchestrated it in the first place. The secret knowledge of the Templar order was closely related to the Ark of the Covenant, which Solomon built his temple to protect. The Knights Templar, nine nobles from France and Flanders, were dispatched on a ten-year mission to search out its secrets. What powers did the sacred geometry offer humankind, and what strength is concealed in Gothic cathedrals, which indeed have all been built on places of power? The Gothic cathedral awakened powers of consciousness that we still cannot fathom today.

Victor Hugo on Notre Dame
"Every surface, every stone of this worthy monument is not only a page in the history of the land, but also in the history of Art and Science." (3)

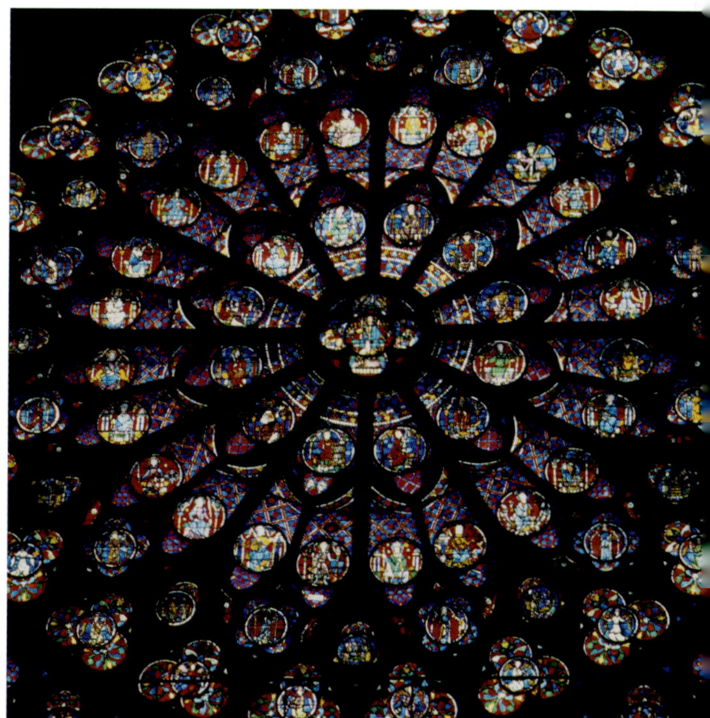

Still preserved after 700 years, the magnificent rose window of Notre Dame de Paris has a diameter of 33 feet (10 m).

Mysterious Artefacts

Artefacts are at least as important as the ancient sites at which they are found. Tools, inscriptions, art and cult objects help us to understand ancient peoples, their living conditions and their cultural context. In studying the physical evidence for the origins of ritual and legend, we have the opportunity to reevaluate our preconceptions and, in doing so, to better understand our own culture.

Innumerable questions about the past have been answered through the study of ancient objects, even if the results have been rather surprising, as has occasionally been the case. We now have evidence for technologies that were forgotten over the centuries, only to be rediscovered or reimagined relatively recently.

Of course, we are equally aware that forgers and swindlers regularly manipulate or even fabricate comparable evidence. It isn't always easy to tell the difference, particularly when, as has happened more than once, false evidence is planted among genuine remains. At the same time, false conclusions can be drawn even without any indications of fraud. It is not uncommon for the true function of an artefact to be identified long after its initial discovery. Misunderstandings can lead to false analysis and published results that frequently give the general public a distorted view of the discoveries, which nonetheless endures.

The following pages review some of these discoveries, present the results of investigations, and attempt to explain their significance.

The Ica stones from Peru portray people, objects and beasts in unlikely combinations.

Geoglyphs

In 1927, while flying over the Peruvian pampa, an arid plain located between the Pacific and the Andes, several pilots reported seeing images that had apparently been drawn on the ground. But it was only after they brought proof in the form of photographs taken during their flights that anyone believed them. These images of apes, birds and geometrical forms extend over an area of several miles.

Lines in stone

The dark stone of the Andes Mountains eroded down onto the plain below millennia ago, where it oxidized over time. Some 2000 years ago, this uppermost dark layer of soil was removed by unknown artists to create images by exposing the red subsurface below. The dark stone that had been scraped away from the subsoil was piled about 3.5 inches (10 cm) high along the edges, strengthening the outlines of the images. When viewed from the ground, the difference between the colours of the subsurface and the dark stone is barely noticeable, and the differences in elevation are barely perceptible. The dark stones, though not piled up particularly high, still block the line of sight. The outlined images are really only clearly recognizable from a great height. Roads had been built directly adjacent to these drawings, in some cases running right through them, without anyone noticing that they were there.

The mathematician Maria Reiche has spent fifty years investigating the Nazca lines.

One of the most unusual characteristics of these so-called Nazca lines is that many of them run perfectly straight for several hundred yards. In German, perfectly straight is *schnurgerecht*, or "string-straight". The double meaning of this term was certainly understood by the German researcher Maria Reiche (1903–1998), who began investigating the lines in 1946. She hypothesized that the designs for the pictures were first sketched on a smaller scale. The next step would be for someone to go to the pampa and extend a string, increase the scale accordingly, and thereby transfer the design onto the ground. Oriented on the straight strings, workers could scrape away the dark surface stone in a correspondingly precise manner.

Sketchbook, divine cult or signs of water?

We don't know why the Nazca lines and images in stone were created. The most popular theory claims that these are landing strips for aliens or deities. There is also a legend saying that a god created the infertile pampa to take revenge on the people living there, who had angered him. This explanation has nothing to do with a landing strip, but says the images were created to placate this angry god. A further theory proposes that the people living there recorded their astronomical knowledge on the ground, and that these images represent constellations. This explanation is much disputed, however, because other civilizations that developed similar astrological cults normally recorded their knowledge in practical, easy-to-use maps of the stars. Some have even connected the drawings with the practical need to locate underground sources of water, which could be identified by means of the aboveground markings. While this last proposal might explain the purely geometric designs, it does not offer much help toward interpreting the depictions of humans and animals.

We also don't know who created the Nazca lines. Since the pampa is not fertile ground, it has been suggested that no cultures settled here at all. The nearest place occupied by humans is the town of Nazca, which lies some 12.5 miles (20 km) away, and there is no evidence at all of other ancient building activity in the pampa. Even other known or researched native peoples seem to have avoided this place. The traces of Indian settlements tend to become lost in the rugged Andes.

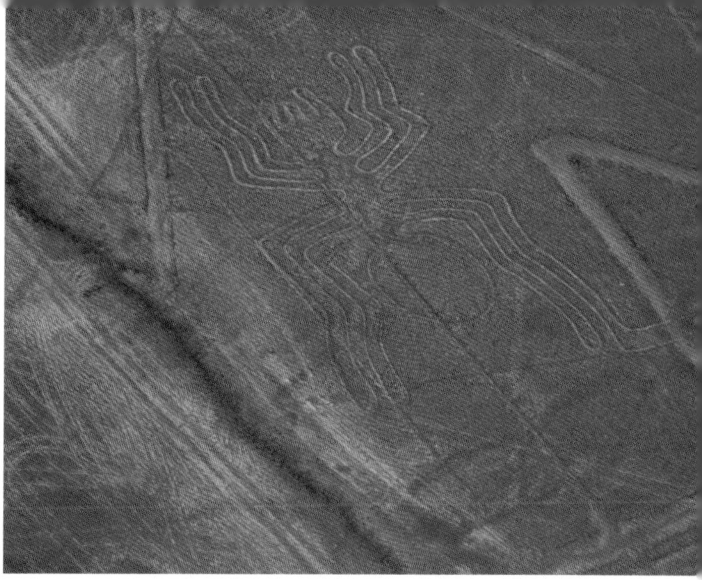

Lines and triangles enclose the spider on the edge of the Pampa de San Jose.

Not all of the 900 geoglyphs are clearly identifiable like the spider (right) or other animal and human representations. It is difficult to say whether what we see here is a symbolic portrayal of hands or some kind of bird.

The White Horse...

Mysterious geoglyphs are not only found in Peru. The "White Horse" is located on a hill named after it near Uffington Castle in Oxfordshire, England. The stylized image dating from the Stone Age is cut into the hill so as to expose the white chalk beneath the vegetation. The image is difficult to recognize from ground level because of its size, almost 360 by 127 feet (110 x 37 m), and also because of the irregular surface of the hill. Over time, wind and vegetation have altered the appearance of the horse, which in the eighteenth century almost disappeared beneath the turf altogether. Since the nineteenth century, English Heritage, England's leading monument preservation organization, has kept the image cleared. The White Horse is so popular that horse outlines have since been dug into other South English hillsides as well.

The exact age of the White Horse and the identity of its creators are not known. Until the 1990s, a date in the Iron Age (800–500 BC) was proposed for its construction, in other words, the same time period as nearby Uffington Castle. Since then, dates provided by a newly developed technology suggest that the horse was created during the Bronze Age (ca. third–first millennium BC). This would contradict the local tradition, however, according to which Anglo-Saxon invaders produced the image during the fifth century AD.

The snake earthwork in Adams County, Ohio is distinctly visible only when viewed from a few specific locations.

... and the Green Snakes

Comparable images are also known in North America, although a different technique was used to create them. Unlike the examples in the Peruvian pampa, the outlines are not dug out, but heaped up into artificial mounds to form outlines of various animals. Up to now most of these have been found in Wisconsin, but others also exist in Iowa, Ohio, Illinois and Georgia. Like other geoglyphs, the animals portrayed are usually only recognizable from a great height (see box, page 71).

Despite its elevation of 775 feet (236 m), the Candelabra is one of the few geoglyphs that can be identified not only from above. Located on the Pacific coast of Peru, it is visible from offshore ships.

The simply represented White Horse of Uffington is really only recognizable when viewed from the air.

It can only be assumed many other representational mounds must have existed, only to fall victim to urbanization. The drawings of the businessman William Pidgeon, an amateur archaeologist and recorder of Native American myths who described his travels and investigations, confirm this. Published in 1858, *The Traditions of De-coo-dah* includes sketches showing animal mounds and processions that no longer exist today. He also includes information provided by the Native American prophet De-coo-dah, who presented himself to Pidgeon as a descendant of the people who built the mounds, supposedly a superior race that preceded the Native Americans. He told Pidgeon that the mounds and the waves were originally characters that spelled out messages for the decendants of his tribe. When asked about the snake form that Pidgeon had seen depicted unusually often on the mounds, De-coo-dah told stories that mingled myth with astronomical descriptions. This led Pidgeon to the conclusion that some images functioned either as calendars or maps of constellations.

Representations

The majority of representational mounds in North America depict snakes, some of which are in the act of devouring an egg. Other earthworks, mainly in Wisconsin, show birds with human heads, two-headed people, and some kind of creature that resembles a dog. In some places, such as McGregor, Iowa, an entire animal parade is portrayed, constructed of several similarly-sized and sculpted mounds arranged in a line with regular spacing between them.

Although many scientists dismissed these words as pompous invention, the investigation of the mounds now began in earnest. Drawings were made of their exact locations, followed by excavations leading into the interiors of the mounds in hopes of finding something that would confirm the Native American's statements. Unfortunately, this did not happen. The riddle of the animal mounds of North America, despite further finds and publications, remains unsolved.

The Ica Stones

In 1961 a group of stones bearing engraved images were found near the Peruvian city of Ica. An analysis of geological sedimentation indicated that the images are more than 10,000 years old. This date was contradicted, however, by the objects and living creatures depicted in the images, which could not possibly have coexisted at that time.

Heart transplants, telescopes and maps of the world

In 1974, the French borderline scientist Robert Charroux reported on a collection of more than 11,000 stones belonging to Dr. Javier Cabrera. The doctor also had other artefacts in his possession, including clay and stone figurines. Dr. Cabrera claimed that the pieces in his collection belonged to an extinct, prehistoric culture. The images engraved on the stones depicted people apparently using a telescope to observe the heavens and using tools to perform heart surgery on an anatomically correct organ. Other stones show people hunting dinosaurs, or depict complete maps of the world. In his publications, Robert Charroux expressed his belief that these stones are in fact millions of years old and represent the library of Atlantis. Dr. Cabrera was of the same opinion, at least regarding the date. He built his own museum (in Ica, Peru) to exhibit his collection, and was always ready to discuss his theories with journalists and scientists.

The Indios' workshop

In 1977, the Swiss author Erich von Daniken eagerly took up Charroux's descriptions and began his own investigations. In his own remarks, von Daniken reports on his discussions with Dr. Cabrera, who he described as "strong willed", and suggested that the doctor was incapable of accepting any opposing arguments. This was clear when von Daniken confronted him with a series of stones that resembled those in his collection, but which had been purchased from an Indio, who had in fact made them himself. Dr. Cabrera nonetheless did not waver for a moment from his opinion that his own stones were the product of an ancient culture.

The very fact that the images included Christian symbols had already led many scientists to doubt Dr. Cabrera's claims. However, because the stones are not made

The Indio who claimed to have made the Ica stones for Dr. Cabrera demonstrated his methods for the BBC. The stones were first blackened with shoe polish, then fired in donkey dung before being engraved. Were all the stones in the collection created in this way?

of organic material, they are very difficult to date and, of course, the engraved images need not be as old as the stones themselves.

In the late 1990s, a television team found an Indio who showed reporters how simple it was to make such an Ica stone. He claimed to have made the larger part of Dr. Cabrera's collection himself, not only the engraved stones, but the clay and stone figurines as well, all while under contract to the doctor. Although Dr. Cabrera protested what he called a misrepresentation, he could produce no counter-evidence. Further investigation by the television crew made it clear that comparable engraved stones were in fact to be found in the Ica region, but with images that were in no way out of the ordinary. The reporters concluded that the Ica stones in Dr. Cabrera's collection were forgeries.

Dr. Cabrera died on 30 December 2001. His collection can still be seen in the museum he built. The investigations of the television team has made it much quieter around the stones, although every now and then there are still scientists hoping that at least part of the collection will prove genuine, challenging our preconceptions about early cultures. Many people, however, are fairly certain that the stone and clay figures are without any historical value.

The French author Robert Charroux was the first to publish descriptions of the Ica stones.

Some of the stones are engraved with living beings, objects and activities that are not in synch chronologically. This prehistoric man using a telescope would be an example.

The Iron Column of Delhi

One relic of an ancient culture that has recently become increasingly popular is the so-called Iron Column of Delhi. According to legend, anyone who can stand with his or her back to the column and fling their arms around the shaft so that their fingers meet in one try will enjoy great happiness in the future. People also claim that despite exposure to thousands of years of weather, the column bears not one trace of rust.

THE IRON COLUMN: DESCRIPTION...

The first mosque to be built in India, the Quwwat-ul-Islam-Masjid (Mosque of the Power of Islam) was erected in New Delhi inside the Qutab Minar Complex, so named because a 240-foot- (73-m-) tall minaret was erected there in 1193 to celebrate a military victory. The mosque's cornerstone was laid at the same time. An iron column some 23 feet (7 m) tall stands within the inner courtyard. It, too, was likely set up contemporarily with the construction of the complex. An inscription in the Sanskrit language explains that the column was originally erected at another site and was moved here later.

In 1969, Erich von Daniken described the iron column in one of his books. According to von Daniken, it was welded together using special iron alloys that are completely unknown today. Because these alloys lacked both phosphorus and sulfur, the column had never rusted, not even in the course of 4000 years.

...AND REALITY

To be fair, it must be said that Erich von Daniken publicly acknowledged the errors in his work several years later. Nevertheless, his original description was so popular and so widespread that it continues to have a hold on popular imagination today. The column is in fact of interest to scientists, but two mistakes made by von Daniken need to be addressed first.

For one thing, the iron column is not 4000 years old. It very likely dates to the fifth century AD, and probably originally stood within or near a temple in the Indian province of Bihar. It was dedicated to Vishnu, the Indian god known as "The Preserver". Its unusual top suggests that it was once crowned by a figure or statue.

The 23-foot- (7-m-) high iron column is located in the inner courtyard of the Quwwat-ul-Islam-Masjid, the Mosque of the Power of Islam.

In addition, the column is not in any way welded together, let alone made out of several unknown alloys. However, on this point we do encounter something unusual. The pillar seems to have been forged as a single piece, which, at a height of 23 feet (7 m), would weigh around 6 tons. In addition, the iron used is of such exceptional purity (99.75%) that, despite India's humid climate during the annual monsoon season, there is in fact no trace of rust to be found on it.

In Europe, work of comparable quality and magnitude would not have been possible until around the end of the nineteenth century, some 1500 years later, when the technical knowledge needed to produce a column such as this would finally be available. From a chemical point of view, its production is also mysterious. While by 1938 it would be possible – under controlled laboratory conditions – to produce iron of comparable purity, nothing like this could be forged under the natural conditions found in a blacksmith's shop. How the column's builders achieved this incredible level of purity has not yet been explained.

The Sanskrit inscription on the column explains that it originally stood in another location.

It is thought that the top of the column originally supported a figure of Garuda, messenger of the gods.

The Glozel Runes

In 1924, a farmer ploughing in the tiny hamlet of Glozel, near Vichy, France, came upon a mass of broken stone with an underground chamber lying beneath. His grandson reached in and pulled out a clay tablet covered with characters that neither of them could decipher. They took their find to a local amateur archaeologist in Vichy. This set off a genuine feud between those who see the runes as fantastically ancient, and those for whom they are nothing more than crude forgeries.

The battle of the runes

There are different versions of how the doctor and amateur archaeologist Dr. Antonin Morlet came into conflict with the professional archaeologist Dr. Louis Capitan over the Glozel runes. We know for sure that Morlet organized an excavation in Glozel after seeing the first runes found by the farmer. He did, in fact, find additional inscribed clay tablets, along with some bones. He wrote these up in a report that he forwarded to Dr. Capitan, who enthusiastically responded, arriving a short time later in Glozel to undertake his own excavation and present the results to the general public.

It seems likely that Morlet did not agree with this plan of action. In any case, Morlet's treatise, in which he dated the tablets to 8000 BC, was published under the names of the doctor and the farmer shortly after the archaeological experts arrived on the scene.

In his later publications, Capitan sharply attacked the claims made by the amateur archaeologist, questioning his competence and even describing the clay tablets as obvious forgeries. He argued that no civilization with writing could have existed in the year 8000 BC. In addition, the rune symbols themselves, in which no word or sentence structure could be recognized, did not suggest that they really represented a language.

The battle of the runes continued into the following years, involving a widening circle of additional experts, who also could not reach agreement about whether or not the runes were genuine. At the beginning of the Second World War the discussion abruptly ended and the runes were forgotten.

Rediscovery and dating

At the end of the 1970s, discussion about whether or not the runes were genuine flared up anew. Due to technical advances that had been made in the decades following the war, it was now possible to determine the age of the inscribed tablets and bones. The oldest find, at 17,000 years, was a bone plate, and the other bones were around 15,000 years old. The clay tablets were considerably later, fired around 600 BC. It is of course possible that additional clay tablets once existed and are now lost.

Deciphering the runes is still considered to be a nearly impossible task. As already mentioned, precise word and

The Glozel runes, discovered by chance, still puzzle scientists today because of their seemingly random arrangement.

sentence structure is lacking. Attempts have been made to interpret these as cultic or astronomical texts, with controversial results.

The opinions of the scientists involved with the Glozel finds today are in any case still not unanimous. While some experts view the runes as genuine, others continue to dismiss them as forgeries. In some publications, even their very existence is contested. In the end, the battle of the Glozel runes has done little more than enhance and preserve the myths surrounding them.

One theory claims that the runes come from a different time period than the objects on which they are written. Therefore, it is possible that Celtic pilgrims inscribed pieces they had found by chance somewhere in the years 700–1000 BC. Nevertheless, the writing still cannot be deciphered today.

These runes found in a Stone Age village in China show strong parallels with those discovered in Glozel.

Other rune finds
The runes from Glozel were long thought to be unique, until clay tablets were found in China with characters that were almost, or entirely, identical to them. The tablets were found in the ruins of a prehistoric village that is estimated to be 8000 years old. Characters with considerable parallels to the Glozel runes are also said to have been found in Australia.

The Antikythera Mechanism

In 1900, divers off the Greek island of Antikythera unexpectedly came across a shipwreck in water over 130 feet (40 m) deep. A great many objects were removed from the hull and brought to the surface, including, among the statues and other art objects, a damaged gear mechanism, the function of which was not immediately recognized by scholars. In the 1950s, the device was analyzed for the first time as an early analog computer.

THE PLANETARIUM WITH DIFFERENTIAL DRIVE

The mechanism found by divers near Antikythera is composed of several bronze rings bound to each other by gears. The rings are engraved with signs and characters that mark it as an astronomical device. These facts were already recorded in 1902 by Greek archaeologist Spyridon Stais. However, because the mechanism was broken into four pieces, it received relatively little attention. Based on other artefacts found in the same shipwreck, it was determined that the ship sank in approximately 82 BC. It is assumed that the device dates to about this time, as well.

In the 1950s, Derek de Solla Price, a professor of the History of Science at Yale University, began to work with the mechanism. His first treatise on the subject appeared in 1955, but the article that really made the mechanism widely known appeared in 1959.

In that article, Price described how the device was manufactured, using evidence that showed that the machine originally had a wooden frame. He came to the conclusion that it was used to facilitate astronomical calculations. This was required at sea in order to determine the position of the ship – that would make navigation possible. Anyone using the device could also calculate the movements of the known planets and figure out the date of certain events, for example, of the equinox. Adjusting the gears would also predict the future phases of the moon as far as a year in advance.

All of this was possible only because the mechanism had a differential drive that, in its modern form, was patented in the year 1828. Leonardo da Vinci (1452–1519) had also designed an earlier version, which was probably never constructed.

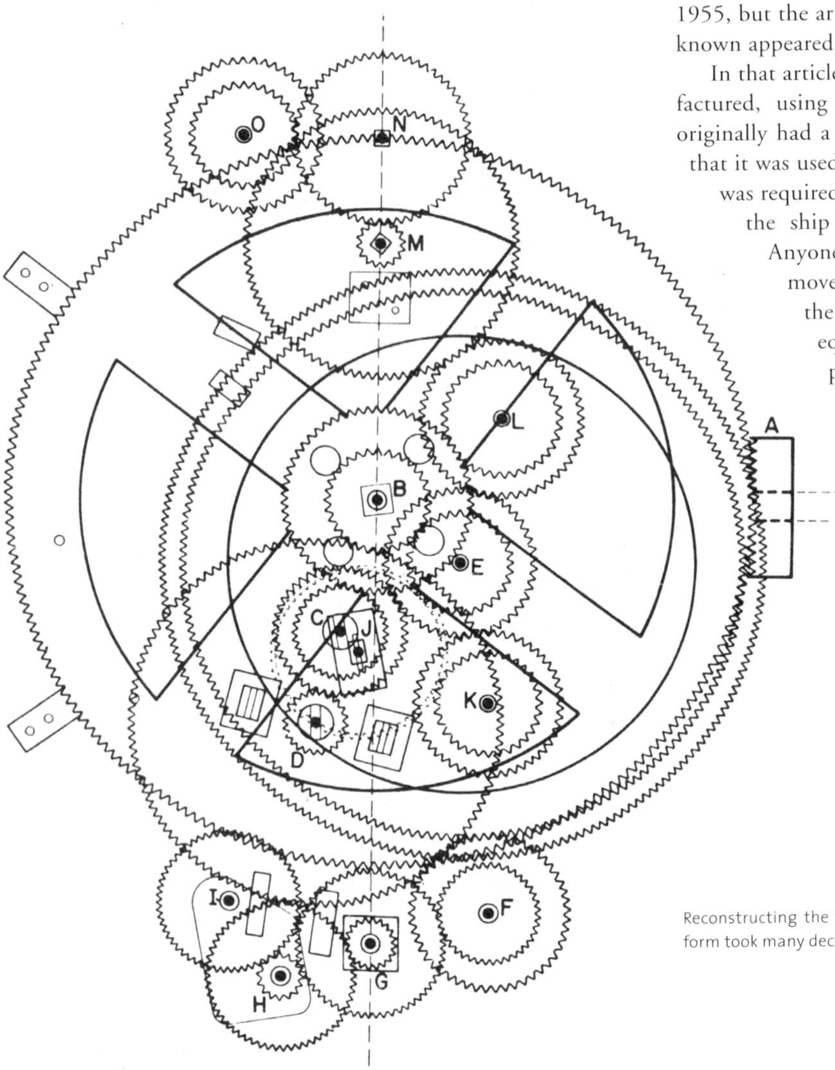

Reconstructing the functions the Antikythera mechanism was built to perform took many decades.

The pieces excavated from the shipwreck are today on exhibit in the National Archaeological Museum in Athens, Greece.

Complex structures

By the 1970s, investigation of the mechanism had progressed so far that individual scientists even attempted to reconstruct it. But it was only after an x-ray analysis in the mid-1990s that a fully functional copy could be produced. The reconstruction based on the most recent research was built in 2002.

The complex gear mechanism, functioning essentially like a mechanical calculator, was probably unique it its day. Although the Greeks already had an extensive background in astronomy and mathematics, and the Arabs proved themselves capable of building a mechanical calendar, modern scientists had never suspected that such a well-thought out device could exist so early in human history.

Oddly, no comparable mechanisms have ever been found, and no mention of any such device appears in any literary sources, making its origin even more difficult to explain. It is therefore still not clear today who made it and why. Its precise function remains uncertain. For the purposes of simple navigation, it provides entirely too much information.

Differential drives

An equalizing or "differential" drive is a construction that makes it possible to regulate the speed with which an axle turns, and to regulate this according a set system of rules. A differential drive mechanism is frequently used with axle-driven vehicles because when driving along a curve, the right and left wheel of a car cover different distances. If both were strictly tied in to the revolutions of the axle, the two wheels would be driven forward equally, making steering difficult. The differential drive mechanically ensures the proper balance.

Until now, no further such device has been found. It is also puzzling why the knowledge that was required to build it ceased to be used, or wasn't applied in other areas.

Ancient Technology

Every now and then, when drawings are excavated or studied, there will be shapes and forms that consciously or unconsciously recall familiar objects. Although evidence such as this can in some circumstances be used to study the development of an early technology, in most cases these are false trails in which fantasy plays tricks on the observer.

The hieroglyphs of Abydos

During the excavation of the Temple of Seth in Abydos, Egypt in 1990, investigators came upon unusual hieroglyphs carved directly above a column. The symbols led many observers to believe that they were looking at a submarine, a tank, a battleship and a helicopter. In fact, the hieroglyphs do have strong similarities with these vehicles. Because these four signs were found directly adjacent to one another, word of the high-tech hieroglyphs spread quickly and was soon making headlines. The inscription was put forward as evidence that such technologies must have already been in existence in 3000 BC, the time period when the temple was constructed.

Disappointment followed a short time later, however, as it became clear that the hieroglyphs to the right and left of these signs could be readily interpreted, and did not depart from other contemporary hieroglyphs. These had at first seemed difficult to understand until the suspect symbols themselves were more thoroughly investigated.

It seemed that someone had made a few corrections. The initial signs had been filled in with plaster or some other material, and then overwritten with new hieroglyphs. Over time, the newer material had decayed, making the older characters visible. The helicopter, battleship, tank and submarine are therefore chance resemblances, which the technically poor execution of the hieroglyphs may have enhanced. Nevertheless, these hieroglyphs are still invoked by different groups as part of the larger argument for an early high-technology culture in Egypt. There is, however, no evidence supporting this at Abydos.

The hieroglyphs from Abydos seem to show a helicopter (upper left), a tank (upper right) and a submarine (middle right).

THE SAQQARA GLIDER

In 1898, a wooden model dated to approximately 200 BC was found in a grave near the Egyptian city of Saqqara. Catalogued together with other bird models, it attracted no special notice at first. It was rediscovered only in 1969 by archaeologist and professor Khalil Messiha (1924–1999), who noticed that the shape of the model strongly resembled a modern glider with a part of its tail broken off. This led to further investigation.

In fact, it does seem that the model would have been capable of flight prior to being damaged. The question as to whether the glider served as the model for a real-life, larger glider, however, could not be answered. Surprisingly, the Saqqara glider became the centre of scientific interest once again a short time later when a collection of gold objects from Columbia was exhibited, and aeroplane-like images were found among the decorated pieces (see illus. below). Although these were certainly not capable of flying due to their weight and structure, there were several details that led to the conclusion that, during this time in South America, people must have been quite familiar with the phenomenon of flight. Whether this led to more extensive experiments in ancient times is not known.

The Saqqara glider (also known as "the pigeon") is now on exhibit in Cairo. It has been interpreted either as a model for a real flyer or simply as part of a weather vane.

Dated to between 500 and 800 AD, some Columbian gold pieces bear a resemblance to modern aeroplanes.

The Baghdad battery

In 1936, during the excavation of Tel Khuyut Rabu'a, south of Baghdad, a ceramic vase was found that contained a copper sheet cylinder pierced by a single iron rod. The Austrian archaeologist Dr. Wilhelm Konig interpreted this find as an indication that early cultures knew about electricity. A few years later, experiments involving a reconstructed version of his find were carried out with some success. If the cylinder was filled with an acidic liquid like vinegar or lemon juice, the current between the cylinder and iron rod measured 1.5 to 2 volts.

This discovery could be connected with other difficult-to-explain finds. Around Baghdad, figurines had been found coated in a very thin overlay of gold. It had always been thought that this kind of figure would normally be gilded either by hammering or by melting the gold over the object. But no trace of hammer marks could be found on these figurines. If galvanization, the thin layering of a material

When different metals, in this case copper and iron, are placed in an acidic solution, an electrical voltage is created. In the case of the Baghdad battery it is likely that an acidic solution (for example, vinegar) filled the cylinder so that an exchange of electrons could take place.

The extent to which the electricity from these simple batteries could be used remains questionable because of their minimal energy yield, which cannot be compared to that of modern batteries.

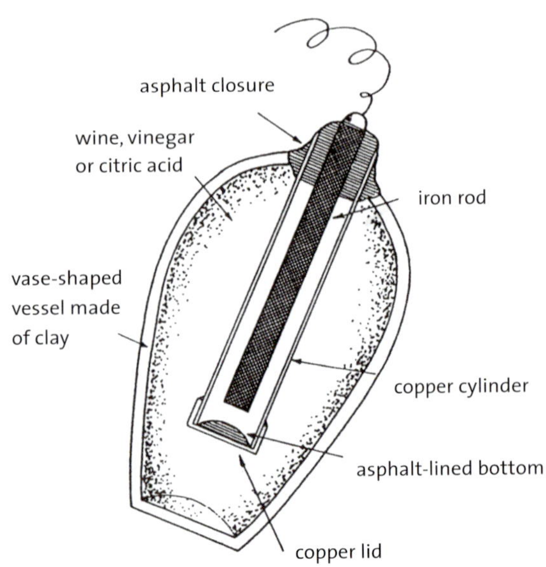

using electrochemical methods, already existed between 250 and 225 AD, this question would be resolved.

Further research brought to light that comparable clay pots had already been found and many more were, in fact, discovered later. Contemporary texts confirm that people were aware of static electricity, if not of the chemical processes that brought it about. Most texts involved simple observations, such as the fact that rubbing two pieces of amber together attracted lightweight particles, such as dust or hair. Therefore, while in principle the invention of a battery was possible, whether this actually took place is still considered controversial.

The jaguar from Panama

This figure is another object that was first viewed as deserving of no particular attention. Found in Panama in 1920, it was dismissed as yet another model of a jaguar. A short time later, though, it was proposed that this could be a design for a machine.

For the depiction of an animal, the figure is unnaturally flat and angular. The tail of the jaguar appears to be exceptionally powerful, with two large, recognizably notched wheels at its end. The claws of the jaguar are bent at unusual angles, running underneath the body to their individual pointy ends, yet bound together on the upper side. All this led to the proposal that the "jaguar" could be a model of an excavator, a construction vehicle similar to a steam shovel. With its "shovel" (the legs and claws), and with a chain mechanism attached to the gear-like wheels located at the end of its powerful tail, a machine such as this built on a large scale could have been used to move tremendous masses of earth.

Technology like this, according to some experts, would have enabled the construction of a city like Machu Picchu, the "lost city" of the Peruvian Andes. Those who are more sceptical of this theory respond that the same work could have been accomplished with muscle power. They also point out that building an excavator would have required additional technologies and skills, such as the ability to smelt iron or manufacture machine parts, for which no evidence exists. This being the case, the theory that this is any more than a jaguar figurine lacks substance.

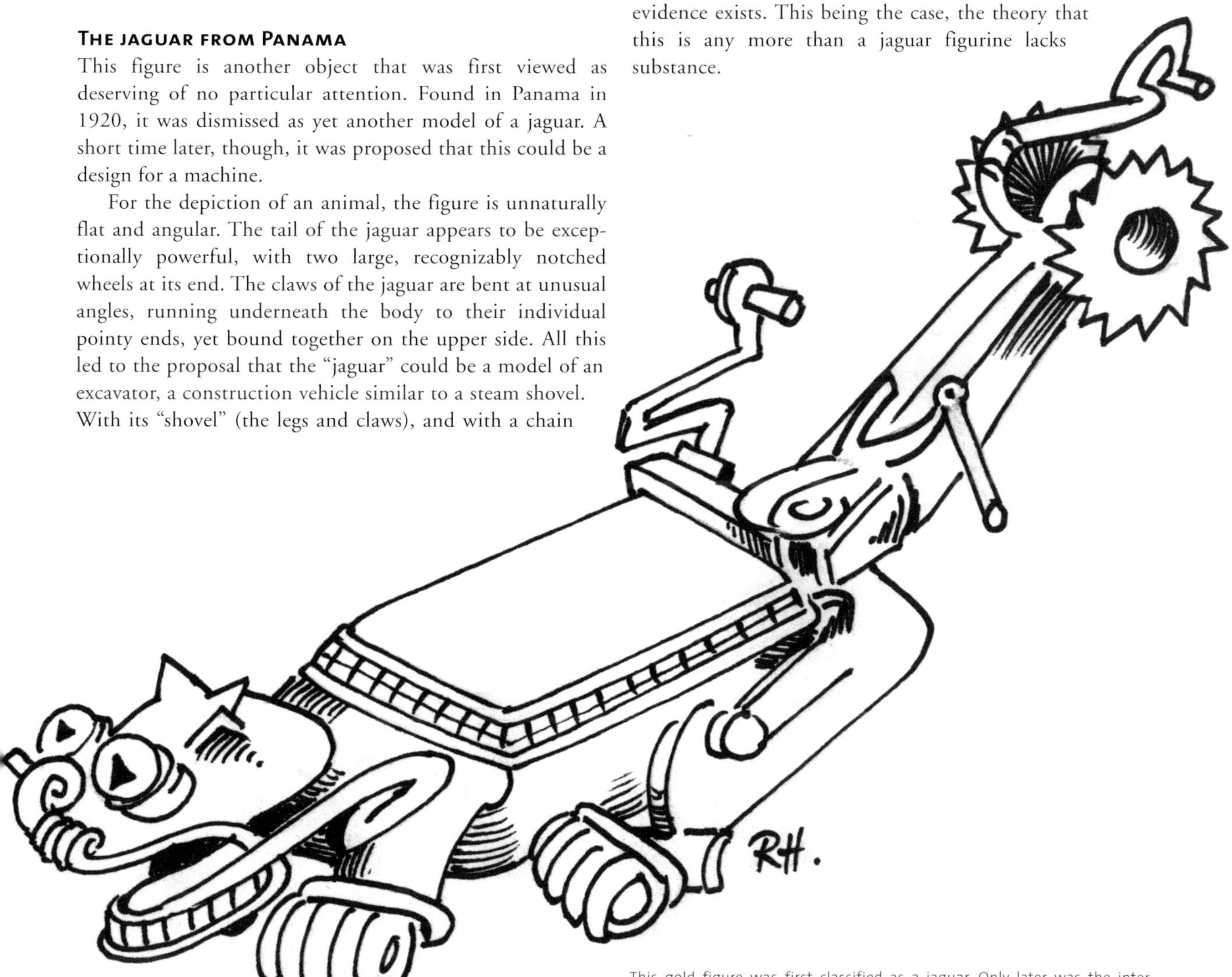

This gold figure was first classified as a jaguar. Only later was the interpretation suggested that this could be a model of a kind of excavator vehicle capable of moving large quantities of earth mechanically.

Crystal Skulls

Few artefacts have sparked as much intense discussion among the general public as the so-called crystal skulls, which can be either death's-head sculptures made out of rock crystal or face masks made of quartz. Over the course of the past decades there has been more and more public speculation and publication of purported research results from both the New Age and the scientific sides of the debate.

A CRYSTAL SKULL FOR A BIRTHDAY?

In 1927, 17 year old Anna Mitchell-Hedges, the daughter of an archaeologist, came across an unusual object near an altar while excavating the ruins of Lubaantun in Honduras. Its skull form was not clearly recognizable at first because the lower jaw was missing; that piece would be found three months later, just a few yards away. Rock crystal is a very common material in nature, but due to its extreme hardness and structure, working it requires specialized tools and skills, in particular when, as in the case with the Lubaantun skull, a high degree of realism is desired.

Shortly after the find was made public, the critics stepped in. The story was derided as stage-managed, for the day the skull was found happened to be Anna Mitchell-Hedges' birthday. The archaeologist Frederick A. Mitchell-Hedges was accused of planting a machine-manufactured skull near the altar as a birthday gift for his daughter. More recent investigations have backed up these claims. Using an electron microscope, traces that could only have come from modern tools were found on the figure.

At the same time, however, this is not the only crystal skull in existence. Additional crystal skulls have been found, sculpted with comparable care.

Frederick Mitchell-Hedges proposed that generations of people had worked over 150 years polishing rock crystal to achieve this perfect skull. He interpreted the skull as the embodiment of evil, employed by the Maya priests as an instrument of power.

Mitchell-Hedges' daughter Anna found the crystal skull during excavation work in the rainforests of Lubaantun. Below is a modern Maya settlement at that spot, in what is now Belize.

Original, forgery or legacy of Atlantis?

For reasons that are not completely clear, it is only this first skull whose authenticity is doubted. After making their own investigations, many scientists described it as a modern forgery, one that was most likely created in Europe. New Age groups, on the other hand, claim that this crystal skull is a piece of work from Atlantis, later passed on to the Mayans.

A relationship with prehistoric ritual had already been proposed by Anna Mitchell-Hedges herself, who estimated that the skull was some 3600 years old. That would place it within a time period when the Mayan culture did not yet exist. She based her conclusion on the date of the geological layers in which she found the skull. Since rock crystal is not an organic substance, there were few other dating methods available.

According to other archaeologists, who because of Mitchell-Hedges' impeccable reputation do not believe that the skull is a forgery, the figure is much later in date. Some say it is 1500 years old, while others see it as a fifteenth-century artefact.

Yet none of these dates can explain how the figure came into existence. Even in Europe, it was not until much later, in the seventeenth century, that knowledge of rock-crystal working had advanced so far that one could in theory work with it, if the appropriate tools were available.

It is still not clear how some of these skulls were made and who was responsible for this work.

Crystal work

Working with crystal is especially tricky because the material itself is incredibly fragile. If its structural composition isn't taken into account very accurately, the crystal can splinter or fracture. There is also always the chance that a flaw deep inside the crystal will expand, causing a crack running through the entire stone. The basic structure of a piece of rock crystal can only be made visible by the light refracted within the crystal, and under strong magnification.

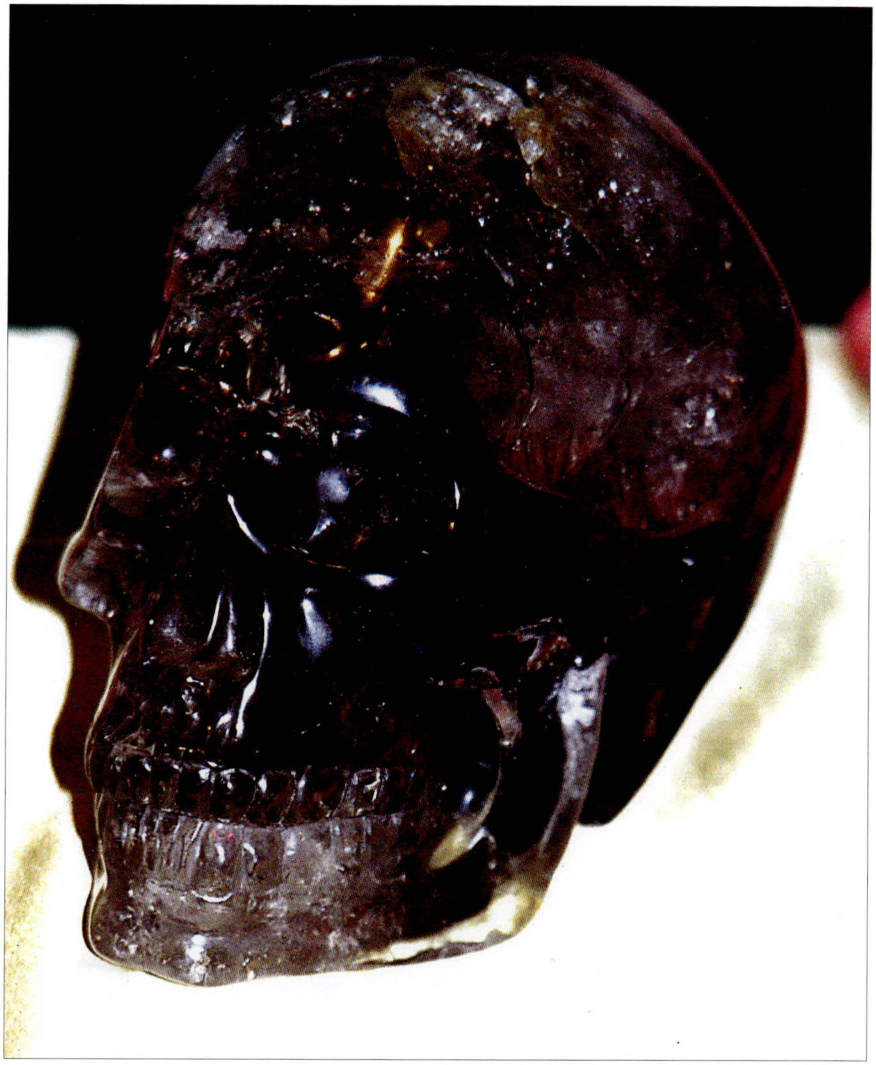

In contrast to the Mitchell-Hedges skull, the smoked quartz skull "E.T.", discovered in 1908 in Guatemala, shows no traces of modern work. It is estimated to be at least 500 years old.

The Stone Spheres of Costa Rica

In Costa Rica there are hundreds of stone spheres. Though not all of the same size or weight, they are all perfectly spherical. Many of the spheres have been damaged or destroyed, primarily during the colonial period, by ploughing or military exercises – not to mention malicious destruction by those searching for gold. Now, many of the spheres decorate private gardens and continue to puzzle researchers to this day.

Mysterious spheres

Where these many intriguing spheres come from has not yet been explained. While several examples can be found in the National Museum in San Jose, and a few more have been uncovered by excavation, the rest of the spheres sit partly or entirely buried in river delta mud or sunken into the floor of the jungle. The information we have about these spheres is meagre.

We do know that the heaviest sphere found thus far weighs 16 tons, and that each of them has a perfectly round circumference with the same diameter at any given point. Many spheres have an extremely smooth surface, probably achieved by polishing them with a mixture of sand and water. How spheres weighing many tons could come to be so perfectly rounded is still under discussion. In addition to the necessary geometrical knowledge, the techniques that would make production possible also must have been in place. The creation of such a sphere is practically impossible without mechanical means, all the more so because the kind of granite of which they are made of is not found anywhere close by. The nearest quarry lies some 30 miles (50 km) up river.

Astrological symbol or perfection of God?

Many native tribes lived in the area where the spheres have been found, but none of their legends mention the creators of these spheres. No tribe claims that their ancestors made them or offers any other explanation that might clear up this mystery. It is fairly certain that they had a special meaning for the natives, however, because smaller spheres are found in their graves.

Some arrangements of these small counterparts are believed to recall constellations. This is an interpretation

One of the stone spheres rests in front of the National Museum in Costa Rica. Although the meaning of the spheres is not known, many front gardens are decorated with them.

Stone spheres were also found some 12 miles (20 km) north of San Jose in Braulio Carillo National Park. These fell victim primarily to gold seekers who were attracted by the gold-coloured water nearby.

that cannot be applied to the larger spheres, which, over the centuries, have moved naturally or by other means. Their original arrangement within the landscape can no longer be determined. In the few exceptional cases where the arrangement of the larger spheres was recognizable, they seem to have been set in patterns of long straight lines, wavy lines or triangles; no astronomical or astrological meaning could be derived. Furthermore, representing heavenly bodies as spheres stands in opposition to the way that other South American groups, like the Incas and Mayas, represented these bodies. Their sun, for example, is disk-shaped. For an astronomical theory to hold some weight, one would have to imagine a completely independent culture living in Costa Rica, which most scholars view as highly unlikely.

Another theory claims that the perfection incorporated into the spheres by their creators can be understood as a form of worship, with the end result of this work a symbol of divine perfection. This would also explain why so few other signs of early religious belief have been found in this region. Whether this theory corresponds to reality will most likely never be confirmed with certainty.

Costa Rican tradition provides no information regarding which people produced the spheres or for what reason.

The Piri Reis Map

Piri Reis (1465–1554), whose real name was Muhiddin Piri ibn Haji Mehmed, was an Ottoman admiral and, as such, familiar with maps of the land and sea. In his day, it was not uncommon to simply reach for a pen to make additions and corrections. It was not unusual to redraw a region on a map more precisely based on new information. The fact that Reis had also, prior to his journeys, acquainted himself with other maps extending past the limits of his own destination, and had made attempts at joining some of those maps together, is in itself nothing particularly mysterious. Yet one of his maps, as it is preserved, includes regions that no one from his time period could have known anything about.

Topkapi Palace in what is today Istanbul was the centre of government and residence of the Ottoman sultans. The Piri Reis map was discovered here by chance.

America on the map

Piri Reis dated his world map to the Islamic year 919, which corresponds to the Christian year 1513. This is probably the first map of the world that he completed. He did not draw the map from scratch, but collected older maps, pieced them together according to the parts they had in common, and then completed them with his own sketches, assembled during his own sea voyages dating back to 1481. Piri Reis himself was primarily underway in the Mediterranean region at this time. Which maps he used to compile this map of the world is unknown, although in his written commentary he mentions using Portuguese material.

In addition to Europe, Asia and a large part of the African coastline, the American continent also appears on this map. This corresponds to the state of knowledge at the time. Only twenty-one years earlier, Christopher Columbus had discovered not the anticipated western route to India, but an entirely new continent.

While the North American part of the world map is full of errors, as is the Caribbean section, where the map leaves out several latitudes and incorrectly joins the coastlines, the eastern part of the South American coastline is easily recognizable. The part of the map that would have showed the western coastline is not preserved, but the east coast already poses more than a few puzzles on its own. It would be decades before the Spaniards and Portuguese, in the course of their conquests, would accumulate enough cartographic information to produce their own map of South America and its coastline. This raises questions as to the origin of the map Piri Reis used for his work.

The discovery of Antarctica
The Antarctic landmass lies hidden beneath an ice cap that is up to 2.8 miles (4500 m) thick. The descriptions of the continent "Terra Australis", which, according to the calculations of the Greek mathematician Ptolemy, should correspond to comparable landmasses in the northern hemisphere, encouraged British sea captain James Cook to search for it in 1772. What he found instead was Antarctica, although he could not actually see any land, as it was covered in ice and clouds. The explorer Fabian von Bellingshausen discovered the Antarctic landmass in 1819, circumnavigating it the following year. The first map of Antarctica was completed in the 1950s as part of the American project Deep Freeze.

The Antarctic on the map?

When the Piri Reis map was rediscovered in 1929 as the Topkapi Palace in Istanbul was being cleared out in order to convert it into a museum, it sparked fierce discussion that only intensified after it was scientifically investigated a few years later. It was generally agreed that the map must have been drawn at a later point in time, perhaps around the middle of the sixteenth century after the South American coast had already been mapped. A further theory proposed that Piri Reis benefited from the knowledge of Chinese or Scandinavian sailors that had been passed along by the Portuguese.

At the end of 1959, the map again became the focus of science, when Charles Hapgood, professor of history at Keene State College in New Hampshire, began a more detailed study and discovered the coastline of Antarctica south of Africa and South America. What was most unusual was that the coastline on the map for the most part followed the actual line of the landmass, although this had been obscured by the permanent Antarctic ice cap since 4000 BC. The continent itself would not be discovered until 1819.

This raised the question as to whether any 6000-year-old cartographic material would have been available in Piri Reis' time, or whether this knowledge had been preserved in some other way. Should the latter be the case, questions still remain. Where did this knowledge come from? Whether or not a civilization capable of travelling to the Antarctic could have existed around 4000 BC is not yet known.

Piri Reis not only drew the coastlines of South America and Antarctica, but included rivers and similar features of the continents as well, many of which would not be investigated for many years.

On other world maps produced at the same time as that of Piri Reis, for example on this one from 1537, the Antarctic continent is missing. The error-filled representation of both the North American continent and the Caribbean is similar on both maps.

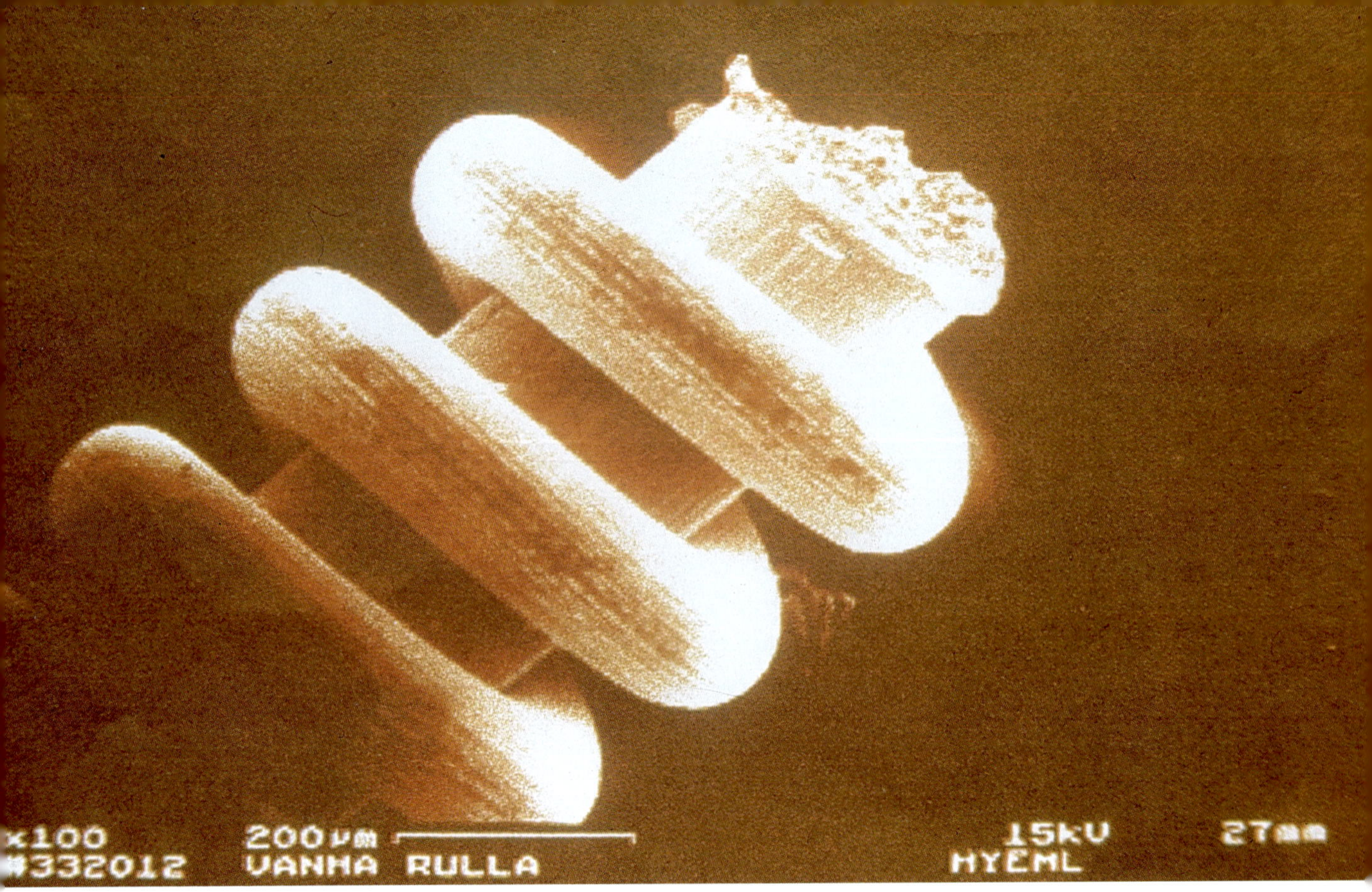

Nanospirals can't be seen with the naked eye. The remarkable regularity of their structure only becomes clear under an electron microscope.

Nanospirals

In 1992, Russian geologists working in the Ural Mountains investigating mineral deposits found microscopically small spirals within material that had to be at least 100,000 years old. Today, their existence is still not explained. Self-named "UFO-ologists" view these structures as definitive proof that aliens were in contact with people of earlier times.

Science fiction?

Throughout the nineteenth and twentieth centuries, theories and supposed proof of aliens visiting the earth were relatively common. This attention began with the fantastic creatures of the novelist Jules Verne in the second half of the nineteenth century, continued with the popularity of H.G. Wells' science fiction stories and utopias at the beginning of the twentieth century, and ended with its absorption into the borderline sciences in the late 1940s. During those decades, these ideas quickly found many adherents. For every phenomenon presented in the course of this chapter,

The use of nanotechnology today

Nanotechnology is currently being applied in a variety of medical fields, for example, with the so-called "lab on a chip" that places a miniature laboratory on a surface the size of a credit card. It is also common in the electronics industry, in particular in the production of computer processors. Further uses include a self-cleaning automobile paint enabled by nanotechnology, and the development of more precise microscopes.

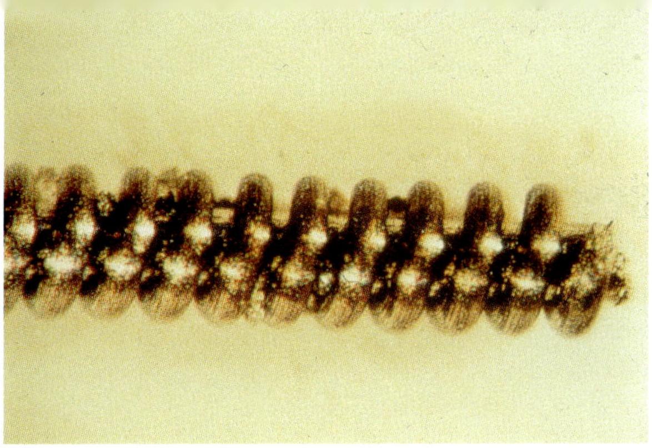

The nanospirals are made of copper, tungsten or molybdenum. The latter two metals, along with others, are used in the fields of electronics and rocket technology.

there are reports that claim that each of these is proof of alien assistance.

The Russians' discovery in the Ural Mountains was therefore a sensation for adherents to the alien visitor theory. The spirals had been detected during a routine investigation and are so small that the human eye can barely see them. The spirals range between 3 cm and 0.0003 mm in size, and their superbly regular structure and smooth surfaces, perforated in places, are only visible under an electron microscope. Largely made of tungsten, their cores are tungsten or molybdenum. Ones discovered at a later date were also made of copper. The proportions of the spirals are so regular that they could only have been produced by mechanical means. Their date of origin, between 300,000 and 100,000 BC, raises the question as to whether people of those times could possibly be capable of manufacturing such a thing.

In our own time, making products like this is no longer a problem, but the technology required to do so only goes back to the 1970s.

Alien technology or forgery?

According to the theory proposed by Dr. Valerie Ourarov of Saint Petersburg, the majority of these pieces were used as part of a receiving and sending antenna. If this were the case, it would provide evidence for the existence of an alien intelligence, for from the point of view of science it is not possible that our ancestors of 100,000 years ago, a time when Neanderthals were not yet extinct, would have been capable of such a project.

The sceptics also stepped in after the first reports on the nanospirals, claiming that the results were compromised by false measurements or that they represented out and out forgery on the part of the investigators. This view is still widespread, despite the fact that additional nanostructures have since been discovered in Koshim and Balbanju. Their investigation points to the same results.

The Ural Mountain nanospirals seem to genuinely support the theory of alien intelligence, if not prove outright that aliens really did visit the earth during a past as fantastic as any "UFO-logist" could desire. It is doubtful that it can ever be proved that these objects really were not manufactured on earth. Toward this end, further finds would be needed.

The smooth surface and unusually regular form of the nanospirals indicates that they are artificial constructions.

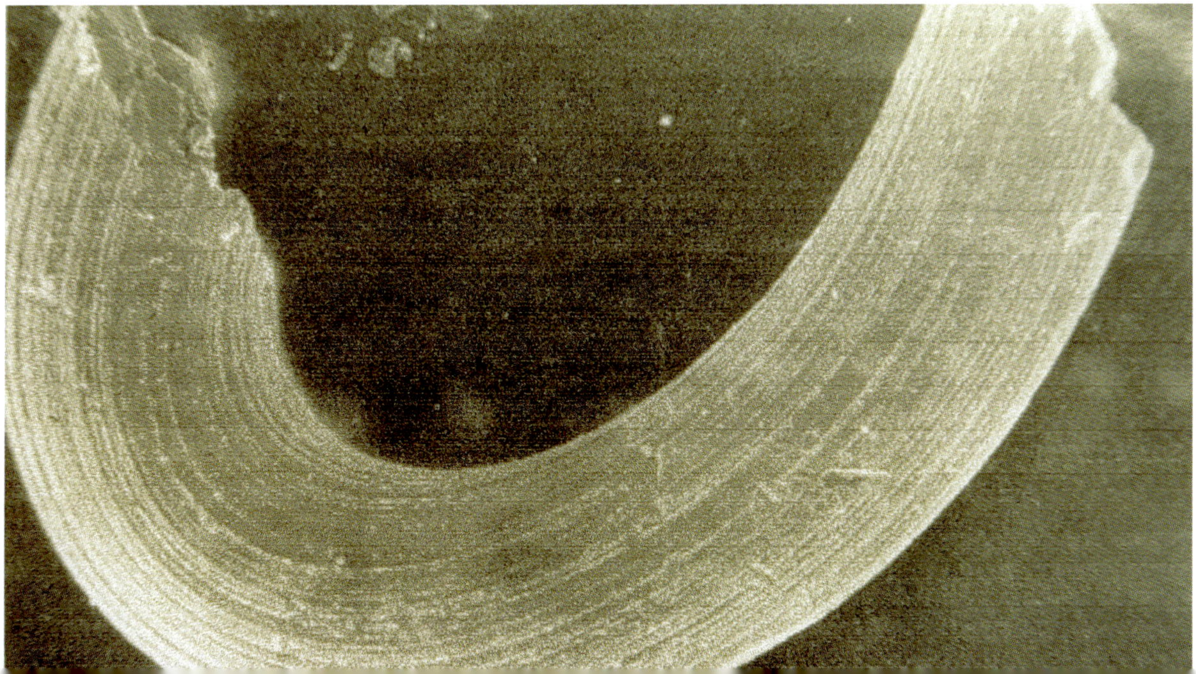

Myth or Reality?

Legendary Places, People and Things

Stories have always been passed along from generation to generation. After some time has passed, no one can be quite sure which parts have been invented and which, if any, are based on fact. Sometimes a kernel of truth is so enhanced by fantastic or historic events, or additional fictional characters, that it is no longer easy to draw the line between fact and fiction.

Interest in times long past has encouraged historical scientists and other scholars to take a good look at legends. Comparison of several traditions can be helpful in determining which events could actually have taken place. While some prove to have historical origins, others are unmasked as pure fantasy. There is also a third group that mixes reality and fiction so seamlessly that it is no longer possible to distinguish between them. In the following pages you will find legends about places, people and things as well as the results of the scientific investigations that have put their propositions to the test.

The Holy Grail is woven into countless theories and legends.

Plato is depicted here with his student Aristotle, who was also the first to criticize the Atlantis story.

Atlantis

In his dialogues *Timaios* and *Critias*, the Greek citizen and philosopher Plato (427–347 BC). wrote a story – supposedly a true one – in which an entire civilization disappeared under the sea, along with the continent on which it stood. Although it has no known ancient historical source, and although it was strongly criticized from the very beginning, the tale of Atlantis is one of the most famous and controversial myths in the world.

Plato's reports

According to Plato, some 12,000 years ago a rich and powerful nation named Atlantis lay to the west of the Pillars of Herakles, or what is known today as the Straits of Gibraltar. The inhabitants of this island ruled over large portions of Europe and Africa. Their lust for power eventually led to war with the Athenians, whom Plato depicted as extraordinarily brave and skilful. When the other Greek soldiers retreated, apparently out of fear of the overwhelming strength of their opponents, Athens crushed her enemies and then freed the slaves of the defeated people of Atlantis. Thereafter, the wrath of Zeus, father of the Greek gods, sent a mighty earthquake and tidal wave to the conquered island. Numerous Athenian warriors were also lost beneath the waves when Atlantis was submerged under the sea.

This is the substance of Plato's account, which he claimed harkened back to the journeys of the Athenian scholar and statesman Solon (639–559 BC). Solon travelled to Egypt and other countries from 571 to 561 BC, and is supposed to have learned of Atlantis from a temple scribe in the Egyptian capital city of Sais, in the Nile delta. It is not clear what sources the Egyptians might have relied upon, given that, according to Plato's chronology, their culture first came into being some 5000 years after the purported fall of Atlantis.

Plato retold the tale of the brave fight of the Athenians as part of two dialogues dissecting the ideal state. The works are organized accordingly. In the first dialogue, *Timaios*, he describes the early history of the Greeks before moving on to the battle between Athens and Atlantis. Specific details about Atlantis are only provided in the second dialogue, *Critias*. A third dialogue on the subject was apparently planned, but never put down in writing.

The first doubts

Although the story told by Plato portrayed Athens in the best possible light, his contemporaries, including his student Aristotle, openly criticized his version of events. Plato was accused of presenting invented material in a sensational manner in order to bring his teachings about the ideal state to the attention of a wider circle of people. It is possible that this is why the third dialogue on Atlantis was never completed. In fact, in the second dialogue, *Critias,* Plato already distanced himself from his description of Athens as the ideal state. Instead, he describes the animal and plant world of the island Atlantis in quite some detail, along with architectural features that included a central, circular canal. The political goals of the dialogue were no longer an issue by this point, and the idealized ur-Athens is only mentioned in passing. At that point Plato broke off his dialogue, and it remains incomplete. Perhaps he was concerned that he would be queried about his sources if he should continue his detailed description. Whether further texts about Atlantis exist is questionable.

Legends tell us that Atlas, eternally damned to carry the heavens on his shoulders, had a daughter who lived on an island to the west and who gave Atlantis its name.

Following its rediscovery during the Renaissance, maps were produced that attempted to locate Atlantis geographically.

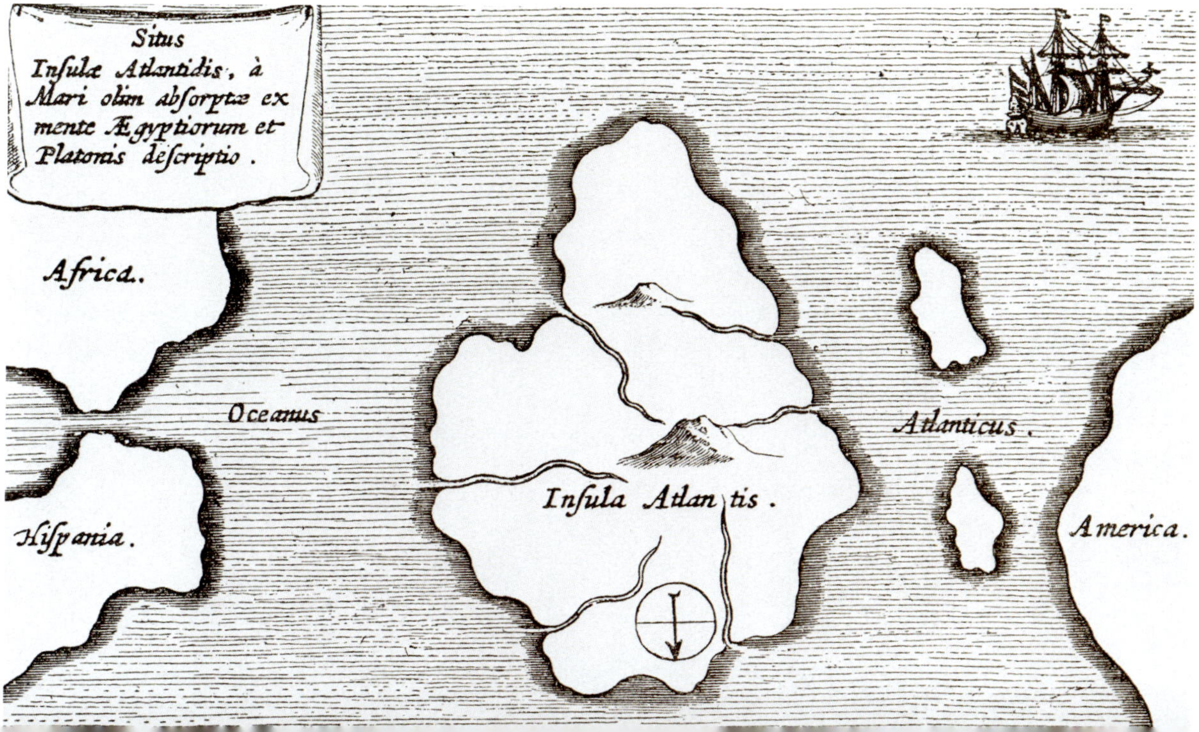

Atlantis sinks

The Greek philosopher Crantor (fourth century BC) considered the question of Atlantis critically. In one of his works he describes a report about Atlantis inscribed on columns in the Egyptian city of Sais. The fact that he talks about inscribed columns, while Plato seems to have had rolls of written text as a source, is a contradiction that would continue to be part of Atlantis discussions in later times. Until the sixth century AD we continue to find evidence that famous philosophers and scholars regularly took up the question of the continent's existence. Later on, Atlantis was dismissed as an invention of Plato's imagination and the story was slowly forgotten.

The rediscovery of Atlantis

During the Renaissance, 900 years later, the Atlantis myth was rediscovered and discussed in various treatises. As in antiquity, there were advocates who were convinced that Atlantis had really existed, as well as scholars who dismissed the existence of the island as fantasy. Despite the growing interest in educated circles, the legend did not reach the general public at this time.

Atlantis only became known to a wider audience at the end of the nineteenth century, following publication of a book by novelist Ignatius Donnelly (1831–1901), *Atlantis: The Antediluvian World*. Donnelly focused on the myths and legends of other peoples, concluding that stories of a submerged continent were widespread.

Descriptions of the lost culture do vary considerably, although in general it is rare for anything negative to be said about the continent. On this basis, Donnelly concluded that paradise-like conditions reigned on Atlantis, and, given the wide geographical range of the legend, that its inhabitants

An underwater complex that brings Atlantis to life can be found on Paradise Island in the Bahamas.

The Greek island of Crete is also a candidate in the search for Atlantis.

may have colonized the New World as well as the Old. The thesis of an ancient "super civilization" was taken up with great enthusiasm in esoteric circles, and in the following years would be repeatedly argued about, discussed and to a certain extent also refined and further developed. The subject would concern not only the continent of Atlantis, but also increasingly its inhabitants, who were attributed superhuman characteristics.

New theses about Atlantis

Although others had published books about Atlantis previously, it was Donnelly's that awakened great interest in the subject outside of specialist circles. When he firmly located Atlantis on the Azores in the middle of the Atlantic, public interest in the sunken continent boomed. In *The Times* newspaper in 1909, archaeologist K.T. Frost presented the thesis that Atlantis could have been a civilization based on the prehistoric culture of the Mediterranean island of Crete. This, together with Donnelly's Azores theory, was the subject of much discussion. Through the course of the twentieth century, there were frequent new proposals for the original location of Atlantis, although reference to Plato's description or the results of archaeological investigations led to most of these being discarded.

Of course, the critical voices did not fall silent, either. In publications that cast doubt on the existence of a submerged continent, the naysayers ceded nothing to the Atlantis supporters. Nevertheless, it has still been neither plausibly proven nor conclusively disproven that Atlantis really ever existed. Both groups are united on one point, namely, that further evidence can only come from archaeology. The 7000 words of Plato and all the later published research based on his descriptions are not sufficient proof.

In 1967, Minoan ruins were found on the Greek Island of Santorini, known as Thera in antiquity. These have also been claimed as the ruins of Atlantis.

The Continents of Lemuria and Mu

Lemuria and Mu are two additional legendary continents that came to the public's attention in the wake of renewed interest in Atlantis.

The path of the lemurs

As envisioned by the British zoologist Philip Sclater (1829–1913), Lemuria was a piece of land that once joined the Island of Madagascar with India, providing a physical connection with that country. Sclater came to this conclusion because, while lemurs are found in both of these places, there are no prosimians at all living anywhere else between East Africa and the Indian coast. For Sclater, there had to have been a direct connection between the continents to allow for this unusual distribution.

Sclater's theory was disproved only a few years after he published it. By the beginning of the twentieth century, no archaeological evidence for his extra piece of land had been found. His observations were, however, later used to prove the theory of plate tectonics.

Refuting Sclater's theory in numerous publications did not stop various groups from giving Lemuria Atlantis-like characteristics, thereby awarding it its very own legendary continent cult. Even if the theory of plate tectonics cannot be proved with absolute certainty, one can easily assign Lemuria to the realm of legend.

Diego de Landa

Diego de Landa (1524–1579) was the bishop of the Yucatan for some thirty years. He came to Central America as a missionary in order to convert the Maya to Christianity. His mercilessness marks him as the man most to blame for the extermination of the Maya and their culture. The so-called Landa alphabet, created by de Landa as a translation aid for the Maya script, is included among his later publications written to justify his actions. As it turned out, this alphabet was fairly useless, although some of Landa's descriptions are useful in understanding the Maya culture.

Mu – the source of Egyptian culture...

Mu is supposedly a continent that sank in the Pacific Ocean, rather than the Atlantic. The British archaeologist James Churchward made this claim in 1926. In his report he described a country with a far superior culture that had disappeared together with its continent in the aftermath of a volcanic eruption.

But this was not the first mention of Mu. The Abbé Charles-Etienne Brasseur de Bourbourg had already published his theory about the sunken continent in 1884. As a source he cited the "Codex Troano", which he had translated himself. The first part of the codex is "Tro-Coresianus", one of the few extensive pieces of Mayan literature that has survived. A few years later, French photographer and amateur archaeologist Augustus Le Plongeon travelled to the Mayan ruins of the Yucatan peninsula to

The unusual distribution of lemurs led Philip Sclater to conclude that there must have been a physical connection between India and Madagascar.

begin an excavation. He completed his own translation of the "Codex Troano", heavily influenced by Brasseur, as well as his own interpretation of the wall paintings in the ruined city of Chichen-Itza. The result was a vivid description of life on Mu, coming to a climax with the princess of the continent fleeing from its destruction to Egypt, where, as the goddess Isis, she is the founder of Egyptian culture. According to Le Plongeon, this explained the similarities between the Egyptians and the Mayans. In his report published in 1896, Le Plongeon claimed to have come across a stone vase containing the remains of one of the princes of Mu.

Le Plongeon believed he had found traces of the mysterious continent of Mu in the ruined city of Chichen-Itza.

... OR A TRANSLATION ERROR?

In his translation, Brasseur made use of the so-called Landa alphabet, named after Diego de Landa, Bishop of the Yucatan (see box on facing page). How his translation of the "Codex Troano" progressed cannot be determined today, but what is certain is that no sensible translation using the Landa alphabet is possible. This means that Brasseur's work cannot be very accurate. Although the Mayan alphabet still has not been deciphered entirely, it is thought that the "Codex Troano" is primarily concerned with astrology rather than submerged continents.

Specialists dismiss Le Plongeon's conclusions. The claim that Egyptian hieroglyphs can be traced back to the Mayan script is unfounded. There can be no connection between them. Doubtful conclusions and a dearth of secure sources ensured that James Churchward's claims would be dropped as soon as they were published. However, although the sunken continent theories remain entirely unsupported, their adherents stand firm.

The form and size of the sunken continents is often discussed, but there is no unified opinion as to their location in the Indian or Pacific Oceans.

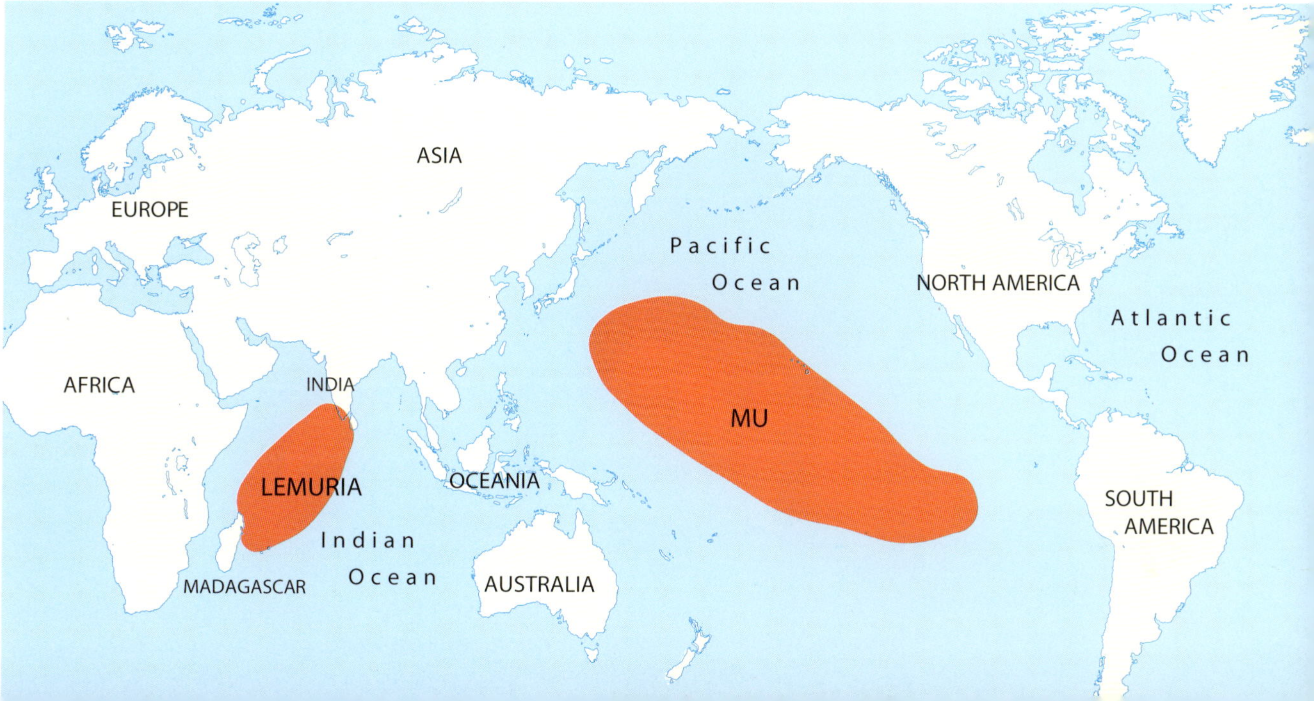

Legendary Cities of Gold

Atlantis and Mu are understood to be extinct cultures. The situation is entirely different for places described as cities or lands of gold. It should still be possible, it is said, to find places where gold can be found in great quantities somewhere on the African or American continents. Over the centuries, many adventurers and conquistadors set out on expeditions in the hope of discovering El Dorado, Cibola, Quivira, Ophir, Piri, Punt and other places. Most met with no tangible success.

Early history

At the beginning of the sixteenth century, the Spanish crown found itself deeply in debt. The collapse of the Moorish kingdom of Granada in 1492 had completed the *Reconquista*, or Spain's re-conquest of lands that had been held by Arabs for centuries. The Spanish king, Ferdinand II, drove out or executed all non-Catholics, thereby crippling the economy. The war machine and the Spanish Armada, still in existence, had consumed a great deal of money and new sources of funds were urgently needed. On his return from his first voyage, Christopher Columbus (1451–1506) provided a solution, promising the royal couple, Ferdinand and Isabella, that he could find a land of gold. But even when Columbus did bring back gold when he returned from his later voyages, and was even allowed to keep some portion of it for himself, it was never enough to satisfy the Spanish king.

The Spanish conquistador Hernán Cortés (or Hernando Cortez) was more successful. He sent enormous treasures back to his king and became legendary among the Spanish people. It is his exploits that form the basis of the legend of

Under the leadership of Coronado, gold seekers stormed out of Mexico and delved far into North America, claiming the lands they encountered for the Spanish crown.

"The Seven Golden Cities of Cibola". As more and more gold treasure reached Spain, this time presumably not only from Cortés, but also from Francisco Pizarro as well, a golden land called Quivira began to appear in poems. Campaigning to the east might lead to its discovery.

Cibola and Quivira

The search for the golden city of Cibola and the golden land of Quivira is closely associated with the story of the Spanish conquistador Francisco Vásquez de Coronado (1510–1554), who emigrated to the Americas following an offer from his friend Antonio de Mendoza, viceroy of the colony of New Spain. In 1539, he was charged with the task of finding both of these legendary sites and taking them into possession for Spain.

The expedition through North America took three years and led Coronado and his people from Mexico into the present-day states of Arizona, New Mexico, Oklahoma and Texas. When the Seven Cities of Gold had still not been located in 1541, Coronado changed his plans and began to move toward the east, as the poems recommended. He and his troops pushed ahead as far as Kansas without finding Quivira, finally giving up, discouraged, in 1542.

With his wealth of captured treasures, Hernán Cortés fostered legends of tremendous riches and golden cities.

Coronado and his men did not return to Mexico empty-handed, however. They had conquered the pueblo-dwelling Native American tribes of the Tiwa, Zuni and Hopi, acquiring an extensive new region for the Spanish crown in the process. Coronado fell out of favour, however, for not coming up with the gold.

Today it is fairly certain that these legends did not develop in the New World, but can instead be traced back to overactive imaginations in Spain. Coronado and all who followed in his footsteps were chasing an Old World fantasy. Nevertheless, the pull of the gold was apparently so great that these legends remained in circulation for centuries, becoming more and more elaborate. One variation on the Quivira material developed a short time later into its own legend – El Dorado.

Francisco Vásquez de Coronado was sent out to explore by the viceroy of the Spanish colony of New Spain. Coronado was for the most part generous to the natives because he hoped they would provide him with information about Cibola.

The first search for El Dorado

In contrast to the legends of Cibola and Quivira, the legend of *El Dorado* ("The Golden One") has its origins in present-day Equador. There one heard about a South American tribe, the Muisca, who made a ritual offering to the sun god every time a new ruler took office. The new ruler would first be covered in gold dust and then rowed out to the middle of Lake Guatavita in the mountains, with four companions, where treasures made of gold would be thrown overboard. Finally the ruler himself leapt into the lake, where the gold dust would be washed away. The ruler then swam back to the harbour while the treasures and gold dust sank to the bottom of the lake.

When the Spanish chroniclers wrote down this legend in the middle of the sixteenth century, the fate of the Muisca was sealed, along with that of many other South American natives. It would be a few years before they were discovered, but accounts of this custom – which was apparently no longer practiced – were related by a few imprisoned Muisca, and naturally caught the Spaniards' attention. The conquistador Francisco de Orellana (1490–1546) had no difficulty finding patrons willing to sponsor an expedition up the Rio Negro.

Between 1541 and 1542 he investigated South America, making his way to the Amazon. Although his efforts were not crowned with success, he described large cities and broad agricultural regions that he believed had once been wealthy. When hundreds of missionaries followed Orellana's route to South America in the mid-seventeenth century, they found only a few hunters living in simple dwellings. Orellana went down in history as a liar. Within a few decades, the El Dorado legend followed him.

Hernán Cortés

Hernán Cortés (1485–1547) was the Spanish conquistador who, within a few years and with some hundred soldiers, conquered Mexico. In his campaigns he engaged in battle with numerous native tribes in order to seize their gold. The Aztec Empire was destroyed through his agency.

The golden raft was considered absolute proof that El Dorado really existed.

The Lake Guatavita in Colombia was thought to be the body of water in which the Muisca sank large amounts of gold. So far, diving expeditions have brought up very little of it, making it unlikely that this is El Dorado.

New information

In the twentieth century, scientists found remains that cast El Dorado in a different light. In 1969, in a cave near an old Muisca settlement, a 7-inch- (18-cm-) long golden raft was discovered. Called the "gold raft of El Dorado", it was engraved with figures that appear to be performing the ceremony on Lake Guatavita that the Muisca natives had described. In addition, scientists from the University of Pennsylvania investigated the ancient forest floor on the banks of the Rio Negro and discovered lines and patterns covering a wide area scattered with thousands of free-standing earthworks. A more precise study showed these to be the remains of a canal system that brought water to agricultural fields. Ceramics and other remains uncovered nearby have confirmed that a great many people must have lived here.

The expedition had still failed to locate El Dorado. The *terra preta*, a dark earth covering several thousand acres, was, however, of interest. Analysis showed that this earth did not represent the natural soil, but was instead a mixture of sand, shell and charcoal. This unusual mixture may have kept soil nutrients from washing away, and is itself exponentially more productive than other known fertilizers. Scientists have concluded that this earth was the true treasure of El Dorado. The gold of the Muisca stemmed not from gold mines, but from trade with other native groups.

Francisco Pizarro

Francisco Pizarro (1475–1541), another Spanish explorer, was a contemporary of Cortés who moved on to South America. Pizarro is responsible for the collapse of the Inca Empire.

It is still not known why this native culture disappeared some 100 years after Orellana travelled through the region. It has been suggested that the white conquerors brought diseases that became epidemics that were disastrous for the native tribes. Unfortunately, there is as much hard evidence behind this theory as there is for the existence of the golden lake of Guatavita.

Orellana came upon a flourishing native civilization on the banks of the Rio Negro, one that vanished within a century.

Avalon

Although scientists have become involved in the search for Atlantis, Lemuria and Mu, the situation with Avalon was somewhat different. The descriptions of the place make it clear that its world belonged exclusively to the realm of legend.

Avalon and the Other World

According to Arthurian legend, Avalon (or Avalun or *Ynis Avalach*, broadly translatable as "Island of the Apples") is a place that lies in another world. A more precise description of that world is not possible because various authors' portrayals vary so widely. It is clearly a mystical, unreal and otherworldly place, like that of a dream, but a dream in which the decisions one makes can have a bearing on reality. Otherworldly places are often tied to places that really exist. Likewise, Avalon, said to be located in the county of Somerset, is associated with Glastonbury Abbey. According to legend, this structure goes back to Joseph of Arimathea or one of his relatives, who brought the Holy Grail back to England or Wales from Israel.

The Road to Avalon

Only a small circle of people were able to enter Avalon. In addition to its female ruler, Morgan Le Fay, and her eight sisters, its only inhabitants were the servants who lived in the Maiden House and Merlin, who is sometimes equated with the bard Taliesin. Only a few additional chosen ones ever made it to Avalon.

The legend describes the way to Avalon. One travels over water in a barque, but first has to learn how to summon the barque and its crew. Only Avalon's inhabitants knew the land road, which never appears in the descriptions, although it is said that some people discover this secret path by mistake. Cloud cover is another precondition for reaching Avalon, which cannot be entered in clear weather. Those who try to enter on a sunny day find themselves in Glastonbury Abbey, instead.

Joseph of Arimathea

According to legend, as Jesus was dying on the cross, Joseph of Arimathea collected some of the blood in a bowl, or possibly in the Holy Grail. After Jesus' resurrection, Joseph of Arimathea was put on trial for stealing the corpse and was condemned to forty years in prison. Jesus appeared to him in his cell, declaring him the keeper of the Grail. Upon his release, Joseph left Israel.

It is sometimes said that the island is hidden beneath the water's surface, with the clouds or mist representing the gateway between the earth's surface and the damp underworld. Avalon itself is a peaceful, healing island, where neither rain, hail, nor snow can fall. Morgan Le Fay and her sisters are said to possess certain healing powers, which is why, with the help of the ferryman Barinthus, they can bring the wounded to Avalon for a short time, travelling along the secret path.

Avalon could only be entered through the mist that lies thick on the water surrounding the peninsula of Glastonbury.

This is how Arthur came to the island. According to Arthurian legend, after his final battle, the Battle of Camlann, the mortally wounded king – in some sources he was already dead – was brought to the island by three otherworldly priestesses and laid there on a golden bed. His fate after that is unknown. For centuries afterward, legend still maintained that the king, either healed or resurrected, would one day return. Thus it was believed that Emperor Frederick I Barbarossa (ca. 1122–1190) was Arthur reborn. Yet, with the description of the road leading to Avalon so imprecise, and given the characteristics assigned it by the storytellers, we can safely conclude that Avalon is purely a product of fantasy.

After his final battle, the dying Arthur was brought to Avalon by ship.

Glastonbury Tor (from *twr*, Celtic for "mountain" or "earth"), near Glastonbury Abbey, is also said to have been one of the entrances to Avalon.

King Arthur

While Avalon might well be an invention not requiring serious investigation by scholars, the situation is entirely different where Arthur himself is concerned. He is said to have fought the Angles and Saxons long before the Knights of the Round Table were assembled around him.

King Arthur is frequently portrayed as the ideal knight and king.

Arthurian legend

As already mentioned, different versions of the Arthur saga exist, and they vary from one another in details. Nevertheless, there are also areas of agreement.

Thus, Arthur has always been the son of Uther Pendragon and Igraine. Most sources say he was fifteen years old when he ascended to the throne of England and Wales. As a military leader he defended his kingdom against the Angles and Saxons, and led successful wars of conquest against Ireland, Iceland, Norway and Gaul. In the Battle of Saussy he was even successful against the Romans. While celebrating his triumph in Rome, the news reached him that his nephew, Mordred, had taken over the kingdom in his absence. Arthur returned to his homeland to wage war against his nephew. He was victorious, though he paid for that victory with death, or, according to other sources, with a serious wound.

Elaborate descriptions of fantastic elements are woven into the legend, like the story of the capture of the giant of Mont Saint Michel, or the journey to Avalon after Arthur's final battle.

Development of the Arthurian legend

All this suggests that the British people saw in Arthur exactly the kind of king they wanted. He is described as wise, just, eager for action, successful and pious. He was a ruler who did not leave his people in the lurch and always kept his word. The figures around this king, like the powerful magician Merlin or Arthur's half-sister, Morgan Le Fay, who ruled Avalon, enhance this image further. This was also the function of the Knights of the Round Table and their mutually agreed tests and trials, including the search for the Holy Grail.

If one compares the earliest Arthurian sources – which in this case are the ninth-century *Historia Brittonum* and the poem *Y Gododdin* by the Welsh poet Aneirin (ca. 535–600) – with the tradition of Arthurian legends in eleventh- and twelfth-century France, there are distinct differences that demonstrate how much the saga has grown since its emergence. By the twelfth century, the poets had attached so many Celtic and Welsh fables to Arthur's heroic deeds that

they give the impression that Arthur himself is little more than a fairy-tale figure.

Arthurian legend has provided the basis for countless works of art, although King Arthur himself is not always the central figure. Many images, texts, musical compositions and films deal entirely with the supporting characters.

Did King Arthur live?

Starting from the presumption that historical events have also been incorporated in the Arthurian legends, numerous scholars began to search for a person who could have been either identical to the legendary King Arthur or whose deeds paralleled those of the legend. In fact, several possibilities presented themselves, although it is not clear that any one of the many knights, generals and commanders who lived between the second and sixth centuries ever achieved kingly status. It can be assumed that the title of king is as much a folk invention as the Round Table, the historical basis for which has been sought in vain.

Excalibur

King Arthur's sword is called either Excalibur or Caliburn. The tale of how it came into the king's possession is related in numerous versions. One variant has Arthur pulling the sword out of a stone, a feat which, according to a prophecy, could only be accomplished by the future king of England. In other versions, Arthur receives the sword from the Lady in the Lake after his first sword (the one from the stone) is shattered in battle. After Arthur's victory over his nephew Mordred, Excalibur was thrown into the lake and thereby returned to the Lady.

The Holy Grail

The story of the Holy Grail is closely tied to Arthurian legend. In many versions, finding the Grail is the primary task to be accomplished by Arthur and his knights. Despite these many sources, the origin, appearance, function and legacy of the Grail remain unclear.

The Ark of the Covenant
The Ark of the Covenant contained the two stone tablets inscribed with the Ten Commandments that Moses brought down from Mount Sinai. The Bible describes it as a gilt chest made of Acacia wood with two carrying poles and a lid with two golden cherubim (angels) atop it. The Ark was kept in the first Temple of Jerusalem until around 587 BC, when King Nebuchadnezzar II carried it off. It has been lost without a trace ever since.

The history of the Grail

The oldest sources for the Arthurian legend vary from one another considerably. Events that are described in detail in one source are barely mentioned in another version, or are portrayed in a completely different way. Thus, the search for the Holy Grail, if included at all, is portrayed in so many different ways that there is little correspondence between them. While in some versions an individual hero tries to acquire the Grail, in other texts Arthur and several of his knights set off after it on a sacred quest. In some cases the court magician Merlin provides direction; in others the search is governed by fate. In nearly every account, however, the Grail lies in an otherworldly realm. With the hero's help, the Keeper of the Grail, who, depending on the version, lies injured or dying, can be healed, after which the hero becomes the new Keeper of the Grail.

From Celtic cult object to Holy Grail

It is now fairly certain that the Grail legend has Celtic roots. Chrétien de Troyes (ca. 1140–1190), who in the twelfth century set down the oldest Arthur saga that refers to it, apparently based his work on myths brought to the continent by Irish refugees and adventurers. This makes it likely that the Grail was one of these tales. Chrétien does not describe the origin of the Grail. It was Robert de Boron, who wrote a little later and apparently independently of

Some members of the Order of the Knights Templar claimed to have the Holy Grail in their possession. The reliquary provided for it is still preserved.

The Apocrypha
Apocrypha (from the Greek word for "hidden") is the name given to texts that have a historical Christian relationship to the Bible, but for a variety of reasons either never were or are no longer considered part of the sacred canon. The vessel used to collect the blood of Christ is mentioned in one of these sources, the so-called Gospel of Nicodemus, which came into being in its current form in the fifth century AD, although fragments of it exist from as far back as the second century AD. Because of its late appearance, the Gospel of Nicodemus is not part of the Bible.

Chrétien's work, who set down a different version of the Arthur saga. In de Boron's version, the Grail was given a Christian background and connections were made to the texts of the Apocrypha (see box).

Joseph of Arimathia is said to have collected some of the blood of the crucified Christ in the Grail.

In some variations of the Arthur legend, it was Sir Percival who received the Grail as reward for his courage and chivalry.

The appearance and function of the Holy Grail

The Holy Grail has been sought for many centuries by Grail seekers or Grail researchers trying to learn more about this magical object. This has everything to do with the fact that the Grail is believed to confer any number of special powers on its bearer, ranging from feeding whoever possesses it to healing illness, and from giving one dominion over a great empire to assuring eternal life.

The search is made especially challenging because the visible form of the Grail is described in so many contradictory ways. In Chrétien's account it is something like a fruit bowl, while Robert de Boron describes it as a drinking vessel. Poet Wolfram von Eschenbach said it was a stone, or at least a stone vase. The view that the Grail can be equated with the Ark of the Covenant is also widespread.

Because it is not described in detail and, last but not least, because it has come to us only through myths and legends that for the most part stem from the twelfth and thirteenth centuries, the tracks of the Grail, if it in fact ever existed, can no longer be followed. In any case, finding the Holy Grail was always a matter of chance.

Miracles and Mysteries

Reports of religious wonders and mysteries have been passed down in great numbers. Most of these come to us through the monks who recorded them in ancient handwritten manuscripts, which were later transmitted to the congregation by priests and ministers. It is no longer possible to know for certain how many of the early traditions of the church actually represent historical events. In many cases the stories are better understood as allegories, tales designed to send a specific message.

Since the Middle Ages, many new mysteries and miracles have entered the picture. These have been more precisely documented, both by the religious and the secular side, which can be explained by the increasing separation between church and state. Secular and religious authorities, both trying to justify their right to power, welcomed seemingly inexplicable phenomena as evidence of their God-given status. During the Renaissance, when most sacred symbols and signs conveyed political meanings, a scientific interest in miracles and mysteries began that continues to this day, leading to an improved standard of investigation.

This section of the book deals with religious miracles and wonders from different epochs, beginning with the period of the biblical Old Testament and concluding with phenomena that only became known in the nineteenth or twentieth centuries. As in the previous chapter, the focus is on the interaction between science and mystery.

Said to be the cloth in which Jesus was buried, the Shroud of Turin is still the object of controversy and discussion.

According to the Bible, the Flood was a worldwide inundation that wiped out all living creatures except for Noah, his family, and the animals with them on board the ark.

The Great Flood

The seventh chapter of the Book of Genesis describes how God made it rain for forty days and forty nights in order to inundate the earth and annihilate all people who lived in sin. Only Noah, who heeded God's warning, was able to save himself and his family from the Flood by building an ark.

Accounts of the Flood

According to current research, the biblical account of the Great Flood was written down in the seventh or sixth century BC, most likely based on prior sources from the Babylonian-Assyrian region. But that is not the only place we find tales about a tremendous flood. Scholars have since assembled more than 250 flood accounts from cultures all over the world.

It should be mentioned that these tales are often quite autonomous and are not easily brought into accord with the biblical Flood. Within the context of a biblical-historical comparative study, as well, certain discrepancies need to be taken into consideration. The theory proposed in the seventeenth century by the Irish theologian James Usher (1581–1656), for example, calculated that the Flood took place in the year 2501 BC. This was certainly false, as later

Even today it is not indisputably clear that the ark, as it is described in the Bible, ever really existed.

finds from the royal library in Ninevah would prove. That library contained copies of an ancient account known as the Gilgamesh Epic (see box, right) that describes the Flood. Based on the language used, the original text has been dated to around 2100 BC; the library itself was built much later.

Traces of the Flood

Scientific circles agree that an earth-encircling flood could not possibly have taken place. Many see an inundation over a large area as equally unlikely. The length of time that it rained has been similarly brought into question, as has the landing place of the ark, named Mount Ararat in the Bible. The widespread opinion was and remains that this is a mountain in Armenia, disregarding the fact that this mountain was called something different during biblical times. Comparison with the more accurate Bablylonian texts reveals that a small plateau in the delta of the Euphrates and Tigris Rivers is also named Ararat.

For centuries, adventurers have been pulled in both directions. Excavation on Ararat supposedly uncovered parts of the ark, including a ship hull, in the Ararat region. In 2003, a Russian group found evidence of stone anchors on the mountain. Needless to say, none of this has survived more exacting investigation.

As already mentioned, since a worldwide flood is not possible, individual scholars operate on the presumption that the biblical Flood was an inundation that covered the land far and wide for a lengthy period of time. Early in the twentieth century, British archaeologist Charles Leonard Woolley (1880–1960) found some evidence that Mesopotamia had suffered such a catastrophe, but it was not until the years 1993 and 2000 that evidence was revealed proving that natural disasters on this dramatic scale actually happen. After the Russian ship *Aquanaut* found remains of freshwater plants deep in the Black Sea in 1993, Robert D. Ballard, who located the wreck of the Titanic, investigated the sea bottom further. He came upon the remains of a human settlement, dated to around 5600 BC, which had been the victim of a natural disaster. Whether this is also evidence of the biblical Flood, is still not clear.

The Gilgamesh Epic

The Epic of Gilgamesh is recorded on twelve stone tablets, the majority of which are well preserved. The tale deals with the legendary King Gilgamesh, who is said to have lived somewhere between 2750 and 2600 BC. Two-thirds divine and one-third human, this king tried to elevate himself to the level of the gods. Toward this end he undertook a journey to the wise Utnapitshim, who was said to know the secret of immortality. Utnapitshim had just survived an unimaginable flood with the help of the ocean god, Enki. By building an ark, he was able to survive, the only human to do so.

According to the Bible, the ark landed on Mount Ararat. Although the mountain was called by a different name in biblical times, many claim that signs of the ark can be found in the area.

Qumran: The Dead Sea Scrolls

In West Jordan in 1947, near the ruins of Qumran (also known as Khirbet Qumran), clay pots filled with scrolls were found stashed in eleven caves. Preliminary investigation identified the texts as belonging to the Essenes (see box, facing page). However, a later review of these results has raised additional questions that are not yet adequately answered.

The plundered library

More than half a year passed between the time a Bedouin youth discovered the clay pots inside a cave near Qumran and the first thorough analysis of the scrolls they contained. During this time interval, the young man first tried to sell the parchment rolls. Later, war between Egypt and Israel (1947–1949) made textual analysis by experts at Jerusalem University even more difficult.

In January 1948, after one of the manuscripts had been identified as a version of the book of the prophet Isaiah, an expidition to search the caves was quickly dispatched. When the caves were finally located, it was quite clear that their contents had been thoroughly plundered. The fragments that remained suggested that between 200 and 250 scrolls had originally been stored here. In ten neighboring caves, still more manuscripts and fragments were found. Based on the biblical content of the scrolls and the caves' proximity to the ruins of Qumran, which had been described by the Roman scholar Plinius (24–69 AD) as the location of an Essene religious settlement, a connection was made between these scrolls and the Essene community.

The scrolls bearing the text of the book of the prophet Isaiah date from the first or second century AD.

Confusing discoveries

Today we know that approximately 500 different scribes produced the 800 or so texts (or fragments of texts) that were ultimately recovered, writing in Hebrew, Aramaic, Greek, or Nabatean. The scrolls were dated between the third century BC and the first century AD. This result encouraged a closer look at the Qumran ruins, triggering a discussion that continues to this day. The unusually high number of scrolls alone, as well as the number of scribes involved, together with the age of some of the texts, raised questions concerning the extent of the Essene complex. Roman coins found during archaeological excavation dated the site's destruction to the time of the Jewish Rebellion (66/67 AD). Among their findings were a storage room filled with hundreds of clay bowls and pots, millstones, a kiln, and cisterns connected with the Essene practice of ritual bathing. A dining room and scriptorium, where texts were written down or copied, were also identified. There were, however, no signs of living spaces or private quarters of any kind, which suggests that the inhabitants retired to the nearby caves to sleep.

Many of the finds were not in line with what one might expect from an ascetic, cloistered religious order. In fact, some scholars claimed that the results point to a Qumran that was in fact a ceramic workshop or even a simple village. Other scholars proposed that texts were written or copied to order there. A further theory claims that the caves and abbey ruins have no direct relationship to one another.

The Dead Sea Scrolls of Qumran are today considered among the most valuable historical manuscripts ever discovered. Yet their history, now as then, still lies shrouded in darkness. Over time it has become less likely that the as yet undeciphered scrolls will tell us anything about their past.

The Dead Sea Scrolls were found inside this cave in West Jordan.

Portions of the scrolls are now on display in a specially constructed museum in Jerusalem.

The Essenes

The Essenes (from the Aramaic for "the pious") were a Jewish religious group in existence from about 150 BC to 100 AD. They can be understood as forerunners of later monastic orders. They lived in isolation from other members of the Jewish faith, practised abstinence, and abjured personal possessions for the good of the group. They were organized into strict hierarchies and had stringent rules governing the day. It is thought that the Essenes were not one unified group, but consisted of numerous distinct groups, each with its own rules and regulation of faith.

The Three Kings and the Star of Bethlehem

The three kings – Caspar, Melchior and Balthasar – were guided to Bethlehem by a star to welcome the newborn king. They brought gold, frankincense, and myrrh as gifts.

THE THREE KINGS

In the New Testament, the story of the three kings is told only in the Gospel of Matthew. A comparison of this account with the popular image reveals that the Bible does not include the name, rank, or number of visitors who came to see the newborn Jesus. Matthew speaks of "wise men", "magi" or "astrologers" and lists the gifts they presented to Jesus. There is also little evidence that the Wise Men were canonized according to the standard procedures of the Catholic Church.

It's likely that the number of gifts was the decisive factor in determining the number of Wise Men. Their names, however, appeared only later, in the fifth century AD, in a book on the childhood of Jesus written in Armenian. It assigned the kings the names Gaspar of India, Balthasar of Arabia, and Melkon of Persia. When we take into account that Matthew, more than any other evangelist, set great store in symbols, it seems best to view the Wise Men as literary figures included to underline Jesus' importance.

What is a comet?
Comets are concentrations of dust particles, gases, and ice. In the course of orbiting the sun, the frozen components turn to steam as comets approach the sun. This gives comets their characteristic tail.

The bones that made their way from Palestra, Byzantium, and Mainz to Cologne, Germany in 1164 under circumstances that are not entirely explained, despite all claims to the contrary, are not the bones of the astrologers. It is thought that the bones were imported to support the position of Holy Roman Emperor Frederick I (Barbarossa) during a politically unsettled period of his reign. This was the emperor who was the first to pray to the Christ Child, but also the man who would elevate secular rulers above the rank of the princes of the Church.

THE STAR OF BETHLEHEM

Just as Matthew was the only Gospel writer to mention the Wise Men, the star of Bethlehem is also missing from the other Gospels. Here again, one can assume that this is an example of the use of a symbol, the conscious placing of a sign on high. Investigations have nevertheless attempted to trace the appearance of the star of Bethlehem back to an astronomical phenomenon.

One of the oldest theories, reported as early as the third century AD, says that the star might have been a comet (see box, above). This sounds reasonable, especially since there

It is written that the Wise Men brought Jesus gifts of gold, frankincense, and myrrh. That three persons were involved was probably derived from the number of gifts at a later time.

were comets visible from the earth in the time prior to Christ's birth. It has since been proven, however, that none of these comets were in any way exceptionally visible.

Other theories propose that a supernova, an exploding star, could have been responsible for the star's sudden appearance above Bethlehem. Since no evidence of this has been found, this claim is probably untenable.

The third possibility would be a conjunction of two stars (see box, right). This theory is supported by the frequent occurrence of conjunctions in the time period shortly before Christ was born. On the other hand, similar to the situation with the comet theory, it is not clear why this one conjunction would be viewed as being in any way unusual to the people experiencing it. In addition, it has been calculated that the conjunction over Bethlehem was not perfect, meaning it would have required little effort to distinguish the individual stars from each other. This discrepancy would have destroyed any impression that the conjunction represented a new star in the sky. Thus, what remains is to consider the star of Bethlehem a miracle or, for the reasons mentioned above, a symbol.

Whether kings or magi from distant places actually followed a star to Bethlehem cannot be proven.

The meeting of two stars

A conjunction is said to take place when, as viewed from the earth, two stars appear to move tightly together or line up one behind the other. When this happens, their surfaces, reflecting the light of the sun, seem larger than normal, making an alignment like this brighter and more visible than any one star on its own would appear.

The Hale-Bopp Comet has been proposed as the star of Bethlehem.

The Shroud of Turin

The Shroud of Turin is said to be the cloth in which the body of Jesus Christ was wrapped and buried, and which was found on the third day after his death in the empty tomb. Ever since the shroud first turned up, people have tried to prove that it is a genuine relic or expose it as a forgery.

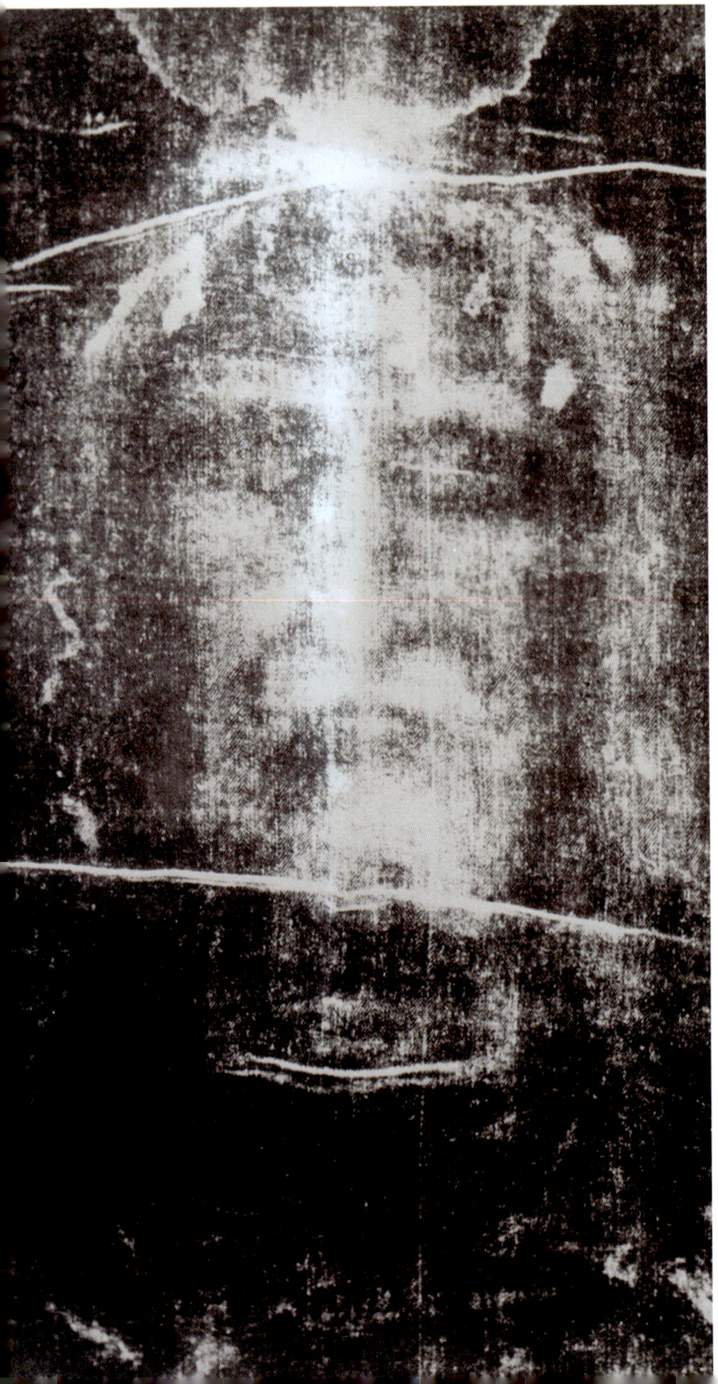

The first exhibition

On 19 September 1356, the knight Geoffrey de Charney fell in the Battle of Poitiers, one of the most important battles of the Hundred Years War between England and France. Afterwards, his widow Jeanne de Vergy found herself responsible for the upkeep of the recently completed collegiate church in Lirey near Troyes, which her husband had built under orders from the king. Toward this end, she organized a public exhibition in the church of a piece of linen that measured 14.3 feet (4.36 m) long and 3.6 feet (1.1 m) wide. On the cloth, the blurred form of a naked human could be recognized. Traces of blood marked wounds on the head, hands, feet, and breast. This piece, claimed Jeanne de Vergy, was the very cloth in which Jesus Christ had been buried.

Shortly after the exhibit opened, the bishop of Troyes took possession of the shroud to stave off rumours that the piece was a forgery. Jeanne de Vergy herself could provide no detailed information regarding how the shroud came to be in her husband's possession.

The road to Turin

Thirty-two years later, the cloth was exhibited once again, this time by Geoffrey de Charney's son with the support of the antipope, Clement VII. The following years were a time of deep schism, characterized by constant strife between Rome and Avignon, each claiming to be the only authentic seat of the Catholic Church. The shroud played an important role in this struggle over church policy. Clement VII used the relic as a means of exerting pressure, arguing that his possession of the cloth alone was proof that he was the true pope. After the Council of Constance (actually a series of councils held between 1414 and 1418) brought about the reunification of the Catholic Church, the shroud lost its political meaning.

The first modern investigation of the shroud made use of the negatives of photographs taken by Secondo Pia.

The shroud was then returned to the collegiate church of Lirey for storage, but was later exhibited in other European cities. It finally fell into the possession of Ludwig, Duke of Savoy, who stored it in the ducal castle chapel in Chambery. It was there in 1532 that the shroud was damaged by fire. The silver of the box in which the relic was stored melted, leaving holes and char marks in the cloth.

In 1578, Ludwig's heir, Duke Emmanuel Philibert, brought the shroud to Turin, where it has remained ever since, though it has since changed hands. It was bequeathed to the Holy See in 1983, and is currently not accessible to the public.

Science and belief

For many centuries, the authenticity of the shroud had only been discussed from a theological point of view. In 1898, the linen finally became the focus of scientific inquiry. The trigger was a man named Secondo Pia, at that time the mayor of Asti, Italy and an amateur photographer, who took many pictures of the shroud during a multi-day exhibition. When he developed the photographs he noticed that the man's body was much clearer in the negatives than in the prints. Many investigations through the following years were made with these negatives close at hand.

Different methods were used to gather more information about the linen cloth and its history. A Swiss botanist investigated the grains of pollen trapped in the material, concluding that the grains could only have come from the area around Jerusalem.

The antipope Clement VII (1523–1543) claimed the shroud was proof that he alone was the one true pope.

The front and back of the body can be recognized on the shroud. This is explained by the manner and method with which the dead were wound in the cloth prior to burial.

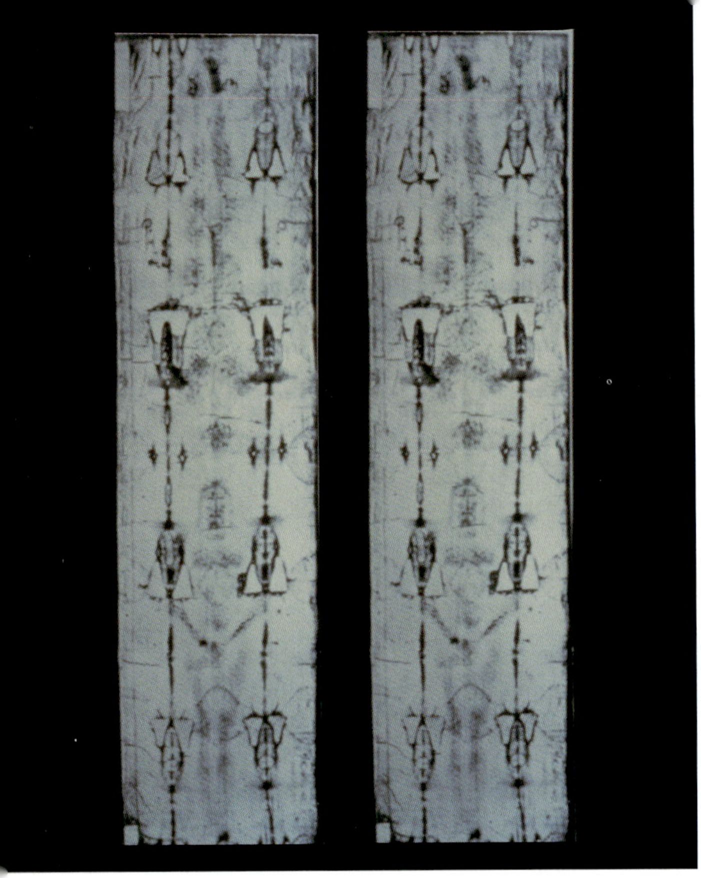

Lignin-vanillin decomposition
Lignin is a solid, colourless substance that is stored in the cell walls of plants and provides physical stability. The investigation of lignin-vanillin decomposition has to do with the fact that the lignin in any woven fabric will, due to a chemical process, decay over time, leaving vanillin behind as a residue. The greater the proportion of vanillin present, as opposed to lignin, the older the cloth will be. A disadvantage of this method is that the rate of decomposition is dependent on the temperatures the cloth has been exposed to over time. This can lead to wide variations in date.

The shroud itself has been damaged many times over the years by poor storage conditions or fire. The repairs and remaining traces of damage are now easier to see than the schematic impression of the dead body.

Wounds caused by nails or a spear during the crucifixion are clearly recognizable on the shroud.

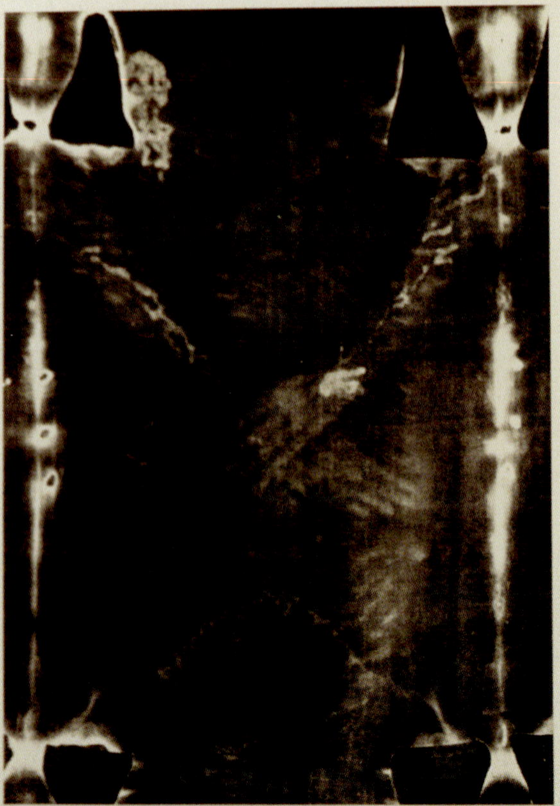

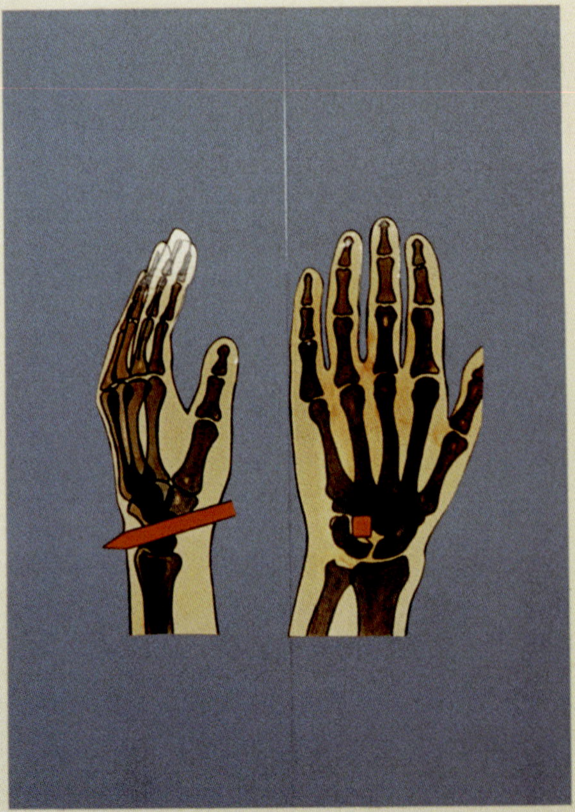

On 12 April 1997, the shroud survived a fire in Turin Cathedral without further damage thanks to a fireman who saved it at the last minute.

Scientific investigations

Forensic medical investigations of the shroud, which began in the 1930s, concluded that the body on the linen represented a man who had died due to crucifixion, who had suffered numerous wounds from a whip-like instrument of torture before his death. He had worn a crown of thorns and his death had been confirmed by a lance thrust into his side. These results were based on the traces of blood found on the cloth.

Great media interest was awakened when the first radiocarbon dating of the shroud took place in laboratories in Oxford, Zurich, and Arizona. The results dated the production of the cloth to between 1260 and 1390 AD. This scientific proof seemed to confirm the cloth as a forgery. However, those supporting the authenticity of the shroud criticized the research protocols soon afterward, some going so far as to accuse the researchers of fraud, perhaps achieved by switching samples.

The most recent investigations used lignin-vanillin decomposition (see box, opposite) as a dating method. These results showed that the cloth was between 1300 and 3000 years old. While this makes it possible that the radiocarbon dates are in error, no further concrete results are forthcoming.

Attempts at explanation

Now as in the past, the question remains unanswered as to how the image came to be on the linen. Although several scientific theories have been proposed, none of these has withstood closer examination.

Statements from the Middle Ages saying that the image on the shroud is a painting have been weakened by the absence of pigment particles. Other proposals, including one suggestion that the image could be the product of a chemical reaction caused by the evaporation of aloe, which can be used to anoint a body before burial, have also proved unfounded. While experiments showed that evaporation did leave an image behind, the contrast wasn't nearly as strong as that of the image on the shroud.

In addition to the question of how the linen came to be imprinted with this intriguing image, speculation continues as to how the shroud could have remained hidden for over 1300 years, as well as how it passed from Palestine to France at all. The question as to whether the man whose shroud has caused a stir for over 650 years really is Jesus Christ is also unanswered.

Radiocarbon dating

Radiocarbon dating (the C14 method) measures relative amounts of carbon isotopes. While alive, the body of all living things absorbs radioactive C-14 isotopes from the atmosphere. This element decays at a predictable rate after the organism dies. Current C14 methods can date organic materials going back 40,000 years.

Our Lady of Guadelupe

It is said that in December 1531, the mother of God appeared to the peasant Juan Diego in the town of Guadelupe, Mexico, entrusting him with the task of having a church built on that spot. When the archbishop refused to fulfil this request, an image of the Virgin appeared on Diego's apron. This relic is still on display at the place where Mary first appeared to him.

Some 20 million pilgrims from all over the world visit the image of Our Lady of Guadelupe annually.

The apparition

According to legends, Juan Diego was on his way to mass in Tlatilolco (where Mexico City is now) when he heard a hymn come down from heaven. The voice of the Virgin Mary spoke to him from a cloud, sending him to the bishop of Mexico to request that a church be built at the place of their meeting. When Juan Diego was finally allowed to meet with the bishop, the prelate did not believe him and sent Diego back home.

The next day Juan Diego went to the same place and again heard the voice of Our Lady asking him to appear before the bishop in her name so that a church could be built on that spot. Again the bishop sent the peasant home. When Juan Diego arrived back at the place where he had heard the voice twice before, he told the Lady that the bishop would not believe him without a sign.

When Diego returned to his house he found his uncle mortally ill. The village doctor was not able to help him, so the uncle told his nephew to go fetch a priest to administer the last rites. On his way to the city he met a woman whose voice he recognized as that of the Virgin. She told him that his uncle was already healed and sent him to pick flowers at the place where they had spoken before, although it was winter and flowers were not in bloom.

Diego obeyed and collected the miraculous blooms in his cloak. When he returned, she sent him to the city again, telling him to open his flower-filled mantle when he kneeled before the bishop. When Diego did as he was asked and presented the flowers to the bishop, there was an image of the Virgin imprinted on Diego's cloak underneath the flowers. The bishop recognized this as a sign from the Virgin Mary and declared himself ready to build a chapel at once at the place named by Diego, and to have a church built there later. The image of Our Lady of Guadelupe on Diego's apron has been kept there ever since, first in the chapel, later in the pilgrimage church built in 1709 and, as of 1976, in the new basilica built next door.

Mysteries and their investigation

Although of great age, the image is still easy to recognize, despite the fact that it is printed on agave fibres, which, under normal conditions, would have decayed within a few decades. The relic was for centuries stored in less than ideal conditions, displayed in a windowless chapel immediately behind burning candles, shrouded in incense, fingered by pilgrims, and sometimes even embraced, kissed, or brought in contact with wounds. Threads were pulled out of the cloth, and in 1791 saltpeter was accidentally poured over the image. In 1921, enemies of the church attempted to blow up the image together with the protective glass that had recently been installed to protect it. Nevertheless, it has never been seriously damaged.

The image was intensely investigated beginning in the twentieth century. It was revealed that the image does not consist of brushstrokes, although in places where the original had been painted over later, traces of individual artists' hands could be discerned. These brushstrokes, incidentally, were more likely to have suffered the ravages of time than the original image underneath. Upon investigation, the eye of the Virgin was shown to include the reflected images of several persons within it. This alone gave researchers new mysteries to investigate, because these figures were at a scale that was almost microscopic. In addition, the rules of optical distortion have been observed, although these were not developed in painting until much later.

The mystery of Our Lady of Guadelupe still has not been explained, and there are no convincing theories of how the image was produced. The imprinted cloth of Juan Diego is visited by millions of pilgrims every year who, now as then, believe firmly in miracles.

How the image of the Virgin Mary came to be on Juan Diego's cloak has still not been explained.

Pope John Paul II visited the place where the Virgin appeared to Juan Diego four times, repeatedly professing his belief in this Marian apparition.

The Holy Grave of Arles-sur-Tech

There's a sealed stone sarcophagus within the church of the tiny village of Arles-sur-Tech, France that supposedly contains the remains of two saints. Inexplicably, this sarcophagus fills itself every day with one to two litres of holy water that is said to possess the power to heal.

Water from the Holy Grave

Reports about the *Sainte Tombe d'Arles-sur-Tech*, the Holy Grave of Arles-sur-Tech in Languedoc-Roussillon, France, can be traced back to the late sixteenth century. The tomb is thought to date from the fourth or fifth century and has served as the reliquary for the remains of Saints Abdon and Sennen (see box, page 128) since at least the tenth century. Many believe it is due to their presence that the grave fills with water again and again, apparently without cause. The water is said to possess an astounding ability to heal, bringing even those on their deathbed back to life.

The sarcophagus sits outside the church behind a metal grille in an unlit courtyard at the foot of a wall. A white cross hangs above it. The air in the courtyard is warm and humid from the winds coming over the south wall, although its northerly orientation admits no direct sunlight.

The holy grave was cut from a single block of marble and stands on two solid socles standing 8 inches (20 cm)

Resting on two solid stone socles, the marble sarcophagus measures 6.3 feet long, 2.1 feet wide, and 1.6 feet high (1.9 m x 65 cm x 50 cm). The walls are about 12 inches (30 cm) thick.

high. It is 6.2 feet (1.9 m) long, 2.1 feet (65 cm) high, and 1.6 feet (50 cm) broad. The prism-form lid is 12 inches (30 cm) high and, like the rest of the sarcophagus, is 4 inches (10 cm) thick. The lid does not meet the sarcophagus cleanly, leaving a finger-thick gap in between them. There is an additional hole on one of the side walls where a pump can be inserted when necessary. This is how the pastor of the church draws off the water to give those who visit the Holy Grave.

A white cross hangs over the sarcophagus. It has been severely damaged by the effects of weathering.

The first investigation

As traditions surrounding holy places accumulate, scientists try to understand the reasons behind the phenomena. In the case of the holy grave, two scientific investigations have taken place, the results of which have put to rest rumours of supernatural aspects of the water in the grave.

The first investigations took place in 1961. Three scientists led a series of experiments over the course of two and a half months in which regional weather conditions were carefully observed. A peculiar set of circumstances came to their aid: it did not rain for two months. Since the investigators had sealed the sarcophagus with putty and a nylon sheet, it was quickly determined that there was no way that two litres of water could accumulate in the sarcophagus. And indeed, the water level inside it remained unchanged throughout that time, except for a slight sinking whenever the pastor removed some of it for pilgrims.

Weather conditions in the Pyrenees play an important role in investigating the holy grave. Warm air currents from the Mediterranean blow moist sea air inland. Since the mountain range makes it difficult for the heavily laden clouds to continue, and the Mediterranian climate often prevents precipitation, the area often experiences high humidity.

It was only when it started to rain again that the level of water in the sarcophagus rose, though very slowly. It seemed to take the water several days to enter the grave. A more painstaking investigation of the surface of the sarcophagus lid showed that it was covered with tiny depressions, only 1 to 2 mm in diameter. When it rained, these were filled with water, emptying themselves again within 45 seconds. Additional observation of the base of the lid led to the conclusion that the water was seeping through it, into the sarcophagus.

The marble of which the sarcophagus is made proved to be porous enough to allow water to enter it. According to the research results, the rain transported dust particles through the porous lid as well. Accumulating inside over time, these particles eventually sealed the cracks and holes in the sarcophagus itself and prevented the water from flowing back out.

Abdon and Sennen
Abdon and Sennen are the names of two martyrs who came from Persia and were condemned to death by gladiatorial combat during the reign of the emperors Decius or Valerian in the third or fourth century. Their bones were sent from Rome to San Marco in 826 and are worshipped there to this day. The martyrs are the patron saints of Arles-sur-Tech, although whether their mortal remains are really to be found in the sarcophagus known as the "holy grave" is open to debate.

Dew formation contributes to the phenomenon, as well. The drops of dew, which soak through the sarcophagus lid, hardly affect the level of the water at all, but do help keep the lid clean. This daily cleansing keeps the depressions in the roof from becoming clogged.

Another factor is the gap between the lid and the body of the sarcophagus, which permits water to condense inside due to differences in temperature. This is the reason for the occasional water overflow, which could be observed in the course of the experiment. It was limited to just a few drops running down the outside of the sarcophagus. Since the surface on the side of the sarcophagus facing the courtyard has a number of irregularities, it was concluded that the overflowing of the water was simple condensation, rather than anything pouring out from a source inside the sarcophagus. The scientific explanation for the phenomenon of water accumulation was therefore already in place by 1961.

Parapsychologists versus scientists: the second investigation

French television broadcast a report on the *Sainte Tombe d'Arles-sur-Tech* in 1992, triggering renewed discussion of the phenomenon. Parapsychologists published articles in which they claimed that the sarcophagus was protected from rainfall by a canopy; this, however, was not at all true. In addition, they claimed that the scientific methods used in the initial investigation were laughable – pointing out in particular the simple student's ruler used to measure the water level in 1961. The scientific community countered that the results from 1961 were entirely credible, and that scientifically precise measurement is also possible with a student ruler.

Since this did not put an end the discussion, a second research group conducted new experiments in 1998 and 2001, this time with modern measurement devices. They succeeded in confirming most of the results from 1961, providing additional support in some areas. The only large variation had to do with the effects of dew and condensation on the interior water level. This was measured at 10 per cent higher than the figures arrived at by the earlier research group.

Publication of the new results may have ended the discussion between the parapsychologists and scientists, but they did not change either the inscription on the plaque in front of the holy grave or the descriptions of the phenomenon in a number of travel guides, all of which continue to describe the water accumulation as "mysterious".

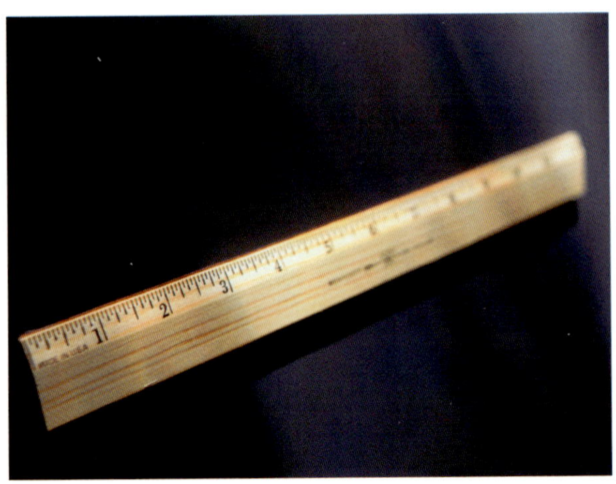

During the first investigation, the water level was measured using a simple student ruler.

Against all expert advice, the sarcophagus does not sit under a canopy, but in an interior church courtyard that is open to the sky.

Human Luminosity and Electricity

Saints are often identified by an aura, which marks their special status as exceptional people. The illumination can be in the form of a nimbus, holy light radiating around their head, or an aureole, also known as a mandorla, which is light surrounding the entire body. The term "enlightened" has even entered daily speech. Over the last few years, the phenomenon has been investigated. Are there really people who radiate light?

The case of Anna Monaro

In 1934, asthma sufferer Anna Monaro became famous within medical circles. Various doctors had examined the Italian woman, but none of them could figure out why light would stream from her chest for several seconds during her nightly asthma attacks. It would sometimes glow blue, sometimes red, and occasionally green. Although Monaro and her doctors were accused of fraud, additional witnesses and even filmed evidence proved that this was in no way a hallucination or manipulation.

While attempts were made to explain the phenomenon, none of the theories reviewed were finally satisfactory. A psychologist spoke of non-specific electrical and magnetic organisms in the woman's body, whereas a medical doctor pointed out a high concentration of sulphur in her blood, a result of her weakened condition. These sulphides could be illuminated through contact with ultraviolet light. This theory was discussed for a long time, but in the end a number of physicians pointed out that the sulphides were found throughout her body, while the light only radiated from her chest.

The light of the sick and the saintly

In the 1940s, researchers began to gather information about human luminosity. It soon became clear that two groups of people were primarily affected: the sick, and exceptionally devout believers.

Reports exist of brightly illuminated wounds, along with other tales that tell of corpses shimmering with a weak light. The existence of glowing bodily fluids, such as sweat or urine, has also been established. There are almost no known cases in which healthy people have been affected by this luminous condition.

There is another group of people who are now and then said to have a certain visible aura. These are people with exceptionally strong religious conviction, that is, the saints.

The Aztec god Quetzalcoatl is frequently shown surrounded by flames similar to divine representations in other religions.

In addition to religious paintings and legends, eyewitness accounts claim that some people, including those who would at a later point be called blessed or saintly, radiate rays of light through their clothing that are strong enough to illuminate an entire room.

It is interesting to note that luminosity is often related to other extraordinary abilities, as well. In his book *The Physical Phenomena of Mysticism* (1952), the respected Jesuit scholar Herbert Thurston wrote about the Blessed Bernardino Realino (1530–1616; patron of Lecci, Italy) and the Spanish Jesuit theologist Father Francisco Suarez (1548–1619). It was independently reported that both of these men were not only luminous, but were also capable of levitation: they were observed hovering in the air.

Can the origin of the holy light found in so many artistic images really be traced back to luminous individuals?

Pope Benedict XIV (1675–1758) wrote a protocol about beautification and canonization that refers to human "fire".

"Electrical" people contain so much voltage within their bodies that a light bulb held in their hands begins to glow.

Magnetized and electrified

Around the same time that human luminosity was being investigated, additional phenomena came to the attention of the scienctific community: human electricity and human magnetism.

One of the triggers was the intriguing case of Mrs. Antoine Timmer, a woman who travelled to New York in 1938 to take part in a competition in which $10,000 would be awarded to anyone who could demonstrate a parapsychological phenomenon that could not be imitated or proven to be trickery. Before a jury that included renowned stage magician Joseph Dunninger, among others, she displayed her ability by lightly touching silverware and other small objects, which then remained stuck to her hands until forcibly pulled free. Although Mrs. Timmer did not win the prize, in part because Dunninger believed he could re-create the effect using string, public interest in this phenomenon was awakened.

A few years later, as electrical appliances became more and more popular, there was a corresponding increase in reports about people who seemed to have an astonishing electrical charge in their bodies. They could cause electrical shorts and blackouts through their touch or, in come cases, by their mere presence. In the 1950s, Brian Williams of Cardiff, Wales found himself featured in newspaper headlines and filmed reports because he could make light bulbs glow by grasping them with his hands. According to a *Daily Mail* article in 1967, Brian Clemens, nicknamed "Flash Gordon", was so highly charged with electricity that he had to ground himself on metal objects before touching another person.

Researchers were also able to locate references to a few examples further in the past, but not too far back, perhaps because the lack of experience with electrical appliances made human electricity more difficult to recognize.

Electricity and luminosity

In the past, before the invention of electrical appliances, electrically charged people might well have existed nevertheless. Here we can sometimes equate the experience of electricity with human luminosity. Reports of persons who gave off sparks might be traced back to either sudden luminosity or the discharge of electricity.

These two phenomena have another aspect in common: illness can either cause these abilities to surface for the first time or strengthen those that are already present. In the 1920s, for example, Dr. Julius Ransom, head physician for the New York state prison system, reported on thirty-four prisoners who were treated for food poisoning. While recovering, one of them crumpled a piece of paper before throwing it away, but it clung to his hand. Investigation showed that the other prisoners had also become so charged with static electricity that their presence could move the needle of a compass or make a hanging piece of metal swing from side to side. This phenomenon disappeared once the men regained their health.

The puzzles of human luminosity, electricity, and magnetism have not yet been satisfactorily resolved. Although scientists have noted some parallels in nature (including creatures like electric eels and glow worms), it is thought that these phenomena have different causes in the human body, which lacks the physical organs necessary for comparable processes to take place. The rarity of these abilities is another factor that makes further study complicated. The magnetism or electricity may only occur during a specific time period, or the ability may require a particular state of mind in order to manifest itself. For science, the field remains highly charged in every sense of the word.

French physicist François Arago was called on during the investigation of an electrically charged woman named Angelique Cottin. He thought she was a fraud, but could prove nothing.

Esteemed American magician and mentalist Joseph Dunninger was one of the initiators of the competition in which a certifiably electrical person demonstrated her abilities.

Stigmata

Nails were driven through the hands of Jesus Christ as he was crucified. A crown of thorns had been set on his head and a lance was driven through his side after his death. In the following centuries, there have been repeated reports of living persons who inexplicably exhibit wounds comparable to one or more of the stigmata of Christ.

Marked like Christ

Stigmata (plural, from the Greek *stigma* = engraved line, sign) refer to marks resembling the wounds Christ suffered that appear on the bodies of some especially devout people. They can take many forms. Some people experience them primarily as brief gushes of blood or changes in skin colour, while in other cases the afflicted spots are excruciatingly painful. The most common variant, if one can use the word

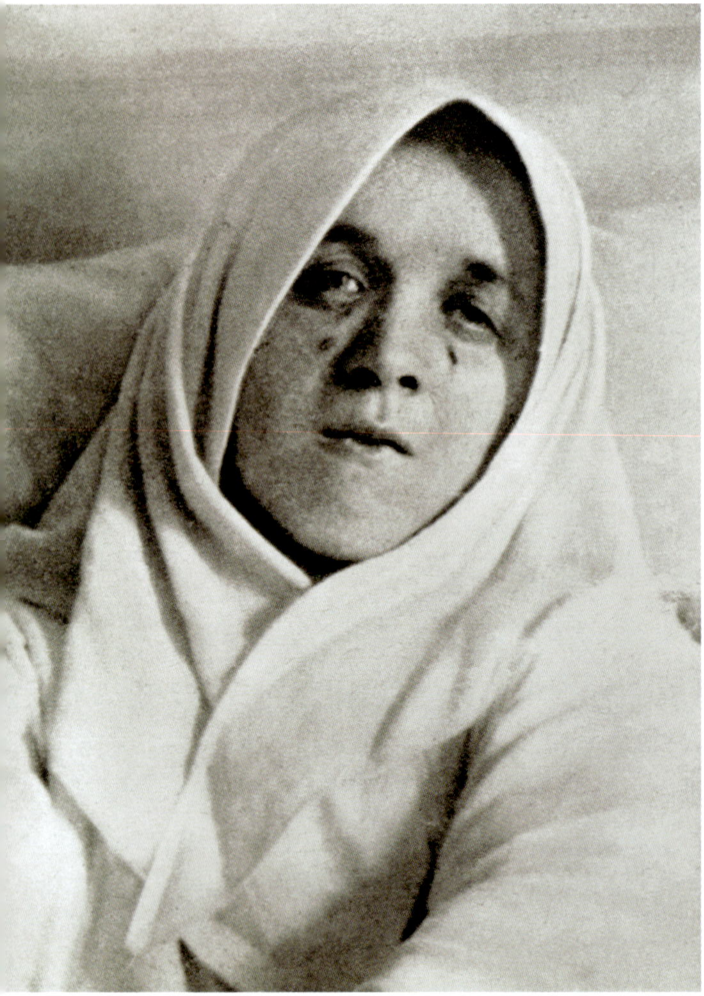

In the case of Therese Neumann (1898–1962), the wounds of Christ first appeared in 1926, leading to a flood of visitors.

The Catholic Church has officially recognized the beloved Saint Francis of Assisi as a stigmatic.

common for such a rare event, is open wounds that are only present for short periods of time. In other cases, the stigmata simply appear and never heal, with the wounds neither forming scabs or scars, nor becoming infected.

Stigmatic people

Although there are eighty people who experienced stigmata who have been canonized, the Catholic Church does not view stigmata alone as a sufficient reason for canonization. The determination that someone should be designated a saint is based on other factors, as well. In particular, the uncertainty inherent in historical accounts can lead to doubts about the authenticity of the stigmata described. In some cases it is thought that reports of stigmata have to do with the desire to more closely associate a certain person with Jesus.

The first person to mention the signs of Christ was the Apostle Paul in his Letter to the Galatians. It is doubtful that he was really referring to a case of stigmata here, however, even if this is claimed again in a later source. There is considerably more evidence that Saint Francis of Assisi (ca. 1181–1226) was a genuine case.

Attempts at explanation

One theory claims that humans have the potential to influence their bodies by means of their spirits. There are reports of persons who were able to perform superhuman deeds in extreme situations, such as being able to lift an object weighing over a ton. Since stigmata overwhelmingly appear on Catholics, it has naturally been suggested that their bodies have produced these wounds themselves. However, in a few cases, non-Christians have received stigmata, as well.

A further possibility is that the afflicted person is suffering from a peculiar form of hysteria, a mania that can produce all manner of symptoms, including bleeding under the skin. There have been attempts to test this theory using hypnosis, and in fact the experimental subjects did produce dark flecks on the spots where the wounds of Christ are thought to have been located.

Real wounds?

Swindlers of varying types also exist. While some only claim to have borne the wounds of Christ, others go so far as to inflict wounds on themselves, presenting the scars as proof. In some cases individuals have wounded themselves repeatedly over an extended period of time, regardless of the harm they are doing to their health.

Although the phenomenon is not common, more recent stigmata have been investigated scientifically. An exhaustive explanation, however, has yet to appear.

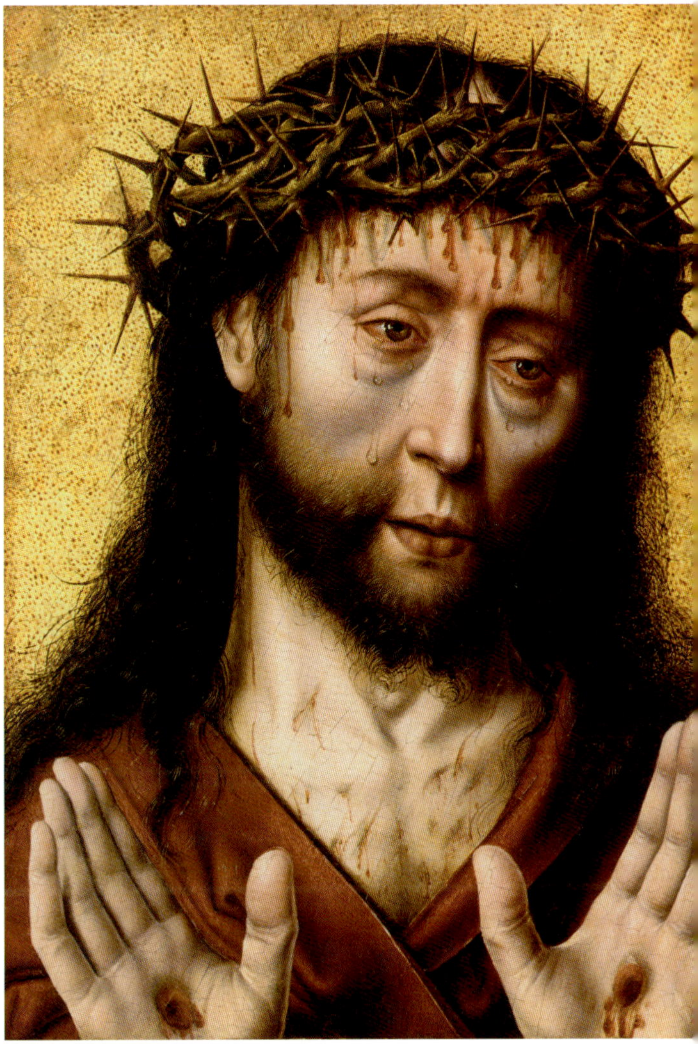

Stigmata may appear on the hands and feet, or less commonly on the brow (from the crown of thorns) or the side (from the piercing with a lance).

Although Marian apparitions take place mainly in front of Catholic witnesses, Orthodox Christians and non-Christians have also described this phenomenon.

Marian Apparitions

Over the past 200 years the number of Marian apparitions has steadily increased, with the Virgin Mary revealing herself to humanity like a prophet bringing salvation. For believers, Marian apparitions are precious and joyful miracles. For doubters, they are the work of charlatans.

What is a Marian apparition?

During a Marian apparition the Virgin Mary makes contact with a so-called seer, often communicating prophesies, expectations, warnings or even apocalyptic predictions. The seers are frequently told not to make the content public. Secret prayers and information are conferred that the receiver might pass on either shortly before their death or, indeed, take to the grave.

The seers are normally simple individuals with strong faith, frequently children. They can usually see Mary as well as hear her. The smell of roses is often reported, as is music and blinding light. Any other believer who might be present

The evaluation of apparitions by the Church

Like all supernatural phenomena, the Catholic Church passes judgment on the authenticity of Marian apparitions. The evaluation is usually conducted by a bishop, but can also be made by other authorities with the Church. An evaluation can lead to one of three decrees:

- *constat de supernaturalite* – confirmation of the supernatural
- *constat de non supernaturalite* – refutation of the supernatural
- *non constat de supernaturalite* – the existence of the supernatural cannot be proven

The first two judgments are final; the third can change if new information is presented.

In contrast to countless refutations, the Marian apparitions at Lourdes (France), Fatima (Portugal), and Guadalupe (Mexico) have been confirmed. Among the "not proven" apparitions are those in Medjugorje (Croatia) and Sievernich (Germany), where Our Lady appeared to the seer every first or second Monday of the month asking for prayers, penance, peace, and love of one's neighbor along with loyalty to the pope.

In 1917, Mary appeared to young children in a field multiple times at Fatima, asking for prayer and sacrifices for sinners. The site has become a famous pilgrimage destination.

at the moment of the apparition do not notice as much as the seer; they often see only light or the outline of a figure. As with all such apparitions, after announcing herself the first time, Mary reappears several further times at the same place. Traditionally, that place becomes a pilgrimage site where ornate houses of worship are built.

Doubt

The number of Marian apparitions has increased steadily since 1830. These often have little to do with matters of faith. The Madonna increasingly issues warnings about political developments and promises her aid to those who believe. It is remarkable that the country reporting the earliest and most frequent Marian apparitions is France, where the period of the Enlightenment and, in particular, the French Revolution of 1789 had weakened religious faith early on. In general one can observe that Marian apparitions increase in relation to the degree of turbulence and "non-belief" within a given period of time.

Therefore, some sceptics consider Marian apparitions the work of charlatans, possibly even originating within the Church itself. They feel this is indicated by the fact that Mary does not speak directly to those with whom she actually wants to communicate, but instead uses simple people or children as agents, individuals who are easier to influence and perhaps also easier to fool.

There is as little evidence for the claims of the sceptics as there is for the assumption of many scientists that Marian apparitions are hallucinations. For the majority of believers, the appearances of Mary are miracles, although the Church leaves it up to the faithful to decide for themselves whether to believe in the apparitions or to question them.

Since 24 June 1981, the Virgin Mary has appeared daily in Medjugorje in Croatia. Her message is clear. The consequences of materialism and the failure of faith are not only war and oppression, but the moral and spiritual collapse of the world.

The Holy Spring of Lourdes

The French pilgrimage site of Lourdes is most famous for its healing spring waters, which are accorded special healing powers. Among the more than seven thousand reported cases of cures recorded by the local medical officials, the Cathoic Church has in the meantime recognized sixty-six of these cases as miracles.

The Grotto of Massabielle

The history of the healing spring of Lourdes begins on 11 February 1858, the day when fourteen-year-old Bernadette Soubirous first encountered the Virgin Mary near a grotto not far from the Gave du Pau River; she met her fourteen times here over the following months, and the spring itself was uncovered during these meetings. Church representatives were initially sceptical, but after Bernadette reported that "the Lady" had called herself the "immaculate conception", a term that Pope Pius IX had only recently added to the dogma, most scepticism disappeared. A shrine consisting of numerous sacred buildings and a procession plaza was erected near the grotto.

After the events that had taken place in the grotto became known, believers from all over the world arrived at this place as pilgrims. Over the next decades "Lourdes grottos" would be built in other countries, either within a Roman Catholic church or in the courtyard, all architecturally similar to the French original.

A short time later the first miraculous cure was reported. This led to the formation of the medical bureau of Lourdes so that individual cases could be recorded.

The Mother of God appeared to Saint Bernadette of Lourdes for the first time in February 1858.

The water from the holy spring is frequently drawn off by visitors and brought home to be given to the sick.

Pope John Paul II prayed at the spring in Lourdes in August 2004. He first visited in 1983, becoming the first pope to do so.

Miraculous cures

Thanks to the work of the medical bureau, statistics are available showing that tuberculosis patients are those who have reported the greatest improvement following a visit. Cures for ailments of the joints and digestive system are also reported to occur. However, the spring has yet to show any healing power over diseases of genetic origin. The water itself has already been the subject of frequent scientific investigations, which, up to now, have shown it to be no different than any other spring water. No medical or any other kind of scientific explanation for the healings has been found.

In scientific circles the spring and its reputation are often strongly criticized. Cases do exist in which the Church has recognized a cure as a miracle, only to have the afflicted person die a short time later of the original disease. The critics are also heartened by the notable decrease in the number of miracle cures recognized following the Church's decision to strengthen the criteria.

Bernadette Soubirous

Bernadette Soubirous (1844–1879) died on Easter Monday, 1879, at the age of 35 due to complications of tuberculosis and asthma. She was laid to rest some 500 miles (800 km) away in Nevers on the Loire. Pope Pius XI beatified her and later declared her a saint. Her body, still on view today, shows no signs of decay after 125 years. Along with the existence of the Lourdes spring, many interpret her preservation as proof of Bernadette's very special relationship with Mary.

Attempts at explanation

The source of the alleged healing powers of the Lourdes spring is unknown. As with the receiving of stigmata, the power of faith and the spirit play a significant role in generating new energy within the body to overcome an illness. This explanation is disputed, however. In some cases spontaneous cures have been reported that should not be possible without medical treatment.

The Gospel of John reports the healing of a man who had been lame for thirty-eight years.

Miracle Cures

In Biblical stories the sick are healed in many different ways. Nevertheless, people who can ease afflictions by means of special rituals, or places that provide cures, or objects and buildings that heal have been controversial for centuries, even within religious circles.

Miracle cures in the Bible

Reports and traditions regarding miracle healings are most often found in a religious context. Cures achieved without medical intervention, but through the power of God, play an important role in Christianity, in particular. Miraculous cures occur in the Old Testament as proof of God's powers: when confronting sceptics, the prophets and others use them as demonstrations of their God's might. These are cures that are for the most part brought about directly by God. Ezechias, the king of Judea, had learned from the prophet Isaiah that the day of his death was approaching. After fervent prayer to God, Ezechias was granted an extra fifteen years of mortal life, after which Isaiah was sent to deliver the message again.

Lazarus was raised from the dead after he had already been buried by the words of Jesus.

Miracle cures and the Church

Reports of miracle cures are actually followed very closely by the Catholic Church, in part because there have always been people who want to use miracle cures to achieve worldly power and riches. As a result, the Vatican established a set of criteria that is still used today to define what is or is not a miraculous healing.

Cures that lie many centuries in the past frequently push these criteria to their limits. Many illnesses have not been adequately documented until recently. Instead, one often set the welfare of the afflicted in God's hands and put off treatment in favour of a "higher power". Cures are inevitably ascribed to "God's Will". For this reason, up to the early Middle Ages there is practically no mention of "miraculous healing": every recovery was considered a miracle of sorts. It is only with the development of medicine as a science, which provided a new understanding of anatomy and symptoms, that illnesses could be better identified. This formed the basis for the concept of a miraculous cure. From the very beginning, however, the Church could attribute miraculous cures to either God or the Devil, depending on the religion practiced, the healing methods employed, and the social and/or religious rank of the healer.

In contrast, the miracle cures in the New Testament take place exclusively through the actions of Jesus and later the Apostles. The four Gospels describe a number of sick and disabled people being healed by a touch or by words alone. Cures can even take place when the sick person is not physically present, as in the story of the centurion who asked that his servant be restored to health (Luke 7:1–10). The description of Jesus raising Lazarus from the dead (John 11:1–44) demonstrates the power of the words of Christ. It is rare that additional materials are used in these healings, but one example is the paste of dust and saliva that brings sight to a blind man as described in the Gospel of Mark (8:22–26).

In the Acts of the Apostles the same abilities are ascribed to Peter. He heals a cripple (3:1–10) and raises Tabitha from the dead (chapter 9). Paul heals by touch on the island of Malta, curing the father of the influential Publius of fever and dysentery (chapter 28).

In this relief, Jesus heals a blind man by coating his eyes with a paste made of dust and saliva.

It is not always a faith healer who is responsible for miraculous cures. On more than one occasion it seems to have been the power of prayer that brought relief.

Modern faith healers

Because of the Vatican criteria, the Church has recognized only very few faith healers during their lifetimes. In most cases the Vatican has been highly critical where miraculous cures were concerned, going so far as to describe the leading practitioners as quacks or charlatans, even when the persons in question came from its own ranks. In some cases, as with Pope John Paul II (1920–2005), claims for supposed miracle cures often come to light only after the death of the person in question.

One modern healer subjected to the prejudices of the Church was the Italian Capuchin monk Padre Pio (1887–1968), who was canonized in 2002. The Church recognizes only a select few of the numerous miraculous cures ascribed to him. That Padre Pio was also a stigmatic is nevertheless still doubted by the Vatican.

Comparable accusations have been raised in the case of the Irish nun Briege McKenna, who is said to have a certain "healing charisma". She herself had long suffered from rheumatoid arthritis until she was spontaneously and miraculously cured. Since then she has tried to channel Christ's healing power to others through prayer.

The young and dynamic Nigerian pastor Charles Ndifon has for many years travelled the world preaching the word of God. He understands his task as helping people who have already given up, bringing new hope through the word of God. When he appears in public, he is said to bring about countless medically confirmed cures.

The Italian Padre Pio was not only a recipient of the wounds of Christ, he was also known as a healer and prophet. He is said to have predicted not only the elevation of Karel Wotyla to the papacy, but also the attempted assassination of him that took place in 1981.

MIRACLE CURES WITHOUT FAITH HEALERS?

Miracle cures are not always dependant on a faith healer, as the following example shows. In 1975, the British physician Jennifer Fendick became infected with meningococcal bacteria. When she was brought to the hospital the morning after she became ill, the diagnosis was Waterhouse Friderichsen Syndrome, a rapidly progressing disease that leads to death within hours if not treated immediately. The first phase of the illness, which Dr. Fendick had already experienced, damages the body to such an extent that a cure is no longer possible.

Informed of her dire condition by a relative, four healing groups from a religious society began to pray for Dr. Fendick at 8:30 a.m. Each of these groups was miles away from Dr. Fendick, and she herself, already lying in a coma, knew nothing of their activities. Nevertheless, she turned a corner and began to get well at almost exactly that same moment. A lung inflammation diagnosed shortly before disappeared within forty-eight hours. Bleeding had occurred in her right eye that should have led to a loss of vision, but when she awoke from her coma four days later, her eye was unharmed. Her kidneys, which had failed during the first phase of the illness, were completely recovered. Upon her release from the hospital she showed no sign of having suffered from any illness at all. A medical explanation was not forthcoming and further investigation provided no answers.

Whether or not such cures can be explained by the placebo effect or are seen as genuinely miraculous, one thing is certain: miracle cures are always connected with the strong belief that such a thing is possible through God.

A nun afflicted with Parkinson's syndrome was reportedly cured following a visit by Pope John Paul II.

Weeping Statues and Icons

There are statues and icons that inexplicably weep water, blood, resin, oil, honey, myrrh or other substances. Reports of this phenomenon have increased dramatically since the 1980s. Some people are convinced that these are signs from God.

Tears flowing from statues

A comprehensive, worldwide survey of all known weeping holy images would be nearly impossible to complete. There are some 200 cases in Italy alone, most involving tears, but also in rare instances "bleeding" or "perspiring" extremities. Some of these images give off so much liquid that it flows down, around, and under the affected statues and icons. The statues and pictures are not all made of the same material; they may be constructed of stone, porcelain, metal, or, in the case of icons, wood or canvas.

The amount of liquid that flows from them also varies. Statues and images with an uninterrupted flow are known to exist, but in most cases the tears fall either irregularly or only within a specific period of time. Because the liquids are thought to possess healing properties, thousands of pilgrims flock year in and year out to the weeping figures that are accessible to the public.

The statue in Seville, Spain known as La Macarena is portrayed with tears and a smile. This "crying statue" has never wept real tears.

Because she had many children, Queen Niobe compared herself to the gods, who then killed them all. Grief caused Niobe to turn into a stone.

The History of the weeping statues

Weeping statues are not unusual in fairy tales or other traditions. They are frequently said to be humans who have been transformed into stone. One of the oldest stories of a weeping statue comes from *Metamorphoses,* a history of the world that contains hundreds of mythical accounts, written by Ovid (43 BC–17 AD). Ovid tells of Niobe, wife of the king of Thebes, whose boastings earned her the wrath of the gods, who therefore condemned her fourteen children to death. Niobe turned into a stone statue that wept perpetually in grief.

It is not known whether Ovid referred to a previous source for this poem. Most of *Metamorphoses* has its origin in Greek or Roman tradition. It has been suggested that the phenomenon of weeping statues was observed already in antiquity, and explanations for it sought.

Fraud or miracle?

In the meantime, we know that not all weeping statues and icons are inexplicable. Their increased popularity and frequency since the 1980s certainly gives the impression that all of these claims are not entirely honest. In fact, some of the so-called "blood relics" have already been exposed as forgeries, after it was proven that their owners were directing the liquid using a hidden tube or the porosity of the stone so as to give the impression that their statue or icon was weeping. The application of certain chemicals directly on a picture surface can create a similar effect.

On the other hand, there are also cases where one can only suppose that fraud is involved because the statue has been placed off limits to scientists, making investigation and explanation impossible.

Nevertheless, some statues and holy pictures have been thoroughly investigated using the most modern methods available, and no manipulation has been discovered. Many scientists remain sceptical where the "miracle" of a weeping figure is concerned. In the absence of proof to the contrary, everyone has to decide for themselves whether or not these are really signs from God.

The weeping Madonna of Civitavecchia, Italy, is one of the controversial statues for which no fraud has ever been proven. The statue is presented during mass on certain holy days. The rest of the time the figure of the Madonna can be viewed as part of an exhibition.

Angels

Angels (from the Greek *angelos* meaning "messenger" or "herald") are creatures that are sent by God to fulfil certain tasks, most commonly that of conveying messages to men and women, whom they also protect. There are many accounts in which angels have affected the course of events on earth in order to save individuals from harm or death.

What the Bible says about angels

The creation of the angels is not described in the Bible. Since they are already present in Genesis as the guardians of Paradise, they, like God, pre-exist the creation of the world. They were not actively involved in that creation, either, which makes it clear that they are not equal to God. In general, the biblical description gives them a passive image. Although the words and deeds of angels can affect humans, their primary function is to serve as messengers or intermediaries between the divine realm and the human one.

There is a clear separation of duties in the hierarchy of angels. Those closest to God praise and pay homage to him, while others protect the Garden of Eden. Only the lower ranks, like guardian angels or cherubs, ever come in contact with humans.

Encounters with angels take place in different ways. While most prophets describe visions of angels, they are also apparently capable of taking on solid form, as when Jacob wrestles with one (Genesis 28). This is not, however, to be confused with human form. Isaiah describes a seraphim as a being with six wings, two covering its face and another two attached to its feet, while the final pair are used for flying. He calls the seraphim a mixture of human and snake.

Many different kinds of angels are named in the Bible. In the sixth century AD it was thought that the various descriptions could be organized into a structured system. The ranks and duties assigned to each at that time are therefore essentially independent of the biblical texts. This hierarchy has been altered slightly over time, with further variations from religion to religion. Judaism and Christianity recognize nine choirs, in the latter case presumably based on the trinitarian principle of Father, Son, and Holy Ghost each having a triad at their disposal. The upper triad is the same in all religions: the seraphim, who stand over the cherubim, followed by the thrones. Archangels and guardian angels occupy the lowest level of the hierarchy, closest to humankind. This does not mean that they stand over people in any way, however, for the Bible clearly states (I Corinthians 6:3) that on Judgment Day it is men who will rule over the angels.

The idea that angels accompany the soul of the dying stems from a story Jesus told about a beggar who died just outside a rich man's house. The poor man was carried by angels to the bosom of Abraham, while the rich man, after his death, was buried in the ground. (Luke 16:22) It is a widespread view that Satan is himself a fallen angel, banished from heaven because he sought to rule over God. As with the organization of the hierarchy of angels, this is not found anywhere in the Bible.

Angels in Art

Angel-like creatures are already present in ancient Egyptian art. Most commonly portrayed as mixed creatures, usually with an animal head and a human body, they have a lot in common with similar descriptions in the Bible. In Greek mythology, Hermes, the messenger of the Gods, plays the role of an angel, complete with wings (though his are usually found on his hat or sandals). Because Christianity tended to avoid physical representations of angels during the Middle Ages, they were understood as existing as pure light. In the Renaissance they were imagined differently again. First they were portrayed as naked, winged youths and later, in an enhanced variation on this theme, as *putti*. There was no unified vision of how angels might appear during the Romantic movement of the eighteenth century.

An angel stood by Jesus on the Mount of Olives to comfort him.

There are no angels in the Bible resembling the Renaissance putti, which were at the time a modern conception.

Encounters with Angels

Reports of experiences with angels or other divine messengers come from all over the world, independent of culture or religious affiliation. Such encounters often occur when someone is in a situation of grave danger, either because of illness or impending death. In many cases the appearance of the angel is connected to averting the danger.

There are numerous accounts of automobile drivers, for instance, who are prevented from continuing their journey as planned by some unexpected circumstance, and thereby escape an accident that would almost certainly have resulted in their demise. That circumstance has been in some cases a radio report that made the driver slow down or or stop the car altogether. Some report seeing a figure waving to them from the side of the road, a figure that just as quickly disappeared. At least one case is known in which the angel actually appeared in the passenger seat inside the moving vehicle. Nearly all of the drivers who have had this experience claim that they were never afraid, despite the unusual situation.

People who are desperately ill, or occasionally their loved ones, are an additional source of descriptions of encounters with angels. The sick person tends to describe a dreamlike state in which an angel suddenly appears in the room with them. Relatives, in contrast, meet angels in the form of doctors, or alleged friends of the sick person, or another person who is there to help. They usually disappear once they have identified themselves as angels.

Swiss psychoanalyst Carl Gustav Jung (1875–1961) described angelic apparitions as the product of unconscious forces of energy that work to stabilize the soul.

Lúcia dos Santos was one of the three children to whom Our Lady of Fatima appeared. Few are aware that the children experienced six separate encounters with angels before Mary appeared to them.

In some cases, angels will also appear to stave off misfortune that would be caused by a third party or otherwise bring comfort. There are reports of people who have awakened from nightmares claiming to have seen an angel at the foot of their bed. The nightmares are usually predictions of events that actually happen later, such as the crash of an aeroplane that a friend was meant to take, or of a suicide attempt by a relative. Thanks to the angel's intervention, steps can be taken to avoid these disasters.

In another case, a child told of a dream in which two angels entered his room, floated slightly above the floor, then disappeared through the ceiling. His sister died the same night.

Science and angels

From the point of view of science, investigating angels is nearly impossible. Immediately following the encounters, the figures or people described disappear without a trace, leaving behind basically no evidence of their ever having existed. Although there are some photographs that are claimed to depict angels or ghosts, the authenticity of these images is exceedingly controversial, not the least because in most cases the photographs are so blurry as to make nothing, let alone an angel, easy to identify; or, in other cases, the angel is very clearly an artificial addition.

One of the significant problems for scientists has to do with the fact that encounters with angels are not as easily equated with hallucinations as was thought to be the case in the past. When encounters with angels are described against the background of a clearly serious or even life-threatening situation, hallucinations are obviously not a factor.

It is unlikely that the existence of angels can be proved or disproved by science. Angels themselves are not bound to any physical form, and proof for the supernatural does not exist. The question of whether or not angels exist remains a question of faith for most of humankind.

Although archangels are frequently portrayed with weapons, their primary duty in the Bible is to announce the will of God.

Alchemy, Magic and Curses

Despite their basic differences, when we compare religion and occultism on an abstract level we find they have many things in common. Both require a belief in the supernatural and organize structured rituals geared toward specific goals. Most significantly, it can be argued that religion and occultism both exist fundamentally because they offer hope. Not suprisingly, there are parallels between the development of religion and the occult. Many religions once included what today would be considered occult practices, although, as the meaning of the word suggests (Latin *occultus* = "hidden" or "secret") this connection is not often publicized.

The essential difference between religion and occultism lies in who controls the expression of supernatural power. While religions are oriented toward one or more gods, within the realm of the occult, that power is the product of individual human will abetted by structured ritual. Although supernatural forces are at work here, as well, the magician is able to control them with his or her mind through a fixed series of ritual behaviours.

The boundaries between some aspects of occultism and religion have blurred over time. It is only fairly recently that practices and traditions originally religious in character have been understood as part of the occult. The next section includes many examples of this. We will also consider phenomena that, because of their threatening nature, have been described as "the Devil's work", as well as modern endeavours that have only recently acquired the taint of the occult.

The vampire Count Dracula (portrayed here by Christopher Lee), can purportedly be overcome with a crucifix.

An alchemist did not consider his laboratory a "witch's kitchen". Alchemists viewed their profession as an attempt to better understand God's creations. For a long time, this kept them from being hunted by the Inquisition.

Alchemy and the Philosophers' Stone

The fabled Philosophers' Stone is the legendary and long sought-after alchemical substance that would supposedly enable base metals to be transformed into gold. As this was not otherwise possible, for several hundred years the search was on for the material that could bring about this transformation.

The history of alchemy

The term alchemy encompasses a range of disciplines, including chemistry, magic, astrology and even theology. An independent variety that devoted special attention to the study of herbs developed in the Far East, in China. Whether Western and Eastern alchemy originally were derived from the same source (or some of the same sources) can no longer be determined today.

Western alchemy is probably best viewed as a melding of prehistoric myths, religions and rituals. One line of thought claims that the birthplace of alchemy was ancient Egypt, where the god Thoth (the god of writing, science and astronomy) in the form of Hermes Trismegistos ("Hermes thrice great") founded the arts and sciences. Historically, European alchemy can be traced back to the fifth century BC in Greece. Alchemical theories already current at that

Paracelsus' (1493–1541) success in healing was based on the new examination and treatment methods he developed.

time – such as the formulation of basic medical principles, Empedocles' observations of individual elements, or Democritos' theory of the atom – would first find a wider following a millennia later. Another important alchemist was Zosimos von Panopolis, who in the third century AD wrote twenty-eight books on the subject, one of which included a description of how to change silver into gold with the help of a tincture of mercury.

From Greece, these teachings next spread to the Islamic cultures. In the eighth century AD, the Persian alchemist Geber, also known by his Arabic name, Jabir ibn Hayyan, concluded that experiments should generally follow a certain method. He developed the basic methodology of chemistry and provided the first description of a chemical reaction, making him the father of the discipline. Geber also mentioned a chemical formula that could create gold out of a small amount of pure sulphur and mercury.

Finally, in the twelfth century, alchemy found more solid footing in Europe. Although medieval alchemists were frequently forced to work well hidden, in general they had a positive reputation. They often enjoyed steady employment as researchers, astrologers or medical doctors, and most of them had one or more wealthy or influential patrons who funded their research.

Paracelsus, an alchemist who paved the way for modern medicine

The alchemist Paracelsus (his given name was Theophrastus Philippus Aureolus Bombastus von Hohenheim) opened up medicine to new possibilities, departing from the textbook medicine of his day in favour of observation and experience. In his own writings, patients and their illnesses are viewed more abstractly. The biological, chemical, or physical cause of an illness was given priority over symptoms. To Paracelsus, fighting an illness meant not only identifying its cure, but also understanding how much of any medicine should be used, since too much or too little could produce undesirable effects. This approach makes Paracelsus the father of modern pharmaceutical chemistry.

Nicolas Flamel

One of the first alchemists who made a name for himself in Europe was Frenchman Nicolas Flamel (ca. 1330–1413), who claimed to have received a book from an angel that contained the secret to the Philosophers' Stone. He said he had used it to turn silver into gold. Flamel generously donated his profits to churches and hospitals, asking only that his name be inscribed on the outer wall of the building. Some time after their deaths, the grave of Flamel and his wife was re-opened, revealing that tree trunks had been substituted for their mortal remains. This may be the reason why the Philosophers' Stone has also been said to grant eternal life. Flamel has been occasionally spotted alive during the ensuing 600 years, making sure that his story survives to this day.

Nicolas Flamel is still considered to be the only alchemist who succeeded in finding the Philosophers' Stone.

Alchemists were not the kind of researchers who withdrew to a lab to experiment in solitude. They typically held professional positions as teachers, astrologers or doctors through which they earned their living.

Unintended discoveries

Over the following decades, Flamel's achievements and reputation ensured that the Philophers' Stone would be intensively pursued. He had not been the first to look for it. People including the Franciscan monk Roger Bacon (ca. 1219–1294), Arnoldus Villanovus (ca. 1235–1312) and the Muslim missionary Raimundus Lullus (ca. 1235–1316) had already described how the Philosophers' Stone would work. But Flamel was apparently the only one who had actually succeeded in making gold, rather than merely describing it, and so the experiments with metals continued.

Although the alchemists never succeeded in producing pure gold – although some could make a gold-coloured metal of ignoble origin – their experiments did result in end products that would prove to have other uses. The Franciscan monk Berthold Schwarz of Freiburg, Germany, for instance, discovered gunpowder while conducting experiments in 1353 or 1359. From a historical point of view this claim is highly controversial, to put it mildly, given that both the Chinese and Arabs had long had access to gun powder by then, and Roger Bacon had already described its production in 1267. In the course of his search for the Philosophers' Stone, Hamburg alchemist Hennig Brand (1630–1692) isolated phosphorus, the first chemical element to be discovered in modern times. Alchemist Johann Friedrich Bottger (1682–1719), together with the mathematician Ehrenfried Walther von Theirnhaus (1651–1708), perfected the production of Meissner porcelain.

Some of the knowledge assembled by the alchemists as part of their efforts would be of great value for the scientific disciplines that came after them. The work of the alchemist Paracelsus (1493–1541), for example, raised medicine to a completely different level. Also in this category is the research Isaac Newton (1643–1727) conducted in the fields of physics, philosophy, mathematics and astronomy.

The end of alchemy

There is evidence that alchemist societies may have existed into the nineteenth century. In the twentieth century there were still a few attempts to put alchemical knowledge to various uses, but by that time most important developments were taking place in other academic disciplines, such as physics, mathematics, chemistry, biology, medicine, theology and philosphy. Basic discoveries in all of these fields, including the organization of the periodic table by Dmitri Mendeleyev (1834–1907) and Lothar Mayer (1830–1895) in 1869, have proved the usefulness of many

Sir Isaac Newton (1643–1727) understood that alchemy and modern natural sciences were kindred endeavours.

of alchemy's basic tenets. Nevertheless, from the point of view of modern science and technology, many of alchemy's endeavours and conclusions are highly suspect, a fact which has led to the negative reputation accorded most of its practitioners.

The term "alchemy" is today too often set aside along with other strange imaginings from the dim, distant Middle Ages. With its murky experiments related to religion, magic and astrology, the people of the Enlightenment took care to distance themselves as far as possible from this ancient science. One should not forget, however, that much of the knowledge base of other natural sciences came into being through the efforts of alchemists, even as the quest for the Philosophers' Stone remained unfulfilled.

The Man in the Moon as described and illustrated with corresponding symbols by a Venetian alchemist.

Black sheep

In the past there were, of course, also alchemists who did great harm to the reputation of their profession through their quackery, lies, or simple lack of ability. Alessandro Cagliostro (1743–1795) coaxed money from his clients with love potions, youth-giving elixirs and beauty mixtures. Other alchemists were said to have made pacts with the devil, like Johann Georg Faust (1480–1540). A third group conducted strange and uncanny experiments that alone were enough to tarnish their good names. One of these is Johann Konrad Dippel (1673–1734) who supposedly worked with corpses and body parts in his castle (Castle Frankenstein). He nearly killed himself when, during a procedure involving nitroglycerin, the keep of the castle was blown sky high.

The Voynich Manuscript

The text known as the Voynich Manuscript is described both in books about alchemy and in more standard scientific works. Its approximately 200 pages are supposed to conceal secrets, but despite the best efforts of the world's leading experts, no one has been able to decipher it. Written in an unknown script and language, perhaps its author had reason to fear the discovery of its contents and their potential repercussions.

Discovery and first investigation

In 1912, the antique dealer Wilfrid Voynich (1865–1913) acquired a heavily illustrated book written in an old-fashioned looking script. The pictures were what first awakened his interest: they depicted unusual spiral forms, plants, constellations, female figures, pipes and other forms. The text itself was rather bizarrely structured around them. In some cases it had actually been worked into part of a drawing, in others it stretched across two pages in geometric forms. And then there was the problem that the text was written in a secret script and language. Although one could recognize character repetition and apparent word and sentence structures, Voynich found it impossible to decipher. He concluded then and there that the text must contain explosive information, perhaps a discovery in the natural sciences or alchemical findings that, at the time it was written, would have caused the author to be burned at the stake. After further research, Voynich traced the manuscript's prior ownership and found out that attempts had been made to decipher the mysterious text already in the seventeenth century, all of them in vain.

Athanasius Kircher was one of many who tried to decipher the manuscript in the seventeenth century.

Some believe that the Franciscan monk, philosopher and scientist Roger Bacon is the author of the Voynich Manuscript.

Deciphering and counterevidence

Voynich sent copies of individual pages to specialists, yet even various intelligence agencies and other respected cryptography bureaus were incapable of translating the text. The drawings contributed nothing to the decipherment because the plants and astronomical sketches were impossible to identify.

The interest of the scholarly world was correspondingly great when William R. Newbold, a professor of philosophy at the University of Pennsylvania, reported the results of his investigations. Using a microscope, he said he had come across miniscule signs that seemed to be a form of shorthand. Replacing each letter produced a text in Latin about germ cells and organic life. It was indeed a natural science text, he concluded, traceable perhaps to the Franciscan monk Roger Bacon (ca. 1214–1294).

Just ten years later, shortly after Newbold's death, his former colleague professor John Manly reviewed the report and came to a completely different conclusion. In his opinion, the supposed shorthand was the result of residues and cracks in the old parchment. He said that Newbold had used an unintelligible system so random as to permit nearly any reading of the text, making his results likely a product of chance.

In the next decades further attempts were made at decipherment, including the use of modern computer systems. Nonetheless, it has still not been possible to crack the code of the Voynich Manuscript. A few questions, however, have been answered in the meantime. We now know that the manuscript illuminations are the product of two different artists, and given that there are no corrections within the text, there must have been a draft version prepared first. We know that the language displays reasonable sentence structure. It is not a random assortment of symbols, but a language that follows certain regular rules. This suggests that the text was either set down in code or is written in an invented language. Another possibility is that the author had only partial command of a language, making this a text filled with grammatical errors. It is questionable whether the text will ever be deciphered.

Despite the efforts of hundreds of experts, no one has yet succeeded in decoding the Voynich Manuscript, now in the collection of Yale University.

The Necronomicon

The Necromonicon is a book described by the American horror author Howard Phillips (H.P.) Lovecraft. It was supposedly written in the year 730 AD by the mad Arab Abdul Alhazred (or Abdul Al'Hazrad). Its 800 pages are said to explain the origins and history of the "Great Old Ones", as well as providing instructions on how to conjure these supernatural beings into existence.

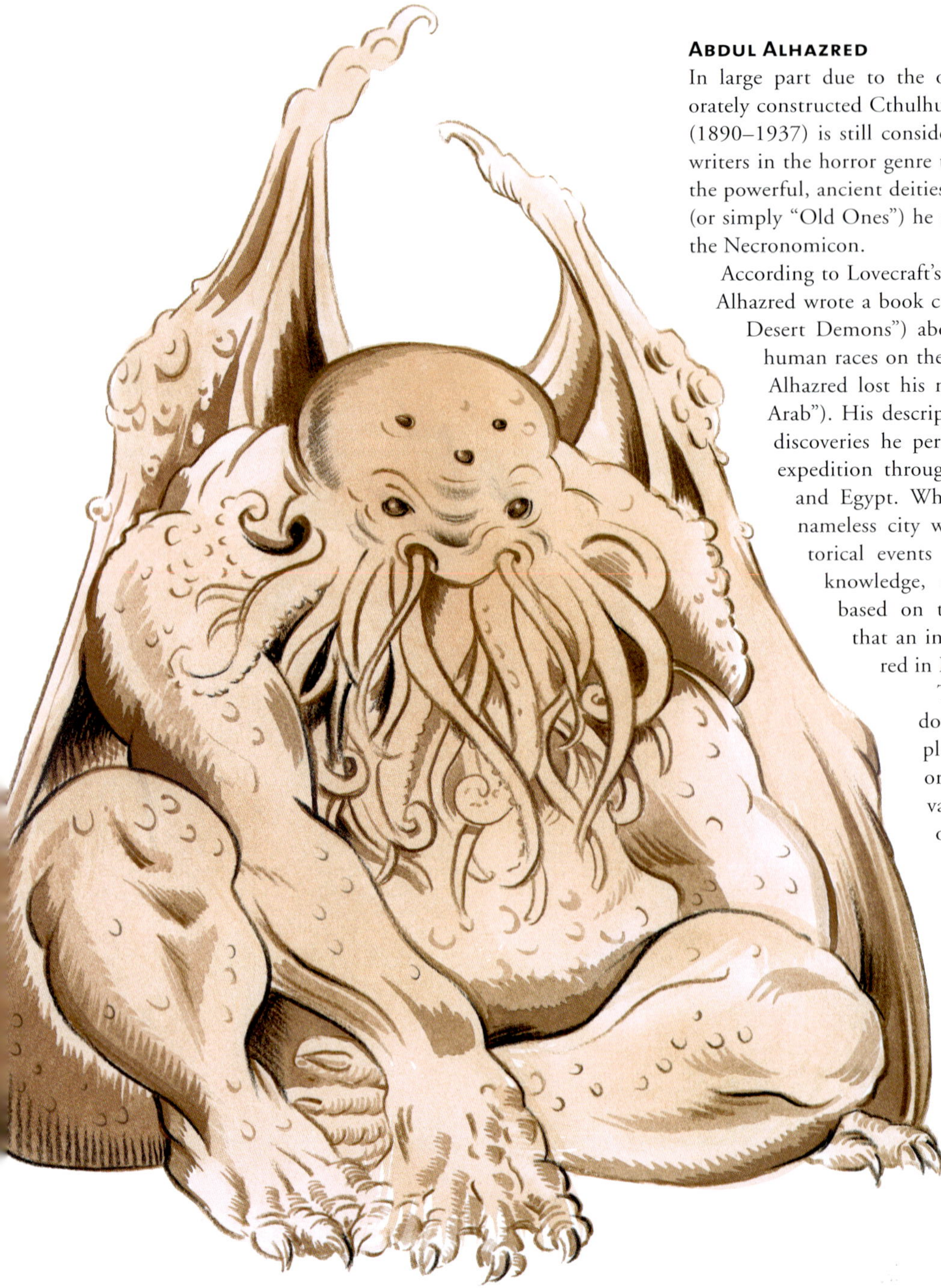

Abdul Alhazred

In large part due to the ongoing popularity of his elaborately constructed Cthulhu Mythos, author H. P. Lovecraft (1890–1937) is still considered one of the most influential writers in the horror genre today. In some of his tales about the powerful, ancient deities he called the "Great Old Ones" (or simply "Old Ones") he makes reference to a book called the Necronomicon.

According to Lovecraft's writings, an Arab named Abdul Alhazred wrote a book called *Kitab al'Azif* ("Book of the Desert Demons") about the various deities and pre-human races on the earth. While writing this book, Alhazred lost his mind (hence the moniker "Mad Arab"). His descriptions are said to be based upon discoveries he personally made during a ten-year expedition through the Arabian Desert, Babylon and Egypt. While underway he came across a nameless city where he found sketches of historical events and texts that imparted secret knowledge, and Alhazred wrote his book based on these sources. Lovecraft reports that an invisible monster devoured Alhazred in Damascus in 738 AD.

The Necronomicon was written down in Arabic, although in some places Lovecraft refers to a "Greek original". The Greek title permits varying interpretations, depending on how the roots of the word are defined. Thus Lovecraft called it variously "The Book of Dead Laws", "Image of the Law of the Dead", "Law of the Dead

In Lovecraft's stories, the Old One named Cthulhu sleeps on an island beneath the ruins of a long forgotten culture.

Images", "Book of Dead Names" or "The Book of the Laws of the Dead".

This is a rough overview of the fictional origins of the Necronomicon. In fact, it is H.P. Lovecraft himself who stands behind the figure of "Abdul Alhazred". He freely admitted that this was a fictional name he gave himself whenever he imagined himself as an Arab in his fantasies.

Cthulhu

The Cthulhu Mythos is a loosely related series of short stories written by Lovecraft in which connections are made leading to the discovery, usually by curious humans, of the existence of the "Old Ones", an all-powerful, non-human, galactic race of unknown origin. One of these beings is Cthulhu, who came to Earth millions of years ago and built a city that later disappeared when the Earth's tectonic plates shifted. Ever since, Cthulhu has slumbered deeply beneath its surface. While some of the Old Ones are more or less neutral regarding people, Cthulhu is apparently one who desires to enslave the human race.

Other authors were already expanding upon the Cthulhu Mythos during Lovecraft's lifetime.

Lovecraft described the Old Ones as powerful, ancient beings with wings, and equipped with supernatural powers, who were terrible for humans to behold.

Horror-genre author H. P. Lovecraft was hardly known during his lifetime. After his death, friends collected his writings, which had appeared in many different magazines, and published them in a clearly organized way.

The contents of the Necronomicon

Lovecraft describes the Necronomicon and its contents in many of his stories, particularly those devoted to the Cthulhu Mythos. Accordingly, it contains detailed instructions on how to conjure the Old Ones, which Lovecraft makes very clear would not lead to mastery over them. It merely opens a path so that the Old Ones can get to Earth. Since the race seems to be immortal, is not subject to any of the laws of nature as we understand them, and is generally beyond the ability of men to comprehend, such conjuring would ultimately lead to the enslavement of humankind, or even to the end of the world.

The Necronomicon also contains information about the development of the Great Old Ones and their civilization. It even mentions individual, long forgotten cults and rituals associated with them.

After the Old Ones fell asleep they were invoked and worshipped anew by the following civilization.

The real Necronomicon?

Ever since Lovecraft's time, now and again different editions of works entitled "Necronomicon" have made their appearance on the book market. One edition is even divided into eight separate volumes so as to keep the reader from falling into madness (a danger associated with this fearsome work). It is questionable whether the necronomica that appear in bookstores have anything to do with Lovecraft's books about the Great Old Ones, apart from their name. It is much more likely that they took this form after Lovecraft's works had already been published.

There are also rumours that Lovecraft wrote a necronomicon himself. Although this is not beyond the realm of possibility, Lovecraft scholars agree that, for one thing, the necronomica on the market are not stylistically in keeping with the author's work, and secondly, that Lovecraft himself kept up such an intense and frequent correspondence with his friends that little time would have remained for him to write it. In addition, Lovecraft made no mention at all of the Necronomicon in his correspondence.

Another persistent rumour claims that sometime in the 1970s, two or more students who needed some money created an independent necronomicon based on descriptions in Lovecraft's books. While this theory has not been disproved, it is generally thought that most versions stem from the 1960s or earlier.

Mad translators

Another claim associated with the Necronomicon is that every person who has ever translated the book has sooner or later gone mad. The editions currently on the market hardly give the impression that anything like that could happen. There are also no medical records mentioning any such cases. This is likely just another part of the legend.

Finally, there is a rumour that connects the Necronomicon with the British Museum in London, where a copy is supposedly stashed and carefully guarded in a cellar room. The Vatican is said to hold the original under lock and key because too many people tried to conjure demons using the rituals described in the book.

Independent of the question as to whether a Necronomicon exists today, one can also ask whether Lovecraft could have had access to such a volume during his lifetime. Based on his publications, this would seem not to be the case. Lovecraft is an author who certainly never lacked for source material. Although he was an exceptionally intelligent child, he was often ill, only attended school intermittently, and never earned a diploma or degree. Largely self-educated, he based much of his wide-ranging edification on his grandfather's library, which did in fact contain a number of books on the occult. Following his early publications in the fantasy genre, Lovecraft then turned to writing books and texts that dealt with old cults. In addition, Lovecraft's patron, Lord Edward Dunsany, was interested in the mysteries of the occult, providing another opportunity for an exchange of ideas in this area.

Lord Edward Dunsany, an early pioneer of fantasy literature, gave his support to young talents like Lovecraft.

Lovecraft also admitted that the idea of incorporating an uncanny book like the Necronomicon as a recurring element throughout a series of short stories came to him from Robert W. Chambers' collection *The King in Yellow,* in which every character who reads a certain play goes out of their mind or experiences a terrible turn of events. If we accept this, then there never was an actual book called the Necronomicon. All the same, there is no doubt whatsoever that comparable occult collections and so-called grimoires (see following page) full of magical information did, and still do, exist.

According to some rumours, the original Necronomicon is stored in an underground chamber in the Vatican.

Ritual Magic

The Necronomicon is an example of a book devoted to the practice of ritual magic. Works like this exist in nearly every culture, although not all of them call the practices "magic". The boundaries between magical ritual procedures and religious practices are often fluid. Generally speaking, the term "ritual magic" means bringing about a result through a set corpus of ritual actions.

Grimoires

The fictional Necronomicon that H.P. Lovecraft refers to throughout his writings has all of the characteristics of a so-called grimoire (from the French word *gramaire,* meaning directions, or guidance), without actually being one, because it does not fit chronologically. Grimoires are practical guidebooks for magical rituals that also include descriptions of supernatural creatures such as demons, angels and monsters. The majority of grimoires were written or compiled during the period from 1250 to 1750. Although owning such a book in those years would have led to prosecution for witchcraft, nearly always punishable by death, most of the standard works from that period still survive, in part because grimoires were kept in monastery libraries as evidence.

Practicing magical rituals

Most grimoires describe highly structured magical practices. Well before a ritual actually begins, magicians must prepare themselves for it, both physically and mentally. Depending on which ritual is involved, this could include fasting, bathing, or prayer. Most grimoires recommend thorough cleansing to improve the flow of magic.

Step two assigns the magician the prescribed instruments, such as chalk, a rod, a knife, or a wand. In most cases the instruments themselves also receive special advance preparation. The knife must be engraved, for instance, the

It is said that Dr. Faust succeeded in conjuring the Devil, with whom he made a pact stating that the Devil would serve Faust for twenty-four years, after which he would take the magician's soul.

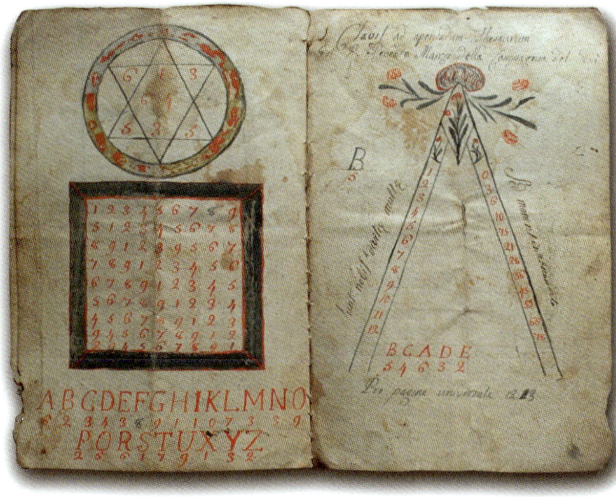

Magic books are more than collections of potion recipes. Their primary use is to provide directions for conjuring demons and spirits.

rod specially prepared, and the wand decorated with a detailed pattern; in addition, it must be added, there is also frequent mention of "virgin" instruments. This means that implements that have been used in certain spells should not be used again.

The third step involves the creation of the magic circle, which is usually a drawn or otherwise demarcated circle decorated with prescribed magical symbols and characters. Thr circle itself is not yet part of the conjuring, but is instead a magically protected space in which the magician is safe from the creatures he or she is about to call forth.

The final steps of the magic ritual will vary widely depending on the type of magic being practiced. The grimoire itself, or at least a list of the beings the magician intends to conjure and their corresponding formulae, is essential. If conjuring is to be performed, a second book is called for so that the conjured creature has a place to set down its mark, thus swearing its obedience.

A grimoire makes it very clear that every step must be precisely followed for the conjuring to be a success. Poorly executed preparations can in some cases be very dangerous for the magician. Accounts describe consequences that range from madness to the loss of limbs.

The difference between black magic and white magic

In fact, there is no real difference between black magic rituals and white magic rituals. The difference has to do with how the magic is to be used. If a spell is cast with the intention of helping someone, possibly with their consent, it is considered white magic. In contrast, rituals meant to do someone harm are black magic. The border between the two is difficult to determine when the magic involves love potions, for example, or spells designed to put someone to sleep.

The effect of a ritual

In most cases, the ability to evoke spirits, angels, demons and monsters is meant to enhance personal power. By subordinating such creatures, the conjurer takes on their corresponding abilities, which he or she can use to benefit or harm people. The hierarchy of creatures, very much emphasized in the grimoire, plays an important role. Conjuring a low-ranking demon gives one the power to give other people nightmares, but a dominating a higher ranking demon imparts the power to heal or sicken. This, however, is much more arduous work requiring intensive preparation that can extend to ritual sacrifice, or even self-mutilation.

The five-pointed star known as a pentagram or "Druid's foot" is one of the most powerful magical symbols and is often used in creating a magic circle at the start of a ritual.

Doll rituals

There are also simpler rituals that are just as widespread and do not require magicians to endanger themselves to that extent. One form of simple magic, today best known in connection with voodoo, uses dolls made of cloth, wax or clay to represent a specific person. The focus of the spell is usually to either harm, or in some way gain power over, that person. In order to make the magic work, hair, fingernails, or bodily secretions – or if all else fails, a piece of clothing – from the intended person are needed. These are brought to the doll, but what happens next varies. In some cases, the "ingredients" have to be burned inside a clay figure. Other sources recommend that they be mixed with the clay, which is then formed into a figure. Other rituals suggest sewing them inside a cloth doll, and so on. All of these serve to entwine the fates of the doll and the person it represents. Tying two dolls together casts a love spell on the two individuals. If a doll is damaged it causes injury to the same part of the victim, and destroying the doll supposedly leads to his or her demise.

During the Middle Ages, magic was viewed as a sin against God. Many people, both those who genuinely participated in magical rituals and those who were falsely accused, were burned at the stake as a result.

Magic rituals and their results

In times past, magic was held responsible for many things. When someone became ill for no clear reason, or suffered an accident or died, or even was unhappy in their marriage, some kind of magic (such as a failed love potion in the last case) was said to be at work. Just how far the slings and arrows of outrageous fortune can in fact be traced to spells and rituals was not at all clear, especially because in the Middle Ages magicians, witches and wizards would have faced certain death had they revealed themselves.

If the ritual does not achieve the desired results, it can happen that the conjurer's health or even life may be in danger when the spell's power rebounds upon him.

There are some documented cases in which the outcome of a ritual was described in detail from the magician's point of view. In 1690, the pastor Arthur Bedford described various grimoire-directed magical rites carried out by Thomas Parkes of Bristol, apparently inexperienced, who cockily undertook the invocation of spirits only to find himself surrounded by demons. When he repeated the experiment he lost all control and found himself confronted with creatures more powerful than the protective circle he had drawn around himself. Pastor Bedford seems to have believed Parkes' every word.

There are many accounts of simple magic in which the victim really did experience injuries corresponding to the damage done to a doll. An American journalist reported on the case of a French concert pianist who left a spiritualist sect after an argument. Someone from the sect made a doll in his image and pressed its arms in a vice. Over the next few days the pianist lost more and more strength in his fingers, to the point where he was forced to break off a concert. The journalist mentions, however, that the members of the sect made sure they were present for the pianist's performances, during which they had incessantly criticized his playing. At this point a psychologist intervened, claiming that the sect's victim, well aware of their methods, had believed in doll magic so strongly that his own unconscious mind had brought about the crippling of his hands. Had the pianist not known of the sect's plans for revenge, the psychologist concluded, he would have been spared its consequences.

Doll magic is not only widespread within voodoo; it was also well known in occult circles in medieval Europe.

Voodoo

Voodoo is a religion that was originally practiced in West Africa. Slavery brought voodoo to different parts of the world, including Asia (India) and the Americas (in particular to Haiti and the Dominican Republic), where the number of adherents increased rapidly. Because of its frequent representations of bones and skulls as well as its wild dance rituals, white populations saw voodoo as a form of black magic or a cult of the dead, with human sacrifice the order of the day. In fact, the voodoo deities much prefer animal sacrifice. They are not, however, simply bloodthirsty. The animals are killed in the open, then later cooked and eaten.

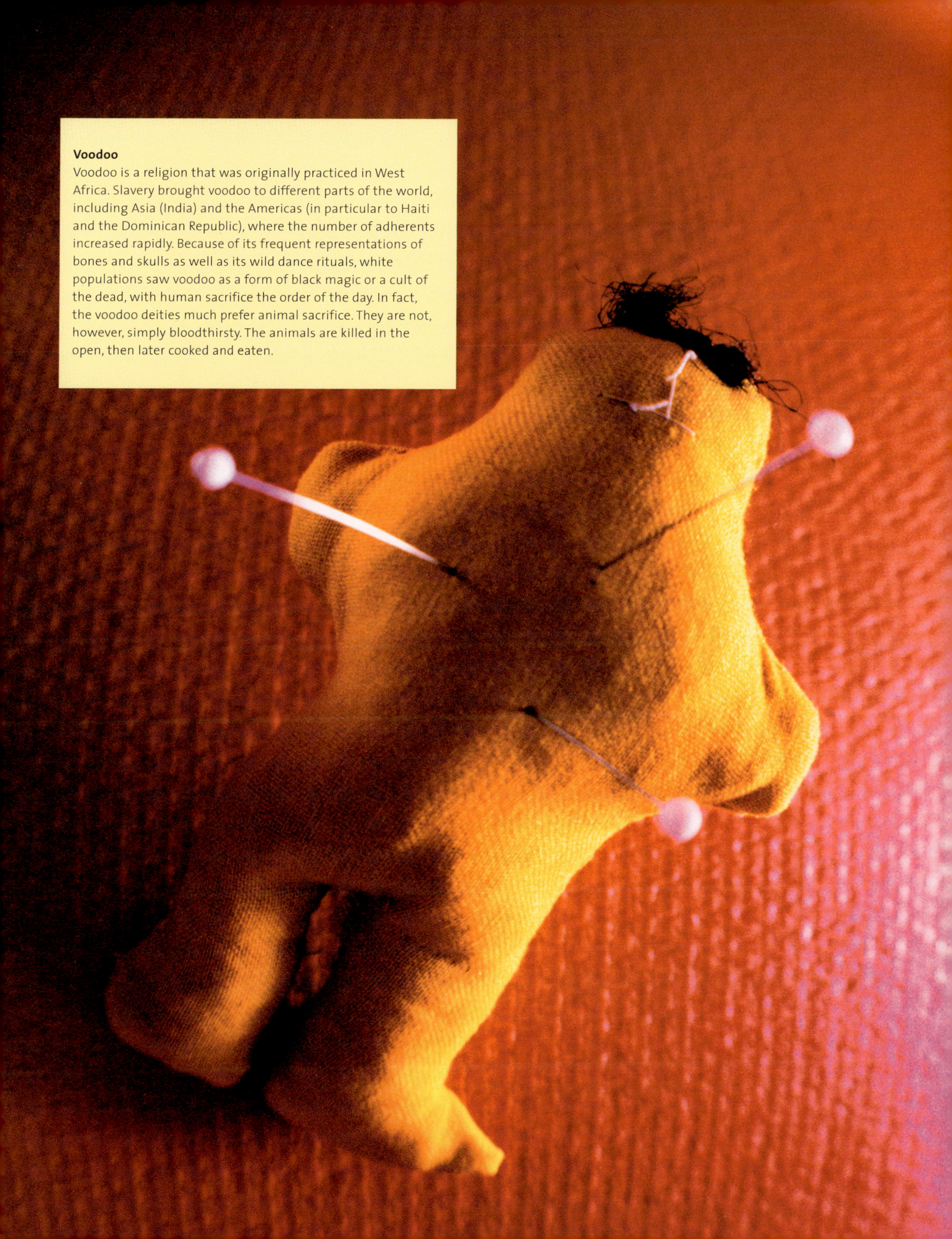

In 1980, when one of the Devil's Marbles of Australia was taken away, tribal elder Mick Taylor prophesied sickness and death. In fact, many children in the settlement did become ill afterward and he himself, aged 50, also died.

Curses

The curse – the exact opposite of a blessing – is one of the most common forms of magic spell. Generally understood as calling unfavourable luck upon a person, curses have been seen as the cause of all manner of misfortune for millennia. The forms they take, their antidotes and their duration vary widely.

What is a curse?

Curses that call down bad luck are very widespread. Many have become parts of everyday speech and are indispensable verbal expressions. Those phrases that are casually tossed about today, however, meant something completely different during the last millennium.

According to the medieval way of looking at things, curses, whether they are expressed consciously or unconsciously, had grave consequences and were therefore to be taken very seriously indeed. The art of cursing underwent a long period of development. In the earliest days, only magicians and witches possessed the ability to impose a curse on a person. In the later Middle Ages, an outburst by a perfectly ordinary person was enough to call up the Devil or his demons. A curse could mean sickness, mutilation, misfortune or even death.

Curses have a corresponding use and meaning when they appear in traditional stories, such as fairy tales. Curses or cursed objects lead humans to suffer a variety of unusual fates, such as being transformed into beasts. It can be years before curses such as these are broken. Fairy tales involving curses are perhaps best understood as a means of conveying what it means to be cursed.

The use and effect of a curse

In occult circles, being placed under a curse has little to do with a casually uttered word. Instead, the curse is itself a magic spell set in action by a spoken or formulaic ritual with the intent of generating a specific effect. This could take the form of a certain gesture, for example, or passing on a particular object accompanied by a fixed sequence of words. As a rule, the gestures that are supposed to accompany a curse are perfectly ordinary. This may have been a means of covering up the fact that a curse had been pronounced at all. A curse can also be activated by its rapid pronouncement in an unguarded moment.

The preparations required for the imposition of a curse depend entirely on the curser's intentions. Curses that have especially weighty consequences require intensive preparation and unusual ingredients. Others work perfectly well when spoken off the cuff. The after effects of a curse are also dependent on its intent. In some cases the cursed person must learn of the curse from the mouth of the person who imposed it before it will have any effect. A curse is, as a rule, intended to harm only the one person who is being cursed, rather than a group or a geographical area. They can bring on sicknesses, great misfortune, or even a transformation, altering character traits, points of view, even memories – and, in the most extreme cases, lead to death.

King Agamemnon of Mycenae was the victim of a curse placed on his family by the god Hermes.

American actress Jayne Mansfield died in a car accident on 29 June 1967. Many people are convinced that her death was due to a curse by her former boyfriend Anton LaVey, who was leader of the Church of Satan.

The evil eye

A well known, specialized variety of curse is the so-called "evil eye". In this case, no particular ritual is required. The person who is endowed with the evil eye need only direct his or her gaze in someone's direction and that person is well and truly cursed. It is not at all clear how one comes to have the evil eye, although it is usually said that the bearer was born with it, and the curse itself is in most cases unintentional. There are also accounts indicating that not every glance by such a person is seen as evil and that this aspect only emerges in certain situations, for example, occasions when praise is offered or envy expressed. It has been said that Pope Pius IX had the evil eye, because people and places he had blessed would experience strange events soon thereafter.

Once encountered, there seems to be no effective defence against the evil eye, although there are plenty of books that offer suggestions of how to protect oneself from it. One can anoint oneself with a special tincture or wear a mask, for example: this is thought to be the reason that hangmen wear their special caps. It is also not at all clear where this belief in the evil eye originated. It has been suggested that it comes from the continent of Africa.

Some cultures try to reduce the effects of the evil eye by placing a special mark on the bearer of the curse.

Ancient curses

Because curses originate from human beings, but can be transformed by magical and supernatural means, their effectiveness is not uniform. In some cases the curse holds sway only for a few days, while in other cases they endure for thousands of years. One example of the latter variety is the legendary curse of Tutankhamon. In 1922, when Englishman Howard Carter (1874–1939) opened the tomb of the Egyptian pharaoh Tutankhamon in the Valley of the Kings, it caused an unprecedented archaeological sensation. The treasures found in the tomb were greater than any found before, and even the mummy and sarcophagus were in perfect condition.

A few weeks after the tomb was opened Carter's friend Lord Carnavon died from an infected mosquito bite. Unrest first broke out among the Egyptian workers at the site,

Native Hawaiians believe that the volcano Mauna Loa is the seat of the goddess Pele, who is enraged when people carry off her stones. Many tourists who have nevertheless done so report twists of fate that only ceased after they sent the last stone back to Hawaii.

Victims of the Curse of the Pharaoh

The curse of Tutankhamon is said to have claimed the lives of sixteen men, including not only members of the expedition, such as Howard Carter's patron, Lord Carnavon, but also people who visited the tomb, like the literary scholar Gardian La Fleur, the millionaire George Jay Gould, or Arthur C. Mace, the head conservator of the New York Metropolitan Museum of Art. Even family members and employees of participants in the expedition were not immune. Richard Bethel, Carter's secretary, was found dead in his apartment, and the circumstances of Bethel's father's death were equally unexplained. The "curse" seems to remain in effect even today. In 1992 a BBC film team documenting the "Curse of the Pharaoh" suffered many small accidents in the course of their work.

however, during the following years, when it was revealed that a total of twelve men who had taken part in the excavation had died. Journalists wrote of the "Curse of the Pharaoh" and speculated about mysterious conditions to which the expedition members might have been exposed. It was suggested that the tomb may have harboured a special fungus or bacteria, put in place by the tomb's builders to ensure the death of any plunderers. Poisons and supernatural powers were also mentioned.

Howard Carter and his archaeologists sharply condemned the sensational journalism, dismissing the reports as "foolish gossip", and assuring the public that there was a reasonable explanation for every death. They insisted that the Curse of the Pharaoh had no basis in reality. Some time later, the British crime novelist Edward Wallace was interviewed for the magazine *Berlin Illustrated*. He said that disaster clung to the mummies of the heathen pharaohs, and explained each and every one of the deaths of expedition members in the most sensational manner possible, chiding the archaeologists for their lack of caution. Howard Carter did not respond to Wallace's accusations.

Although one can still read about the Curse of the Pharaoh now and again in the tabloid press, numerous investigations of the tomb for viruses, bacteria and fungi led to the conclusion that these could not have survived over millennia, given the conditions inside the tomb. Supposedly inexplicable phenomena could also be due to natural causes. The Curse of the Pharaoh does, in fact, seem to be no more than a series of unhappy events and the invention of imaginative journalists.

Genuine curses?

The Curse of the Pharaoh might have been invented by the press, but there are numerous other descriptions of places and objects that seem to be genuinely cursed. These kinds of reports are sometimes refashioned as ghost stories. There is no one answer to the question of the extent to which these stories correspond to reality; the same is true for the extent and duration of curses.

The Curse of Tutankhamon is supposedly responsible for the death of many of the men who took part in opening his tomb.

Raining Fish

"It's raining cats and dogs", goes the familiar saying, an everyday, fanciful visualization of a heavy downpour. Since antiquity, however, there have been reports that suggest this may be more than just a proverb. Accounts exist of unusual rains of fish and other animals suddenly falling from the sky.

Fish fall from the sky

Fish and frog rains were long considered to fall strictly under the heading of legend, this despite the fact that a fair number of different cultures have reported this phenomenon, often explaining it in conjunction with a divine curse or bad omen. In the meantime, however, there have been other cases that have been documented scientifically. One example is the rain of living stickleback fish that fell over Mount Ash in Wales, in 1859. This event led to the closer investigation of animal rain.

One theory claims that aeroplanes flying overhead cause it to rain fish. Since reports of animal rain predate the invention of the aeroplane, this theory cannot be sufficient.

Over the last few decades, researchers have uncovered numerous historical cases, going all the way back to the second century BC. It is now known that the phenomenon is not limited to fish or frogs, but that there are also other categories of untypical rain, involving insects, snails, birds, flesh, blood and stones. These varieties are, however, much less common.

Attempts at explanation

One recent theory associates fish rain with aeroplanes flying overhead and dropping cargo over the area. Although this idea is favoured in some circles, and may explain some specific events, it can be easily discounted as a blanket solution by the fact that many accounts come from periods that predate mechanical flight.

The most current theory claims that fish and frogs are sucked up into the air by the force of tornados and waterspouts as they pass over bodies of water, only to be dropped in a different place at a later time when the storms become too weak to carry them further.

At first glance this theory seems to explain at least some instances of the phenomenon, although there are other factors that speak against it. Firstly, in many accounts, only fish of a certain species are transported, as with the sardines that fell over northern Greece in 2002, or the sticklebacks in the Welsh mountains. Sticklebacks are not schooling fish. Any whirlwind collecting them would have had to do so over a large area while avoiding all the other species of fish, plants and earth. Secondly, the Mount Ash sticklebacks fell over an area of 240 x 36 feet (73 x 11 m) in two intervals, with eyewitnesses reporting a ten minute gap between the two "showers". This would mean that any tornado would have to remain on the same spot for fifteen minutes or more in order to drop the fish in two batches. This is certainly not possible and would, of course, be a unique event if it were.

A third argument against the whirlwind theory is the varying condition of the animals. In two cases documented in India, in 1833 in Futtepoor and in 1836 in Allahabad, the fish were not only dead, but desiccated as well. In Essen, Germany, a variety of carp fell from the sky in 1896, all encased in ice. The Mount Ash fish were not only alive, but did not even seem to have been harmed in any way by their journey and fall.

We can conclude that, although a good start has been made in investigating the phenomenon of animal rain, it is not yet sufficiently explained.

According to one current theory, the powerful winds of tornadoes suck fish up into the air over a wide area and release them later, as the storm winds decrease and lose power.

With the help of artistic representation and accounts in literature, we now know that animal rain has been occurring for centuries, even millenia.

The Sliding Rocks of Death Valley

In the infamous Death Valley in California, there is a dry lake called Racetrack Playa. It has long been rumoured that the place is cursed because of evidence found there indicating that heavy boulders move themselves across the lakebed.

Racetrack Playa

Racetrack Playa is the bed of a dried up salt lake measuring 2.8 miles (4.5 km) long and 1.35 miles (2.2 km) wide. Because of Death Valley's extraordinarily low level of rainfall (less than 2 inches annually on average), the lakebed only fills with water once or twice a year. There are some 160 stones in the lakebed, ranging from big to enormous, with the largest weighing over 700 pounds (320 kg). The perfectly flat, dry ground is scoured and scraped with paths that suggest these boulders are being moved along the ground at great speed, perhaps as fast as three feet per second according to some estimates. There is no indication of how this movement could have been brought about by outside forces, and no stone has ever been observed actually making its way across the ground.

In the 1990s, the boulders were accurately mapped and their movements documented over several months. It was found that many of the stones followed similar paths to others lying close by. This suggests that identical forces are at work in moving each individual boulder.

Attempts at explanation

Many explanations for this phenomenon have been proposed. One possibility is that Racetrack Playa is only superficially "flat". If it slopes instead, the stones are simply moving downhill. A further theory suggests that the boulders are reacting to local magnetic effects. Both explanations can be discounted by the same argument. The scrape marks clearly show that the stones abruptly change directions, sometimes by as much as 90°. For the first theory to stand in face of this evidence, the slope would have to make a sudden change to a comparable degree. For the second, it is the magnetic poles that would have to change. Neither of these are considered physically possible at this site.

The theory that resonates to the greatest extent in the scholarly world argues that, because of the meagre rainfall and the tremendous temperature variation for which Death Valley is famous, ice or dew will form a slippery coat on the surfaces of the boulders, causing them to slide relatively easily across the fine, sun-baked sand. This effect would be enhanced by the extremely strong winds that blow through the Playa, which would set the stones in motion. As the lakebed dries out, the boulders settle again into the ground and any sand pushed ahead by their forward movement quickly blows away.

This theory, while plausible, has yet to be supported by direct observation. Geologist Bob Sharp conducted the only investigation of the phenomenon between 1968 and 1974, and no further studies have taken place since then. While it has certainly been proven that ice and dew can accumulate in Death Valley, and that powerful winds blow across the Playa, these effects are even more characteristic of parts of the region lying well away from Racetrack Playa. It remains to be seen whether any new expeditions will endure the harsh conditions of Death Valley and study this particular phenomenon further.

The base of Racetrack Play consists of dry mud. A mosaic-like pattern is formed when the surface contracts irregularly in the intense heat.

Death Valley is renowned as one of the hottest and driest places on Earth. In Badwater Basin temperatures as high as 134.7 °F (57 °C) have been recorded, and the average temperature in July is over 115 °F (46 °C).

Death Valley National Park lies in the Mojave Desert in California.

Vampires

As already mentioned, in some circles, curses are often a handy explanation for anything out of the ordinary. Unexplained incidents and events create a breeding ground for myths and legends such as those associated with vampires, werewolves and zombies.

Vampires from all over the world

Stories about vampires or vampire-like creatures can be found in cultures throughout the world. The monster itself is called by many names. The Slavs call vampires *moroi*, in the Philippines they are *danag*, on Java they are known as *sundal bolong*, and as *kuang shi* in China. Even the ancient Romans had a name for them: *strigas* (note the similarity to the Italian word for witch, *strega*). Although they also have varying characteristics, the creature is always human, or at least human-like in appearance, and always feeds on human blood. Belief in vampires is so varied and widespread that some suspect a common origin, although a more likely reason is the universality of the kinds of observations made by people all over the world that lead them to suspect the existence of vampires in the first place. Each culture develops its own kind of vampire independently.

Vampire bats don't actually suck blood; they bite their victims and lick the blood that flows from the wound.

Characteristics of vampires

Listing all known vampire characteristics would require an entire book devoted to the subject. The points they have in common, however, can be briefly summarized here. Nearly all "traditional" vampires can transform their victims into vampires with a bite or by drinking their blood. Most vampires are described as young and attractive, and their stunning appearance is usually achieved by means of magic. Sometimes they have the ability to transform themselves into a different animal, such as a bat or a wolf. Vampires are frequently described as aggressive and endowed with supernatural physical strength. Finally, vampires are, of course, only active at night.

The sculpture is of Elizabeth Bathory (1560–1614), the "Countess of Blood". She led gruesome rituals in which more than 600 women died, leading some to believe that she was a vampire.

Rabies
Rabies is a viral infection spread by the bite of an infected animal, causing an inflammation of the brain. The infected person or animal is exceedingly aggressive as well as over-excited and highly sensitive to light, sound and smells. As the disease progresses, paranoia, mania, and hallucinations set in, accompanied by muscle spasms, cramps and, in the final stages, paralysis and death.

Prince Vlad III (known as *Tepes*, "the Impaler") was the ruler of Wallachia in the fifteenth century. He served as a model for Bram Stoker's *Count Dracula*.

The question as to whether a vampire is a living, superior variety of the human species, a member of the walking dead, or a supernatural demon is not easily answered. Likewise, it is not always clear whether vampires can actually be killed. In some traditions it isn't possible at all, while in others they succumb to sunlight, fire, Christian symbols, and having a stake driven through their heart. Water and strong-smelling plants, like garlic, are often thought to keep vampires at bay.

The origins of belief in vampires

The belief that those who are presumably already dead might climb out of their graves and feed on human blood is very likely based on the observation of a number of unrelated phenomena. Some descriptions of how vampires behave correlate to the symptoms of rabies (see box, above), as does the fact that vampires are created by another vampire's bite. The vampire's ability to transform itself also comes into play, since people infected with rabies, having been bitten by animals, take on beast-like characteristics as the disease runs its course.

In the past, it was frequently observed that the dead had undergone inexplicable changes after burial that could be interpreted as supernatural. Perhaps they had been drinking blood? Today, these changes are better understood as a natural part of the decomposition process.

Just a myth?

That blood is the sap of life is a central belief in many cultures. Nearly everywhere in the world there are rituals, some religious and some secular, which revolve in some way around blood. Symbolizing life, strength, and frequently youth, blood often serves as a kind of sacrificial offering. There are also reports of people intentionally drinking the blood of animals or of other people so as to take on their characteristics.

Werewolves

Werewolf is the term given to a creature that can take on either the form of a human or that of a wolf. In the majority of cases, werewolves are ascribed characteristics similar to those of vampires.

What is a werewolf?

The same topography of belief holds true for werewolves as for vampires: they are mythological cousins in every sense. There are strong parallels between the stories associated with both creatures in terms of their respective origins and where they are most widespread.

While there are similarities in various descriptions of werewolves' appearance and characteristics, as with vampires – another similarity – many cultures imagine werewolves in their own particular way, starting with their external form. Occasionally, some tales describe werewolves as mixed beings, half human and half wolf, that walk standing upright on two legs. More commonly, though, they look just like an ordinary wolf. A third variation reports of people who begin to behave like a wolf, but without any physical changes.

Lycanthropy

There is no clear answer as to what causes a person to transform into a werewolf. There are several descriptions and opposing explanations, even found within the same culture. One popular explanation claims that people become werewolves as the result of an illness or a curse. The disease is called lycanthropy, named after Lykaon, a mythological Greek king of Arcadia, who angered Zeus and was turned into a wolf as a result. There are other possibilities as well. One can be cursed, or find oneself in a bewitched place, or inadvertently use certain objects with the power to transform people, such as the belt made from the skin of a hangman or an animal pelt.

There is no unified description of how a person transforms into a wolf; many alternative theories exist.

Werewolf trials

Parallel to the witch trials, werewolf trials also took place in the Middle Ages, in which suspected werewolves were confined to stocks. The accused were not always human, however. In 1685, a wolf with its muzzle cut off and dressed in clothing was hung from the gallows.

According to most sources, the transformation from human to werewolf is usually triggered by external forces, such as when a person is transformed into a wolf under the influence of the full moon. In some cases the setting of the sun is stimulus enough.

The transformation is not always involuntary. It is said that there are objects that can help one transform into a wolf and then back to human form again. In some stories this can be accomplished completely without the aid of magic objects. In cases like this the werewolf may also be described as good-hearted and wise, a mediator between the animal and human worlds and a supporter of both.

In many films, werewolves are portrayed as tragic figures with no means of stopping their transformation.

Already in antiquity, the full moon was ascribed special powers. It is said to encourage or otherwise trigger werewolf transformation.

Do werewolves exist?

As with vampires, the behaviour attributed to werewolves can be traced back to physical illness, in this case once again to rabies (see box, page 175). But the werewolf mythos also includes descriptions, and even images, of people who seem to prove that wolf men really exist. There are a number of illnesses that can lead to overgrowth of body hair, such as the genetic disease hypertricosis. An infectious disease similar to porphyria can interrupt the production of white blood cells, which leads to heavy growth of hair, hypersensitivity to light and skin irritation. It can even cause the gums to recede, making the teeth look like fangs.

Finally, independent of the werewolf myth itself, there continue to be people today who are so fascinated with the creatures that they identify with them. There are many cases known in which people have made excuses for themselves for violent crimes by claiming they were werewolves at the time they committed them.

Zombies

These days the term "zombie" either means a reanimated corpse or a living person robbed of their will by supernatural or magical forces. The word comes from *zumbi*, the African spirit of the dead. Belief in zombies is generally supposed to have originated in West African and American voodoo.

Voodoo zombies

Limiting the belief in zombies to West Africa or the Caribbean is essentially false. Traditions of the wandering, soulless dead have existed for centuries, under names including *draugr*, which is what the Vikings called them. Within the realm of magic, individuals have tried to come up with spells that would permit them to control the will of another person, bring the dead back to life, or animate a lifeless object like the golem (see box, right) in order to exploit them as slaves.

The Golem

A golem (from a Hebrew word meaning "unformed") is an artificially made creature, typically with a human-like form. Built by a person, the golem is subjugated to the will of their creator. Making a golem requires some sort of natural material to begin with, and most sources report using mud, clay, or wood. Whoever performs the magical ritual that infuses this creation with life has power over the golem forever and can command it to do their bidding.

In films, zombies are usually inhuman, disfigured murder machines, that are driven only to kill.

The zombie spells cast by a voodoo priest are fully grounded in magic. They begin with a curse placed on a specific individual by the *houngan* (priest), *mambo* (priestess), or *bokor* (black magician). This either kills the person or causes them to fall into a death-like trance. Days later, whoever pronounced the curse conducts a special ritual to make the dead person rise again, now fully subservient to their will. The zombie itself is, from that point onward, incapable of independent action or thought.

Zombie powder

Many accounts mention one or more powders that the voodoo priests use in order to transform someone into a zombie. A few scientists have approached voodoo priests and taken samples of their powders. They found it to be a mixture of animal and plant substances, including extract of toad and puffer fish. Both of these can lead to hallucinations as well as paralysis of the circulatory system. With proper dosage, the victim falls into a death-like stupor. There may be other substances, as well, that cause the seemingly dead person to lose his or her will.

Do zombies exist?

It must be said that all of the above information, with the exception of the scientific analysis of voodoo powder, is almost entirely dependent on claims made by voodoo priests or their followers.

The actual voodoo spell seems to be employed very rarely. At the same time, the island of Haiti is full of stories that have awakened scientific interest. One of these that made headlines around the world in the spring of 1918 was the case of the plantation owner Ti-Joseph du Colombier. He employed a crew of ragged and apparently will-less men during the sugar cane harvest, driving them on brutally, without, however, leaving any recognizable marks on their bodies. It was reported that many inhabitants of the nearby city recognized the labouring men as their deceased relatives or friends.

A further case was reported in 1980 after a tattered, apathetic Narcisse Clairvius, who had died eighteen years previously, appeared before her horrified sister in the village marketplace. Both cases were investigated and, although not every element could be confirmed, there did seem to be some kernel of truth in each.

In regions where voodoo is practiced, widespread false information about the religion is exploited for profit through the sale of devotional objects.

Zombies are described as the "living dead" because they occupy the threshold between life and death. Nevertheless, representations of the dead rising from the grave are for all intents and purposes absent from voodoo.

Exorcism

Exorcism is another form of ritual. Whether it is a magical ritual or a religious rite is difficult to say, and very much dependent on who is conducting it. Essentially, exorcism involves driving out the Devil, demons or evil spirits from humans, animals, objects and places.

Contact with evil

Some believe that the actions of a person or animal behaving abnormally can be caused by demons or spirits that have taken up residence in their bodies for various reasons. This concept of "possession" is older and more widespread than Christianity, with widely varied accounts coming from many different cultures.

The measures to be taken against possession are also known. A person capable of driving out demons, perhaps a shaman, a priest, a hero or a tribal chief, meets the evil spirit head on and drives it out of the creature it occupies. This casting out is conducted in different ways, depending on the cultural setting. In addition to prayer, intellectual arguments or trickery may be called into play to persuade the demon to leave the body. Dance and often drumming are used to help the facilitator enter a trance state, placing the shaman on an equal spiritual plane from which to battle the unwanted

The evil spirit must be forced to leave a body. Many aboriginal peoples believe this is best accomplished by weakening the body itself through beatings and charms.

A seventeenth-century image of a biblical exorcism, showing the evil spirit leaving a man's body through his mouth.

spirit. There are parallels between exorcism and magical rituals, in particular when the person or animal has apparently fallen into this abnormal condition as the result of a spell or being otherwise bewitched.

Signs of possession

It is hard to say exactly what "abnormal behaviour" might be for any given individual or animal. There is little written evidence explaining the symptoms of demonic possession. Speaking in an unknown or incomprehensible language, or with more than one distinct voice, is a common aspect of possession. An unnatural fear of religious objects, throwing fits, howling or exhibiting supernatural strength and extreme physical changes are also thought to be signs. In some cases, other phenomena, such as telekinesis – the ability to move objects around a room – have been reported, as have sudden changes in temperature and inexplicable sounds that seem to come from nowhere.

Exorcising the demon

Although only a few grimoires describe how to perform an exorcism (see pp. 162–164), the collective instructions in several sources make it clear that a very specific set of conditions is required for an exorcist to successfully call forth the afflicting demon and order it to leave the body of the one who is possessed. Procedures vary from case to case, but most accounts include the same basic ideas.

First, the exorcist must threaten the evil spirit. This upsets the demon, making it lower its guard. Next, the exorcist asks the demon its name. This very question presupposes that the organization of all demons and spirits is strictly hierarchal. Here, Christianity differs from some other cultures in that knowing the name of the demon conveys special powers on the exorcist; knowing its name is what allows the exorcist to call the demon forth and order it out of the body. This was also true in ancient Egypt, for example. In other systems of belief, a magic ritual is conducted with the victim, instead. Finally, the exorcist forbids the demon to repossess the creature it has just left.

How long an exorcism lasts depends on the strength of the demon, the ability of the exorcist, and the energy of the victim. There are known cases in which the possessed person died from exhaustion or wounds received in the course of the ritual.

A person can usually do very little against a demon intent on taking over his or her spirit.

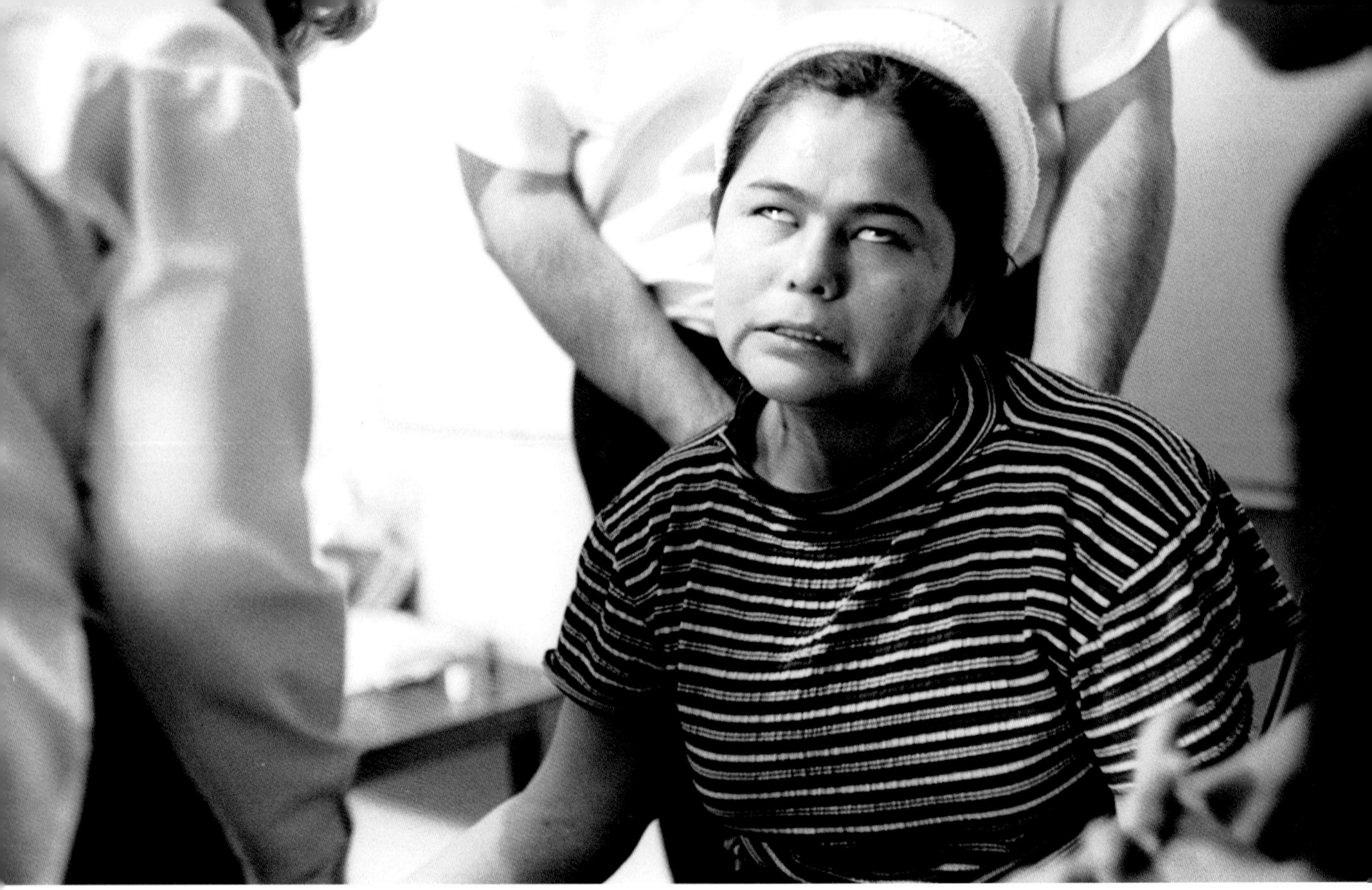

On 27 February 2002, Pastor Hugo Alvarez of Mexico City conducted an exorcism in the village of Iztapalapa.

Exorcism and disease

Scholars have studied accounts of possession from the Middle Ages in regard to developments in medicine, and psychology in particular, that have taken place since then. Nearly all the cases in question could be connected with medical conditions that are quite easily recognized today. These include epilepsy, which causes muscle spasms and cramps in those "possessed", and Tourette's syndrome, which results in uncontrollable, unintelligible utterances and twitching. Finally, there is schizophrenia and related personality and psychological disorders, which also lead to unusual behaviours.

The less common phenomena described in some of the older sources, such as smoke emanating from the body, for example, or short term physical malformations, are considered by scientists to have more to do with fantasy than any actual physical condition. It has been speculated that they were perhaps included in some accounts to enhance their symbolic power. Possession, therefore, is not recognized by science, which, accordingly, discounts the effectiveness of exorcism as well.

Exorcism and the Church

In modern times, the Catholic Church has differentiated between simple and solemn exorcism. Simple exorcism takes place during the sacrament of baptism, in which the baptized child is freed from sins and snatched away from the devil. Solemn exorcism is be carried out by a priest with permission from his bishop, who will usually first ask for a medical opinion of the case.

Even in the Middle Ages, the church tried to guard against the tendency to perform exorcisms on the sick. If the illness was believed to have been caused by a curse, it was still considered curable and a doctor was called in to take care of the matter. But in a case of possession, medicine is powerless, and when all other means and methods proved useless, the church sanctioned an exorcism.

It goes without saying that medieval physicians did not have the knowledge of modern psychologists today. As a result, exorcisms were commonly performed on the mentally ill. In 1999, the Catholic Church officially recognized mental illness as a possible alternative interpretation for demonic possession. Nevertheless, the Catholic Church has kept

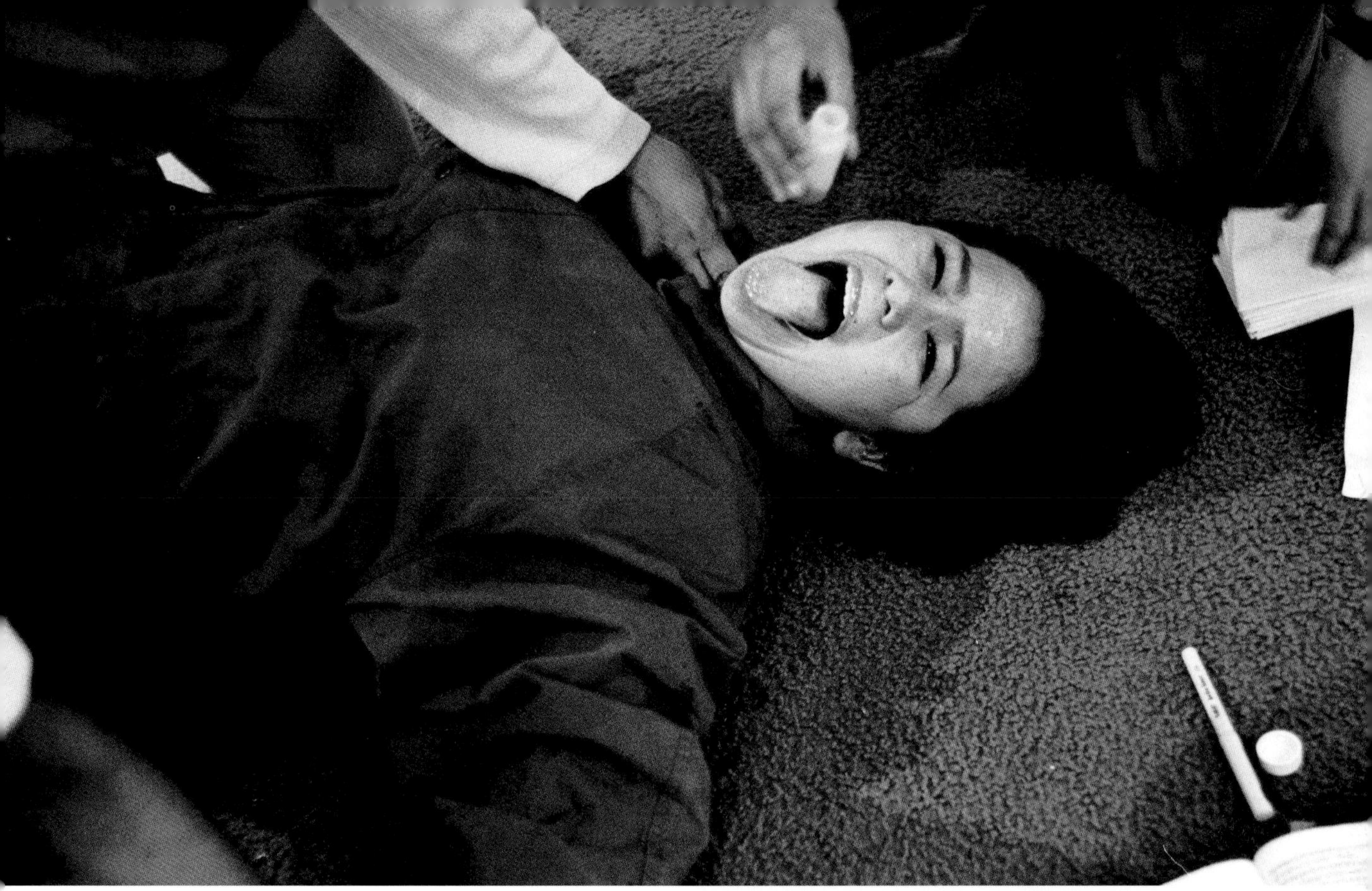

No two exorcisms are the same. The behaviour of the possessed varies, as does the length of the procedure. Some exorcisms have gone on for years.

exorcism as an option. Even today one can take a course in exorcism at the Vatican, and the first conference on the subject was held in Mexico in 2004.

In contrast, many Protestant churches no longer practice exorcism. Here, as well, advances in the field of psychology have led to most cases being handed over to people with appropriate training for therapy.

The Orthodox churches have, for the most part, retained their traditions regarding exorcism. These involve, among other procedures, a ritual in which the possessed person is crucified. There are accounts of this taking place up to the present day. In many tribal religions, the medicine man or shaman still battles it out with demons, meeting them on that spiritual plane.

We don't know exactly how exorcists achieve their successes. In cases of possession, investigations after the fact nearly always point to mental illness as a cause, an illness that is almost inevitably present after the exorcism as before. Everything else is shrouded in mystery.

Depending on the culture, dancing or threatening gestures can be part of an exorcism ritual.

Parasciences

Parapsychology

On the fringes of psychology, parapsychology is concerned with potential qualities like extrasensory perception and telepathic communication that exceed accepted human abilities. German psychologist Max Dessoir (1867–1947) coined the term in 1889, making anything related to one's inner life that falls outside of "normal" the object of study.

While parapsychology deals with supernatural occurrences and the occult, it does so on a purely scientific basis. Parapsychologists have made it their job to investigate whether certain phenomena exist. These include telepathy (mindreading), precognition (predictions and foretelling the future), telekinesis or psychokinesis (moving objects without physical contact, poltergeist phenomena), psychometry (knowing a person, place, or thing intimately through touch or close contact), near-death experiences, spiritualism and bilocation (being in two places at the same time). Parapsychology also deals with certain subcategories, such as the special abilities of individual yogis and fakirs.

Parapsychologists are especially interested in the circumstances surrounding these events: when, where, who is involved, etc. Although parapsychology claims to be a working science using scientific methods, many of the phenomena that fall under its area of study cannot be reliably verified using the senses or scientific observation. As a result, the reports produced are often criticized for their subjectivity. Objectivity in the classical scientific sense is not always possible, casting doubt on the validity of their conclusions. Until now, many of the phenomena could not be explained conclusively, despite the existence of evidence that in some cases, such as Ted Serios' "thoughtographs", is well documented and tested.

A couple looks on as a medium tries to make contact with the other world.

Telepathy

Are there really people who, thanks to special abilities, can look into another person's soul? People who can read and send thoughts, even over a great distance? Do they really have the ability that Frederick W. H. Myers (1843–1901), founder of the London Society for Psychical Research, first called telepathy in 1882? This phenomenon, which is probably the best known of all of the parapsychological disciplines, is one of the greatest mysteries of human existence.

Communication channels with restricted acccess

Telepathy is not nearly as controversial as many of the other parapsychological phenomena, and serious scientists have been interested in it for many decades, perhaps because quite a number of people have already had some experience of it in their own lives. After all, who has not thought of someone out of the blue and then found that very person suddenly standing at the door, or calling on the phone? We usually call it a coincidence, not yet ready to admit that the approach of another person can be announced on a spiritual channel, direct access to which lies just out of our reach.

The many uses of telepathy

Long before the beginning of the Cold War and even earlier, during World War II, the Soviet Union, the United States and England conducted experiments with people who could read the thoughts of others, with suprising results. Telepathy offers a lot of opportunities for military intelligence and spying – the term used for its practioners in this sense is "psi agents". However, these days the term telepathy is more often replaced with the designation "remote sensing". The agents try to describe places and objects by means of their thoughts. In 1940, the telepath Wolf Messing was introduced to Josef Stalin. This could be viewed as the beginning

Is it possible to send or receive information or feelings in some way other in addition to the usual forms of communication?

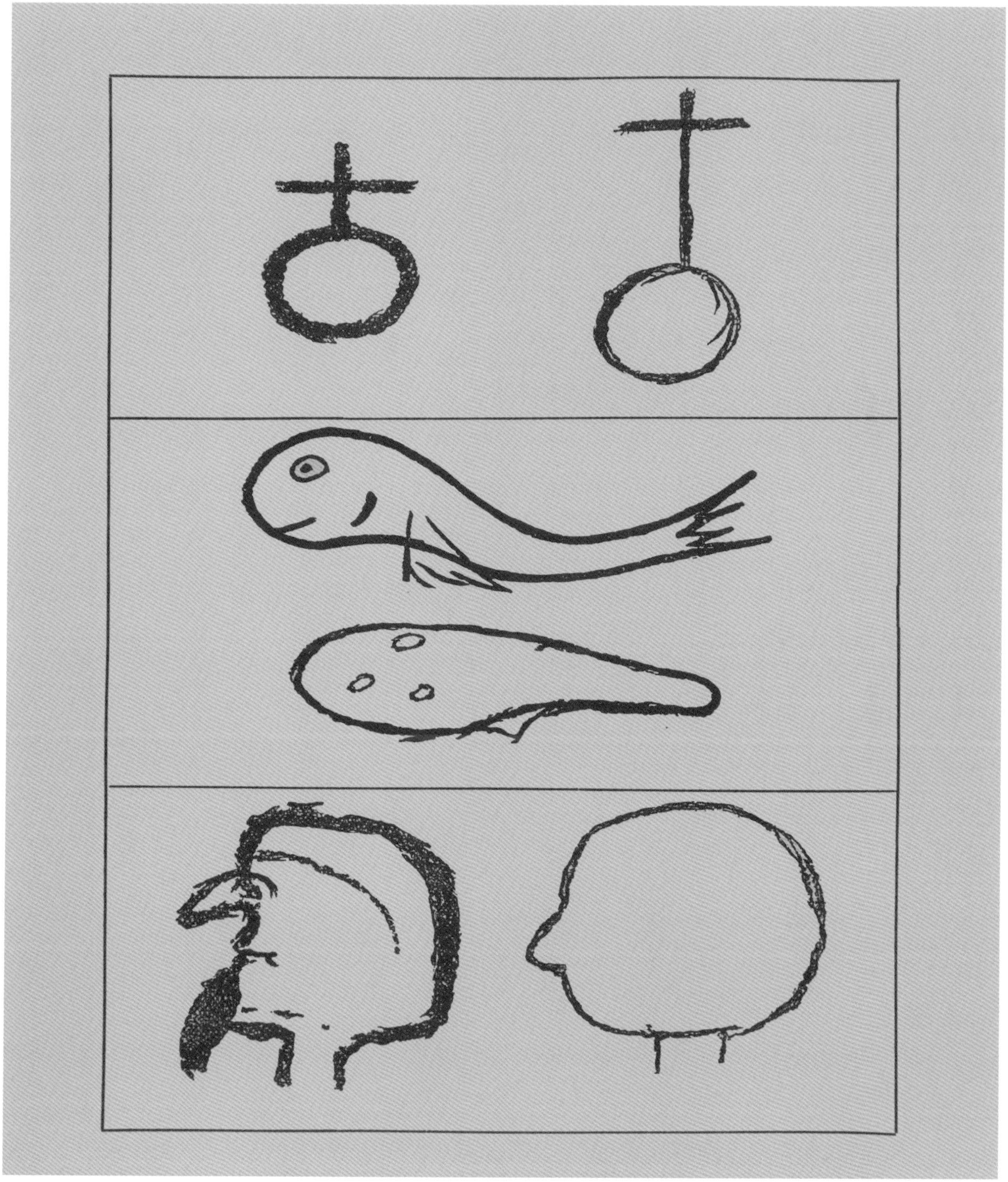

These pictures are the result of a telepathy experiment from 1883 conducted by English scientist Samuel Guthrie. In each case the original is shown next to the image reproduced by the telepath.

An experiment by the British television channel BBC had a suprising result. At the exact moment that its owner decided to return home, this dog got up and waited by the door.

of government interest in the use of telepathy. Telepathic phenomena were also researched in the Western world. Between 1934 and 1939, S. G. Soal (1889–1979), professor of mathematics at the University of London, tested 160 people in 100,000 individual experiments. Similarly, in 1941, parapsychologists Basil Shakleton and Rita Elliot were also able to produce results that could not have been due to chance alone.

The reasons why one person is blessed with this ability and another is not, is a grey area within the field. Many scientists are convinced that every person has telepathic abilities, at least to some degree, and that this sixth sense need only be trained using proper sensitization.

Experiments in the realm of telepathy have a simple pattern. The subject sits across from an examiner, who looks at symbols or pictures randomly generated on a monitor (which the subject cannot see). The telepath is supposed to name or draw the picture that the examiner is looking at. Telepathic subjects can actually "read" what the other person thinks and draw pictures of what the other person sees. Years of repeated experiments have produced impressively consistent results.

Morphogenetic fields

English biologist Rupert Sheldrake, who has been studying telepathy for years, has developed the theory of morphogenetic fields. It states that nature stores information in fields, which are then made available to others. In his most famous example, he describes a British variety of chickadee (*Parus caeruleus*) that learned to open the aluminum cover of a milk bottle and steal milk. Once learned, the behaviour quickly spread to many other areas. Very soon, even the continental European birds learned to steal milk in exactly the same way. They had learned it thanks to morphogenetic fields because telepathy is boundless, surrounding people and animals alike.

Sheldrake has proved this in an impressive experiment with a parrot and its owner. The animal was able to speak in whole sentences with a vocabularly of over 500 words. The parrot sat in front of a running camera with its owner, Aimee, two floors below. Aimee opened envelopes containing pictures and looked at them. In a surprising result, the bird seemed to receive thoughts from its owner, as the parrot repeated – in English – whatever Aimee saw. This is an unparalleled result. Since then there have been no other known cases of animal-human telepathic communication at this level of precision and consistency.

Other experiments with animals and people

The BBC has documented other experiments involving people and animals, as well. In one example, dogs were filmed whose owners left them at home and moved around town without a certain destination. At a set time, the person received a signal and decided to return home to his or her dog. The film teams recorded that at the exact moment the owner decided to return home, the dog got up, went to the door, and waited. Countless recurrences of this experiment prove it could not be coincidence. The results were always the same.

It is still unclear how telepathy really works. However, after years of research it can be said with some certainty that the phenomenon exists. Questions remain regarding why it exists. In addition, no one is sure what makes certain individuals telepathic and others not.

Biologist and philosopher Rupert Sheldrake (born in 1942) developed a theory that information is transferred from generation to generation over time and space by a kind of morphogenetic resonance.

The Dutch medium Gerard Croiset (left) was famous for being able to predict events and find missing people. Professor Hans Bender tested him in numerous so-called location experiments in which Croiset predicted who would sit in places drawn by lots.

Precognition

Precognition is knowing something before it happens. It is also called clairvoyance, second sight, prophesying and seeing the future. In parapsychology, precognition means the ability to see and foretell events in the future using extrasensory perception. There are and have always been active psychics, but the question of the reliability of their interpretations of horoscopes, palm lines, cards and other oracles remains. How reliable is a glance into a mysterious future, and what does this mean for humanity and its values?

Fear of death and the afterlife

For as long as humanity has existed, there has been an interest in what is coming next, in that obscure time that lies before us, in the possible dangers hidden within it. But people also want to know about joyous events and whether their hopes will be fulfilled. Since prehistory, people have feared death and wondered about the afterlife. Oracles were people with special talents who could see the future, so people sought them out and asked them for that secret information.

As great as the desire for such knowledge was in the past, it seems actually to have increased in modern times. Due in part to the New Age movement, soothsayers and mediums are more popular today than they have been since the Middle Ages. It seems no small town is without someone willing to read palms or tarot cards, and there is no lack of faithful believers. Statistics show that 38 per cent of the

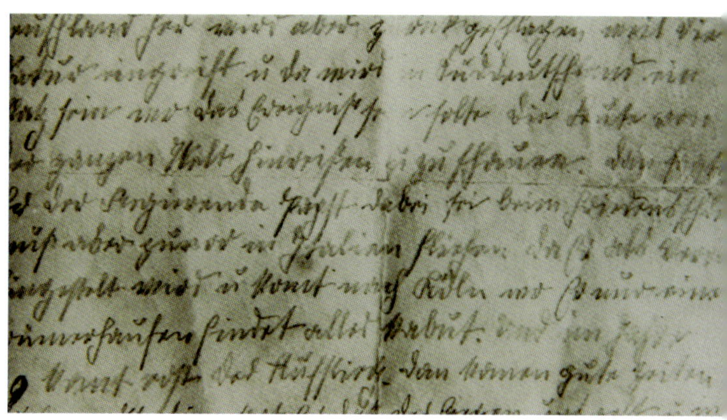

In 1914, Bavarian soldier Andreas Rill wrote in two field posts about a "prophetic Frenchman", who among other things imparted precise information about the end of World War I and the duration of World War II. The letters were forensically tested and proved to be authentic.

Helmut Schmidt, a German physicist and parapsychologist living in America, constructed a testing tool for precognition called the "four button machine", a device with four lamps and a button for each one. The test subject presses one of the four buttons to foretell which lamp will light up next. The lamps are programmed to light up randomly. A talented medium will know which one will light ahead of time.

adult population is convinced that the future can be predicted. But how clearly do psychics see the future?

Probably the greatest psychic of the last millennium, Nostradamus (1503–1566) made a series of genuinely startling predictions. Among other things, he said that the end of the world would occur in a year when Easter falls on the 25th of April. This has already happened in the years 1666, 1734, 1886 and 1943. The next time will be in 2038.

Precognition itself is a fact

While there are still problems defining other paranormal phenomena, after over 100 years of parapsychological research involving clear-cut cases, thousands of lab tests and experimental studies, precognition has been generally accepted as having proven worth. The research has little to do with individual events, but rather works from the theory that everyone is able to sense the future. American parapsychologist William Cox examined accidents with regard to human behaviour preceding them. He compared the passenger count in train collisions with the average number of passengers on the same stretch on ten different days. On the days when there were accidents, there were consistently far fewer people travelling than on the other days. He concluded that without being aware of it, people had sensed what was going to happen and avoided those routes.

Life as a series of predetermined events

In spite of – or perhaps because of – the possibility of precognition, efforts to discover the future are often criticized. If it is possible to see the future, our entire collective knowledge, Western morality and system of religious beliefs would be thrown into question, or at least need to be redefined. We like to think that personal freedom and responsibility exist, but if the future is already determined and can be "seen" by those who are able, then this freedom is an illusion, leaving our lives little more than a sequence of predetermined events. Our concept of time and causality would be fundamentally changed, requiring a new kind of physics with a radically different point of view, one that includes precognition in our perspective on the world.

We don't see the future, we see the past. That's odd, because we don't have eyes in the back of our heads.

Eugéne Ionesco

Famous Visionaries

Classical fortunetellers

We know from myths that there were well-known fortunetellers in ancient Greece, the prophets and preachers of the will of the gods. Prophesying in sanctuaries and at oracular sites like Delphi, the most famous are Teiresias, Amphiaraos, Bakis, Calchas, Mopsos, Epimenides and Amphilochos. There were also women who were seers, for example, the sibyls. Representing a prophetic tradition that originated in Asia Minor, they were respected in Greece, and later Rome, as oracles of fate and disaster. Cassandra is the prophetess in the story of Troy. It was her destiny to predict the fall of the city, and to be punished for doing so.

Michel de Notre-Dame, a.k.a. Nostradamus (1503–1566)

Nostradamus, probably the most famous visionary of the last millennium, prophesied events that would take place through to the year 3000. The verses in his books, which encompass all of world history, are written in Latin and in a special code. For this reason, each new generation brings new interpretations; yet, suprisingly, the verses also continue to fit with the earlier interpretations. Some of his greatest predictions were the assassination of John F. Kennedy in 1963, the terrorist attacks on 11 September 2001, the Iraq War begun in 2003, current religious conflicts and even global warming.

Michel of Notre-Dame, a.k.a Nostradamus, was one of the most famous seers of all time.

Stefan Ossowiecki (1877–1944)

Stefan Ossowiecki was a Russian seer with a number of exceptional paranormal talents.

Psychometry (knowledge of people and situations gained through objects), telekinesis (moving objects without any physical contact) and bilocation (being in two places at the same time) are among the extraordinary talents of Stefan Ossowiecki, a Russian seer with many paranormal gifts. He was condemned to death by the Bolsheviks in 1917, but managed to flee to Warsaw, where he remained. He participated in numerous experiments and during World War II helped many people locate missing relatives. Ossowiecki was murdered by the Gestapo in 1944, a fate which, sadly, he also foresaw.

Erik Jan Hanussen (1889–1933)

Hanussen worked as a magician in variety shows during the 1920s. As a psychic, he advised film stars, politicians and bankers. He supported the Nazis in their early days and campaigned for National Socialism. He may even have been Adolf Hitler's psychic. His predictions about the Reichstag fire, the Nazi takeover of power and Kristallnacht all came true. In 1933, his Jewish identity was revealed and, tragically, he was murdered by Nazi storm troopers.

Margareta Meerstein, a.k.a. Madame Buchela (1899–1986)

Madame Buchela predicted the marriage of Princess Soraya to the last Shah of Iran and advised Konrad Adenauer on the repatriation of war prisoners from Russia. Willy Brandt, Leonid Breshnev, und Ted Kennedy all asked her for advice. She predicted the death of John F. Kennedy, the Balkan War and the advent of AIDS. Called "the fortuneteller of Bonn", it is said she saw up to eighty people a day.

Telekinesis

One of the most puzzling categories within the parasciences is telekinesis or psychokinesis, an ability demonstrated by certain people who, using only mental power and concentration, can move and change objects or leave them suspended in space. Although this ability may well lie dormant in everyone, only a few people have succeeded in rousing this elemental force of the human mind.

Mysterious ability due to unknown energy

A person who is able to use telekinesis, or psychokinesis, (both expressions refer to the same phenomenon) draws on an energy source that is as yet unknown to us. Researchers suggest that everyone who has mastered this mysterious ability creates a particular interaction between their own energy and the energy of the object they are moving.

Uri Geller in 1978 with a bent spoon that he is said to have shaped simply with the force of his mind.

We are also familiar with macro-psychokinesis, in which objects are visibly bent, for example what Uri Geller was able to do with spoons and other metal objects. This subject includes poltergeists and ghost sightings, as well, which we will examine later on. Other related phenomena are the changing of particulars of the past (retropsychokinesis), starting fires using mental powers (pyrokinesis), transforming water into ice (cryokinesis) and manipulating wind (aerokinesis).

Fixing dots on dice and other experiments

In 1934, a gambler approached the psi researcher Joseph Banks Rhine with the claim that he could fix the roll of the dice. This encounter led Rhine to launch a series of experiments in which the subjects first threw the dice a number of times to provide a statistical basis for comparison. The subjects and groups whom Rhine tested often rolled "snake eyes" (two) far more often than the predicted statistical probability, which suggested to Rhine that they could indeed fix the dice.

Other experiments were designed to show how people could divert water drops with their minds. William E. Cox (Rhine's former assistant) and Dr. Werner F. Bonin investigated this phenomena with surprising results. However, Bonin also concluded that we do not know the real reason behind telekinetic events and cannot explain them scientifically. The term telekinesis is often extended to refer to poltergeist phenomena, because people decribing poltergeists describe the objects as literally being moved by "the hand of a spirit".

Uri Geller

Uri Geller was born in Tel Aviv in 1946 and currently lives in England. During the 1970s he became famous around the world for being able to use nothing more than the power of his mind to bend cutlery, start nonfunctioning clocks and move compass needles.

To release telekinetic energy one should:

- be in top shape, emotionally as well as physically
- be able to sense the energy of an object within its surroundings
- easily be able to go into a trance-like state
- be able to focus completely on one thing
- be able to replenish and bundle one's own energy
- interact energetically with and control the object

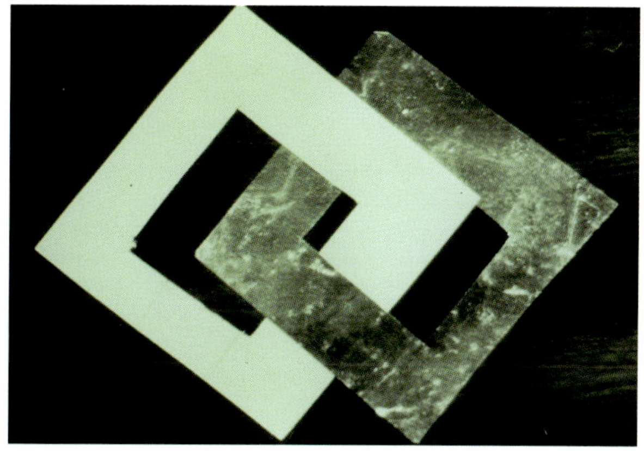

The "impossible object" of Silvio Mattioli. Taking two square pieces of paper, Mattioli intertwined them psychokinetically leaving no visible cuts or tears.

Doubts in telekinesis

Since the eighteenth century, people have conducted experiment after psychokinetic experiment in an attempt to prove the phenomenon scientifically. Some observations involved moving tables and glasses; in any case, results clearly showed that certain people were able to manipulate inanimate objects without exerting physical force. In those days, quite a number of people were fascinated by paranormal and extrasensory activities, in large part due to the philosophical movement of the Enlightenment. People wanted to redefine scientific, social and moral parameters while distancing themselves from what they considered to be religious superstition and general ignorance.

Unfortunately, in our day, a tidal wave of fraud has inundated psychokinesis. The perpetrators use methods similar to those of the magicians and trick artists in variety shows. This ensures that the existense of telekinesis remains controversial. Critics of parapsychology constantly refer to the fact that reproducable, and therefore genuine, proof is lacking. They also point out that the more precise measuring instruments become, the smaller the objects are that are moved.

One test subject of parapsychologist Richard Broughton is said to influence the roll of virtual dice on a computer screen psychokinetically. The dice are controlled by a randomness generator.

Psychometry

A house in which a traumatic event took place, perhaps a murder or a suicide, is perceived as an intolerable place to live by empathically sensitive people, called psychometrics. At the same time, an old toy can evoke positive feelings. For them, places and things are full of feelings and memories. How is it possible for certain people to "read" so much about a place or thing?

Umberto di Grazia at a pre-Etruscan burial ground with dolmen graves. The talented medium, based in Rome, specializes in the paranormal discovery of archaeological sites.

Crime understood by touching the weapon

Within parapsychology, psychometry is the particular ability to discover and relate details about past events or actions by the mere act of being in the place where the events occurred or by touching a related object. Psychometrics are the psychics who maintain that they are able to unterstand a crime and can even see it unfold if, for example, they touch the weapon used. As is the case with many parapsychological abilities, this is hotly contested. Stefan Ossowieki, the famous Russian psychic and engineer, delivered an extraordinary performance at an international conference on archaeology. He touched a hand axe on display and related astonishingly detailed descriptions of prehistoric life. Years later his claims were substantiated both by classical archaeological and newly developed scientific methods.

Medical applications

Psychometry can play a crucial role in medicine. Physician Tino Merz believes that tests on patients who have suffered chemical damage can only be successfully carried out using this extremely sensitive approach, and that psychometry can also treat these same sensitive people. In Merz's opinion, studies on organophosphates would have been impossible without these tests because contamination could not have been detected in any other way.

English architect Frederick Bligh Bond (1864–1945) is considered the founder of paranormal archaeology. During séances, while in a trance, he would draw sketches that contained information about archaeological finds. The drawing below is a sketch he made of Edgar Chapel of Glastonbury.

Auras

The literal translation of the word aura is "breath". Many parapsychologists agree that an aura is a collaboration of the one who releases it and those who see it – a kind of give and take. One person illuminates his or her aura by means of a specific ability to express their life force, and in response particularly sensitive or skilled persons can perceive the aura. But what do auras express?

An emotional and health force field

It was Zeus who turned Aura, companion of the goddess Artemis, into a spring. She is still understood as the embodiment of mild breezes, a cool breath from the water.

In parapsychology, an aura refers to the emanation of a person's emotional state made visible to certain psychics or mediums. Depending on its colour and quality, they can even determine the individual's medical condition and treat them accordingly. This is because the aura not only diagnoses, but recommends a therapy as well. An aura is a kind of emotional or health force field. Up to now, we still do not know which particular abilities are required to see another person's aura and interpret it correctly.

In the fine arts, the nymph Aura was always portrayed with a large cloth over her head, but the best known auras are found in religious depictions of Buddha, Jesus, or saints with a nimbus or halo surrounding them.

Kirlian photography

The Ukrainian Semion Davidovich Kirlian accidentally discovered this type of photography, also called the corona effect, while repairing medical machinery in 1939. A person, body part, or object is subjected to a high-voltage electric field against a photographic plate, creating an image on the plate that resembles a coloured halo or aura. A diagnosis of the energy then takes place according to the colour of the field. Some healers maintain that even cancer can be diagnosed this way. Whether diseases or emotional dispositions can in fact be diagnosed using the Kirlian technique is still open to debate.

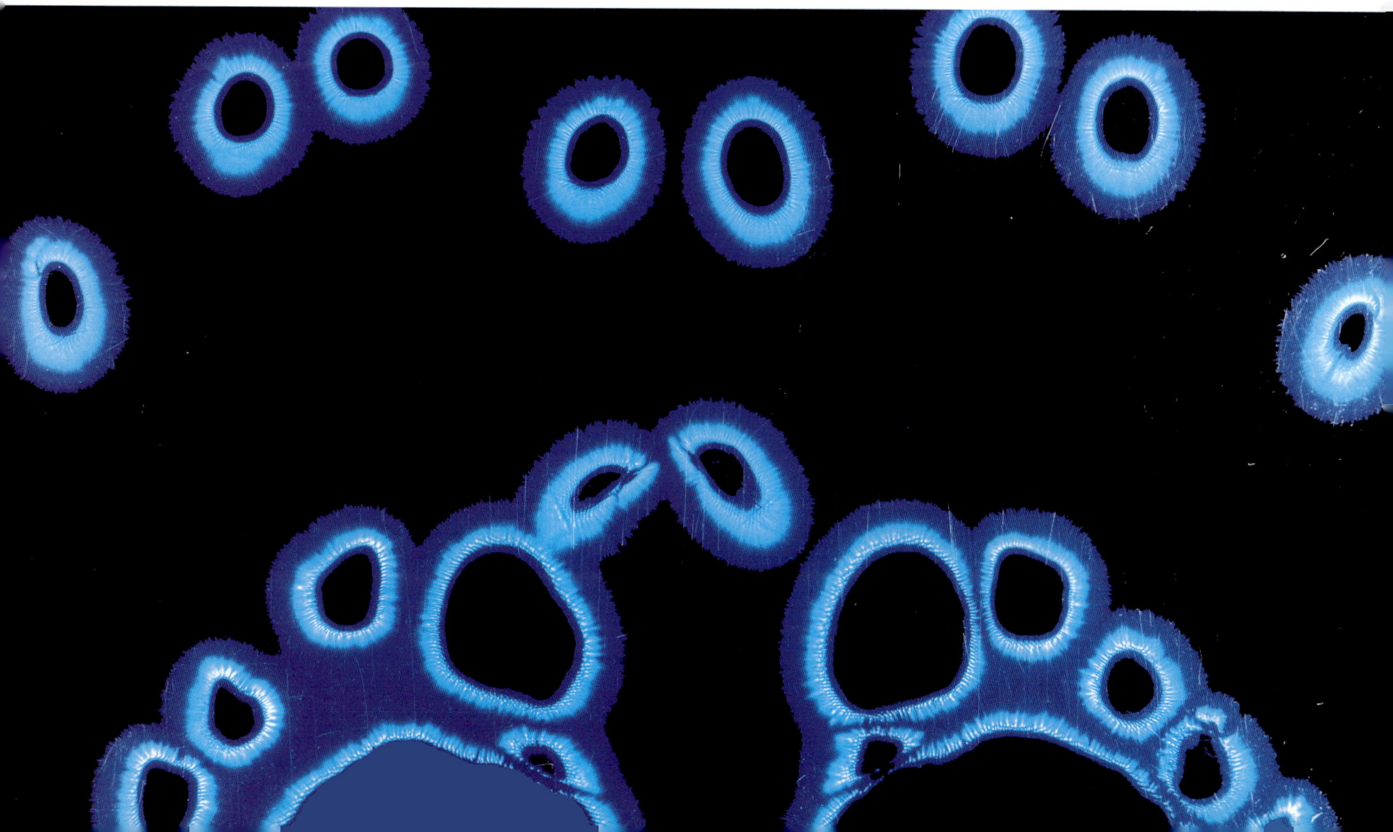

In 1939, Semion Davidovich Kirlian accidentally discovered a type of photography that makes visible the aura of a body, organ, or limb. The auras of a person's fingertips and toes are shown here.

Castles are often thought to be haunted. The lore surrounding Fyvie Castle in Scotland includes blood stains that cannot be washed away, reports of ghosts and cold winds blowing from unknown sources.

Spooks and Poltergeists

Poltergeists usually announce their presence by knocking, moving objects and static discharges, but they can also be *Naturgeists*, spirits tied to a particular place who want to take out their wrath on the living. Then they are transformed from rather harmless, if annoying, spirits into dark visitors. In many places around the world, poltergeist phenomena are considered among the worst paranormal events.

Connection to the Dark Side

Within parascience, poltergeist phenomena are generally viewed as a subcategory of telekinesis, because in both cases objects are moved seemingly without cause, as if by the hands of spirits. Upon closer examination and detailed investigation, what at first appeared to be an apparition often turns out to be a practical joke or a natural effect of wind or weather.

However the spectre actually manifests itself – whether by knocking or moving objects around – and whether or not this phenomonon could ever be scientifically proven, poltergeists would still have earned a firm place in parapsychology. They continue to fascinate us because they connect us with the other, darker side.

Strange Occurrences as the Result of Emotional Excitement

Research has shown that poltergeists surface most often in the presence of adolescents and people who are psychically gifted. In 1958, two American parapsychologists, J. Gaither Pratt and William G. Roll, defined a "poltergeist" as recurrent, spontaneous psychokinesis (RSPK). According to their investigations, the poltergeist is not a ghost, spirit, or phantom, but a projection by a person under emotional stress, like a teenager going through puberty. In their tests. this tense energy was expressed as telekinetic discharges.

In the 1960s and 1970s, Hans Bender, a parapsychology professor from Freiburg, Germany, researched such phenomena in teenagers further and came to the conclusion that

DE INFESTIS OB MOLESTANTES DAEMONIORVM ET DEFVNCTORVM HOMINVM SPIRITVS, LOCIS, LIBER VNVS.

IN QVO. SPIRITVVM INFESTANTIVM genera, conditiones, vires, discrimina, opera, mala quæ viuentibus afferunt; rationes item quibus partim cognoscuntur, partim proscribuntur; modi denique, quibus loca ab ipsorum molestia liberantur, hisq; similia discutiuntur & explicantur.

AVTHORE PETRO THYRÆO NOVESIENS, SOCIETATIS Iesu, D. Theologo, & Professore Ordinario Herbipoli.

Accessit eiusdem Libellus de TERRICVLAMENTIS nocturnis, quæ hominum mortem solent portendere.

IHS

One of the earliest books on haunted places is *Loca Infesta*, written by Petrus Thyraeus of Cologne, Germany in 1598.

he was dealing with a type of unconscious personality split that was bringing about telekinetic events. His work shows what is generally accepted in parapsychological research: if the haunting is taking place openly, from the inside out rather than the other way around, then the first place to look for the cause is among those most affected by it.

Parapsychologist Theo Locher proposed schizophrenia, hallucination or severe emotional disturbances as additional scientific explanations for ghostly apparitions.

Haunted houses

It is scary when a ghost or poltergeist apparition does not fit into any of these currently accepted categories or catchy descriptions. One example of an unusual occurence that cannot easily be explained involved a house in Breslau, Germany where people heard singing. The scientists who investigated the singing ran into dead end walls from which the sounds seemed to come and found themselves lost in basement vaults. No law of acoustics could explain the singing, and individual mental confusion was excluded as a cause because too many people had heard it.

In Stans, Switzerland there is a haunted house open to the public that belongs to the Joller family. The inhabitants kept track of what happened in their house over a long period of time. It began one day with knocking and scratching and, as in Breslau, the whole family heard it. Witnesses were summoned and scientific explanations were sought. But science failed them, and the reason for the events is still unknown. One morning Mr. Joller, a local politician, awoke white-haired and confused. A year later, in 1865, he died. His book, "Personally Experienced Mystical Events", has been lost, but we know of its existence based on other sources that mention it.

There are also reports of machines that stopped working, only to develop a life of their own. For many, this kind of event is proof that a parallel world of spirits exists, inhabited by the messengers of the dead. Does a mysterious and unknown spirit world really exist parallel to our own?

This special instrument registers sudden fluctuations in temperature. It is set to detect the "cold air" in hauntings.

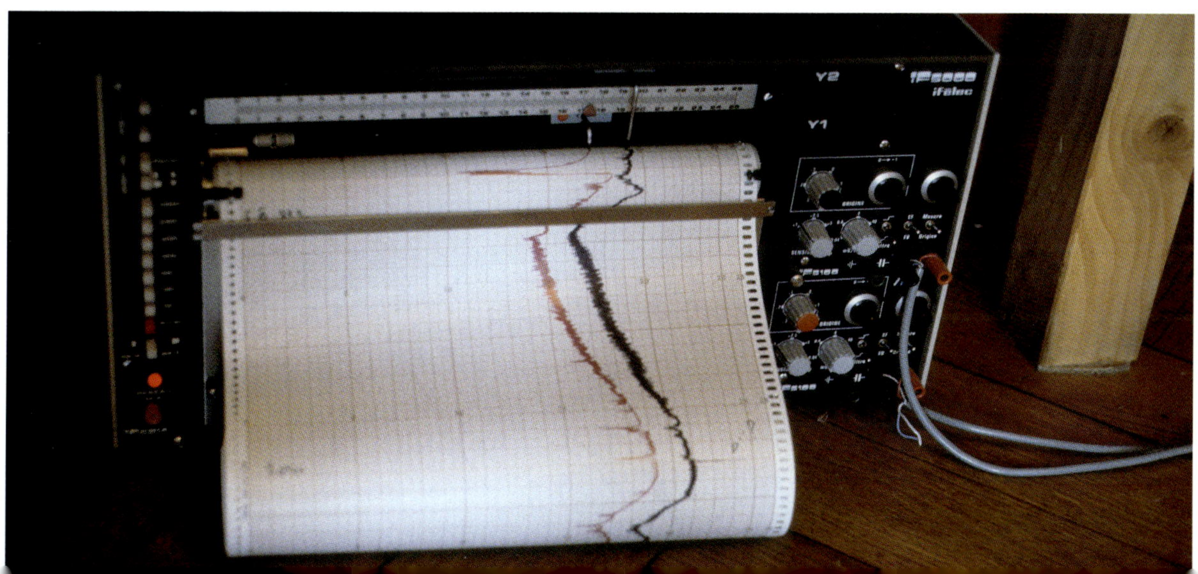

Levitation

A person or heavy object rises from the ground and hovers there. Within the Catholic Church this phenomena is understood as a common manifestation of the charisma granted to saints. Saint Joseph of Copertino, Italy, who lived in the seventeenth century, was famous for such events. What kind of energy concentration makes people able to raise objects off the ground mentally?

Water can float

In the form of ice, water is solid, tangible and visible. When the temperature is increased, the water molecules move faster and the ice melts, becoming a liquid that is still tangible, if not as easy to grasp as the hard ice. By raising the temperature even further, the water turns into a swirling cloud of steam, no longer tangible and barely visible. It is still the same water, yet its qualities differ in its three aggregate states: solid, liquid and gas. When it cools down, it becomes water or ice, but when the molecules are moving their fastest as steam, it blows away. In other words, water is able to move, float in the air and travel over distances. This analogy is not only a way of explaining levitation, but also bilocation in the next chapter.

The dream of flying

In parapsychology, levitation is considered a form of psychokinesis. It is defined as the ability to float in the air without physical support. There are reports of such events from nearly every culture and time period. The Bible states that Jesus could hover above and walk on water, which is why levitation is considered a sign of sainthood in the Catholic Church, an ability that has so far been ascribed to over 230 saints. A few saints, such as Saint Teresa of Avila, mention it in their autobiographical works. Flying is, after all, a continually reccuring motif in dreams, one of the great shared dreams of humanity.

A sleeping beauty levitated by the English magician Adelaide Hermann.

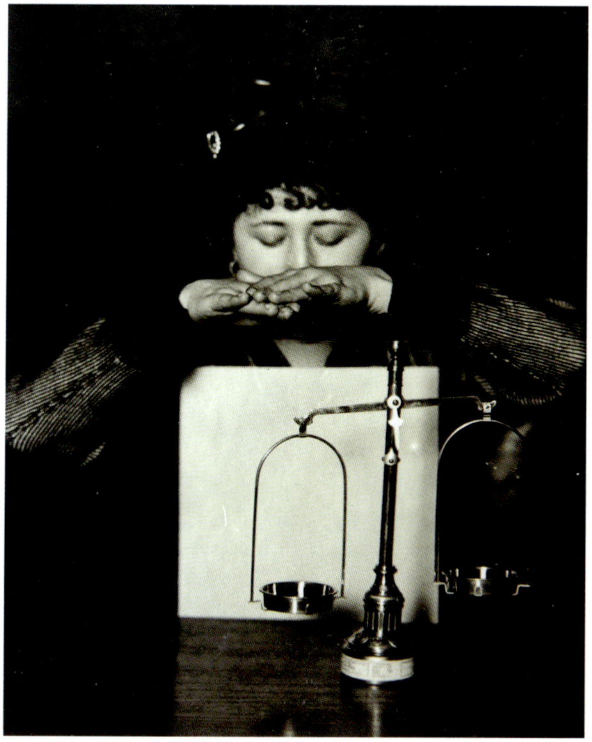

The Polish medium Stanislava Tomczyk was able to influence scales telekinetically.

Jesus' walk on water according to the Gospel of Matthew
"When evening came, he was there alone, but the boat was already a considerable distance from land, buffeted by the waves because the wind was against it. ... When the disciples saw him walking on the sea, they were terrified, saying 'It's a ghost!' And they cried out in fear. But immediately Jesus spoke to them, saying 'Take heart, it is I; have no fear'."
(Matthew 14:23–27)

Yogic flying, a technique of transcendental meditation

New Agers and spiritualists consider yogic flying one of the advanced techniques of transcendental meditation (TM). In the first stage of this advanced meditative practice, people sit with their legs crossed in the lotus position and hop up and down, but in the second stage, after much practice, they levitate. Photos of the second phase show people in the lotus position not touching the ground.

The TM Sidhi program, as transcendental meditators call the practice of hovering, provides its practitioners with improved mind-body harmony. Research has proven its positive effects on mind, body, behaviour and environment. People believe that, through transcendental meditation, a group of 1000 people practicing yogic flying at the same time would be enough to alter the collective consciousness. Interpersonal bonding, harmony and positive thinking would increase; while stress, violence and social tension would be reduced. There are even statistics to back this up, including a 20 per cent reduction in criminal activity, in auto accidents by 25 per cent and in the unemployment rate by 35 per cent.

Flight out the window

In the middle of the nineteenth century, the American Daniel Douglas Home (1833–1866) caused a sensation in European circles with his ability to fly. Important figures like Mark Twain, John Ruskin and William Crookes, President of the Royal Society, were witnesses to his flying demonstrations. In the *Quarterly Journal of Science*, Crookes wrote that he had overcome his own inner conflict between what he could see and touch with his hands and what he described as the irrefutable logic that a man could not fly. He wrote that in London, he had seen Mr. Home fly out of a third storey window and then back inside again through another window.

Saint Teresa of Avila is thought to have had the ability to levitate.

Bilocation

A person appearing in two different places at the same time is called bilocation. Some in the Catholic Church recognize this as another mysterious gift associated with the special charisma of saints, but there are also other people with this particular ability who have succeeded in letting their astral body travel.

Astral travel to two places at once

The astral body is the indestructible body of souls that have ascended to the stars, comprised of miniscule particles. According to Paracelsus, the astral body is a visible source of powerful energy. Meditation and the highest level of mental concentration allow individuals with the requisite abilities to separate the astral body from the physical body and project it, so that they appear in two different places at one time. Parapsychology uses the term "ethereal" to describe everything that takes on a physical form outside the imagination, but cannot be assigned to the material plane. Therefore, the physical manifestations in instances of bilocation are ethereal bodies. Other common designations are "doppelgänger" or "double". There have been individuals, such as English poet and adventurist Lord Byron (1788–1824), who took advantage of both astral projection and the iconography of the occult. To establish his image as the Devil incarnate, he hired doppelgängers to make appearances at the same time in different places in Europe, a trick he claimed to have carried out via astral projection.

Religious examples of simultaneous presence in two places

According to psychologists, the numerous examples of bilocation or multilocation among the religious, such as the bilocation of Padre Pio, indicate that deeply religious people can trigger this phenomenon through their faith. Padre Pio was seen in countless places around the world, saving people from accidents or, as in the case of the Italian general Cadorna, preventing suicides. The fact is that Padre Pio never left his monastery, right up until the day he died. Critics and doubters accuse the Catholic Church of overexaggerated expressions of piety, calling these accounts a deliberate strategy designed to fascinate and attract believers through mysteries.

The phenomenon of astral travel is familiar to many people as an aspect of near-death experiences (see page 188);

During experiments on out-of-body experiences at the Psychological Institute of the University of Cologne, Germany, the Indian yogi Pushpal Behen (right) was examined and the results documented.

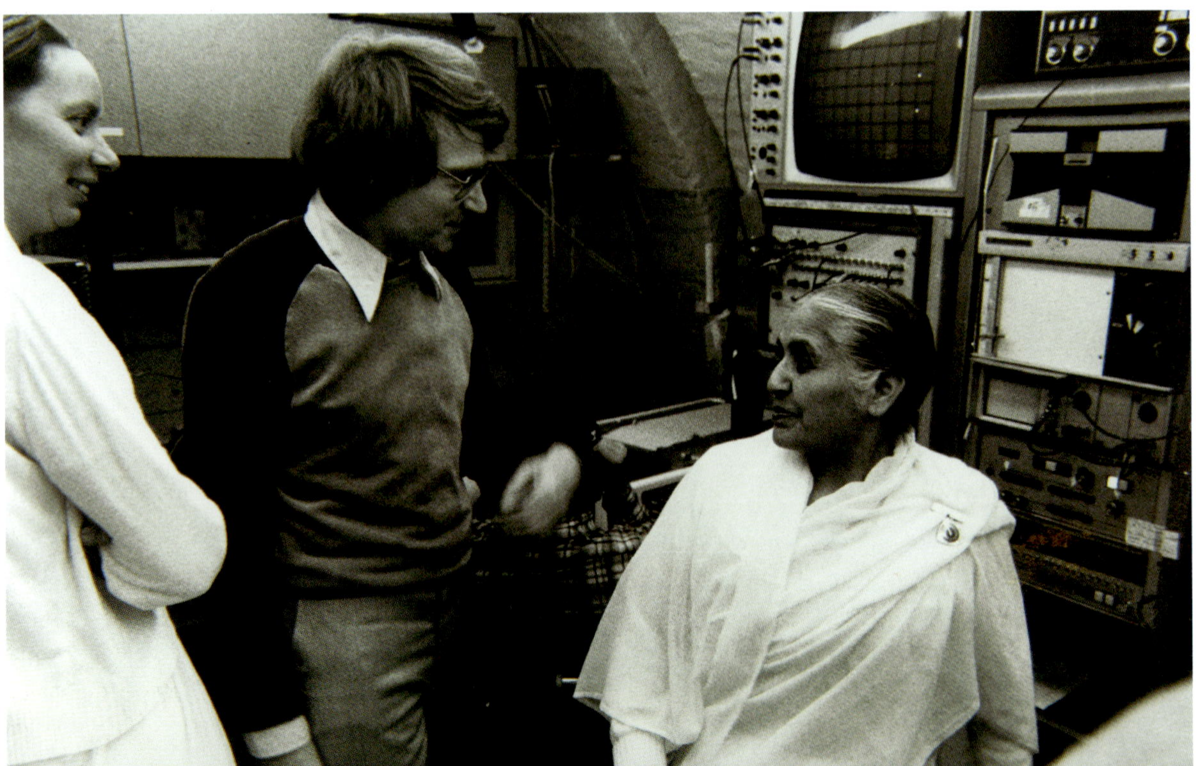

During a phase of astral projection, Behen's electroencephalogram (EEG) shows increased low frequency waves, suggesting a deep state of relaxation as well as heightened attention.

however, parapsychology is the field responsible for proving that bilocation and astral travel are genuine. The Catholic Church has commented that all of a proposed saint's acts are very carefully examined over a long period of time prior to their canonization: witnesses are questioned and accounts corroborated, and only then is a person pronounced a saint. The question remains whether bilocation, which is attributed to so many saints, can thus be considered proven.

An eyewitness report of the bilocation of Padre Pio
One day, a former Italian army officer entered the sacristy and, seeing Padre Pio, said "Yes, he is here. I am in the right place!" He approached Padre Pio and, kneeling in front of him crying, said "Father, thank you for saving me from death." The man told the people present, "I was a captain of the infantry. One day, in a terrible hour in the middle of the battlefield, I saw not far from me a friar, who said "Sir, get away from there!" I approached him, and as soon as I moved a grenade burst in the exact spot where I had been standing just a few seconds before. The grenade ripped a chasm in the ground. I turned around again wanting to find the friar, but he was no longer there." (3) Padre Pio, who was bilocating, had saved his life.

The English poet and adventurer Lord Byron (1788–1824) enjoyed cultivating an image as the incarnation of the Devil.

A séance, as depicted in the silent film *Dr. Mabuse, the Gambler*, directed by Fritz Lang. The members of the séance sit around the table touching the tips of their little fingers to one another in order to close the circle and concentrate the energy in their midst.

Spiritualism

Spiritualism claims it is possible to contact the dead, either through a medium or by invoking the dead person's spirit. Grounded in occult practices, spiritualism enables the spirit world to influence the world of the living. Are there really ghosts? Can the living contact the dead and communicate with them?

A SHORT HISTORY OF SPIRITUALISM AS A MASS MOVEMENT

Modern spiritualism has enjoyed massive popularity since 1848. By moving tables and glasses during séances, mediums laid the foundations of a movement that currently has 4.6 million believers and has achieved the status of a religion in Brazil. In that year, the Frenchman Hippolyte Léon Denizard Rivail, better known under his pseudonym Allan Kardec, compiled a list of questions for mediums and channelers to pose to spirits. He eventually published the results in *The Spirits' Book* and *The Book of Mediums*. Both are still used as manuals of spiritualism today.

Spiritualist circles, societies and magazines also emerged in the United States and England during the nineteenth century, in part due to the work of outstanding mediums like the American Daniel Douglas Home (see page 201). In 1882, the groups united to form the Society for Psychical Research to examine allegedly paranormal phenomena in a scientific and unbiased way. Modern parapsychology has its roots in this movement.

Since World War II, spiritualism has experienced an upswing in Europe and the United States, although people today are looking for a more objective presentation of the hereafter based on scientific research and fact. They are interested in practical solutions rather than romantic ideals and religious dogma. Author and afterlife researcher Hans Geisler thoroughly examined, with scientific accuracy, these questions of eternity, life after death and the meaning of life in his book *Die andere Welt* ("The Other World") in 1962. Focusing on propositions testable by experiment, Geisler estimates that approximately 200 million people worldwide are actively or passively involved in the field of spiritualism.

The techniques of spiritualism

Techniques for invoking the dead vary, and all are successful in their own way. They all permit communication with spirits, and the manner itself is less important, be it through moving tables or glasses, automatic writing, or in spoken form. A séance can even be successful using a tape recording of the medium's voice. If used correctly, all methods lead to the same goal, which is communication with the world of ghosts and spirits. The best results occur when a talented, energetic medium with outstanding abilities is present.

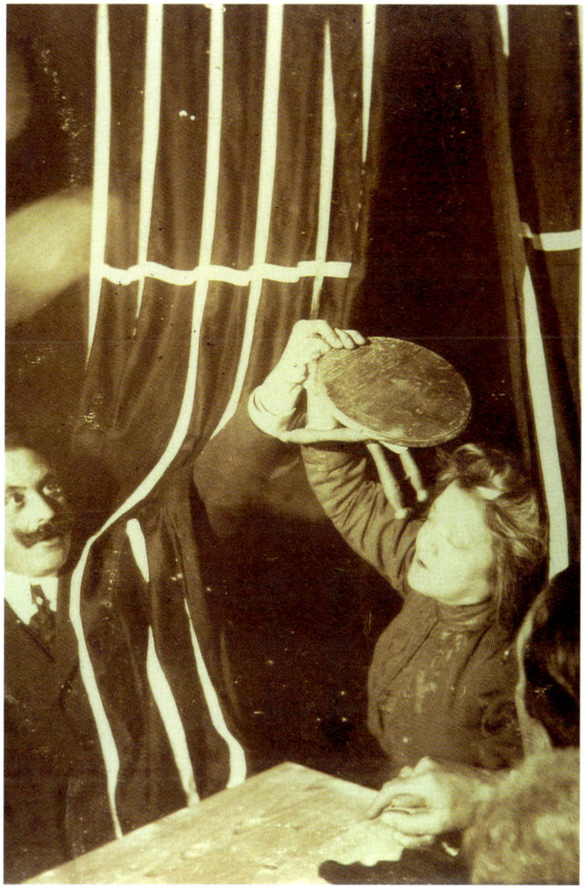

During a spiritualism session with the Italian medium Eusapia Paladino, a small table supposedly moved itself telekinetically, but in this case it is obvious that the medium is holding it in her hand.

A woodcut from the nineteenth century depicts the appearance of a spirit who reveals itself to the members of a spiritualist circle in order to convey information from the other side.

There is also always a question as to the identity of the spirit present; one cannot assume that the spirit that makes contact is always the spirit that was called.

In the early nineteenth century, German physician and author Johann Heinrich Jung-Stilling wrote in his romantic work *Theory of Pneumatology* that the world is full of ghosts, and that they see us as little as we see them. If an unexpected contact occurs, they are as afraid of us as we are of them. If the contact is positive, it can result in an exchange beneficial for both parties, but one cannot always assume that a ghost is well-disposed toward the relationship. Just as there are dangerous people among the living, the same is true in the spirit world. There can be no doubt that contact with the parallel world has its own dangers.

Moving glasses

Moving glasses is the simplest technique for calling spirits and, since it is often successful right away, the one preferred by amateurs. You need a table with a smooth surface, a glass and a piece of paper with the alphabet, the numbers zero to nine, and the words yes and no written on it. The glass is placed upside down on the paper, and the participants each place a finger on the bottom of the glass. After careful concentration, someone calls a spirit. It can be a specific spirit, perhaps a deceased loved one of someone present or another chosen for the session. If contact is made, the glass will begin to move by itself. The participants ask questions that are then answered by the glass's movements over the letters. A problem sometimes arises when, as is often the case, the answers are communicated telepathically to one or more of the participants. One also needs to learn how to tell whether one is actually communicating with a spirit, or whether the thoughts are messages from one's own subconscious.

Ectoplasm

In biology, ectoplasm ("outer plasma") refers to the outer regions of the cytoplasm of a cell. In parapsychology, ectoplasm is the name given to the hypothetical form of dense bioenergy that rises as a grey-white substance like a veil from a medium when contact is initially made with a spirit. Ectoplasm is thought to be an unstable, organic substance that is sensitive to the light emitted from spirits, allowing them to materialize and carry out telekinetic acts. Ectoplasm is invisible to the naked eye, but shows up in photographs. Many scientists, however, consider the otherwise undefinable substance to be manipulated gauze, cheesecloth, or similar material.

The dangers of spiritualism and communicating with the dead

Parapsychologists are very firm in the opinion that there are dangers involved in spiritualism. Too many people approach these activities lacking a positive frame of mind and are blindly unaware of the potential dangers and consequences. Author Johann Edgar describes the dark side of spiritualism under the headings below.

In séances, the participants often form a spirit circle by touching fingers or holding hands to make a linked circle of energy. Ectoplasm appears behind medium Linda Gazzera (centre).

Dependency and blind faith

Contacting the spirit world is often done to help an individual make decisions. This can weaken one's own ability to make choices. In particular, weak-minded people are at risk when they are only willing to make decisions based on spiritualist consultation. Edgar warns against allowing your free will to be too heavily influenced by the parallel world. Not all spirits have good intentions. Some like to play with people who blindly ask them questions, while others have more evil intentions.

Feelings of anxiety

Many laypeople experience feelings of anxiety for a period of time following a séance, especially if the séance was improperly conducted. This is especially true if materializations (visions, or ghostly appearances) occurred. In some cases, the level of anxiety becomes unbearable and requires medical attention.

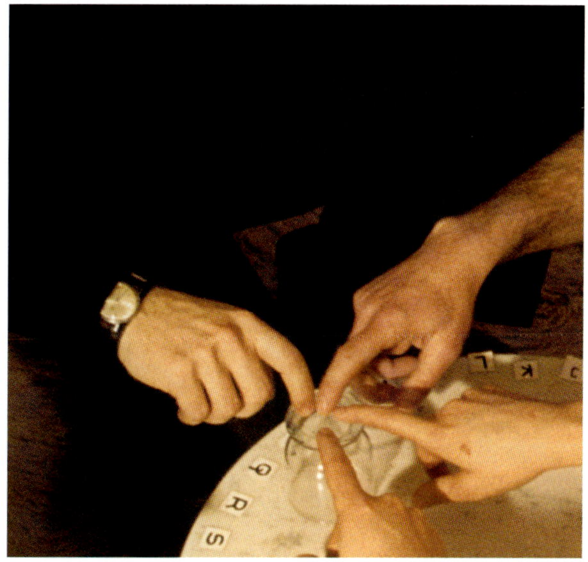

Through the power of a spirit called up during a séance, a glass moves from letter to letter on the table to formulate a message, usually the answer to a question asked by one of the séance participants.

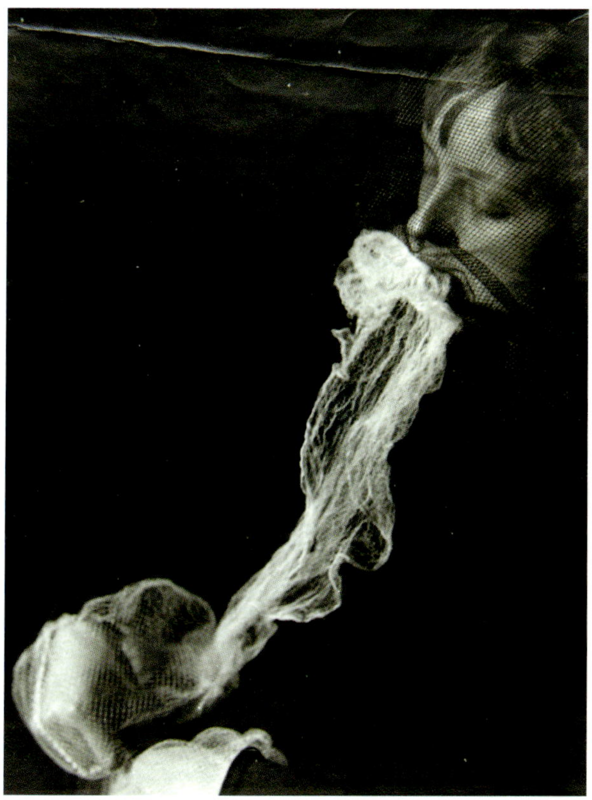

Polish medium Stanslava P. was sewn into a special shirt and wore gauze around her head and hands in order to prevent fraud during a séance, but ectoplasm still appeared to issue from her mouth.

Obsession and possession

Edgar describes obsession as the negative influence of a spirit from the parallel world. The affected person is literally "dispossessed" by spirits, which influence his or her life to the extent that the victim is no longer capable of acting independently. In its most extreme form, this can lead to possession, in which the spirit takes control of a person's body and mind. As with drug addiction, this can lead the person into a deep depression requiring clinical psychotherapeutic treatment, or even end in suicide.

Allan Kardec

Allan Kardec (1804–1869), the pioneer of practical spiritualism, was a student of Johann Heinrich Pestalozzi, becoming a teacher and later a spiritualist researcher. Hundreds of thousands of copies of his books have been sold. His books were especially well-received in Brazil, where a postage stamp featuring his picture was issued in 1957 to honour the 100th anniversary of the first edition of *The Spirits' Book*.

The French physiologist and Nobel Prize winner Charles Richet acknowledged Kardec's importance to spiritualism, saying "Allan Kardec's intellectual energy certainly deserves admiration. He always supports his findings with experiment so that one must recognize his work not just as a grandiose, homogenous theory, but also as an impressive summary of facts." (4)

Diviner King Faria, formerly a cattle rancher, was often hired during the great drought in California to identify the location of underground water for wells on private properties.

Dowsing Pendulums and Divining Rods

There are drawings of divining rods from Roman and Egyptian times. Diviners are said to be capable of locating underground water, gold, coal, bronze, petroleum, minerals, and even hidden treasures using divining rods. That explains why a divining rod is also called a magic rod, because when it actually does help find bronze or gold, the effect is magical.

Finding esoteric energies

A divining rod is a V-shaped twig or branch, usually hazel or willow, but also occasionally made of plastic or metal. The divining rod is held loosely with one hand on each end of the branch, with the pointed end directed away from the diviner's body. This is the end that moves in reaction to the Earth's energy. According to diviners, the perceived energy is esoteric, i.e., not physical energy. Diviners describe what they do as a mental process, rather than simple detection. They say that when they are divining, they are capable of finding any material, essentially "calibrating" themselves according to the task. Diviners believe that every material gives off its own vibration that penetrates everything, and this is what they can feel. Some diviners can also divine disease and illnesses. As natural healers, they can divine

As this etching shows, there are various ways to hold a divining rod.

intolerances to pharmaceuticals or food. Critics assign these activities to the realm of the occult, as with any process that is difficult to analyze scientifically.

The history of the divining rod

In its current form, the divining rod has been used since the sixteenth century. People believe that the branches of certain trees, especially the mistletoe, are endowed with special powers. This belief was derived from an ancient method of foretelling the future by casting a series of sticks on the ground, or from magic wands, which had to be made from special wood. Moses struck the rock with his staff to find water, and the Greek god Hermes had a magic staff decorated with two intertwined snakes (the caduceus) that he used to open the gates to the Underworld. The Teutonic god Wotan was the god of both desire and the staff.

The first accounts of diviners who used branches to locate bronze come from the Middle Ages. The method was considered controversial even then. Hazel branches were cut on the eve of the summer solstice and have been considered particularly well suited to divining ever since. During the seventeenth century, French diviner Jacques Aymar claimed he could detect crimes with his divining rod. Some thought he commanded supernatural powers, while others criticized him heavily.

The Carpenter Effect

The Carpenter Effect, named after British physiologist Walter Benjamin Carpenter (1813–1885), claims that just imagining a movement can trigger it involuntarily, on a small scale. One example is an audience at a sporting event. Spectators unconsciously feel compelled to perform the movement they see or want to see happen. Researchers thus view unconscious movements like this as a function of the power of suggestion. Critics of parapsychology attribute phenomena such as moving glasses, swinging a pendulum, or divining to this effect.

Divining rods were widely used well into the nineteenth century, also by geologists and physicists. Some believe there are special electrical force fields that can result in physical manifestations, and these are triggered in sensitive people by the presence of underground metal or waterways.

Scientists continue to conduct experiments designed to prove the genuine effectiveness of the divining rod or expose it as fraud. Critics consider these experiments to be unreliable, preferring to attribute the rod's deflection to the so-called Carpenter Effect (see box, above).

A diviner attempts to determine which homeopathic medication is best suited for a patient by alternately examining the medications and the patient with a divining rod.

Hypnosis

For a long time, the superstition was widespread that hypnosis, once attributed to magnetism, was a supernatural art. Hypnosis is actually an altered state of consciousness that is induced by a hypnotist. Just how capable is a talented hypnotist of influencing the condition – even the physical condition – of a person? Do certain mental processes occur while under hypnosis? Is a person who has been placed in a trance a submissive plaything? Questions like these contribute to hypnotism's supernatural reputation.

Exerting influence on the mind

Researchers have been studying hypnosis for 200 years. The term itself was coined in the middle of the nineteenth century by Scottish surgeon James Braid (1795–1860). However, the first directed scientific study of the phenomenon of making an individual (the client, as he or she is usually called) receptive to certain influences took place between the years 1950 and 1980. The effects of hypnosis include limited attention and memory, the appearance of certain illusions, responses and feelings, as well as certain physical changes.

The definition of hypnosis from a medical standpoint
The Merck Manual of Medicine defines hypnosis as follows:
"Hypnosis is a process in which the client loses control of certain mental content (memories, illusions, feelings, perceptions) while in a state of diminished consciousness and loss of free will." (5)

Hypnosis has a long tradition. A group of French physicians observe their colleague hypnotizing a patient in this photo, taken in the late nineteenth century.

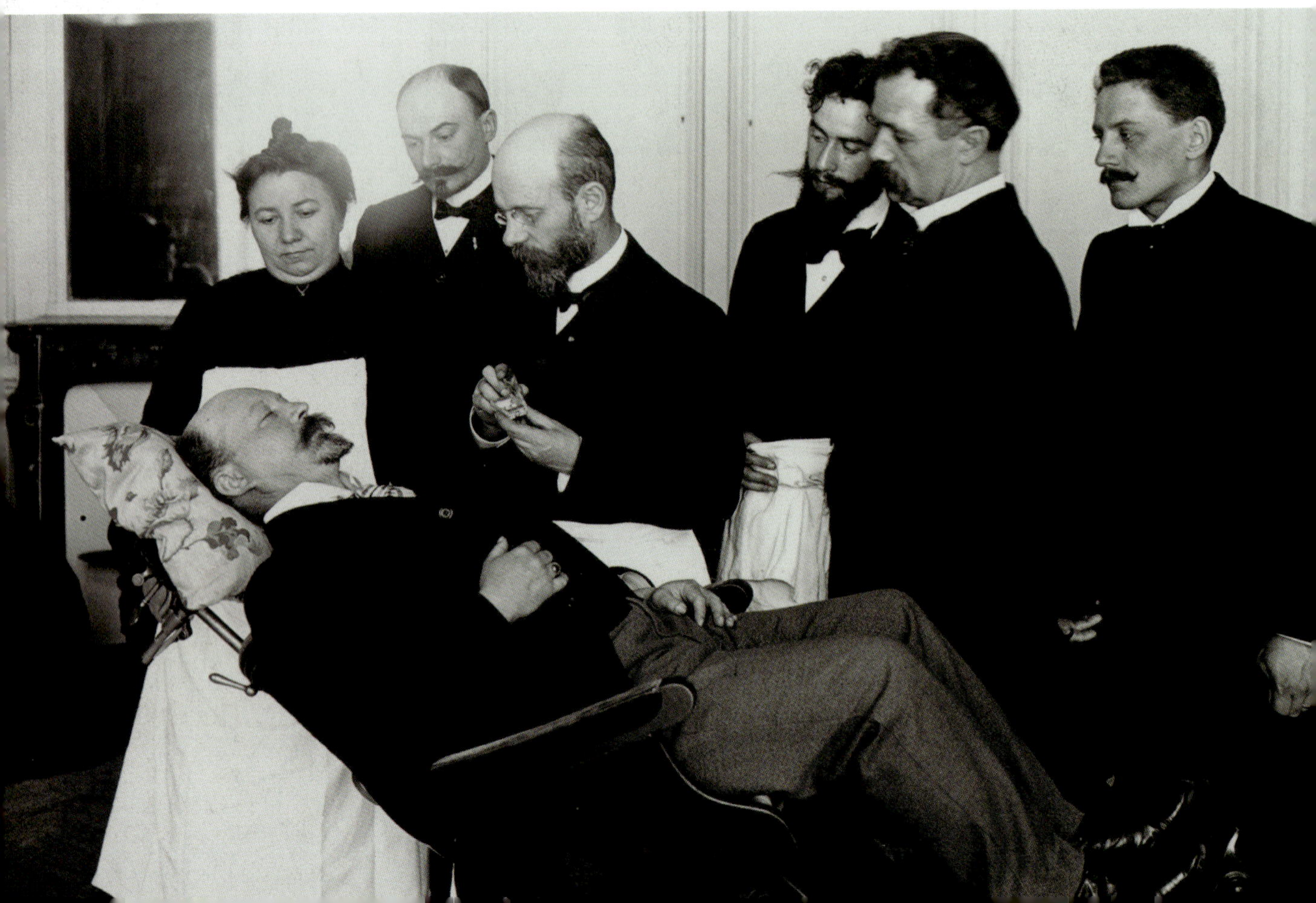

The use of hypnosis as a medical therapy

- To lose weight
- To stop smoking
- To eliminate drug or alcohol dependency
- To relax; to prevent or reduce stress
- To improve concentration
- To cure phobias
- To reduce the fear of flying
- To increase success

Post-hypnotic commands are instructions given to a person while under hypnosis that will be carried out by the subconscious once the person wakes up. In the process, the client believes he or she is acting on their own initiative. It is false to assume that psychic processes are activated during hypnosis. Hypnosis is actually just an extreme form of suggestion (see below).

Since the discovery of the relationship between the nervous and immune systems and their importance for a person's overall health, hypnosis has taken on new significance in the treatment of illnesses and substance dependencies (nicotine, drugs, alcohol). However, classic hypnosis research shows that people respond to hypnosis in different ways, and there are even plenty of people who do not respond to it at all.

Psychologist W. J. Ousby stands on top of the stiff body of one of his hypnotized patients. He often used hypnosis to cure his clients of psychological problems.

Three methods of hypnosis

According to popular prejudices, a hypnotist is a kind of magician who looks deep into a person's eyes and mutters "Sleep, sleep!" That is no longer the case and, if it happens at all, it is in the context of a circus or variety act.

There are various methods employed to achieve a hypnotic state. One of the most common is the fascination method, in which the person to be hypnotized stares at a shiny or reflective object, such as a pendulum. Using the counting method, the hypnotist states, "I am going to count to ten. When I get to ten you will find yourself in a deep sleep." Using the fixation method, the hypnotist stares into the client's eyes and explains that he or she is getting sleepy until their eyes actually close.

All of the methods are similar in that the client is encouraged to relax and show signs of being tired by means of suggestion. It is also suggestion that brings about the hypnotic state by erasing any doubts that might hinder the hypnotic process, because a person cannot be hypnotized if he or she fights it off in the grip of fear. The popular belief that people can be placed in a trance against their will and made to do terrible or embarrassing things is groundless. It is always the clients who place themselves into the hypnotic state. Experts call it "guided self-hypnosis".

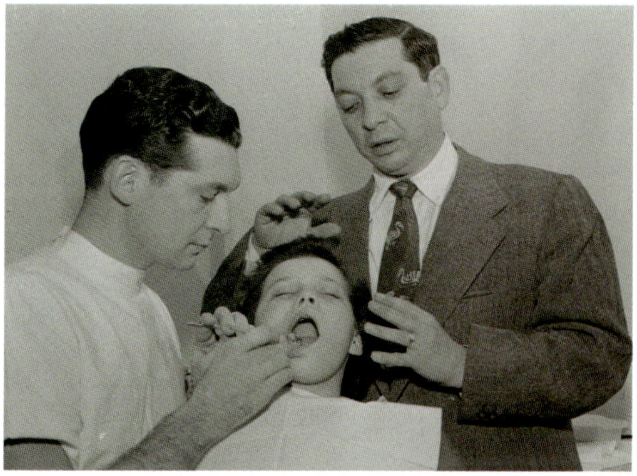

Hypnotist Edwin L. Baron placed Karen Shafer in a trance in Chicago in 1954 so that the dentist, Dr. Arthur M. Krause, could work on her teeth without need for anesthesia.

Thoughtography

There are supposedly people who are capable of projecting pictures, ideas, or feelings onto unexposed film, making them visible using only the power of their thoughts. Do psi phenomena such as thoughtography obey the laws of nature? If so, some of these laws must be considered unexplained even today despite all the accomplishments of science.

Thoughts become reality

Thoughtographs are psychogenic mental projections that are realized by means of extreme concentration, emotional outbursts, or, indeed, a well-developed imagination. A medium visualizes something in their thoughts as an object before them. If the image is that of a person, that individual can contact the medium and, through an exchange of powers, in a sense become real. The solidity of the mental picture depends on the psychological energy being poured into it. Actual thoughts are not depicted, but rather pictures from the imagination, thus making the term thoughtography inaccurate. Nonetheless, thoughtography falls under the heading of psychokinetic phenomena.

An excerpt from Dr. Jule Eisenbud's book *The World of Ted Serios: 'Thoughtographic' Studies of an Extraordinary Mind*:
"It is possible ... that the laws of physics, which I believe are subordinate to psi phenomena, will never be capable of incorporating these kinds of thoughts. Perhaps we will only gain insight into these matters from someone who is capable of reaching a state of mystical consciousness, a person who doesn't insist on looking at them from some abstract, external perspective, but instead can facilitate a clear and direct understanding of psi phenomena, and thus of nature as a whole."

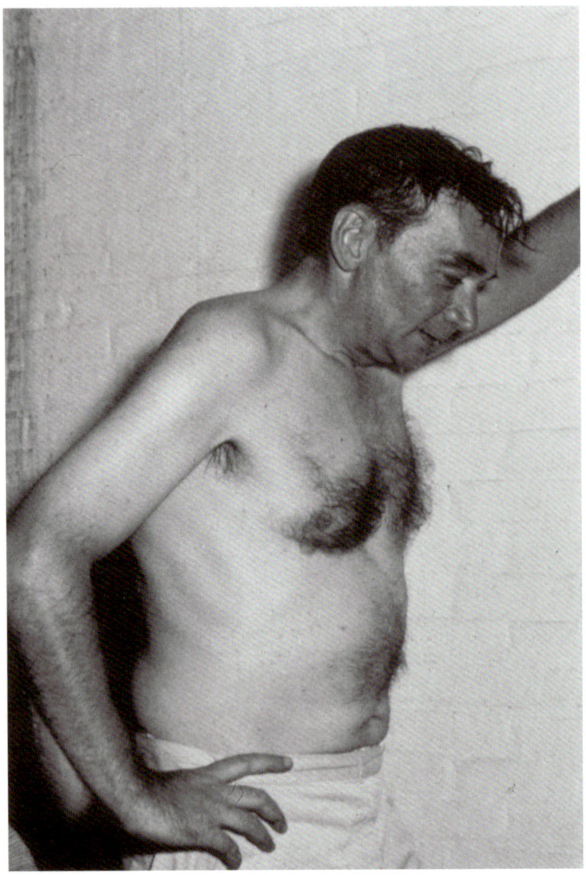

Ted Serios is the most well-known medium for thoughtography.

The spectacular story of Ted Serios

In parapsychological research, psychiatrist and parapsychologist Dr. Jule Eisenbud (1908–1999) is considered the father of thoughtography, or psychophotography. In his 1967 book (see box, above), he describes his spectacular experiments with Ted Serios, a hotel porter from Denver, Colorado, who could make images of his thoughts simply by pointing a camera at his head. Many of the pictures show only his concentrated face, but others were more surprising. They showed famous people or places that Serios focused on so that they could be captured on film.

Dr. Eisenbud and other scientists had Serios medically examined, but the results were inconclusive. His environment and his body were closely studied and monitored in order to investigate any possible fraud, but, once again, the results were not conclusive. The case must therefore be ranked as an authentic parapsychological phenomenon, one of the most astonishing of all psi research.

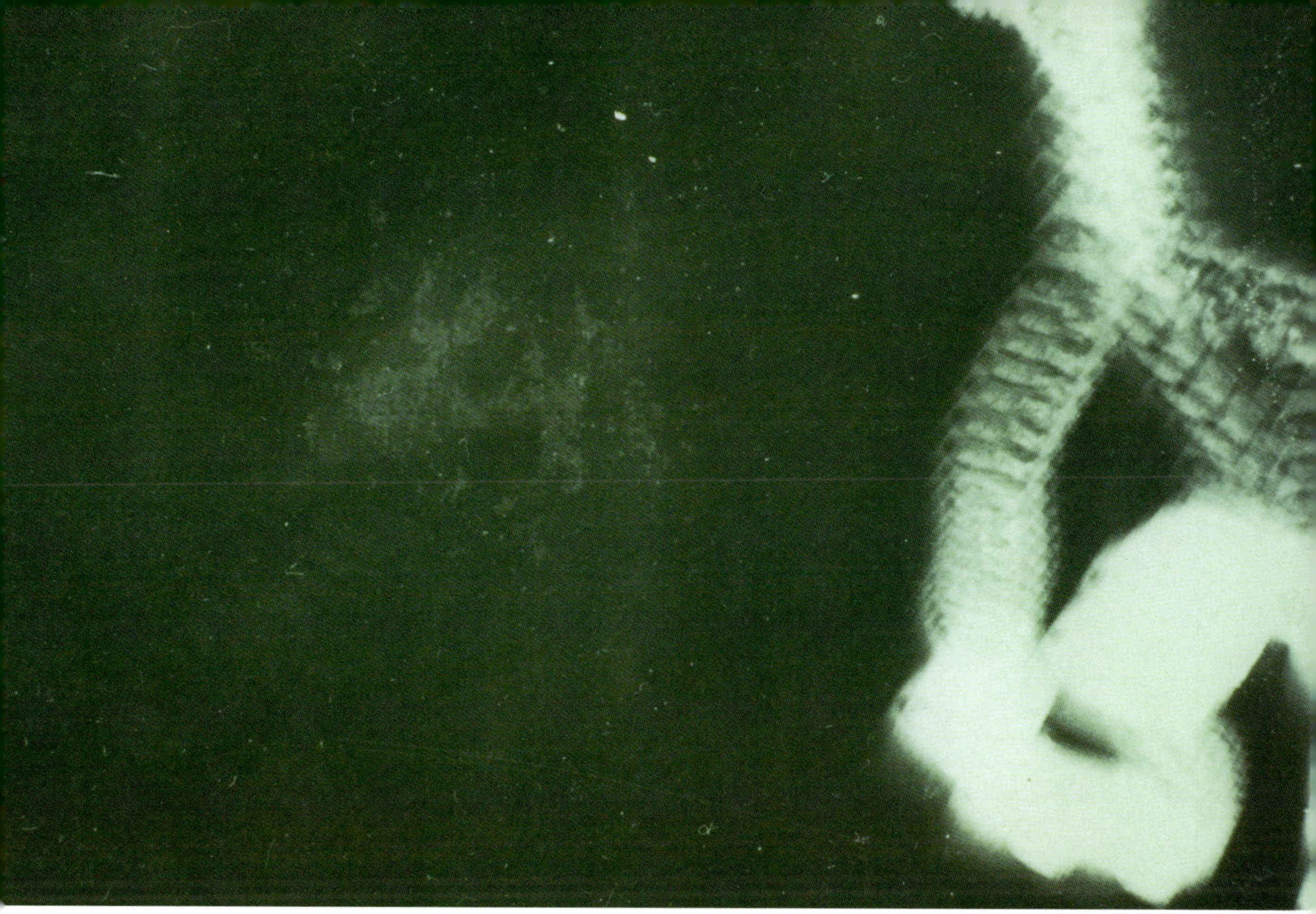

This thoughtograph image by German-American Willi Schwanholz shows a baseball player with a baseball glove.

Buried wisdom from the distant past

The interest in Ted Serios and his abilities can be in part traced back to a general fascination with the paranormal and supernatural during the early 1970s. New religions, mind-expanding drugs and new approaches to life in general characterized the time period. Serios was in this respect only part of a larger cultural phenomenon. In some respects, Eisenbud treated Serios as if he were a wild animal, a beast from the modern jungle of the big city. But he also saw him as someone who had access to long-lost wisdom and skills from a dim and distant past, skills that the modern age had relegated to the realm of superstition and the uncivilized. Serios connected us all to something that, parallel to our own world, lies slumbering inside of us.

Willi Schwanholz (left) during a thoughtography experiment with psychiatrist Jule Eisenbud, who also conducted the majority of the experiments with Ted Serios.

Near-Death Experiences

There are accounts from almost every known culture about what happens at the threshold between life and death. For over 2000 years people have described journeys in which heroes, prophets, kings and sometimes even mere mortals, manage to cross the threshold twice. They die, only to return to the world of the living, carrying a message for humanity.

Plumbing the Depths of the Afterlife

The subject of death appears in all the world's epic poems, myths and religious texts. As depicted, the afterlife is approached in three different ways, the first of which is a descent into the Underworld. In this variety, heroes such as Hercules go down to the Underworld to snatch a dead person from the kingdom of the dead or to retrieve some other form of knowledge. The Eleusian Mysteries, which re-enact a descent and return form Hades, served as an initiation ritual and preview of death in ancient Greece.

The second variety involves an ascent to a higher world accompanied by ecstasy and consecration. The prophet Mohammed set off on a heavenly journey and returned with knowledge of a paradisiacal world still revered today in the Muslim religion. Zarathustra (the priest and prophet), the apostle Paul, Mani (prophet and founder of Manichaeism, an ancient Persian gnostic religion, once widespread but now extinct), or Henoch (the seventh patriarch in the book of Genesis) also return to Earth from above with stories of heavenly splendor. Jesus died on the cross and was resurrected from the dead.

The third variation involves fantastic adventures, such as Homer's *Odyssey*, in which Odysseus descends into Hades, as well as accounts from great sailors, among them Marco Polo (ca. 1254–1324) and Juan Ponce de Léon (ca. 1460–1521), most of which seem to be fairy tales. All these adventurers returned to their familiar world after crossing the threshold, and came back to report unimaginable treasures, enchanted gardens, ghosts, mythical creatures and monsters.

People who have had near-death experiences frequently report that they found themselves in a dark tunnel with a bright light at the end.

In light of the reports of near-death experience, the question arises whether death is really the end. One of humanity's deepest mysteries is what death really represents.

Witnesses of the Afterlife

In modern times there are countless reports of journeys to the hereafter by people who were considered clinically dead for some time, only to be brought back to life. These are not ornate retellings of exotic trips, but serious accounts. The modern visitor to the other side is witness to what takes place in between the worlds of the living and dead.

This kind of report was popularized in the 1970s by Raymond Moody's book *Life After Life*. Since its publication, a flood of books and reports on this subject has dominated the popular culture market. American engineer Tom Sawyer appeared on a TV talk show reporting how he was pinned under a truck for 15 minutes:

"My heart stopped beating ... this darkness took the shape of a tunnel and then I saw an extremely bright light. It was the brightest thing I'd ever seen in my life. The light I am describing is whatever most people would describe as God. That's the description. It meant the same to me as the word God. It was in fact the light of Jesus Christ." (6)

The following report is attributed to Saint Salvius and comes from the sixth century:

"When I died four years ago, I was raised by two angels and carried up to heaven so that I not only had the unhappy Earth under my feet, but also the sun and moon, clouds and stars. I was then led through a gate that glowed brighter than sunlight, and I entered a house in which the floor gleamed like gold and silver. It contained an indescribable light, and its expanse cannot be described." (6)

Both reports are based on the same experience, even though they are separated by fourteen centuries. The correspondence is impressive. The same pattern can be found all over the world, irrespective of age, gender, social position or ethnicity, and as these examples show, in every age. Nearly everyone who has had a near-death experience reports emerging from the body, a tunnel, a bright light, reviewing their life, an encounter with a mystical being, judgment and, finally, the reluctant return to the mortal body.

When one sees what medicine can do today, one reluctantly asks: how many levels does death have?

Jean-Paul Sartre

Charon, the "infernal boatman", rows the damned souls to Hades in his boat in Michelangelo's *Last Judgment*. The fresco was commissioned in 1536 by Pope Paul III and completed in 1541. It is located in the Sistine Chapel in Rome.

Swiss architect Stefan von Jankovich (left) was clinically dead after an accident. After he was reanimated, he remembered many details of a vivid near-death experience, which he later captured in numerous watercolours.

No measurable brain waves

According to a recent study of sixty-three patients who survived cardiac arrest in England, seven of the patients reported a near-death experience. The study provides the best indication to date that life exists after death, says the chief investigator of the study, Dr. Sam Parnia of the University of Southampton. The patients who were brought back to life told of joy, hope, light, warmth and meetings with departed relatives and mystical beings. None of these patients exhibited brain wave activity during this period.

How is it possible to feel without a brain? Some researchers say oxygen and carbon dioxide in the brain are responsible for these experiences. However, Dr. Parnia explains that these seven patients had high concentrations of oxygen, so a lack of oxygen cannot be the reason for the near-death experiences. He said that we can also rule out hallucinations, because the reports are too realistic and detailed. Their brains were not capable of facilitating such clear processes, nor were they able to call up memories.

Is there life after death?

In 1994, test subjects in other experiments were asked to hyperventilate until they lost consciousness. The subjects experienced similar conditions and sensations to those who were clinically dead.

Parnia wonders if all of this proves that there is some kind of life after death. But many more studies need to be carried out to conclusively answer this question. The astonishing correspondence between stories remains a mystery. Is it possible that death is a beginning and not an end? Is there a further form of existence once the physical, worldly life comes to an end?

A British study of patients who survived cardiac arrest, all of whom had no brain wave activity for some period of time, suggests that there may be life after death.

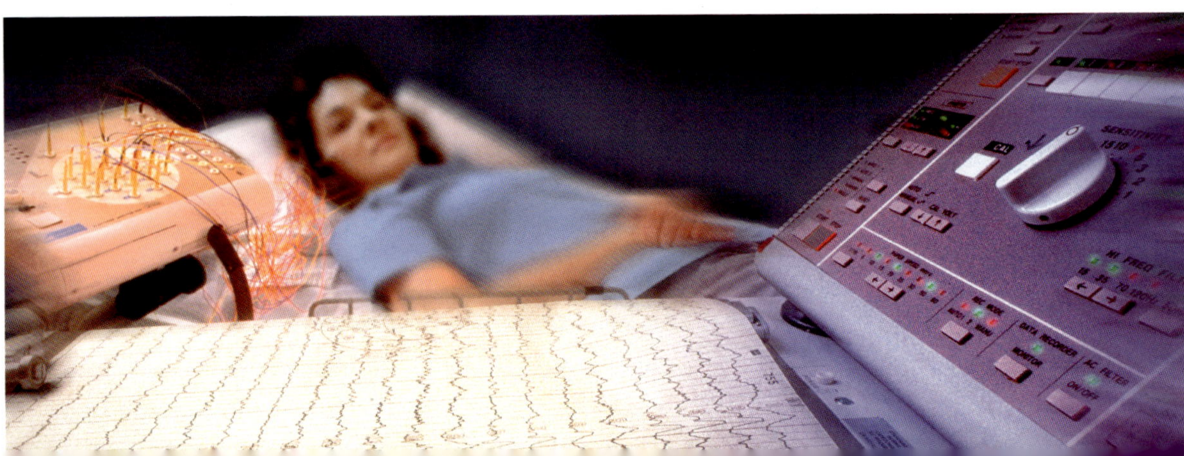

Life after Death

A variety of interdisciplinary studies reveal that in all time periods, in all places, in all cultures and religions, people long to maintain their existence, strive for immortality, and hope to achieve this through religious, ascetic, or ecstatic means. Is the hope for life after death the driving force behind our lives?

Hope for life after death

Human beings are created from the fusion of two cells, from the bare minimum of our genetic inheritance. Everything a person needs to live develops during the first nine months inside the mother's womb before birth. The question of what happens to the energy that represents each individual person after their death has occupied humankind since the beginning of time. While in their mother's wombs, people prepare themselves for life on earth, and during their existence on earth they prepare themselves for life in the hereafter. Everything they need for the afterlife must be acquired during life on this side. These are ideas common to every religion determined by the hope of a life after death,

But it is not only in religion, but also in more general popular belief, that we find the presumption of a life after death. Accounts of the "undead" and places or areas haunted by spirits, who usual appear at midnight, occur in all cultural regions. The Catholic and Anglican Churches fight these phenomena with exorcism (see pp. 180–181), a ritual designed to help the "tortured" souls to find peace. By accepting this ritual, the existence of the undead is recognized as a regular part of Anglican and Roman Catholic church dogma.

The Catholic and Anglican Churches combat the possession of a human being by an incubus, evil spirit, or demon through exorcism, which supposedly helps the "tortured" soul find peace. The picture below is a scene from the film *The Exorcist*.

AN OVERVIEW OF THE BELIEFS OF VARIOUS RELIGIONS

Eastern religions are based on the idea that the world is neverending and is subject to unchangeable laws of being. In contrast, Western religions teach the transitory nature of a world governed by a benevolent God. Despite some variation, Western religions are dominated by the belief that the soul lives forever and will be judged according to its deeds in order to determine if it will spend eternity in Paradise, linger in Purgatory, or be eternally damned.

Hinduism

Karma is the term for a person's destiny or fate, which is itself dependent on an individual's actions during previous incarnations. Belief in the transmigration of souls is also closely related to karma. If people do good things, good things will happen to them. Souls are eternal, but they are manifest in various bodies, which are nothing but temporary exteriors.

Buddhism

Buddhism also believes in reincarnation through the law of karma, i.e., one's subsequent life is based on behaviour in a previous life. However, unlike Hinduism, Buddhism believes that a person can break the otherwise endless rebirth cycle of reincarnation and achieve nirvana, a supreme state of perfect peace, freeing the soul from its journey.

This thangka (a religious art form) depicts the wheel of life. The thangka is a permanent part of Tibet's religious culture. This wheel hangs on the wall of the Tibetan Refugees Self Help Centre in Darjeeling, India.

Universalism

Universalism is an amalgam of Chinese religions sharing a common belief in ancestor veneration. Deceased ancestors participate in the fate of their relatives and help them as protecting spirits. The dead take pleasure in sacrifice and receive money, food and even automobiles from the living, indicating that they continue to exist in a form similar to living human beings.

Detail of Christ's Resurrection in a seventeenth-century fresco by Francesco Figini Pagani.

Judaism

Judaism is based on the written Torah, or Tanakh. Neither the principles of belief nor the existence of God are established dogmatically in the Jewish faith. Unlike Islam or Christianity, Judaism accepts that members of other religions can also share in life after death as long as they have led a moral life.

Christianity

Christianity is based on the Old Testament (Jewish Tanakh) and the teachings of Jesus Christ in the New Testament. Life after death is an integral part of the Christian faith and is considered dogma.

Islam

In principle, Islam shares the same God as Judaism and Christianity and is also built on the Hebrew Bible. The description of Paradise as a place of eternal life is primarily based on the account of Mohammed's journey there.

Past Life Regression

The spiritual experience of past lives can help people discover special abilities and talents in their current life and thereby enable them to better conquer fear. Many recall their reincarnations while hypnotized in an effort to learn something about their life between lives. This knowledge reaffirms the meaning of life, bringing vitality and joy. Those who regress under hypnosis journey back into their own existence without relying on any religious means. Have we lived other lives before our current one, and can we retrieve them?

Past life regression

Past life regression can be achieved using various methods. Hypnosis (see pp. 210–211) is the easiest and most direct method, since it requires no special meditation techniques, which would usually have to be learned first. With hypnosis, people are so relaxed that, in the hands of an experienced helper, regression takes place without any problems. Free of fear, because hypnosis is a pleasant state, people can undertake a journey into their own minds, while mentally alert and inwardly focused. Everything that they have experienced along the journey of their existences can be remembered and retrieved.

Fear of nothingness

As long as the human race exists, we will fear a death that means disappearing into a void without a trace. This fear leads every culture in the world to question the meaning of life. Where do we come from, and where will we go?

It is logically consistent that the wish of a person to continue to exist is one of the central concerns of almost all religions, with rebirth or reincarnation an integral part of the faith.

People who are led back into their past lives through hypnosis report ecstatically about what they discover there. Every researcher who has studied this phenomenon of regression is convinced that we all have stored experiences from previous lives in our subconscious; the problem is only retrieving the experiences again. By recalling past lives, people can understand themselves better, become the master of their existence, learn from the past, and thereby be better able to overcome present and future problems.

Regression into past lives can be conducted using a variety of techniques, including hypnosis.

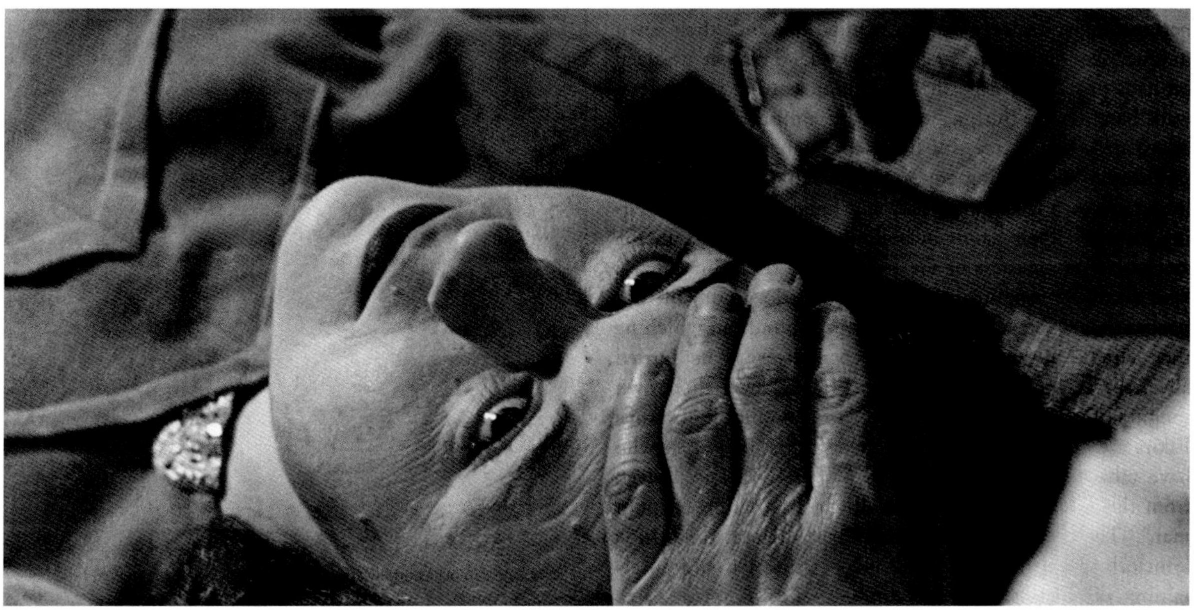

This fakir allowed himself to be buried, remaining in this condition for years.

Fakirs

Fakirs are fascinating, exotic characters who exemplify the mystical culture of ancient India. They are part storyteller, part saint, yet also something like our image of a circus performer. How are genuine fakirs capable of demonstrating such remarkable control of their bodies? Are they con artists, or people endowed with mysterious abilities?

Miracle workers and magicians

Fakirs are considered to be holy men, magicians capable of performing miracles through meditation and their own unique, God-given, supernatural powers. They sit or sleep on beds of nails or glass shards without cutting themselves, walk barefoot on burning coals, and conjure *vibhuti* (holy ashes) or jewels. They run hooks through their backs and pull automobiles using ropes attached to the hooks, ram long nails through their cheeks and tongues without bleeding, immerse their hands in boiling oil, and levitate in the air. Farkirs are masters of the Indian rope trick, in which a fakir throws a rope up into the sky that does not fall, but hangs straight like a pole rooted to the ground, up which he then climbs. Other fakirs allow themselves to be buried alive, surviving for months at time. They sever their own tongues, then restore them, and also conduct exorcisms. Fakirs are Sufi or Hindu ascetic mendicants, holy men who have taken a vow of poverty. The name "fakir" is derived from the Arabic word *faqir* – its literal translation is "poor man". They wander through villages, dressed only in a loincloth, performing miracles, healing the sick and entertaining the masses. This last aspect is the role most often

In India, one can occasionally come across a fakir by the side of the road lying on a bed of thorns.

associated with them in the Western world, where we think of fakirs primarily as variety artists and magicians.

Sai Baba, the fulfillment of all religions

Some fakirs become very famous in India, functioning primarily as holy men. The best known fakir is the inscrutable and mysterious Sai Baba. He was born in 1926 and his life has been characterized by mysterious events. It is said that a poisonous cobra appeared in his crib without harming him, musical instruments in the house began playing by themselves, and jasmine blossoms thrown into the air spelled out his name as they fell to the ground. These were followed in 1963 by his revelation that he is the embodiment of Shiva and Shakti, Indian deities that symbolize the male and female energies, respectively. He is Hindu, and he worships Brahma, the creator. His followers consider him to be an avatar, an incarnation of a higher being equipped with divine power. He demonstrates countless wonders and has even been credited with raising the dead. Sai Baba claims every religion will be fulfilled through him, repeatedly identifying himself with Christ. Sai Baba has avoided all scientific study of his claimed phenomena, leading his critics to dismiss him as a con artist.

Holy man or imposter?

Scientists from the Science and Rationalists' Association of India (SRAI) travelled from village to village pretending to be fakirs. They are so convinced that fakirs are frauds who use sleight of hand, tricks and other dishonest means to convince villagers of their wondrous powers that they, the SRAI scientists, lie down on glass, walk over burning coals, and show everyone how these things can be done without supernatural intervention. Their goal is to expose fakirs, who use the ignorance and superstition of villagers to make money out of them. However, one should keep in mind that many of these miracle workers, who perform at public festivals and markets, are truly religious. How can people separate the wheat from the chaff? Are we dealing with wonders or tricks, miracle workers or imposters? The question has not yet been conclusively answered.

The "human pin cushion", Fakir Yvon Yva, demonstrates his ability to lie on a bed of nails with heavy weights on his chest without being hurt. His assistant can even strike the stone on his chest with a sledgehammer without injuring the fakir.

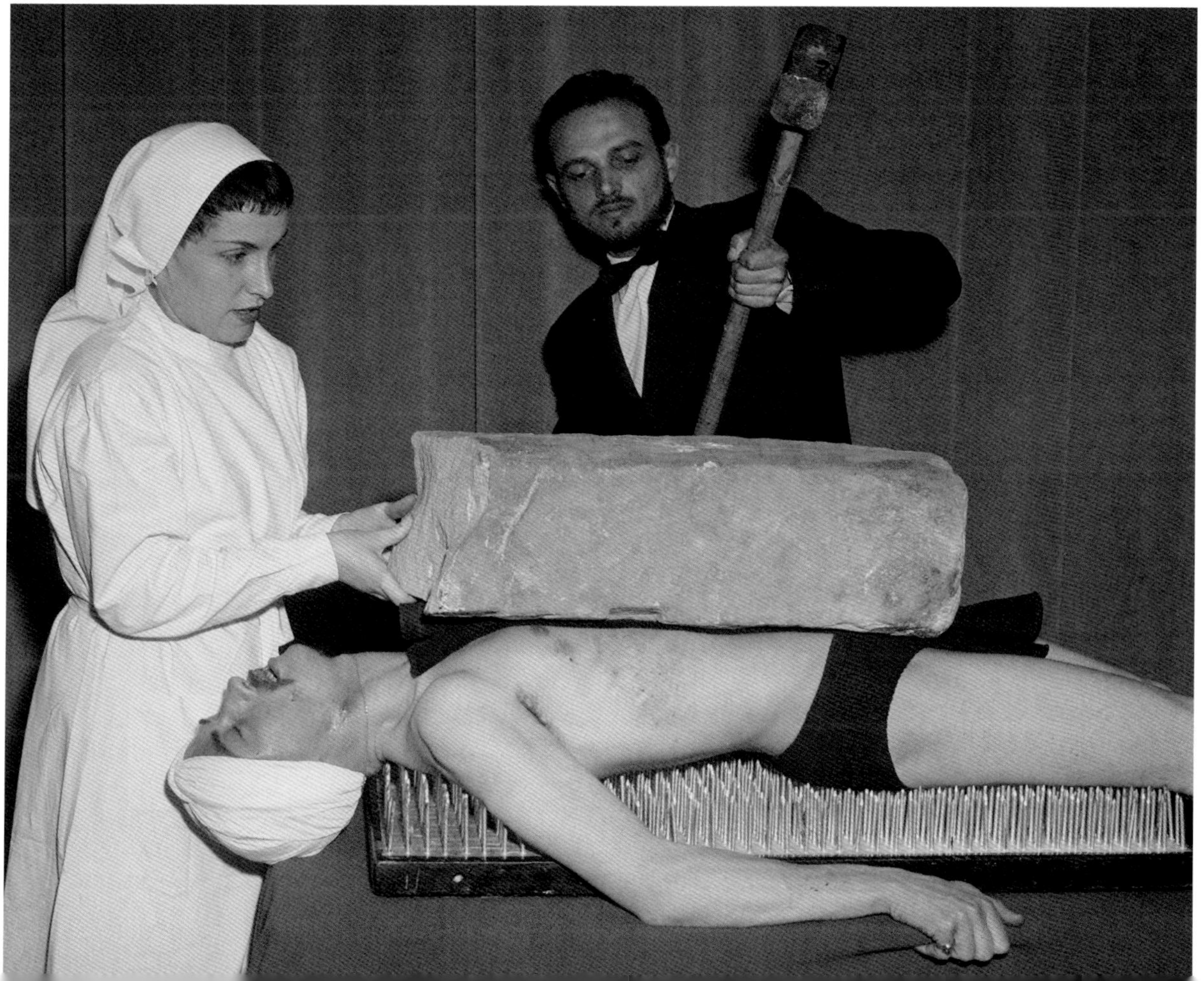

Yogis

Translated from Sanskrit, yogi means "one who practices yoga", a meditating, practicing follower of yoga. For a yogi, immortality as the mystical experience of eternity is a state of consciousness that already exists in this world. What energies are these holy men capable of focusing and releasing, giving them their remarkable inner strength?

Red clothing in honour of the goddess Amba Mata

Yogi Prahlad Jani, a hermit and holy man, lives in a cave near a temple in the West Indian province of Gujarat. The yogi always wears red in honour of the goddess Amba Mata, because, according to him, she was the one who gave him his special abilities. Thanks to a hole in his palate from which liquid streams to feed him, he is able to do completely without food or drink. Prahlad Jani claims he has neither eaten nor drunk anything, neither urinated nor defecated, since 1965. Believers who visit the temple in Gujarat and have known the yogi for many years confirm his claims.

Maharishi Mahesh Yogi next to a picture of his master, Shankaracharya. Maharishi Mahesh Yogi was the spiritual guru for the Beatles.

A life without eating or drinking

Neurologist Sudhir Shah, who has known the 76-year-old Prahlad Jani for many years, was finally able to convince him to admit himself to the hospital in Ahmedabad for observation of his special gift. A team of doctors examined the mysterious man and confirmed the existence of a hole in his palate as well as the flow of liquid, but they have not been able to say what the liquid is.

One of the doctors remarked that the yogi is a challenge for scientists. The thin man with a long, white beard lay on a bed in the hospital for ten days without food or drink, and did not urinate or defecate. The yogi was monitored by a video camera around the clock, but no one found an explanation that could shed light on this mystery. Prahlad Jani is physically fit, and all his medical tests are completely normal. The tests showed that urine does form in Jani's bladder, but it is reabsorbed by the bladder wall, which explains why he does not urinate. In the meantime, the yogi has achieved the status of a holy man. His followers assure everyone that he has never been sick.

Masters of the Diamond Way

A yogi is a practitioner of yoga and, for many, the explanation for the host of mysterious abilities that yogis such as Prahlad Jani possess is that simple. Some yogis are capable of lowering their pulse to the extent that it is barely measurable, bringing them close to clinical death. Others can meditate themselves into a state of suspended animation, while still others specialize in walking over burning coals. The Yoga Sutras, which were written down by Patanjali in the second century BC, prescribe adherence to the Holy Path with Eight Limbs, or steps (see the box, opposite page), which may help make the yogis capable of accomplishing these miracles. Yogis cleanse and transform their bodies through fasting, breathing techniques and almost acrobatic postures. Science, meanwhile, continues to be baffled by the riddle of how yogis, who in Tibetan Buddhism are called Masters of the Diamond Way, are able to achieve these states purely through meditation.

An Indian yogi, using great powers of concentration, is shown here lifting extremely heavy stones with his genitalia.

A yogi in the meditative lotus position.

The Holy Path with Eight Limbs of classical yoga by Patanjali

As set down by Patanjali, the eight steps are the foundation of yoga methods. The path is organized according to progressive steps and the methods that belong to them according to increasing states of awareness.

- Restraint
- Observances
- Posture or physical exercises
- Breath control
- Withdrawal from the senses
- Attention
- Concentration
- Meditation

The Thaipusam Festival

The Thaipusam Festival is one of the most amazing and astonishing Hindu rituals. Young believers, having taken a vow, pierce their cheeks and tongues, attach hooks to their skin, stick sharp objects into their bodies and dance through the streets as if in a trance. Strangely, no blood flows from any of these believers due to the application of holy ashes.

Pain as a gift for Lord Murugan

When the star Pusam is at its highest point during the full moon in the Tamil month of Thai (Jan/Feb), the tenth month of the Hindu calendar, devout Hindus celebrate one of their greatest festivals, one that can be traced back 2000 years. Thaipusam commemorates the birth of the youngest son of the Hindu gods Shiva and Parvathi. Their son is the six-headed lord Murugan, the fulfiller of wishes. Everyone who prays to Murugan and asks for his benevolence takes a vow to offer him their pain along with honey, milk and flowers during the Thaipusam Festival.

The night before the festival, believers gather in the courtyards of Sri Srinivasa Perumal temple in the Indian district of Singapore, where a large and most opulent festival takes place. Accompanied by family and friends, the participants begin their procession for lord Murugan's favour.

Holy men put the faithful in a trance

Fakirs and yogis prepare the pilgrims by piercing their backs and chests with dozens of small hooks. Courage, endurance and insensitivity to pain are the virtues called for here. The participants look within themselves with their eyes almost closed. The young Hindus have fasted and prepared for the preceding six weeks in order to keep their promise to the god. Oranges or limes are hung from many of the hooks that pierce their skin. Then the pilgrims pierce their cheeks, after the holy man has rubbed them with consecrated ashes. Music plays, it is infernally hot, drums and flutes lull the believers until their eyes turn inward and skewers with diameters as great as the thickness of a finger are shoved

Covered with holy ashes, this young woman did not lose a single drop of blood as skewers pierced her cheeks and tongue.

through both of their cheeks. Somehow, not a single drop of blood is shed. The fakir extends the tongue of a young man and pierces it from top to bottom with a small skewer until the skewer crosses the one running through his cheeks. There is no blood. The young believer opens his eyes and straightens the skewers in his face and mouth. He seems to feel no pain. Helpers trickle water in his mouth, which will now remain open until the following morning.

Those who accept the pilgrimage must have courage, endurance and insensitivity to pain. Limes were hung from fish hooks inserted in the back of this devotee.

Adorned with peacock feathers and flowers

Edifices up to 10 feet (3 m) high built of aluminum and adorned with peacock feathers, flowers and pictures of Hindu deities are called *kavadis*. These are often carried or pulled by the devotees with chains and ropes anchored in the skin of their hips, backs, or chests. The structures weigh up to 130 pounds (60 kg). Some attach wooden wagons to the hook in their back as they make their way to another temple. They appear dazed, with a look of joy on their faces. Some of those carrying a *kavadi* begin to dance, spinning barefooted on the street's asphalt. Family members continually dribble water into their open mouths, held open by the crossed skewers. At the entrance of the Sri Thendayuthapani temple, the helpers smash coconuts on the ground as a gift to the god. The pilgrims are then relieved of their painful burdens, which they appear not to have felt. Fakirs are again there to skilfully pull the skewers out of tongues and cheeks and rub the holes with ashes. There are not even any scars. The pilgrims are exhausted, but the procession was a pleasure, not at all agonizing.

During the Thaipusam Festival this man carries the *kavadi* on skewers that pierce his face and body in honour of Murugan.

Some Sampedranos carry another person on their back while they run across the glowing charcoal coals.

Fire Walkers

For thousands of years, people of all cultures have been walking across burning coals to pay homage to the holy element of fire. Fire burns, but it also purifies. Shamans perform fire-walking ceremonies to heal their communities, for example. For all those who walk through fire, the experience becomes a dance with the fire of life itself, in which, mysteriously, no one is hurt.

Fire walking as an initiation ritual

The walk over burning embers is an ongoing ritual of initiation for many cultures. In the field of parapsychology, it is considered a higher path to self-awareness. From the point of view of spiritualists, fire walking seminars offer the opportunity to perform this ancient ritual without injury in order to activate resources, increase concentration, and release stress. Firewalkers can be found all over the world. The best-known firewalkers live in India, Sri Lanka, Fiji, and some southern European countries. In Fiji, they walk on hot stones, rather than on hot coals as in most other places. In Agia Eleni, Greece, people walk over hot coals holding icons of Saint Constantin and Saint Helena in a three-day ritual celebrated at the end of May. Europe's most famous fire walking ritual takes place in the small Spanish village of San Pedro Manrique, in the province of Soria. In Spain, the village is considered to be the "end of the world", with Soria not just adjoining other provinces, but other worlds as well. The custom of fire walking has pagan Celtic roots, rising from the belief that people are invulnerabile on the eve of the summer solstice.

Sampedranos, the fire walkers of San Pedro Manrique

A gigantic bonfire of oak, which, according to tradition, is gathered from the neighbouring village of Sarnago, is lit in front of the chapel of the Virgen de la Peña (the Virgin of Sorrows) at around ten o'clock on the night of the summer solstice. The red-hot coals are arranged into a rectangle. The venue is mysterious. Hundreds of years ago the Madonna appeared here in a whitethorn bush that has never dried out since then, and faith healings have apparently taken place here too, verified by ancient documents. Many of the villagers who walk across the red-hot coals on that night do it because they have taken a vow to run through them for the sake of the Virgin Mary. Barefoot, sometimes carrying another person on their back, they pound through the glowing embers without burning their feet, without pain and without screaming.

Those who walk the coals claim the red-hot coals can radiate up to 1800 °F (1000 °C). How is it possible to run through glowing embers without the least sign of burns, much less walk across them as if it were an everyday stroll?

A man rests after a traditional firewalk in Rukua, on the Fijian island of Beqa. His feet are black from the ashes, but they show no sign of injury.

Scientists who have studied the phenomenon explain it as follows: the glowing coals burn because of their heat and conducting capacities, not due to their absolute temperature. The ash that surrounds the embers is a poor heat conductor. The surface of the coals is also uneven, which keeps the contact area small.

In addition, if a fire walker strides through the coals quickly, contact with the embers is short, less than half a second. Finally, the heat is quickly dissipated by the blood, which is why the feet are not harmed. In total they spend no more than seven seconds on the coals, but the feet must be well-supplied with blood and already warm before making contact. The feet must be dry, too, so that glowing embers cannot adhere to them. Despite all the instructions, recommendations and examinations by sceptics, it remains a mystery how the Sampedranos, as the villagers are called, are able to run through red-hot coals without getting injured.

With determined steps the firewalkers of San Pedro Manrique stamp through the embers on the eve of the summer solstice.

Cryptozoology

The scientifically based search for unknown animals, including those familiar to us primarily from myth and legend, is the subject of cryptozoology. Is the hunt for these creatures, which are known in the most diverse cultures, a serious science, or are the cryptozoologists the last romantic adventurers?

Dr. Bernard Heuvelmans coined the term "cryptozoology" in the 1950s. Cryptozoology is considered a parascience, occupying the realm between serious science and fantasy. The Greek word *kryptos* means "hidden", "unknown" and "secret". In relation to zoology, therefore, cryptozoology is the study of hidden animals.

There are some 1.5 million identified animal species. There are, however, many more that have yet to be discovered. Some scientists estimate a total stock of more than 15 million animal species. Cryptozoology covers the grey area between these two figures, because traditional zoology ignores animals that fall outside any typical classification system. For example, the coelacanth was thought to be extinct until its existence was proven in 1986. Giant squid (also known as kraken) were thought to exist only in sailors' tales until 2005, when a Japanese team photographed a live specimen. For cryptozoologists, the existence of these animals, as well as others like the Komodo dragon and Java rhinoceros, validates the importance of their field.

However, cryptozoology also deals with creatures which do not and could not exist, but whose existence has nevertheless been attested throughout the centuries. Cryptozooloogists are convinced that undiscovered species lie behind these accounts of animals that have been, up to now, filed away as fantastic or mythical.

Ever since humans began to think, strange animals have played an enormous role in our fantasies, enlivening our myths and legends. Sightings of remarkable creatures have always fuelled the imagination. This aquatint shows a sea monster attacking a ship.

Cryptozoologists, the Last Romantics

The search for hidden animals might seem strange at a time when human activity has hastened the rate of species extinction to some hundred or even a thousand times faster than that which would occur under the influence of nature alone. Nearly all of the world's most threatened 794 species can survive only in one place, and the majority of these places are in developing countries, where the rate of extinction is by far the highest. But this is also the primary field of operations for cryptozoologists. In their own way, these scientists are the last romantics, searching for adventure on the final frontier.

Two fields of cryptozoology

Cryptozoology is divided into two subfields, one of which deals with creatures of myths and sagas, like dragons and sirens. Many people still believe that there is a real creature behind every legend, one that either once lived or still lives undetected. The second subfield investigates animals that are either thought to be extinct already or that have yet to be discovered. The animals sought by cryptozoologists, ranging from the Yeti to the chupacabra, are called cryptids. The field has undergone a renaissance during the past few years as nature detectives, working on the borders of conventional zoology, continue to come up with data in support of cryptozoological theories.

Komodo dragons live on the small Indonesian island of Komodo. This reptile, found nowhere else, is the largest in the world, reaching up to 10 feet (3 m) in length.

In 1989, sightings of a panther in southwest Germany, supposedly witnessed by many people, were reported in the press. None of the local zoos were missing any animals. Was this a case of mistaken identity, fuelled by fear, or are there big cats living out of sight in Germany?

THE FOUR KINDS OF CRYPTIDS

The methodology of cryptozoology, although it is still considered a parascience, mirrors that of of zoology. Accordingly, cryptids are subdivided into four groups.

1. Unidentified animals. These deviate from known and identified animals to the extent that they cannot be categorized according to any existing zoological system. Examples include Mothman and Bigfoot.
2. Potentially extinct animals. These are organisms that are considered to be extinct already, like some forms of modern reptiles.
3. Animals that are identical to familiar types, except for one or two exceptional qualities, perhaps due to mutation or parentage that is a mixture of more common animal varieties. Zoological classification is easiest in this case.
4. Known animals found in unusual places, such as the panthers reported in the Odenwald region of southern Germany. It is important to verify that these sightings represent a genuine population, rather than simply an animal that has escaped from captivity.

Confirmation of existence by cryptozoology

The discovery of a few species that were thought to have died out has given cryptozoology a boost, much like the discovery of new species did in earlier times. These discoveries include:

Coelacanth (Latin order *Crossopterygii*) a predatory, bony fish with tassel-like fins. Until discovered alive in 1938, they were known only from fossils. They live at depths of 2500–3500 feet (765–1065 m) and can weigh up to 150 pounds (68 kg). Their body structure resembles that of quadruped vertebrates.

Javan Rhinoceros (Latin *Rhinoceros sondaicus*), a forest-dwelling rhinoceros that once lived throughout Southeast Asia. The remaining population lives in the protected Udjung Kulon Nature Reserve on the island of Java.

Komodo dragon (Latin *Varanus komodensis*), with a length up to 10 feet (3 m) and weighing up to 300 pounds (135 kg), it is the largest living reptile. It was discovered on the Indonesian island of Komodo in 1912.

Bernard Heuvelmans

Bernard Heuvelmans was born in the town of Le Havre in north western France in 1916. He earned his doctorate in zoology in Brussels at the age of 23. In 1938, he began to compile systematic reports and articles on everything that fell under the heading of zoology. His book *On the Track of Unidentified Animals* was published in two volumes in 1955 and translated into over twenty languages. He founded the International Society of Cryptozoology (ISC) in 1982. As a philosopher of science, he never questioned whether cryptozoology is properly a parascience or a pseudoscience. Bernard Heuvelmans, the father of cryptozoology, laid the foundations for the field's modern methodology. He died in August 2001. Today, the Museum of Zoology in Lausanne houses a unique archive of cryptozoological research.

Dragons, Unicorns and Mythical Creatures

Mythical creatures have played a role in human life for centuries. Constellations are named after them, including Pegasus, Hydra, Phoenix and the Centaur. They function as powerful symbols in both religious and secular contexts, and their images have appeared on Western and Asian currencies since antiquity.

Mythical creatures in cryptozoology

Mythical creatures appear in songs, in stories, in medicine and as the subjects of films all over the world. Our ancestors would frequently find oversized or oddly shaped bones that they could not connect to any known creature, human or animal. Later, travellers brought home animal remains that also could not be identified. This led to the creation of legends and mythologies involving mysterious beasts. An enormous mammoth bone dating to the Pleistocene era would be transformed into the bone of a giant. The most modern approach to dealing with such inexplicable finds is cryptozoology. Many researchers think mysterious beasts should be studied under the banner of cryptozoology rather than being dismissed as merely legendary, mythical creatures.

The dragon

The dragon is probably the best-known mythical creature. Steeped in symbolic meaning, it appears in all cultures in the form of fairy tales and legends, including stories in the Bible, and is especially prominent in Chinese mythology. Dragons breathe fire and are close to invincible. In some cultures they are a bane to humanity, but in others are bringers of good luck.

Dragons appear in all cultures, at all times throughout human history. They have surprisingly similar characteristics in all of them. This sculpture of a dragon keeps watch on a bridge in Ljubljana, Slovenia.

Saint George slaying the dragon, which represents the heathen that must be brought low and conquered. Places where dragons were slain were declared holy sites because they mark areas where Christianity had triumphed.

A fantastical creature

In a zoological sense, the dragon is not an animal, but a creature that incorporates different parts of snakes, lizards, birds, bats and lions. Often dragons were guardians of some kind of treasure, and anyone who managed to kill a dragon won the princess or some other special prize. A dragon could be a good creature or an evil one, depending on the culture. In Christianity, it is considered a form of the devil, an incarnation of evil, an enemy of God and humanity. In Asia however, especially in Chinese culture, the dragon brings good luck and wisdom and is the personification of masculinity.

The dragon in world mythologies

Well into the sixteenth century, most people believed that dragons genuinely existed. Swiss natural scientist and humanist Konrad Gesner (1516–1565) differentiated three types of dragons in his six-volume work on the animal world. One type was like a gigantic snake without wings, another resembled a winged snake, and a third creature had a snake's body, membranous wings, a horned head and armored claws.

But dragons appear in all cultures. After the death of Osiris in Egypt, the gods Nephtys and Isis transformed themselves into dragons, hovering over the embalmed body until it was buried. In Greek mythology, Ladon is a dragon with 100 heads guarding the gold apple tree in the garden of Hesperides. The father of the Greek gods, Zeus, put the dragon Typhon under Mount Etna, where bursts of his foul, fiery breath cause the earth to tremble. Apollo took control of the Oracle of Delphi by fighting off the dragon Python. Jason, the hero of Greek legend and leader of the Argonauts, sowed dragon teeth that sprouted into invincible giants in the field of King Aeetes near Colchis. The Golden Fleece, the goal of Jason's quest, was guarded by a dragon who wound himself around the oak in which the fleece hung. Cadmus, the founder of Thebes, was another hero who sowed dragon teeth and harvested monsters. Medea, a female archetype in the plays of Euripides, flees Corinth in a wagon pulled by two winged dragons.

In Christian legends, Saint Martha overcame the dragon Tarasconus in southern France, much like the better-known Saint George. The Germans have the dragon Niddhogg, who sits at the foot of the ash tree, Yggdasil. A squirrel carries messages down to him from the eagle sitting in its uppermost branches. Fafner is the dragon that Siegfried kills in order to bathe in his blood and become invincible.

In contrast to dragons in the West, the Asian dragon is charitable and brings luck. It lives in rain clouds, lakes and springs. In China, the emperor sat on a dragon throne as a sign of his power.

Why all dragons look alike

Cryptozoology asks how it is possible that all cultures have a creature endowed with the same attributes and sharing a nearly identical appearance. One theory says that dragons were dinosaurs that were able to survive longer than others of its kind because they learned to fly. Humans were already in existence before it died out altogether, leaving behind a common image to be passed down through different cultures. Another – highly adventurous – theory is that dragons were UFOs once seen by people all over the world. This, too, would explain why dragons everywhere look alike.

There are even dragons in the German Nibelungen sagas. The warrior Siegfried kills the dragon Fafner and bathes in its blood in order to become invincible.

The unicorn is a horse with a horn on its head – a mythical creature that appears in a number of cultures. Christians see it is a symbol of purity and therefore of Christ.

The unicorn

The unicorn is a mythical creature with a horse's body and a single, elegant horn on its head. Saint Ambrosius said it was a symbol of Christ. The horn has been ascribed magical qualities in a wide range of cultures throughout the ages. Amulets made from unicorn horns play a role in folk medicine and superstition.

The life of a unicorn

At birth, a unicorn has a very small horn or none at all, but will grow one throughout its lifetime. A broken horn takes ten years to grow back. At some point, the young unicorn leaves the forest of its mother and looks for its own forest to inhabit. Some sources say unicorns live a very long time, while others say they live forever. Unicorns are afraid of people, who hunt them for their horns, and will only show themselves to those who believe in them. Anyone who does not simply sees a horse. Only a virgin can soften the unicorn's wild nature. It is said that they will readily appear to virgins, and that if such a woman sits at the edge of the forest a unicorn will lay its head in her lap and fall sleep. Often this trust is used to capture the animal. A maiden waits for the creature, summoning the hunters once it has fallen asleep.

The horn of a unicorn or narwhal

The tusk of a male narwhal can grow to be up to 10 feet (3 m) long. People have long questioned the purpose of this sword-like tooth. The length of the horn supposedly determines the pecking order of the creatures within the pod, or group. The narwhals use it to bore through layers of ice, dig up the ocean floor and to spear fish. We have also learned that it is a sensory organ with 10 million nerve endings capable of testing water temperature, pressure and salinity.

The legend of the unicorn

Our ancestors often found bones that were oversized or oddly shaped and therefore difficult to identify as belonging to any animal they were familiar with. This must be how the legend of the unicorn began. Powdered unicorn horns were ascribed miraculous healing powers. Our forefathers must have often found objects on the beach that, while resembling the popular image of a unicorn horn, was probably a washed up tusk from a male narwhal (see box, left). A few cryptozoologists believe that *Procamptoceras brivatense*, an equid that died out a million years ago, is the true ancestor of the unicorn. This ancient beast was a kind of antelope with two horns so close to one another that they could easily be mistaken for single horn.

Sprung from the body of Medusa and tamed by the Greek mythical hero Bellerophon, Pegasus is a poetic symbol.

Other mythical creatures

Pegasus

The winged, magical horse of Greek mythology was born of Medusa when Perseus cut off her head (its father was Poseidon, god of the seas). It was later tamed by the hero Bellerophon. Pegasus symbolizes poetic fantasy.

Hydra

In Greek myths, the Lernaean Hydra is a nine-headed sea monster killed by the hero Heracles, who, as he chopped off each head, seared the neck stumps to prevent a new one from growing back.

With the torso of a human and the body of a horse, the centaur is usually a lecherous, wild creature in Greek mythology.

Centaur

A mythical quadruped with a human torso atop the body of a horse, this lustful, wild creature lived in the mountains of Arcadia and Thessaly.

Sirens

Sirens are demons of death, visualized in Greek mythology as women with the bodies of birds. In Homer's *Odyssey* they appear as sea demons living on an island, where they lure sailors to their death with their song. In later myths they are envisioned as half woman, half fish, and became symbols of immortality. Columbus sailed near the Antilles because he wanted to see the sirens that had been sighted there. The British Museum in London exhibited a specimen in the eighteenth century, supposedly captured in Japanese waters.

Cerberus

Greek mythology's hound of Hell has three heads and a snake's tail. He allows people to enter Hades, but does not let them out again.

Nessie

When we talk about Nessie, we are speaking about the unchallenged queen of the cryptids. She has sparked myth and legend in the Scottish Highlands for over 1500 years. In the last century, she became famous well beyond the shores of Loch Ness, and scores of people set off in search of her.

The Loch Ness monster

If there were such a thing as a list of the most sought-after creatures of cryptozoology, Nessie, the monster thought to inhabit Loch Ness in Scotland, would have to be at the top. Nessie is usually described as looking like a plesiosaur, a marine reptile thought to have become extinct in the Mesozoic era. Loch Ness, the lake in which Nessie is said to live, is about 1 mile (2 km) wide, 23 miles (37 km) long, and up to 750 feet (230 m) deep. The surface temperature hovers between 40 and 55 °F (5–12 °C) in the summertime. The bottom of the lake is muddy, making the water cloudy and hindering investigation of any life forms that may live in its depths.

The first reference to this "monster" is found in a biography of Saint Columba written by Abbot Adamnan in 565.

Columba, an Irish monk, was assigned the task of converting Scottish heathens. Once, from the shore of Loch Ness, he and his followers saw a man being devoured by a monster, which then tried to attack one of them. The saint held off this "devil" with a cross, making the monster retreat to the depths of the loch. Since then, Nessie has been a constant presence in the mythology of the Scottish highlands.

Loch Ness is an elongated, relatively narrow and quite deep lake that lies in northern Scotland. It is thought to be the place where the legendary creature Nessie lives.

Next to the Yeti, Nessie is probably the most famous cryptozoological creature in the world. Her existence is still uncertain. This picture from 1934 that was said to show the beast was later exposed as a fraud.

Nessie, a magnet for tourists

The modern history of the lake monster begins in 1933, after the construction of a road along the loch. Mr. and Mrs. John MacKay were among the first to see the creature from a distance of about 500 yards. They thought Nessie looked like a whale. Fifty additional sightings followed that same year, one of them even occuring on land. A couple from London related seeing a long-necked, dragon-like creature about 26 feet (8 m) long holding a lamb in its mouth. Some of the sightings lasted up to ten minutes, and some witnesses claimed they had seen the creature up to eighteen times.

Since then, there have been countless sighting and photos, most of which have proved to be something other than a lake monster: drifting branches, the wake of a fishing boat, whirlpools, a large salmon, or a sea lion. Modern technology, including sonar and underwater photography, have, after many expeditions, produced very little results. Even the underwater caves where Nessie is supposed to be hiding have yet to be located. Sonar equipment repeatedly recorded large underwater objects, but no corresponding photographs were ever produced. Whatever was down there had either quickly disappeared or dissolved into pieces.

The literature on Nessie fills libraries. Many authors consider the creature to be an unusual fish, while others, particularly the sceptics, think the legend of Nessie is kept alive as a tourist attraction. Still others think Nessie may be the last in an evolutionary line. There are flora and other fauna in the lake that go back as far as the last Ice Age.

The latest phase of the search for Nessie has the loch under observation via Internet camera around the clock.

On an expedition in 1976, a diver holds an ultraviolet light in the muddy depths of Loch Ness. The surface temperature does not reach more than 55 °F (12 °C) even in summer.

Other Water Creatures and Sea Monsters

Nessie is not the only purported water monster, and Loch Ness is not the only body of water said to contain unusual life forms in addition to the known fish populations. Sightings have been reported for centuries in three Canadian lakes and, over just as many years, accounts of sea serpents ranging from Massachusetts to Tasmania have also been common. Many of the descriptions of these creatures resemble the monosaur, otherwise known as the ichthyosaur, considered to be long extinct. The last monosaur presumably lived during the final phase of the Tertiary period some three to five million years ago. Could these creatures have remained hidden in the depths of oceans, only to surface occasionally today?

Manipogo

Around Lake Manitoba in the Canadian province of the same name, people believe in the existence of Manipogo, a snake-like, humped, dark brownish black sea monster. Its estimated length ranges between 12 and 50 feet (3.5–12 m). In 1962, two fishermen managed to photograph it, but the quality of the image was terrible – it could just as easily show a drifting branch – and thus is not accepted as proof.

Igopogo

North of Toronto, Canada, many people believe that Igopogo, also known as Kempenfelt Kelly, lives in Lake Simcoe. It is said to have a long neck and a dog-like head. All descriptions of the beast are in agreement, supporting the theory that an unidentified creature really does inhabit the lake. In 1970, John Kirk, president of the British Columbia Scientific Cryptozoology Club, organized a search for it, which was unsuccessful. Amateur video recordings show a dark shadow, after which a head surfaces, looks around for a few seconds, and then goes under again. Kirk categorizes the creature as a seal or sea lion.

Additional water creatures in various countries and regions

- Cardborosaurus, or "Caddy" (Vancouver Island, British Columbia, Canada)
- Piast, Peiste, Paystha, Ollphiast, Ullfish (Ireland)
- Morgawr (Cornwall und Wales, England)
- Chessie (Chesapeake Bay, Maryland)
- Rocky (Rock Lake, Wisconsin)

In 1550, Sebastian Munster drew many sea monsters based on accounts of the explorers who had returned to Europe from the other side of the Earth.

Ogopogo

In Lake Okanagan in Canadian British Columbia, there is a beast by the name of Ogopogo. Long before white men arrived, the indigenous peoples had believed that a mythical creature lived in the lake, which is why they always carried a few live chickens when crossing it. There is no proof of this sea monster, although the first recorded sighting took place in 1937. It is said to have been nearly 30 feet (9 m) long. In 1986, six humps were seen rising up out of the water. Those present at the time guessed that the creature was about 50 to 60 feet (15–18 m) long. Experts think it was probably a reptile or a whale.

Basilosaurus, or sea snake

A few cryptozoologists assign these creatures to the same order as the extinct *Basilosaurus*, the earliest whales. But because the lakes freeze in the winter, a mammal would be

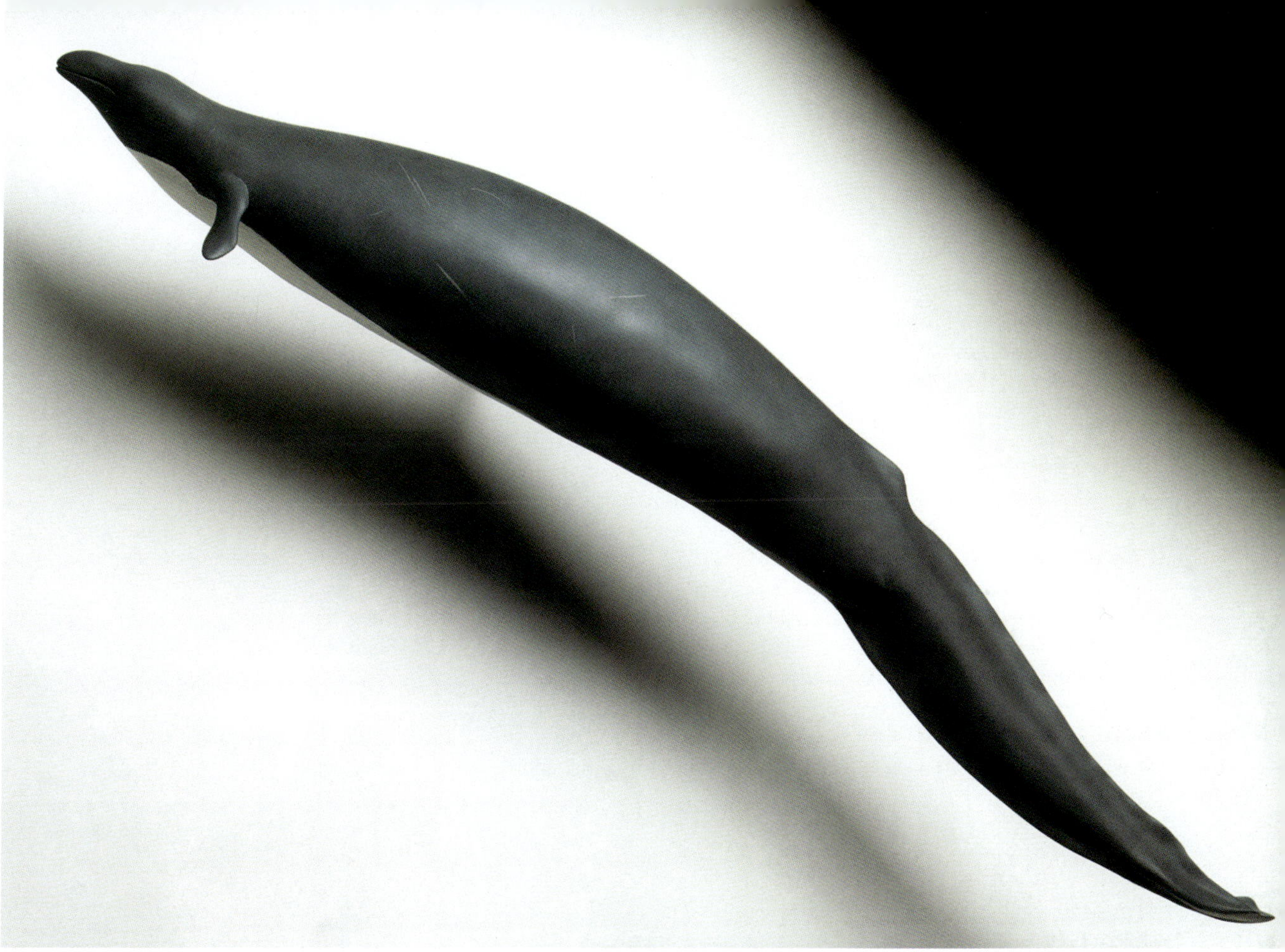

This model of a predecessor of modern whales, the *Basilosaurus*, which reached a length of up to 80 feet (25 m), was made in 1993.

unable to get to the surface to breathe. Besides, a *Basilosaurus* could reach a length of up to 80 feet (25 m), making it highly unlikely that it could simply disappear into an ice-free river during the winter. Other cryptologists believe they are dealing with a large sea snake, which could both live under ice and swim through rivers undetected.

Zoologists say the sightings only prove that seals occasionally find their way from the ocean into inland lakes, and that all of these sightings are in fact seals. After analyzing 587 reported sightings, Bernard Heuvelmans summarized the data set: "sea snakes with a typical long neck and a cigar-shaped body, four legs, webbing and quick movements; a rarely observed marine saurian that looks like a crocodile and lives in tropical waters; seahorses; multi-limbed super-otters; fins; super-eels; and varieties of turtles and yellow-bellied reptiles." (7)

With a diameter of 100 yards (90 m), Lighthouse Reef, or the Great Blue Hole, as inhabitants of Belize (in Central America) call it, is another place said to harbour sea monsters in its underwater caves and shoals.

Bigfoot

There have been sightings of exceptionally tall creatures with enormous feet (hence the name Bigfoot) and a thick covering of hair on their bodies in remote areas of the United States and Canada – in the Rocky Mountains and the Appalachians – from the earliest times onward. Are we dealing with ape men, human-like apes, or as the latest theory proposes, aliens?

Bigfoot: extinct creature or legend?

Bigfoot, or in Native American languages, the *Sasquatch*, like the Yeti, is considered by some cryptozoologists to be a survivor of the extinct Gigantopithecus. Zoologists, on the other hand, consider it to be a purely legendary creature. Increasingly, scientists and lay people alike are nevertheless on the lookout for Bigfoot.

An early encounter with Bigfoot was described in a newspaper article in 1818. Since then, there have been numerous sightings of the creature. The descriptions are always the same. Bigfoot is up to 8 feet (2.5 m) tall, stands upright and is covered in thick reddish-brown hair. Its piercing red eyes are close-set and can put people into a trance. It has a large, massive head set directly on its shoulders, makes whining noises and gives off a foul, musty odour.

The DNA of an ape

Time and again, Bigfoot tracks are discovered – and then dismissed as forgeries. Cryptozoologists maintain that one can discern the genuine from forgeries by looking for evidence of the weight shift that takes place when a living creature takes a step, which should lead to differences in

In 1981, C. Thomas Biscardi, a cryptozoologist from California, was able to capture a fleeing Bigfoot on film. Will anyone ever succeed in proving the existence of this creature that has been seen so many times?

An upright grizzly bear, which can reach a height of over 7 feet (2 m), is often mistaken for Bigfoot.

depth throughout the imprint, differences which cannot be credibly replicated using wooden or rubber feet.

In addition to the foot and body prints left by this human ape, hair and excrement have been found, also supposedly from this creature. Test results show that the DNA from these samples is comparable with that of a primate.

Sightings of Bigfoot often turn out to be grizzly bears, which also can move about on their hind legs and have a human-like physique.

Firing away at a phantom

There are sound and video recordings of Bigfoot, but as is often the case, there are strongly opposing points of view on the issue. Cryptozoologists believe in the authenticity of the Patterson/Gimlin film, for example. This was shot in 1967 by Roger Patterson while Gimlin stood beside him. Its advocates say the film does indeed show a female Bigfoot crossing a river. Sceptics, on the other hand, including Heuvelmans, believe the film to be a fake. Upon closer examination, say the film's supporters, one can see that the creature has a torn muscle beneath its fur on the right leg. They maintain that no one would have thought to add that kind of detail while filming.

The German author Roland Horn entitled his chapter on Bigfoot *Feuer frei auf ein Phantom* ("Firing Away at a Phantom"). It is interesting how often those who want to see Bigfoot take a gun and shoot at the creature, although it has never posed a threat. Also noteworthy is that no one has ever found a dead Bigfoot, although in some cases people claim to have unloaded entire gun magazines into the creature. Either the cadaver fell into a crevice and could not be immediately salvaged, only to disappear the next day, or the bullets had no effect on the creature and so it survived, or disappeared into thin air.

Gigantopithecus

Gigantopithecus an enormous primate thought to have inhabited southern China and northern India between 12 million and 500,000 years ago. It was described in 1935 on the basis of individual teeth from a Chinese apothecary. Since 1956, four large fossil jawbones have been identified. *Gigantopithecus* would have resembled the mountain gorilla.

Bigfoot and UFO sightings

New theories connect UFO sightings with Bigfoot encounters, claiming that both have happened simultaneously. The question is now not only whether Bigfoot is human or animal, but whether it should instead be categorized as an alien being. Some say Bigfoots are holograms because this is the only way to explain their imperviousness to bullets and their ability to appear and disappear just as quickly.

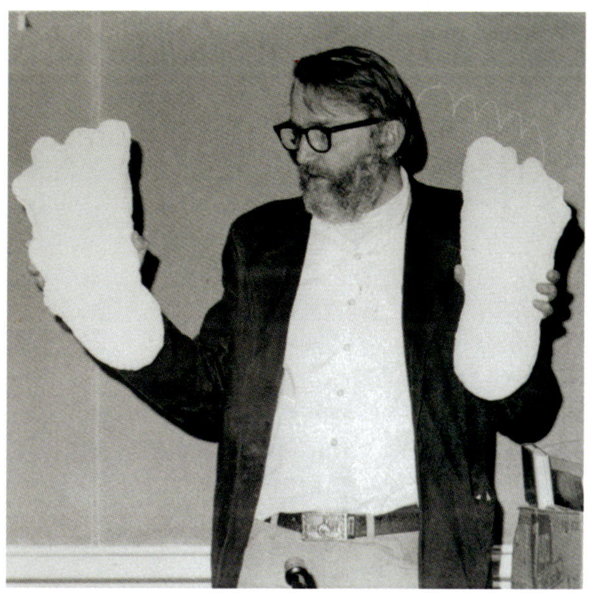

In 1974, Washington anthropologist Dr. Grover Krantz presented this cast of a Bigfoot. From the height and depth of the print he surmised the creature must have been about 8 feet (2.5 m) tall and weighed 550–775 lbs (250–350 kg).

Yeti

Is there anyone who has not heard of the "Abominable Snowman", or Yeti, or Metoh Kangmi, as the inhabitants of the Himalayas call it? It seems to make its home in the Himalayan Mountains, where it leaves behind its tracks and is sometimes even seen fleetingly. Is the Yeti a remnant of our earliest ancestors, or the member of an as yet unidentified species?

Mysterious tracks in the snow

The Himalayan Yeti is another classic cryptid. This world-famous creature has actually not been sighted very often. Mostly people find its tracks, which range widely in size between 6 and 18 inches (15–45 cm) long.

Yet accounts of sightings of this mysterious creature continue right up to the present. In his book *My Quest for the Yeti*, first published in German in 1998, world-famous mountain climber Reinhold Messner writes that he saw a Yeti, or at least was given the impression that he had by the locals accompanying him on a trek. Upon closer examination, Messner was able to ascertain that what he saw was in fact a Tibetan brown bear. Bears are often confused with cryptids because of their physical similarities and the fact that they can walk upright, yet people who insist that they have seen the Yeti up close are all agreed that what they saw was neither ape nor bear.

Three types of Yeti

Himalayan natives who believe in the Yeti's existence distinguish between three different types: the small *yeh-the*, the larger *meh-the* and the gigantic *dzu-the*. These size distinctions would also explain the different sized footprints. The two smaller creatures are probably varieties of apes, which are often mistaken for Yetis in the Himalayas.

If there really is such thing as a Yeti, it would have to be a *Gigantopithecus*, a giant ape that is thought to be extinct (see box, page 241). As *Gigantopithecus* was dying out half a million years ago, the elevation of Mount Everest was actually increasing 1600 feet (500 m). It is possible that some species were isolated during that time.

Another theory for the origin of the Yeti suggests that they live in the forests and valleys that lie below the snow line, at lower elevations. These hidden, lush and extremely foggy Himalayan valleys are only very rarely visited by humans. The only way for Yeti to move between such valleys would be over the snowy peaks, which would explain the footprints that are regularly found in the snow.

An essential element of Himalayan belief

In his book on the Yeti, Reinhold Messner concludes that a wild, frightening human-like creature is a firm element of religious belief among the Himalayan natives. It is a fact that, apart from a few bad (and mostly debunked) pictures and references in Tibetan religious texts, there is no real indication of the existence of the Yeti. Remains of the creature can always be found in remote Tibetan monasteries, where they are exhibited as proof of its existence, but when

The Yeti has fascinated people for a long time. Quite a few onlookers were drawn to the film set of the production *Yeti, Giant of the Twentieth Century*.

tested these have always been shown to belong to a known animal. In 1960, Heuvelmans investigated a purported Yeti scalp that was used as a ritual object by Himalayan natives. After comparing the hair to that of a Himalayan mountain goat that he found in a natural history museum in Brussels, Belgium, he was able to demonstrate that the same hair on the scalp was also found on this relatively unknown species of goat.

In other words, there is no substantiated proof. Despite the accounts of thousands of witnesses, accounts that continue up to today, this cryptid remains a mysterious riddle in the dizzying heights of the Himalayas.

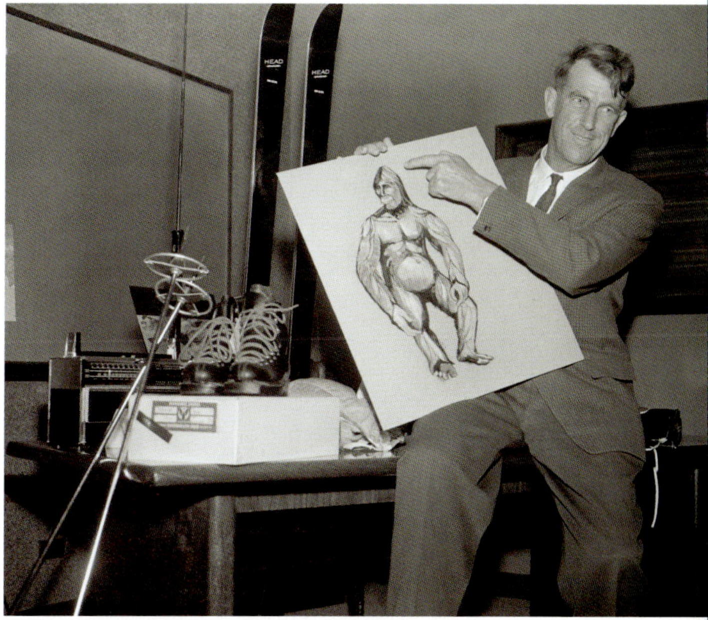

At a press conference in 1960, Sir Edmund Hillary, the first man to conquer Mount Everest, shows drawings of a snow creature that he had seen while in the Himalayas.

In the early 1990s, the skin of a creature found in a small village of Khumbu Tal in Nepal was said to be that of the mythical Yeti.

Ape-Men

In addition to the hominid-like Yeti and Bigfoot already described, other ape-men sightings from a number of countries on different continents have been documented throughout history. There are always notable reccurring characteristics in these sightings. How is it possible that identical features are consistently described, independent of time or place? The following cases represent only a selection of the most important cryptids. The existence of all of these creatures has not been scientifically verified.

De Loys' ape

De Loys' ape (Latin *Ameranthropoides loysi*, also known as *didi*, *vasitri*, *guayazi*, or Fallhammer), is a kind of humanoid ape, or apelike human, that is said to live in South America. There have been reports of this creature for more than 400 years. Sir Walter Raleigh (1552–1618) brought the first account of it back to Europe in 1595. Two hundred years later, Alexander von Humboldt (1769–1859) related Indian stories of man-eating apes, which he himself thought were probably bears. According to the natives, these aggressive creatures kidnap women and kill men.

An expedition in 1920, led by François de Loys (1892–1935), was looking for oil near the River Tarra in the jungle between Colombia and Venezuela when the group was attacked by creatures that were larger than apes, had no tails, and were running on their hind legs. Defending themselves, the men killed one of them, a female. To photograph it, they posed the cadaver on a crate, propping a stick under its chin. The animal was supposedly about 5 feet (1.5 m) tall, with reddish-brown fur, long arms, prehensile feet and thirty-two teeth (as a rule, South American monkeys have thirty-six teeth). Superficially, the genitalia could be taken for either male or female. De Loys' friend, French zoologist George Montandon, put the animal in a new class, *Ameranthropoides loysi*, (otherwise known as the de Loys' ape). Zoological experts greeted the find with much scepticism, maintaining that de Loys had cut the tail off an indigenous monkey. They classified it as a spider monkey because of the animal's hair colour and genitalia.

Supporters of this new species said that the crate on which it was photographed was 18 inches (45 cm) high, making the ape about 5 feet tall, much too big for a spider monkey, which would have been much smaller and would have had thirty-six teeth. But neither the height of the crate nor the number of teeth could be independently verified.

This reconstructed drawing of *Homo floresiensis* shows the creature whose skeleton was found on the Indonesian island of Flores. It was nearly 40 inches (1 m) tall.

What speaks of the authenticity of the creature is that de Loy himself never publicized the discovery; but Montandon did. De Loys was a geologist in Rio Tarra to search for oil. He was not aware of or interested in the fame that discovering a rare animal would bring.

In 1920, near the border of Venezuela and Colombia, Swiss geologist François de Loys shot and killed this ape-like creature, which was then photographed. It turned out to be a female about 5 feet (1.5 m) in height. What appears to be a penis is in fact a part of the female genitalia. Zoologist George Montandon classified the animal as a new species: the de Loys' ape.

Orang pendek

Orang pendek (or "short person", because it only stands about 30 inches, or 75 cm, tall) resembles the orang-utan ("forest person") and supposedly lives in the jungles of northern Sumatra. This cryptid is probably a new kind of primate. It differs from its similarly named cousin in height, but also in its upright gait. The evidence for its existence is limited to single footprints, an unidentifiable fur specimen and some webbed tissue. The footprints are clearly different from other humanoid cryptids, such as Bigfoot or Yeti.

To date, no conclusive proof for its existence has ever been presented. While it is certain that the hair specimen does not belong to any known monkey or any other mammal, all pictures of this creature have either been debunked or are unusable. Those who have seen it say it resembles the Paranthopus, a bipedal relative of the ancestors of early humans. Thanks to the discovery of *Homo floresiensis* bones in 2004, a very short human that lived on the Indonesian island of Flores and has been extinct for a few thousand years, some conclude that orang pendek could be a relative or descendent.

This South American species of monkey is called a spider monkey because of its long, thin arms and legs. Although it only grows to about 16 inches (40 cm), classical scientists classify the de Loys' ape as a spider monkey.

What secrets are still hidden in the South American rain forests? Do any creatures we do not yet know about live there in hiding?

People have always portrayed apes as a kind of person, depicting them with human qualities. This study is from the eighteenth century.

Yeren

In the Chinese province of Hubei, there is a creature known as "Yeren", the wild man from Shennongjia, or Yen Hsiung, an ape-man that lives in the mountains. It is covered with reddish-brown fur and is supposed to stand between 5 and 6½ feet (1.5–2 m) tall. Since its first sighting in 1920, there have been over 400 reports of encounters. Cryptozoologists assume that they are dealing once again with a remnant population of the otherwise extinct *Gigantopithecus* (see page 241) because this is the region where its fossils were first found.

Alma

The Alma is the legendary ape man of Mongolia, said to be up to 6½ feet (2 m) tall. It has long arms, is covered in reddish-brown fur, and has a notably flat forehead. Thought to be very shy, Almas are seen in the mountains of Mongolia and in the Chinese Tien-Shan range. The earliest accounts go all the way back to the year 1420. Natives describe the creature as a "wild man". Several expeditions have gone in search of this ape-man. Other than what may be footprints and bits of unidentifiable fur, no conclusive proof of its existence has ever been presented.

Minnesota Iceman

In 1968, zoologists Ivan T. Sanderson and Bernard Heuvelmans visited a travelling exhibition in Minnesota, where they saw a hominid frozen in ice inside a trailer. They documented the creature with photographs and detailed drawings. "This is the first time in history that a fresh cadaver of a Neanderthal-like human has been found. This means that this type of hominid, thought to be extinct since prehistoric times, still lives today", wrote an excited Heuvelmans (7). He thought that the Minnesota Iceman might have actually come from Vietnam, brought back to the USA in a body bag meant for American soldiers. Captain Hansen, the man who displayed the body, had been stationed there in 1966 during the Vietnam War. The true origins of the creature in ice will probably never come to light, because the information given out, mostly by Hansen himself, changes continually. He first claimed that the creature was shot in Minnesota, left behind, and after many years frozen into a block of ice, only to be rediscovered later. Next, he said that he had fished the floating block of ice out of a lake near Siberia. Finally, he claimed that he had discovered the cadaver in a plastic bag at a Chinese house in Hong Kong. The Minnesota Iceman of the travelling exhibit disappeared, probably because the body decayed. It was replaced by a fake, as the two zoologists were able to confirm after comparing their details. Another hominid that resembled the Minnesota Iceman showed up in France in 1997. Bernard Heuvelmans identified this as a fake, as well.

Other names for ape-like creatures in various countries and regions

- Yowie (Australia)
- Moehau Monster (New Zealand)
- Chuchunaa (Eastern Siberia)
- Jag-mort (Ural Mountains)
- Mechenji (Western Siberia)
- Kaptar and Almastij (Caucasus Mountains)
- Hibagon (Japan)
- Dwendis and Duende (Belize and Guatemala)
- Shiru (Ecuador and Columbia)
- Didi (Guayana, Surinam and French Guayana)
- Mapinguary or Maricoxis (Brazil)
- Ucumar, Umahuaca and Ucu (Argentina)

"For the first time in history a fresh cadaver of a Neanderthal-like human has been found", wrote an excited Bernard Heuvelmans upon seeing the Minnesota Iceman on display in a travelling exhibition.

Chupacabra

Somewhere between legend and reality lies the chupacabra, literally translated from Spanish into English as "goat sucker". The manner in which it brutally kills, sucking the blood dry from household pets and farm animals, often going so far as to remove their organs, has pushed it into the spotlight of cryptozoological attention from its very first sighting in 1995. Many questions surround this creature and its origins. Some have suggested that it is an alien, while others consider it to be a horrible result of genetic experiments.

A mixture of reptile, dragon and vampire

The chupacabra, the "goat sucker", received its name from the local press because it leaves its victims without a drop of blood. It was first sighted in the 1990s in Puerto Rico. Then people found evidence of this fear-instilling creature in Latin America, in the southern United States and later in Africa. The descriptions are, for the most part, very similar. The creature is 5 feet (1.5 m) tall with a pronounced lower jaw, large red eyes, small nostrils and a razor-thin mouth with curved fangs. It has a rough black coat and, according to witnesses, can change its skin colour like a chameleon. Jagged spikes are said to grow on its back. The creature is described as being able to run very fast as well as jump long and high. Author Vladislav Raab describes its appearance as follows: " ... it looks kind of like a dinosaur, comparable to a Deinonychus or Velociraptor. The vampire myth, which is widely known in South America, also plays a role in the reports, thanks to the classic bite marks a la Dracula that are found on the cadavers." (8)

Did aliens bring it here?

Some cryptologists believe that the origins of the chupacabra can be related to UFO sightings. UFO researcher Tito Armstrong thinks the chupacabra is a wild alien pet wreaking its havoc on Earth. Cryptozoologist Scott Corales describes the creature as a cross between the "grey alien" and a terrestrial animal like a porcupine or kangaroo. The creature, he continues, is active day and night. Other animals panic when it comes near them. The chupacabra is very skilled at making itself invisible and its appearance is nearly always associated with UFO sightings. Some groups go so far as to claim that the aliens have an organized

Some creatures thought to be chupacabras at first sighting have turned out to be coyotes.

Many dead animals in Puerto Rico were blamed on the Rhesus monkey, for which killing is apparently "sport", but witnesses claiming to have seen the chupacabra counter this theory, saying that whatever it was that they saw, the beast was bigger and stronger than a Rhesus monkey.

program designed to eliminate large numbers of people by vampiric means so as to rid the planet of humans, thereby freeing it for alien colonization. Thus far, however, no humans have been attacked.

A mixture of different species

Professor Juan Riviero from Puerto Rico offers a natural explanation for the many dead animals in his country. He claims that Rhesus monkeys, which were brought to an island near the coast for experimental purposes, are responsible because they are known to kill for "sport". Contraindicating his theory are the many witnesses who say they have seen the chupacabra.

Other theories mention genetic experiments conducted by NASA that went awry. In Nicaragua, a chupacabra was allegedly killed by a shepherd during an attack on his herd. The corpse had deep inset eye sockets, soft skin like a bat, notably large claws and fangs and something resembling a ridge extending down the length of its spine. Veterinarians who examined the creature thought it looked like a combination of species, but certainly not like any known animal. The coroner let the body soak in embalming fluid. No further information has been obtained since.

The strange thing about the dead animals (mostly goats) that were found is the fact that the meat was not eaten. Instead, they were literally sucked dry – not one drop of blood remained in their bodies.

The Mothman, with its hypnotizing red eyes, is one of the most unsettling creatures of cryptozoology. It terrorized the state of West Virginia for months.

Mothman

With its hypnotic red eyes, Mothman is one of the most fantastic creatures of the century, steadfastly refusing to fit into any set of explanations laid out by the scientific establishment. More than 100 witnesses reported seeing this strange creature, apparently half man, half bat, which for over two years had the state of West Virginia in a panic. It disappeared without a trace in 1967.

The bird creature from West Virginia

In 1966 and 1967, there were numerous sightings in West Virginia of a gigantic winged creature, an "animal", witnesses called it, which appeared suddenly out of the darkness. It had large, round red eyes that glowed in the dark with hypnotic effect. The creature was shaped like a man, but at about 7 feet (2.1 m) was taller than any but the tallest of men. It had no recognizable head and its eyes seemed to sit directly on its shoulders. Large wings were folded and lay close to the back of its body. When the wings were extended, its wing span was around 12 feet (3.6 m). Witnesses reported that the beast made squeaking noises like a mouse.

The creature was grey, walked on strong human legs and must have had super-human strength, because it lifted heavy iron gates from their hinges and moved at speeds of over 90 mph (145 km/hour). According to witnesses who tried to escape from it in a car, it hovered above them at a constant height. The press dubbed it "Mothman" from the first night it appeared, and the name has stuck.

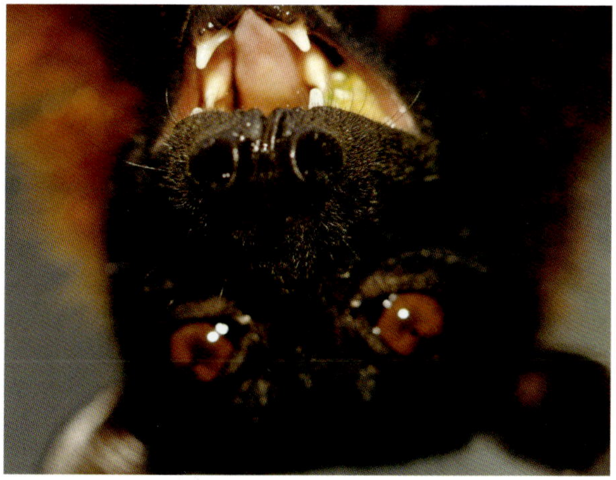

This close-up of a bat shows the terrifying power of their teeth. Bats have always been considered frightening creatures with magical powers.

Other puzzling flying creatures

- Between 1877 and 1880 there were sightings of flying creatures in Brooklyn, New York that were not a kind of bird, but rather some winged, black creature.
- A human-sized bat was seen in Kent, England in 1963.
- In 1969 a bird-woman with bat wings appeared near Da Nang, Vietnam.
- In 1971, witnesses in Kristianstad, Sweden saw a large flying creature.
- In 1973 there were numerous sightings of so-called smallygasters (mythical, nocturnal creatures that are half bird, half reptile and covered with hair) in Maryland.

The paralyzing effect of its glowing eyes

Some of the people who sighted this creature, predominantly women who were menstruating, were literally followed by it right up to their front door. Some said it was a huge bird, while others called it an enormous bat because it had no feathers and smooth skin. One thing all the descriptions have in common is that the glowing eyes, up to 2.5 inches (6 cm) wide, are attributed a paralyzing effect. Because it was seen in West Virginia so many times that year, a kind of panic broke out, although no one was ever harmed. In one week in late 1966, there were reports of strange looking, tall birds resembling the Mothman in Ohio and Pennsylvania as well. Since the press at the time was full of news about the strange creature, it is hard to say if these really were sightings or whether it was just mass hysteria.

The mysterious connection between UFO sightings and Mothman

John Keel states in his book, *The Mothman Prophecies*, "Those who saw the Mothman also saw UFOs. Those who saw them also had contact with the aliens." (9) The appearance of each of these three phenomena is accompanied by a cacophony of static (dissonance) that some call a loud squeak or distorted noise. Many witnesses in West Virginia reported that the noise sounded as if someone were playing a recording much too fast.

The creature remains a mystery. On the one hand, it is a biological impossibility, because it is too large to fly. On the other hand, it did not really use its wings in that way. According to witnesses, it flew more like a helicopter.

The total count of people to have seen this "winged impossibility", as Keel calls it, numbered more than 100. In 1975 there was another Mothman-like appearance in Texas, but it was not documented. In 2001, a film was made based on the book *The Mothman Prophecies*, starring Richard Gere in the lead role.

In another attempt to clarify the unexplained, Mothman has been portrayed in different ways in art. This is a bat that was styled to look like the Mothman.

Kongamato and Thunderbird

In Indonesia, Africa, Australia and on both American continents, there have always been sightings of enormous birds. In particular, cryptozoologists have intensively investigated the African Kongamato and the North American Thunderbird. Some even equate them with extraterrestrial flying objects

Kongamato

The Kongamato (or "overwhelmer of boats") is an ancient flying reptile with a wingspan from 4 to 7 feet (1.2–2.1 m). It is believed to still inhabit the Jiundu swamps in the western part of the Democratic Republic of Congo (formerly known as Zaire). It is described as having no feathers, but instead smooth red or black skin and a long, tooth-studded beak. This animal gets its name from the natives, whose fishing canoes apparently have been capsized by its attacks. Folk tales go so far as to say this creature brings death to anyone who looks upon it.

In 1923, British explorer Frank H. Melland heard reports from native Kaonde tribesmen of a "swamp demon". In an attempt to identify the creature, Melland showed the natives images of pterosaurs (often called pterodactyls). Without hesitation, they identified them as their Kongamato.

A few years later, journalist J. Ward Price and the future King Edward VIII were on an expedition in the then British colony. Near the Jiundu swamps, they encountered a native who had a terrible injury on his back that he said an enormous bird with large teeth had inflicted. This man also immediately recognized the animal that had attacked him

A panicked person might confuse a flying stork with a mythical creature, maybe even the Thunderbird.

from pictures of flying reptiles. In 1957, a man en route to the hospital with flesh wounds on his chest claimed that a large bird attacked him in the Bangweulu swamps in southern Rhodesia (now Zambia). He drew a picture of his attacker, sketching the outline of a flying reptile. There were sightings in the aforementioned areas up to the late 1950s. The one photograph of a Kongamato turned out to be a hoax upon further analysis.

It is unclear what people were actually seeing when they claimed they had seen Kongamato. Zoologists think it may have been the indigenous shoebill stork, which lives in the swamps. However, there are no known cases of this kind of bird attacking a person. A further theory attempts to explain it as an unclassified variety of large bat. Cryptozoologists, however, still believe reports involve a genuine flying reptile, falsely believed to be extinct.

Zoologists think the Kongamato is the indigenous African shoebill stork. There is no known case, however, of this bird attacking a person.

THUNDERBIRD

The Thunderbird is a mythical North American Indian bird that has quite a lot of similarities to the African Kongamato. From the time North America was first settled, there have been sightings of large, unidentifiable flying creatures. In the northern states, one can actually speak of a veritable wave of sightings. The physical description hardly differs from that of Kongamato, but Thunderbird is powerful and cunning, associated with flight, lightning and thunder. It is a majestic creature, but can also be threatening.

A number of cryptozoologists, in particular American researcher Ivan T. Sanderson, are of the opinion that sightings of the Thunderbird are of the same surviving species of flying reptile as the Kongamato in Africa. The only flying animal that comes into question is the long extinct North American Teratorn, a truly enormous forerunner of the modern vulture, which had a wingspan that could reach up to an impressive 26 feet (8 m).

When classifying both of these animals, some scientists involved in the study of prehistoric astronaut theories would like to go so far as to assume that the Thunderbird's role in Native American mythology can be traced back to prehistorical sightings of UFOs.

The American Indians have always worshipped the Thunderbird as one of their totem animals.

This creature, an axolotl, was photographed in the Baja region on the California-Mexico border in the 1980s. With its small front feet, it resembles the mythical tatzelwurm, providing support for its existence.

Tatzelwurm

In the German language, a *tatze* is a paw or a leg. A tatzelwurm is a mythical reptile from the Alps that possesses two or four legs. Since the fifteenth century there have been accounts of this cryptid, which is said to have terrified hikers.

A small dragon or "white worm"

The tatzelwurm is often described as scaly, then again as hairy. It is supposed to resemble a snake, or sometimes a mammal, occasionally even having the head of a cat. In some reports, the animal is 1 foot (30 cm) long, and in others, over 3 feet (1 m). The tatzelwurm, resembling a small dragon or the legendary "white worm", is described as an aggressive beast that readily attacks animals and people. It lives in caves and tunnels dug into cliff faces. It is said to secrete poisonous gases and spew fire. In some reports, it spits poisonous slime and its skin is also poisonous.

Almost no sightings in fifty years

Similar creatures were sighted all over Europe. In 1924, two hikers found a 4-foot-long (1.2-m) skeleton of the legendary worm, which has in the meantime, unfortunately, been lost. Photographs brought forward as evidence have always been identified as fakes. One of the last sightings occurred near Palermo, Sicily in 1954. Farmers saw a creature with the head and front legs of a cat attacking a herd of sheep. There have been almost no more sightings since then.

Heuvelmans suspects that the tatzelwurm is a relative of the Gila monster or the *Heloderma suspectrum*, or an Asian giant salamander called the Megalobatrachus. Other cryptozoologists think it is a relative of the European legless lizard, *Ophisaurus apodus*.

Can the biome of a creature, one that practically lives on our doorstep in densely populated countries, be so reduced by tourism and development, that the animal dies out before our very eyes? Cryptozoologists tend to think that a few tatzelwurms are still alive, hidden somewhere deep in the mountains.

Mongolian Death Worm

The vast, inhospitable expanse of the Gobi Desert is the home of this mysterious creature, *Allghoi khorkhoi*, the Mongolian death worm, which is supposed to be able to kill people and animals on the spot, even from great distances.

Deadly creature under the desert sand

The death worm is between 2 and 4 feet (60–120 cm) long and is described as a thick, bright red, snake-like animal. The Mongolians fear the creature to the extent that even mentioning it is considered bad luck. It apparently either sprays a deadly poison that kills instantly or emits a strong electric shock.

Czech author Ivan Mackerle was the first person to investigate this creature. Mongolian nomads told him the worm is attracted to the colour yellow. They told Mackerle about a child who had a yellow toy box into which the worm crept. When the boy touched it, he died instantly. His parents saw a tail disappear into the sand and pursued the worm in order to kill it, but instead they were killed by it, as well.

The Mongolian death worm is said to live here in the Gobi Desert. With an area of about 500,000 square miles (1,300,000 km²), it is the largest desert in Asia. Parts of it are over 3000 feet (900 m) above sea level.

Desert death adder or relative of the Tatzelwurm

There is a lot of speculation about this creature. One theory says that the Mongolian death worm is actually a desert death adder. From the description, they are physically identical, and both spray poison. The death adder could very well live in the Gobi Desert, but they have only been proven to live in Australia and New Guinea. Sceptics say no traditional worm could possibly survive in a desert because it would dry out in no time. Either an undiscovered type of deadly adder lives in the Gobi Desert, although its appearance and the level of danger it poses have been blown out of proportion by exaggeration or superstition; or the creature is an invention of imaginative nomads trying to find a reason for inexplicable deaths.

There are countless theories about the Mongolian Death Worm. One involves the Desert Death Adder. It looks just like the Death Worm and also sprays poison.

Contemporary Mysteries

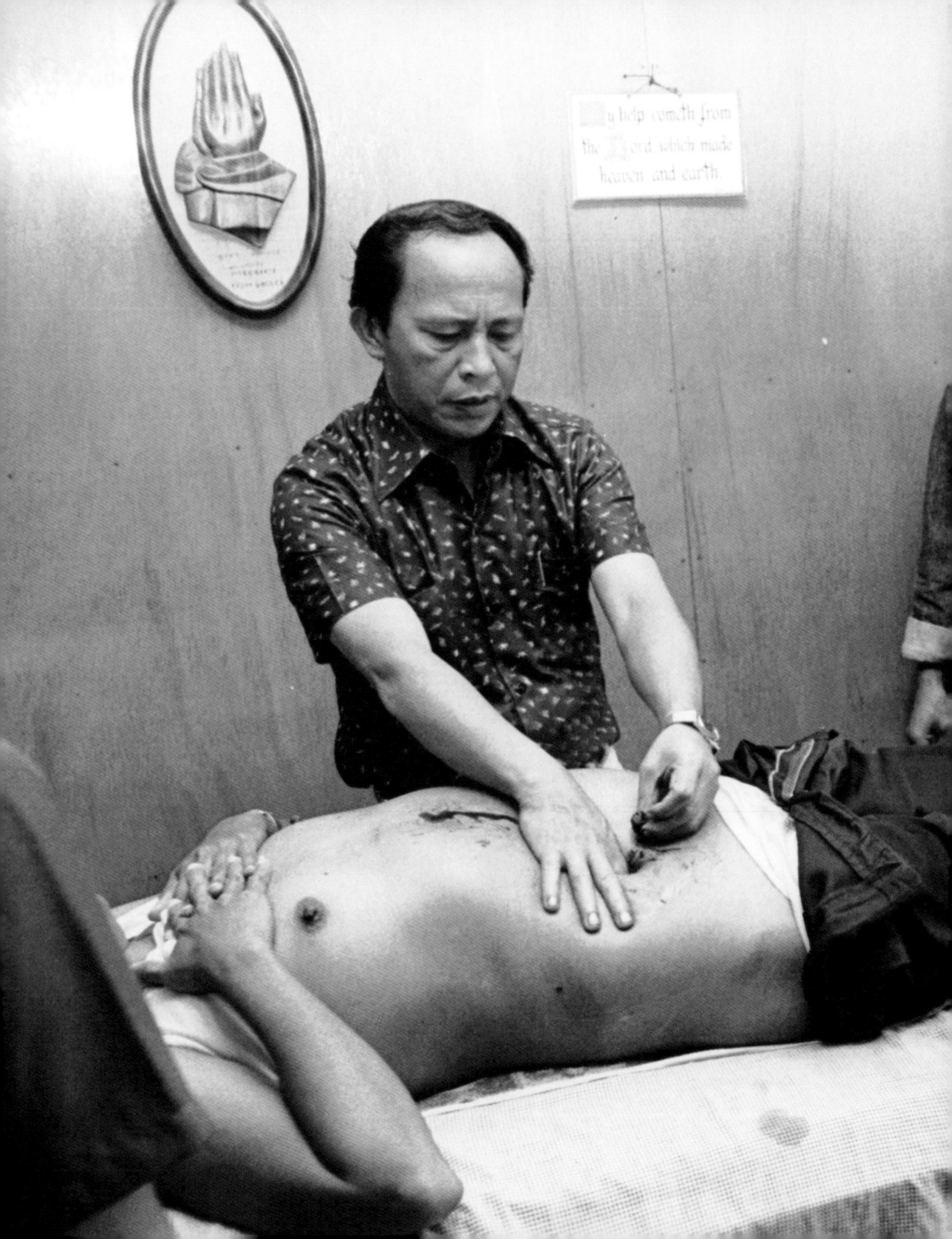
y help cometh from
the ord, which made
heaven and earth.

Medical and Psychological Phenomena

After Sigmund Freud and C.G. Jung established the study of dreams, and thus the subconscious, as a fruitful subject of study and it was recognized as a legitimate scientific discipline, researchers from different fields were inspired to take another look at comparable borderline disciplines that were not yet part of any respectable canon. Most of these non-traditional fields of investigation focus on phenomena that most people would normally consider paranormal.

Included here are the various kinds of alternative healers, including tribal shaman, spiritual healers and psychic physicians. Also investigated are documented cases of remote healing, successful operations with bare hands, and the spontaneous healing of the sick, as if by magic, without conventional treatment. But many other types of phenomena are also considered relevant, including corpses that do not decay and individuals endowed with special talents, such as the Russian children who, thanks to their mysterious gift of X-ray eyes, can see right through people, even diagnosing their diseases.

No conventional medical practitioner would risk his or her reputation by relying on these methods for fear of being dismissed as a charlatan. But where does this fear of the inexplicable, or better yet, the unexplained come from?

This chapter probes not only the physical dimension of healing, but also questions and illuminates the psychological aspects.

Filipino spiritual healer Laurence S. Cacteng operates on a patient with his bare hands.

Spontaneous Healing

Cases of spontaneous healing, such as the sudden remission of malignant tumours, are known to every physician, although no one knows how it happens. Because doctors consider themselves scientists, they seldom speak of miracles. Explanations should fit accepted medical dogma, and alternate interpretations are not permissible. The question that medicine as a science should ask itself is: what does healing actually mean?

Blind can see again

In 2004, Joyce Ulrich, now 74 years old, suffered a severe heart attack, then fell into a coma. The doctors in Coventry, England fought for her life. When she awoke from the coma three days later, the woman, who had been blind for twenty-five years, could see again. The medical experts have so far not been able to explain the unexpected cure. Joyce had contracted glaucoma in 1979 and over time become nearly completely blind. At the time of her cure, she could only see very dimly and could no longer get around on her own. She had lost her eyesight gradually, but regained it all at once. The doctors were mystified, as spontaneous cures lie outside their previous experience. The patient and her family, however, speak of a miracle.

Two additional patient histories

Two German patients had cancer, one a bronchial tumour and the other a malignant skin cancer. Both patients developed metastases, additional tumours that had attacked several critical organs. Doctors gave up on the first patient, prescribing only pain relief. Suddenly, and without the help of any other treatment, the cancerous tumours went into remission. The patient lived cancer-free for another ten years, dying from a pulmonary embolism.

The skin cancer patient had already had his tumour removed surgically, followed by chemotherapy to prevent further growth, and radiation to prevent metastases in the brain. Although doctors continued to treat him, they had already given up hope that he would survive. The patient began alternative therapies, switching to a vegetarian and whole foods diet. Within three years all his tumours disappeared. The man has been considered completely cured since 1986. Medical experts are mystified.

Spontaneous healing does occur, as in the case of the blind woman who, after surviving a heart attack, could see again. Her doctors were baffled.

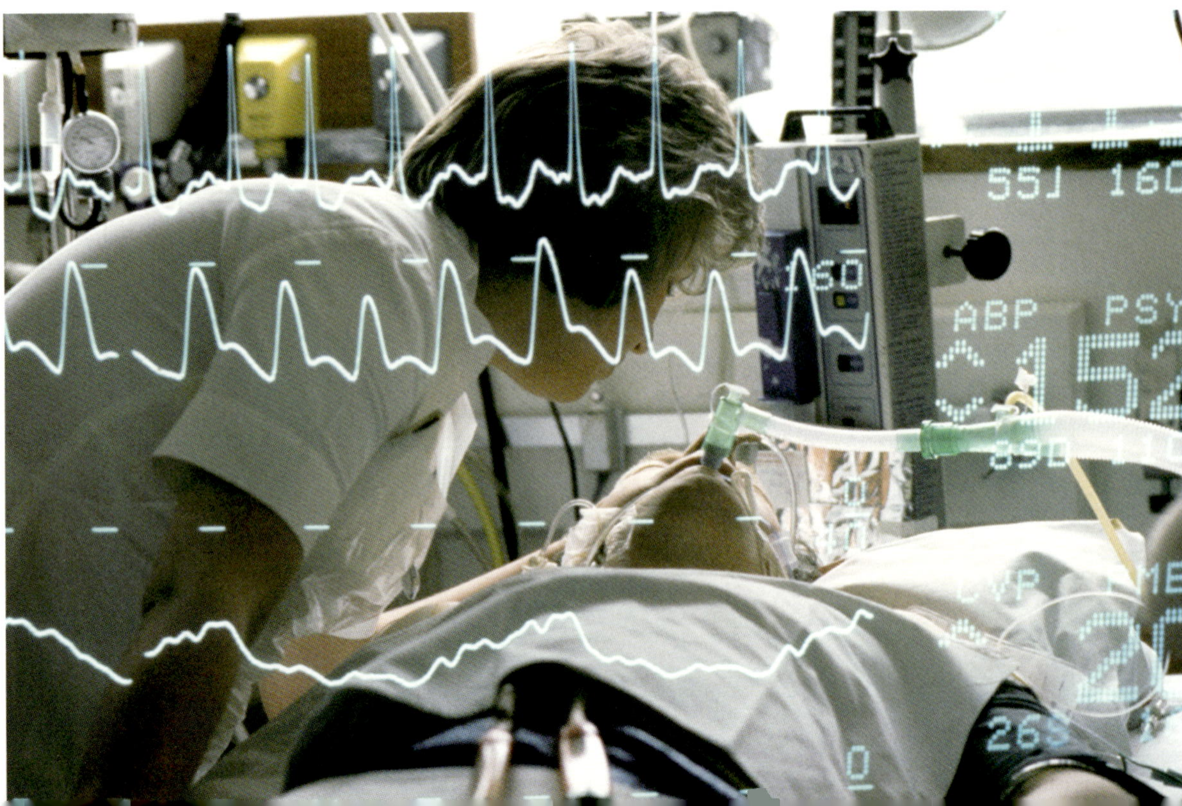

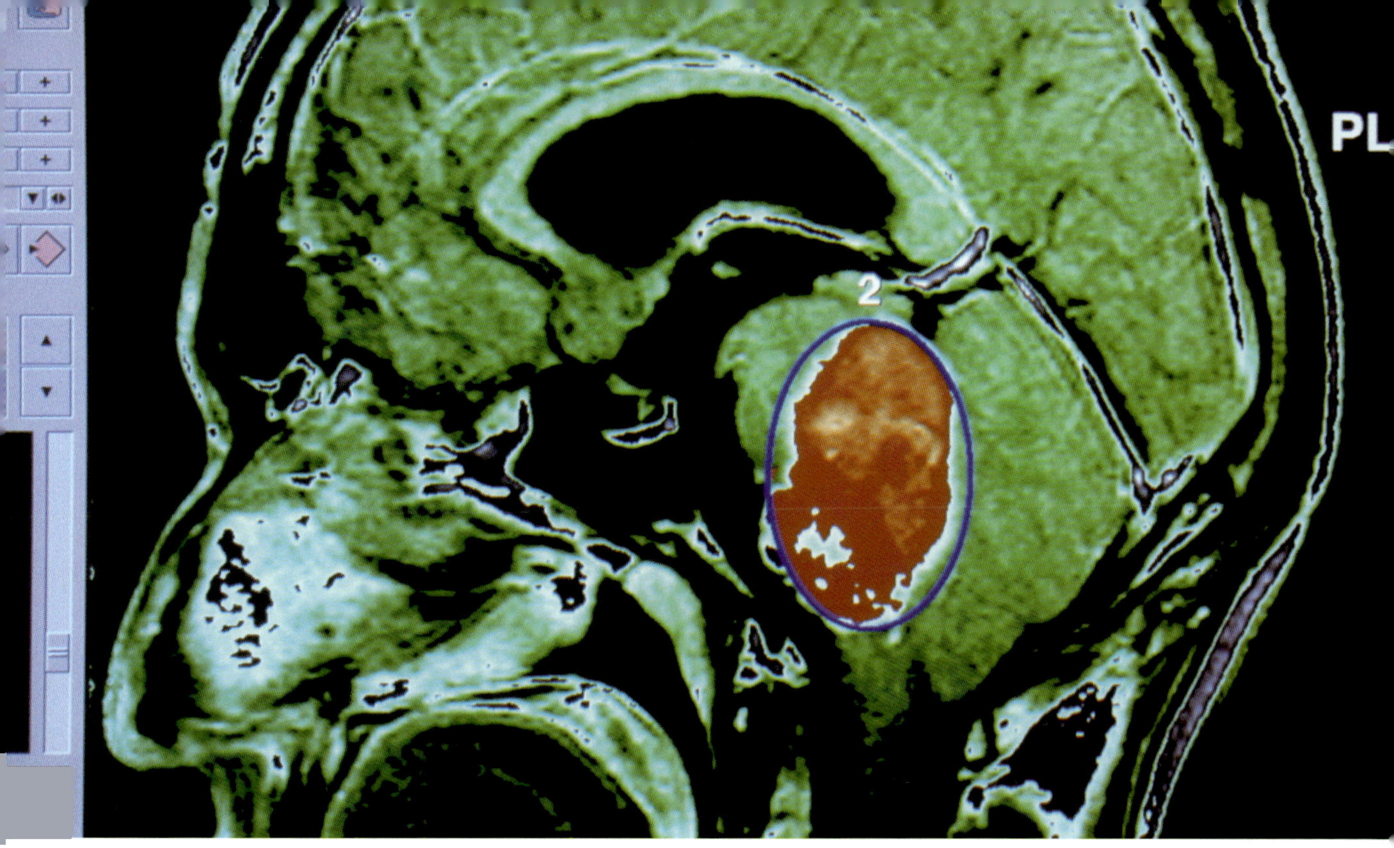

Does personal effort play a role?

People who have experienced spontaneous healing often feel that the reversal of fortune came about either due to their own efforts or from the application of alternative therapies. International scientists have been collecting data on spontaneous healing for a number of years and are trying to analyze it statistically, but they have yet to reach any conclusions. Investigative teams from Nuremberg Hospital and from the University Hospital of Heidelberg, Germany, have stated that their analysis has yet to lead to any new patient recommendations, nor was new information forthcoming regarding how spontaneous healing comes about.

Particularly with alternative therapies and in parapsychological circles, repeated attempts are made to draw on particular personality traits, behaviour patterns and spiritual powers in the hope of a cure. The best-documented cases of spontaneous healing are those that have taken place against a background of deep religious faith. Medical science, however, typically rejects such a causal connection, considering each such case a matter of chance. The question of what was responsible for the cures, whether chance or spiritual power, remains unanswered.

There are cases of inexplicable spontaneous cures in which brain tumours, like this one shown above on a CAT scan, go into complete remission.

A scientific explanation of spiritual processes

A number of factors, including a patient's attitude toward life, current quality of life and personal means of coming to terms with disease, play a major role in their recovery. Scientists acknowledge the phenomenon of "existential transformation". This is what happens when, in the course of a severe illness, an individual discovers a state of "being", or alternately, acknowledges the existence of God, the result being a sense of gratitude for their affliction. Researchers have found that mental processes of this kind stimulate the immune system, which in turn can lead to healing.

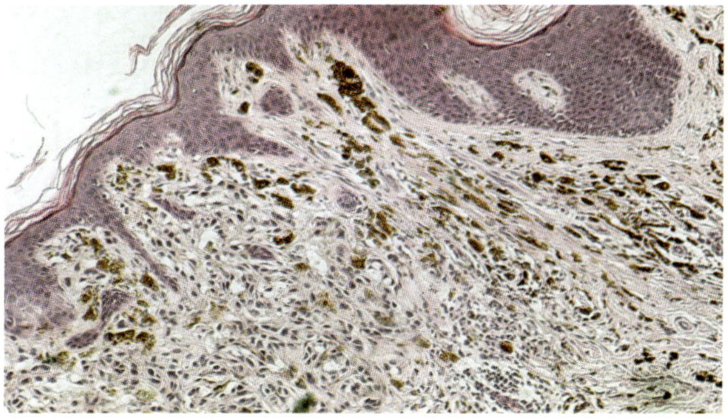

A section of a late stage melanoma (skin cancer). A statistical study showed that the chance of a spontaneous cure is one out of every 500 cases.

Miracle Cures

Today, fewer and fewer people put their complete trust in orthodox medicine, preferring to consult so-called healers to alleviate their suffering. The methods of alternative healing are varied, ranging from the laying on of hands to swinging a pendulum. Many healers treat patients from great distances, perceiving the vibrations of the disease and sending out a healing energy. Where is the boundary between the swindlers and those who use their mysterious abilities for the good of their fellow humans?

In London, in 1951, a group of people gathered in the Royal Festival Hall served as witnesses when the miracle healer Harry Edwards helped a disabled woman walk again.

Making the inconceivable conceivable

For years now, success stories from the alternative healing community have surprised the world. Tumours disappear and cancer patients regain their health. The lame walk, mortal diseases are cured, and patients who were declared dead go on living. Healers have to work very hard to maintain their reputations, which is why many of them offer their services only selectively. While orthodox medicine has long refused to recognize alternative forms of healing, or even to make use of alternative methods, more and more serious scientists are getting on board. Given the pervasive doubts of the medical community, researchers try to make the incomprehensible understandable, carrying out tests involving infrared cameras, heart rate monitors and highly complex cellular studies in order to determine if there is such a thing as healing energy.

Two European healers

More people are trusting healers, and scepticism toward conventional medicine is on the rise, because healers more often provide what orthodox medicine seldom can: attention, hope and help.

Christos Drossinakis, born in Greece, is today probably the most famous healer in Germany, as well as one of the world's most tested miracle healers. He can completely

The success of alternative medicine

In the United States as elsewhere in the world, acceptance of alternative medicine, or CAM (complementary and alternative medicine), is on the rise. An extensive study conducted by the Centers for Disease Control in 2002 demonstrated that 36 per cent of adults currently use some form of CAM, and when prayers for improved health are included, the number increases to 62 per cent. These findings "confirm the extent to which Americans have turned to CAM approaches with the hope that they would help treat and prevent disease and enhance quality of life", said Stephen E. Straus, M.D., Director of the National Center for Complementary and Alternative Medicine. (10)

Quote from Christos Drossinakis
"I do not actually heal anyone; with God's help, the sick heal themselves. My job is to create the conditions to make that possible." (11)

transform the molecular structure of water from several miles away. How does he do it? How can he influence the body temperature of a patient through mental concentration? How is it possible for him to cure a patient of an asthma attack from hundreds of miles away?

Piotr Elkunoviz, who lives in Germany, also cannot explain how he heals people of their ailments, saying it must be the power of God working through him. One patient with advanced osteoporosis left his office after minutes without any further pain. Piotr cured another woman with a tilted pelvis by just waving his hand, making her legs even again. Thousands of people, having benefited from his healing expertise, extol Piotr Elkunoviz's abilities. One patient described him as a combination of God, Indian guru healer Sai Baba (see page 221) and Mother Teresa.

In Baltimore, Maryland, miracle healer Olga Worrall lays both hands on a man to cure him of his ailments.

The spiritual healer as an intermediary between worlds

Orthodox medicine treats miracle cures as frauds, claiming that they rely on a combination of the placebo effect and blind faith. Increasingly, however, doctors are making use of abilities that fall outside the realm of the medical model. Professor Kasper Rhyner, a senior physician at Kanton-Spital [Canton Hospital] in Glarus, Switzerland, works with a female healer. He has demonstrated that patients of his who were ready to terminate traditional treatment have regained their health through her intercession.

Spiritual healing employing powerful mental abilities works in different ways. Energy and light are transformed into healing currents by a process that remain mysterious. The spiritual healer is never the source of energy, but instead functions as an intermediary between "worlds". The source of the healing energy is instead the universal divinity or cosmos, whose energy stream can be regulated and focused by the healer. This also explains the success of healing over great distances.

Each cure also brings increased spiritual awareness. Most spiritual healers explain their actions to their patients with words like "It is not I, but your faith, that has healed you."

Greek born Christos Drossinakis is one of Europe's most famous miracle healers and the most tested healer in the world.

Spiritual Healers

Psychic surgery, which originated in the Philippines, involves penetrating the body with the bare hands, making negative energy tangible so that it can be removed. Psychic surgeons explain their abilities as the power of the Holy Spirit working through them. Their hands can also enter the body and remove diseased tissue. What is most baffling thing about this form of healing is the fact that the skin closes up again with no sign of a wound or scar.

The readiness of patients to be healed

They reach into the body of their patients, operating with their bare hands, neutralizing diseases of all kinds. Patients all over the world swear by them. Considered charlatans by orthodox medicine, they're revered as miracle workers by the

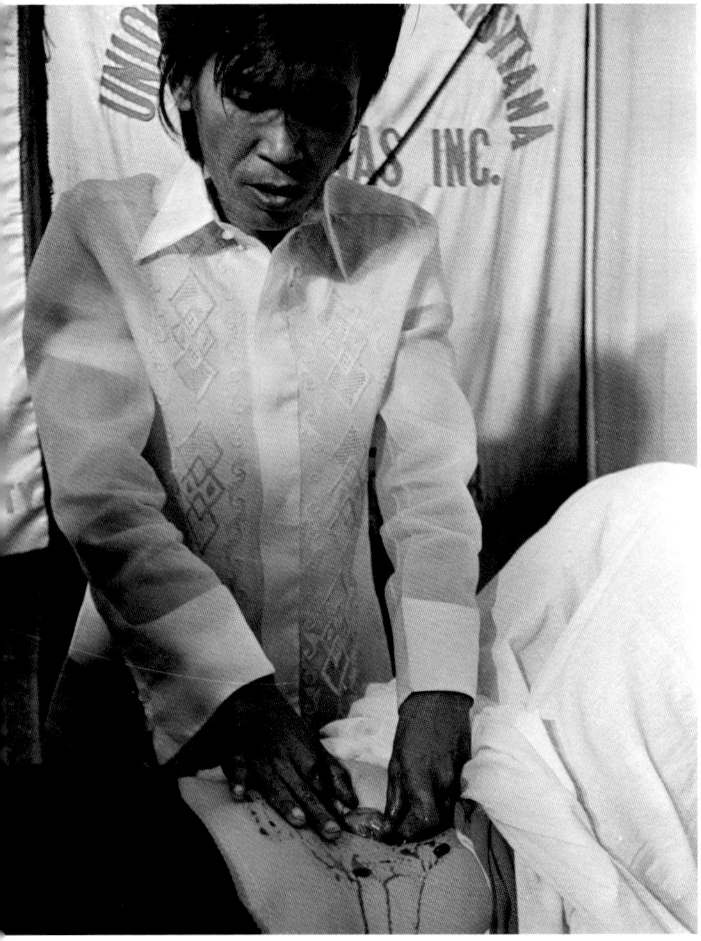

Alex Orbito is one of a great many spiritual healers in the Philippines. The picture shows him performing an appendectomy with his bare hands.

cured. How do we categorize these people with their unconventional healing abilities? How important a role does autosuggestion play in their success? Are these miracles?

An increasing number of individuals who have not been cured by conventional medicine lose faith in chemotherapy and high-tech medicine as a means of recovery. At the same time, there is also increasing interest worldwide in alternative treatments, whether naturopathy, spiritual healing, or psychic surgery.

Matthias Kamp, a physician in Hamburg, Germany, is head of a medical science group that investigates spiritual healing phenomena. The results of his research are mixed, he says, and as one should expect, it seems as though the positive elements of society are not the only ones drawn to this new field. Clearly, spiritual healing attracts frauds as well as saints, in full accordance with the general nature of things, but this should not detract from the positive achievements of genuine healers.

Dr. Donald McDowall, an American physician, has studied spiritual healing and psychic surgery for many years. Anyone who decides to follow that path to a cure, he explains, should first verify the surgeon's references. He sets two preconditions for patients before committing to treatments of this kind: they must have faith in the healing power and must be ready to be cured. Both conditions must be met without qualification.

Healing powers since time immemorial

All cultures are aware of healing powers, but the more technological a society becomes, the more it believes it can renounce them. There is also the question of the dubious reputation of spiritual healers, a reputation fomented by orthodox medicine and pharmaceutical companies, both of which would like nothing better than to expose all healers as charlatans in order to strengthen their own positions.

Yet the quantity of medically verified results continues to grow. Doctors' reports, laboratory analyses and patient histories verify that actual healing takes place. Accounts of recovery are on the rise, coming from the hard of hearing,

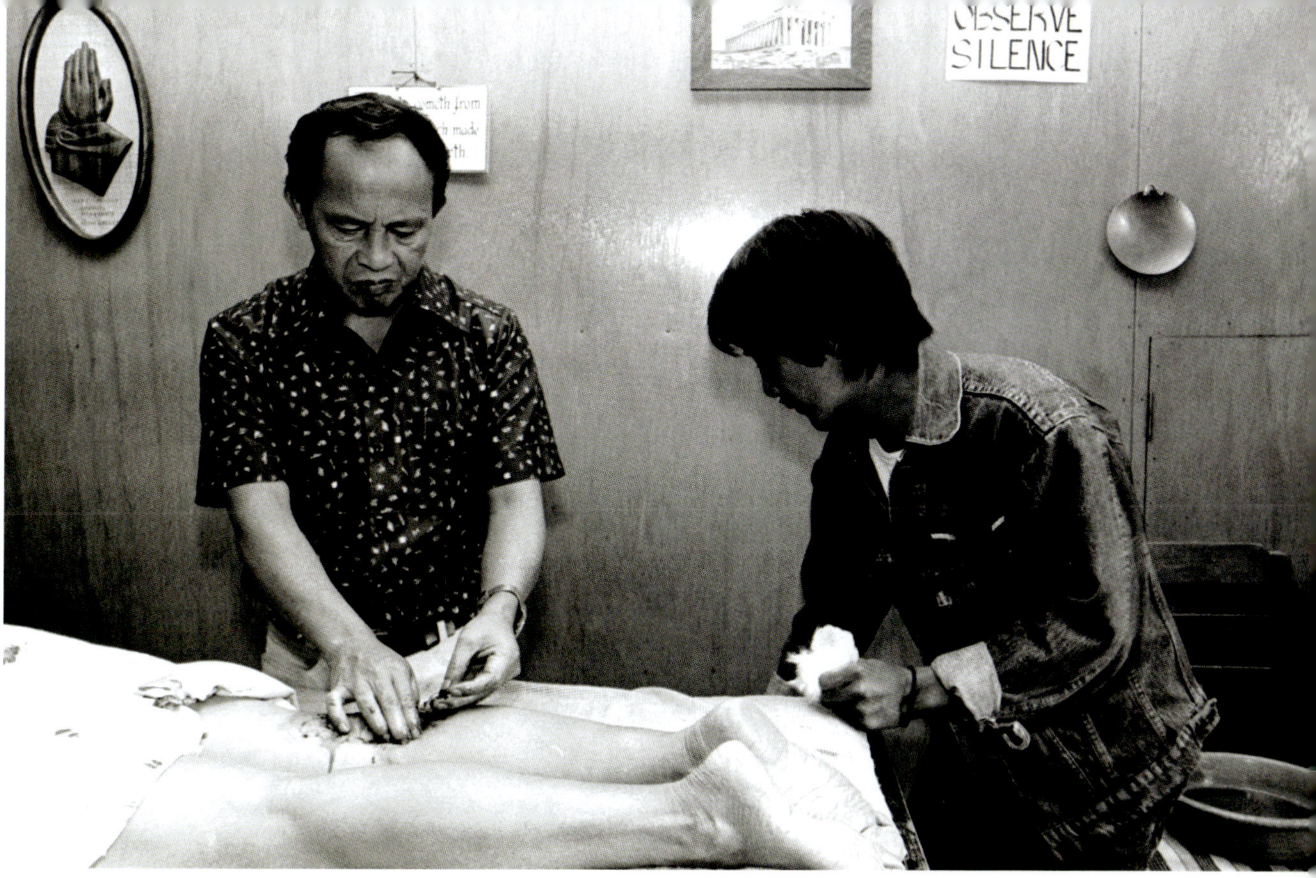

Laurence S. Cacteng, a famous Filipino spiritual healer, treats a patient who has vein problems in his calf.

the wheelchair bound, the lame, and from rheumatics who have had enough of conventional therapies. While spontaneous healing can take place, more typically the healing process is spread out over a longer time frame. But the cures are in fact medically verifiable. Dr. Kamp maintains that the most important part of the healing process is the willingness of patients to be open to the healing power.

Mediums with divine energy

Spiritual healers work with energy that they themselves call divine. They feel that the energy works with them or through them, and that they are therefore nothing more than conduits or intermediaries. The sensation of energy passing from the healer's hands to the patient's body so that they can operate must be an extraordinary experience. To be present and see healing taking place without pain or side effects is an indication of how far we have travelled away from ourselves and our roots.

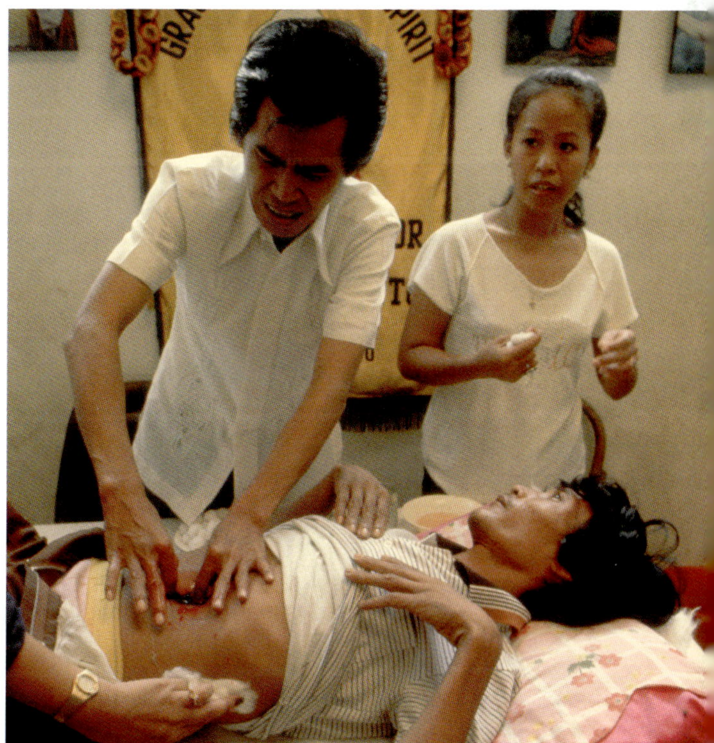

Another spiritual healer during an operation. The spiritual healers call themselves "God's surgeons". They claim that they can treat people whom orthodox medicine can no longer help.

Cases in point

The four cases studies presented here describe people who were healed by João Teixeira da Faria, a spiritual healer who also goes by the name João de Deus (João of God). The accounts come from the records kept by his secretary in Abadiania, Brazil (12). According to the secretary, it is difficult to determine exactly how many people João has cured, because the volume of those healed at a distance is nearly impossible to calculate.

A pastor of a church in Victoria, Brazil, 1996

"I was operated on twice, but my injured spinal disc problems kept recurring. My leg muscles had atrophied to the point that I had to use crutches to move around. I entered the treatment room. João de Deus appeared, laid his hand between my legs, and then on my spine. Immediately after the treatment, I threw away my crutches and went home. I will never have to use crutches again."

Allesandreo Nardes Krug and Terezinha Krug, mother and son, Brazil, 1995

A healthy 15-year-old boy developed agonizing pains in his legs, to the extent that he became wheelchair-bound. The doctors were puzzled and no longer knew what to do. They thought it could be osteoporosis, multiple sclerosis, or a slipped disc, but they could not be sure.

Following treatments with João de Deus, his father says, "Allesandreo can walk again, as if nothing was ever wrong

The Brazilian spiritual healer João Teixeira da Faria, aka João de Deus, treats a patient for angina.

with him. He was cured by a psychic operation, herbs and spiritual energy. I paid for nothing except the trip to Abadiânia." Terezinha Krug, Allesandreo's mother, could no longer walk because of a malignant tumour in her uterus. The pain was intolerable. Mr. Krug reported, "She was cured by painless surgical removal of the tumour and without anesthetic. The operation took only took five minutes."

Dr. Romeu Correa de Araujo Filho from Goiania, Brazil, 1996

Dr. Romeu's colleague Dr. Divaldo Matos Sautana and three other physicians observed the operation performed on him. Romeu was asked to sit down on a low stool. An in-house medium stood before him, providing energy, while João "traced" an incision approximately 3 inches (6 cm) long down the right shoulder blade. Part of an ulcer was removed as he worked his way around the main tumour until it could be removed almost in one piece. The cavity was then rinsed with "charged" water to sterilize the area. Two stitches closed up the incision and the young doctor went on to the recovery room for postoperative rest. The other doctors observed the entire operation and were allowed to take the tumour for pathological analysis.

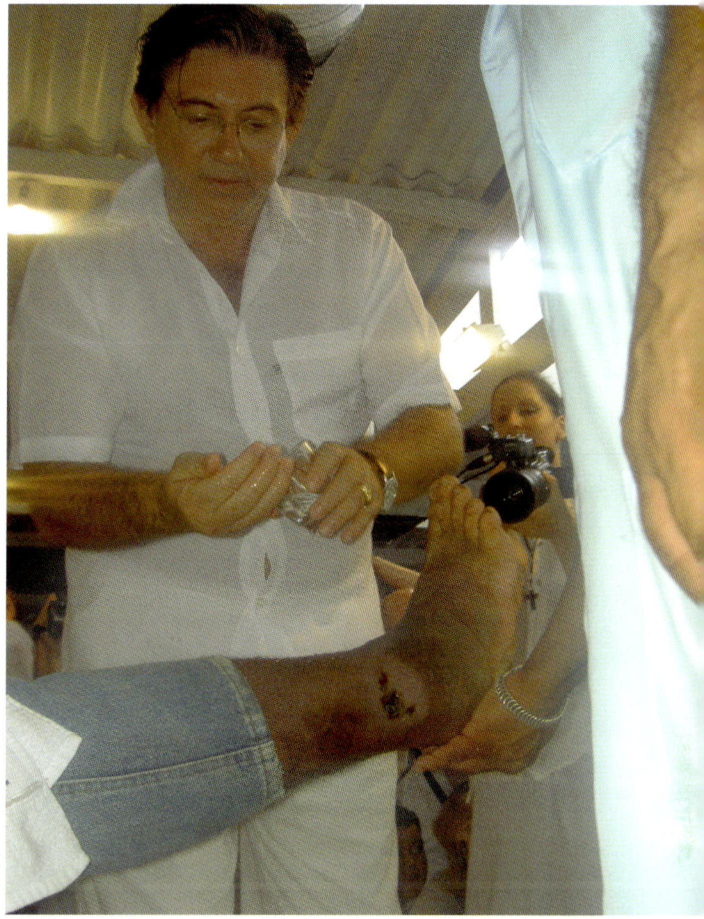

João de Deus spreads consecrated oil on the foot and leg of a man suffering from severe burns.

Many disabled individuals do not give up hope, but instead look for help from alternative medicine or spiritual healers. Some are able to leave their wheel chairs behind forever.

Thank you note from Caterina Pellgrino of Florence, Italy, 1996

"I'm writing to thank you for the psychic operation that I had last week in Abadiânia. Dr. Augusto de Almeida [one of the so-called entities, or manifestations, who works through João to accomplish healings] removed a large tumour from my small intestine, other tumours from my right kidney, and a small marble-sized tumour from my neck. The intestinal tumour was diagnosed some time ago in Australia, but I was too afraid to have it removed by a conventional operation. I can never thank you and your being enough for alleviating my suffering.

"My visit to your hospital was a remarkable experience, and I thank you for it.

"Respectfully, Caterina Pellgrino"

A shaman from the Ndebele tribe in South Africa watches the sun go down. On his head rests an *isiba*, a headdress made of porcupine needles. It is part of his job to read the future by casting bones on the ground and observing how they fall.

Shamans

A shaman is a person endowed with unusual spiritual abilities who is able to heal the sick, ward off disaster and influence the weather. One can only become a shaman by being called in a dream or a vision. Shamans have a direct connection to the world beyond this one, with the task of restoring the distorted relationship between humans and the gods. Thus, shamans are mediators between humanity and the spirit world.

The female magicians of Manchuria

The literal meaning of shaman is "he (or she) who knows". The term comes from the Manchurian-Tungusic language with roots in Siberia and Central Asia, and was first documented in 1194. Predecessors of the Manchu associated it exclusively with their female magicians.

Shamans are not tied to any one religion, and shamanism has spread with the spiritualist and New Age movements. Shamans mediate between the spiritual and material worlds by means of their store of ancient human knowledge. This knowledge gives them access to special techniques and rituals placing them in contact with the invisible reality that surrounds us all. They are also often called medicine men (or women). The practices and responsibilities of a shaman to their community are nearly the same whether in Asia, Africa, or India. Their intense experiences can lead to physical and spiritual healing, but also to transmigration, the means by which they contact the otherworld.

To counsel, heal and bring self-knowledge

From the beginning of human history, there have always been certain people whose task it has been to preserve and pass on ancient knowledge about medicine and healing. There are still shamans who live and work in Europe and North America today, often in secret, because, as they say, our society is not yet ready to accept their mysterious gifts and abilities. Individuals seeking help turn to them for the most part in private.

The World Health Organization (WHO) has recognized shamanistic healing rituals and also documented that these often work just as well as orthodox medicine. In the USA, orthodox medical practitioners are increasingly working together with shamans in hospitals. Western medicine has something to learn from ancient ritualistic traditions. Because shamans view the natural world as animated and spiritual, they treat diseases as invaders of the organism. Some shamans have also mastered the diagnosis of disease. They see their task today as tracking down the invaders causing disease and removing them.

This photo by Edward Curtis portrays a medicine man from the North American Arikara tribe.

Ecstasy through dancing and drugs

Shamans, male and female, achieve their ecstatic states by means of drumming and dancing, but also often with drugs. Although the state of ecstasy they achieve may resemble possession, the magical situation is at all times consciously led and under the shamans' control.

Through ritual, the shamans offer themselves up as a means of transmitting superhuman powers and as a contact point for potentially useful energies. In the process they are never themselves controlled by the spirits they invoke. Instead, they are the intermediaries between the otherworld and Earth, between humankind and the divine. They are on a journey of the soul. While underway they are able to see the future, guide the dead to the afterlife and, most importantly, serve their community by healing the sick.

Shamans have special knowledge that gives them access to an invisible reality. This shaman from Nigeria is shaking a rattle during a ritual.

Druids

Druids were Celtic priests and priestesses whose deeds were woven into many legends. They were also responsible for teaching mythology and morals to young people. By observing the heavens and stars, and by performing occasional human sacrifices, they were able to predict the future. The cult of the Druids has managed to endure to the present day.

The Celtic spiritual elite

As religious leaders, the Druids were a kind of spiritual elite within Celtic society. They were other things as well: poets, doctors, astronomers, philosophers and magicians. Everything we know about Druids today comes from ancient sources that are not necessarily objective, given that their authors were not always interested in a neutral account. Whether they really were as they are portrayed in literature can no longer be determined. The accounts from Christian Middle Ages as well as those of a more recent vintage written by spiritualists or followers of neo-Celtic religions, are extremely subjective and therefore not easily proven.

The very meaning of the name is not conclusively documented. "Druid" comes from the Celtic *dru*, which means "steadfast, solid" and *uid* means "seer". Other etymologists see the name as stemming from *drus'*, which means "oak".

Female Druids

Female Druids are mentioned frequently. Medb of Connacht and Ceridwen appear in Celtic myth. Ceridwen makes a potion that conveys knowledge about the past, present and future. She first mixed it for her son, Affagdu, to make up for his ugliness by giving him knowledge. Having been led into temptation, her maid drank three drops and then fled to escape her mistress' wrath. While running away she is transformed into a variety of creatures and objects, ultimately changing into a kernel of wheat, which Ceridwen swallows down. She became pregnant as a result and bore a second son who would be the first Druid. This legend leads one to believe in the existence of female Druids with significant functions within the belief system.

A group of modern Druids celebrate the summer solstice on June 21st at Stonehenge (see pages 38ff).

The oral transmission of knowledge

Julius Caesar mentions the Druids in his history *The Gallic War*. Plinius the Elder describes them as men dressed all in white carrying gold sickles and mistletoe branches. They were Celtic priests at the height of their powers during the period of the Roman campaigns. Other sources say that they were already active much earlier at Stonehenge. Critics point out that Stonehenge was already a ruin by the time the Druids arrived on the scene. We also know from Roman accounts that the Druids did not build temples, instead holding their rituals in groves or forest clearings.

The above-mentioned texts also tell us that the Druids passed on all the necessary knowledge in the form of oral rhymes, known as gnomic verses (from the Greek word *gno*, "to know"). The histories say it took an individual twenty years to learn them all. Although the Celts did have writing at that time, Druids were forbidden to write down their knowledge of astronomy and natural history; it could only be passed on orally. The rhymed verses made everything easier to memorize, considering just how much material there was to learn. It was not uncommon in other cultures

Druids were Celtic priests. It is said that they could tell the future from their observations of the heavens and stars.

for orally transmitted information to be organized in verse form so that information could be passed on from generation to generation. We know, for example, that the sailing guidelines needed for sea travel in the Pacific were passed on over many centuries as part of an oral tradition.

Neo-Celtic Druids

The antiquarian William Stukeley (see pages 40ff) is considered the father of modern Druidism. Based on his ideas, a solstice ceremony that included Druid initiation was held in Wales in 1792. With the sprouting of nationalism, Ireland and Wales no longer saw themselves as part of Britain, but as independent states with their own language and culture. The secret societies that supported political and cultural independence often included Druids, who in any case, as priests, were sworn to secrecy. Today, Neo-Celtic Druidism is one of many neo-pagan religions. Present-day Druids see themselves as direct descendents of the Druids of the past.

Druids used mistletoe as an ingredient in magic potions. For high priests, mistletoe was a holy plant because it was a sign of the presence of the gods of the tree. That is why mistletoe branches were cut only with a golden sickle and caught by a white cloth as they fell.

Spontaneous Combustion

The human body can burst suddenly into flame. In the past three centuries, nearly 200 cases of this mysterious phenomenon have been described, but no scientist has yet been able to explain conclusively how it happens. Interpretations from the parasciences include divine punishment, atomic chain reactions and unknown chemical processes. What manner of energy is released that can set off spontaneous combustion?

A known alcoholic burns to death on his straw bed

Individuals spontaneously burning to death without any visible cause is one of the most mysterious phenomena of all. The undisputed specialist in this area, Larry Arnold of England, identified the earliest report of spontaneous combustion, which dates to the year 1671. It took place in Paris. A known drunkard was completely consumed by fire except for his fingertips and head. Although lying on a straw bed at the time, the straw itself had not caught fire. Ever since, police investigating similar cases have explained the phenomenon as resulting from the ignition of gases produced by alcoholics. This explanation no longer suffices, however, given the sheer number and variety of instances. The most frequently posed question remains: "How is it possible for a person to be completely consumed by flames without setting fire to the immediate surroundings?"

Attempts to explain the inexplicable

A characteristic of all cases of spontaneous self-combustion is the generation of tremendous heat. Its victims do not suffer a normal death by fire. Rather than dying from suffocation or burns, they are literally consumed by the flames. Typically, the only thing left is a heap of ashes. Over the years, scientists from different disciplines have proposed explanations for these mysterious events. Some claim it is God's way of punishing alcoholics who have so saturated their bodily tissue with alcohol that even the smallest flame,

Is self-combustion a punishment from God, as parascientists often propose, or is it the result of an atomic chain reaction? The riddle of this remarkable phenomenon is still not solved.

Sir David Brewster invented the kaleidoscope at the beginning of the nineteenth century. An independent scholar, he also studied incidents of self-combustion, contributing a famous account of one of these cases.

The victims of self-combustion usually burn completely. Some researchers attribute the fact that, in some cases, only the legs are spared to the wick effect.

perhaps merely the embers from a cigarette, would be enough to set them ablaze. Experiments with meat marinated in alcohol, however, did not support this hypothesis. Other researchers proposed that ball lightning was responsible, but this theory was also refuted because there is not nearly enough energy in ball lightning to account for it (see page 306). More recent theories suggest that atomic chain reactions within the body's cells could be responsible, or cold fission, which would be capable of releasing that kind of energy. All of these would explain the extreme heat generated. However, there are no known radioactive elements in animal or human bodies that could either produce an atomic chain reaction or enable nuclear fission. Most scientists maintain that the phenomenon of self-combustion simply does not exist. The body is two-thirds water, they say, making it too wet to burn that way.

Characteristics of spontaneous self-combustion

- 80% of victims are women.
- Most of the victims are overweight and/or severe alcoholics
- Almost all victims are alone and often known to be heavy drinkers
- The bodies are nearly completely burned, but not the rooms in which they are found
- The bodies are usually burned, but not the head and/or extremities; and the clothing often remains undamaged
- A yellow, foul smelling oil surrounds the victims

The wick effect

If the affected person can be said to burn like a candle, then the clothes function as the wick and the body's own fat supplies the "wax". Parapsychologist Larry Arnold maintains that this would explain the yellow, foul smelling oil often found on the floor around the victims. What has never been explained is how bodies can be so completely consumed, something that does not typically happen, even during cremation, which always leaves bones behind. Arnold's argues that once there is enough heat generated to ignite the body fat, the wick effect takes over, leaving the body to burn over an extended period of time at a temperature of over 1450 °F (800 °C). This should be more than hot enough to break down the bones. The legs are sometimes left unscathed, he explains, because of the position of the individual when the fire began. If the person was sitting up, the fire, subject to the wick effect, will only burn in an upward directon, like a candle.

Crystal Tears

An age-old fairy tale tells the story of a young woman, the good sorceress Aryuda. She felt rejected because her magic had only stirred up jealousy. Disappointed by people and other magicians, she withdrew to a high mountaintop to be alone. Saddened by her experiences, she began to weep, whereupon her tears solidified into sparkling crystals. She wept until her body was completely covered by crystals, transforming her into a crystal statue.

Not just in fairy tales

The ability to weep crystal tears is not only something that happens in fairy tales. It is one of those mysteries that science cannot explain. In March 1996, twelve-year-old Hasnah Mohamed Meselmani, a student in Lebanon, was in school when she complained about something caught in her eye. It was accompanied by a stabbing pain as if something sharp was lodged there. And in fact, to the great surprise of her teacher, a small, sharp-edged fragment of sparkling crystal emerged. To everyone's amazement, her eye appeared to be uninjured. Witnesses went on to describe how, a few minutes later, another crystal tear fell from her eye.

Doctors remain at a loss

Hasnah's father took her to an eye specialist, who admitted her to a hospital for two weeks of observation. She produced crystal tears every day during this period, yet the doctor could not determine their source. In spite of his scepticism that such a thing was possible, he had no other choice but to acknowledge the authenticity of the tears, which, meanwhile, had become so sharp-edged that they could shred paper or cut glass, but still, mysteriously, did not injure the girl's eye.

Hasnah's father brought his daughter to see another eye doctor, Dr. Salomoun, from the American University Hospital in Beirut, but he was also unable to explain the phenomenon. To this day, doctors have yet to provide an answer. Dr. Nasib El-Lakkis, an eye surgeon, drew up a detailed case study, but he could not help, either. Hasnah's father also tried, unsuccessfully, to consult with European and American specialists.

In the fairy tale, tears turned a sorceress into sparkling crystal. Twelve-year-old Hasnah Mohamed Meselmani complained about something caught in her eye, and also wept crystal tears.

In many cultures, crystals are said to be tears of the gods and are ascribed special healing properties.

Night visits from a white knight

After a few weeks of uncertainty and daily crystal tears, Hasnah told her family that nearly every evening someone was knocking on her window. When she looked up, she would see a knight dressed all in white, asking her to come outside. They began to talk. The white knight announced that she was to be messenger of God on earth, with her crystal tears serving as proof. He told her she should not be afraid, because everything comes to pass by God's will. She asked when the crystal tears would stop, but received no reply. The divine messenger appeared many times, even once when Hasnah's brother present; but he only saw and heard his sister, never the white figure.

Authorities keep the case quiet

The case received worldwide attention at the time, but its Christian aspects unsettled the Islamic authorities in the region. They ultimately succeeded in swearing Hasnah's father to silence with the help of a large sum of money. Later, after some fuss the story became public. Many considered it to be a fraud, insinuating that the father had placed the crystals in his daughter's eyes to make money.

The case remains unsolved to this day and Hasnah continues to weep her mysterious tears.

When Hasnah Mohamed Meselmani cried crystal tears, she said she would see a white knight, with whom she also spoke.

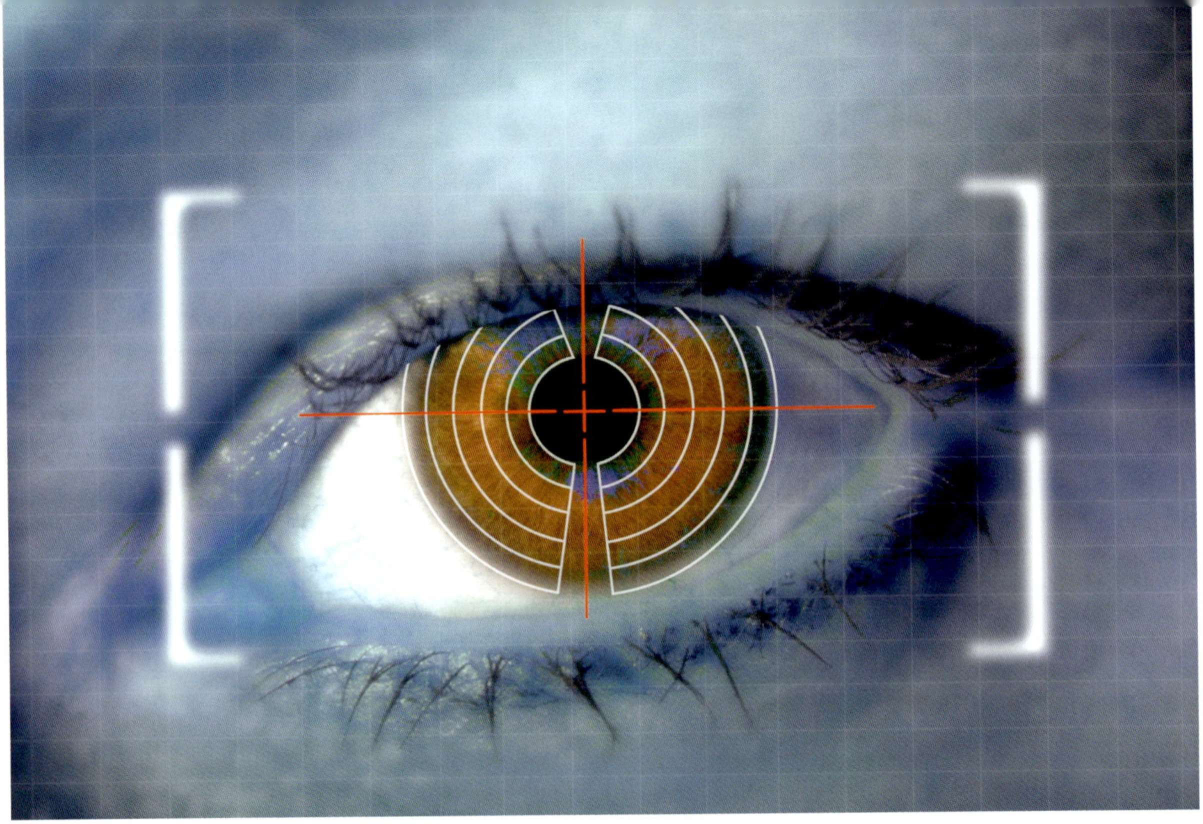

Is the human eye able to see through bodily tissue like an x-ray?

X-Ray Eyes

X-ray machines generate beams that penetrate a person's body in order to detect damage to their organs or bones. In everyday parlance, a person with x-ray eyes is someone who can see through things without an x-ray machine. In Russia, two young people have become known for their mysterious gift of being able to literally see into other people and diagnose diseases.

From a normal view to a medical view

Seventeen-year old Natalia Demkina is from Saransk, a town in Russia east of Moscow. When she was 10, scientists discovered that she could, at will, switch her vision from normal sight to what she called "medical" vision. She could clinically look inside other people. Despite her gift, however, she cannot see into her own body.

Demkina had first attracted attention after she drew sketches of her mother's inner organs and those of some other members of her family. They found the subject a bit morbid and brought the child to see a doctor. While she was at the medical office she drew the doctor's stomach, including an ulcer. The doctor, who knew he had an ulcer, was flabbergasted.

A God-given gift

Early in 2004, the BBC produced a television program about Natalia's mysterious ability. She was asked to scan four unknown people brought before her. In each of the four cases, her diagnosis was correct: a failing kidney, a spinal defect, an injured shoulder and a surgical scar on a spleen. The moderators and the doctors invited to observe were visibly impressed. Natalia really was able to see into other people. Naturally, she became famous overnight and since then people have been standing in line outside her door. Natalia looks into every case, providing her diagnoses for free. She feels that she owes it to her fellow men and women to share her gift, which she sees as God-given, but which no one has yet been able to explain.

Irina Katschan, chief of staff in the local hospital, recognizes Natalia's abilities, declaring "The percentage of cases that she diagnosed correctly is exceptionally high."

People come in droves to be cured

Rafael Batyrov, from the southeast Russian province of Bashkiria, is 11 years old. He has the paranormal gift of being able to diagnose diseases in other people using a mirror. From the accounts of those who have consulted him in increasingly large numbers, he is also able to heal them. Like Natalja Demkina, his family and home received a great deal of media attention, and therefore is regularly besieged by masses of people. The boy discovered his gift some years ago when his father mentioned that there were individuals who could see through other people. Rafael told his father to stand in front of the mirror, which he uses for his diagnoses, whereupon he was able to detect his father's lung cancer. Rafael's mother, Rasima Batyrov, is an elementary school teacher. Full of pride, she reports that her boy has already managed to cure a great many of her colleagues.

The Laser Boy from southern Russia

His supporters call Rafael "Laser Boy". Convinced that his gift is divine in origin, this intelligent youth is a vegetarian, avoids dairy products and spends his time reading the Holy Scriptures. He, too, would like to use his paranormal gift in the future to serve humanity. Like Natalia, he wants to study medicine and, above all, devote himself to furthering the parasciences. The medical world remains bewildered by the abilities of these two young people. Even the most extreme sceptics have not yet been able to cast any serious doubt on the children's well-proven abilities; neither can they explain them.

Eleven-year-old Rafael Batyrov from southern Russia can diagnose diseases by looking at a person's reflection.

The German physicist Wilhelm Conrad Röntgen discovered x-radiation, the first technology to provide an immediate and direct image of internal organs. But do some people really have x-ray eyes?

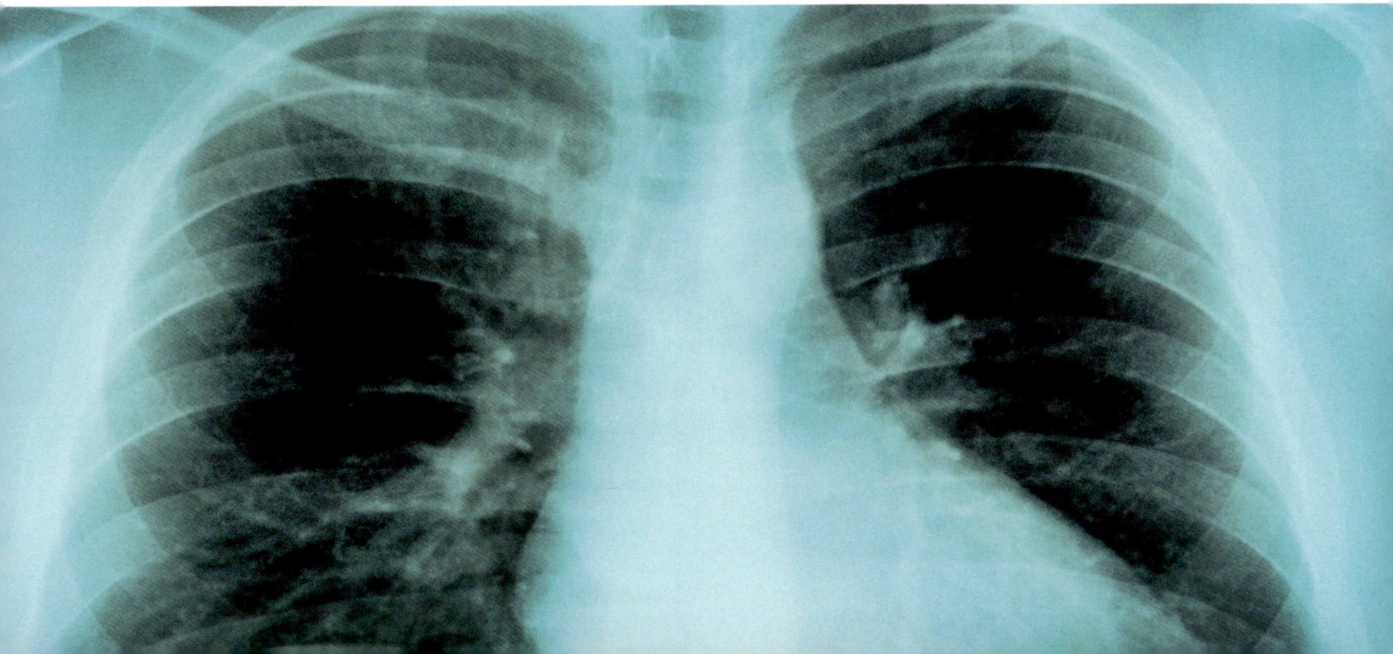

Déjà vu

Translated from the French, the words déjà vu literally mean "already seen". In the field of psychology, the term describes a false memory in which a new situation is perceived as feeling familiar. Psychology usually classifies such an experience as a psychotic or neurotic disturbance, but spiritualism believes that reincarnation and past lives explain déjà vu experiences.

It is not uncommon for a person to encounter an individual with whom they have the intense feeling that they have met in some other time or place.

Soul transmigration as an explanation for déjà vu

According to parapsychologists, when you meet a person who seems somehow familiar, but you do not know anything about them and have never before met them in your present life, what you perceive is the energy of a kindred soul from a past life. Exceptionally sensitive individuals may meet many former acquaintances throughout the course of their lives, considered by some to be their "real" family. Ordinary people unconsciously seek out places in which they've already lived and find signs of themselves when they were other people. There are also people, clothed in various human bodies, who are in touch with the elemental power of their own souls.

People who experience déjà vu frequently seek out places where they believe they have lived at some point in the past.

Lives pass on only to blossom again in another place

Déjà vu is the strange sensation of having already experienced a situation or seen a person or place before, when that is not the case. The expression comes from French philosopher and linguist Emile Boirac (1851–1917), who used it for the first time in one of his novels. While informed by the past, déjà vu actually has more to do with the present because it deals with that precise moment when one senses that something has happened before, leading to questions like, Have I seen this film already? Have I been in this city before? Do I know these people? Parapsychologists explain experiences like this as the retrieving of buried memories, usually those from an earlier life, but sometimes also associated with clairvoyance. To spiritualists, every life in all its incarnations touches on all other lives, as well as all the persons who have been part of those lives. A young child may die for what seems to be no obvious reason because it is not happy in its chosen milieu. Lives pass on only to blossom again in another place.

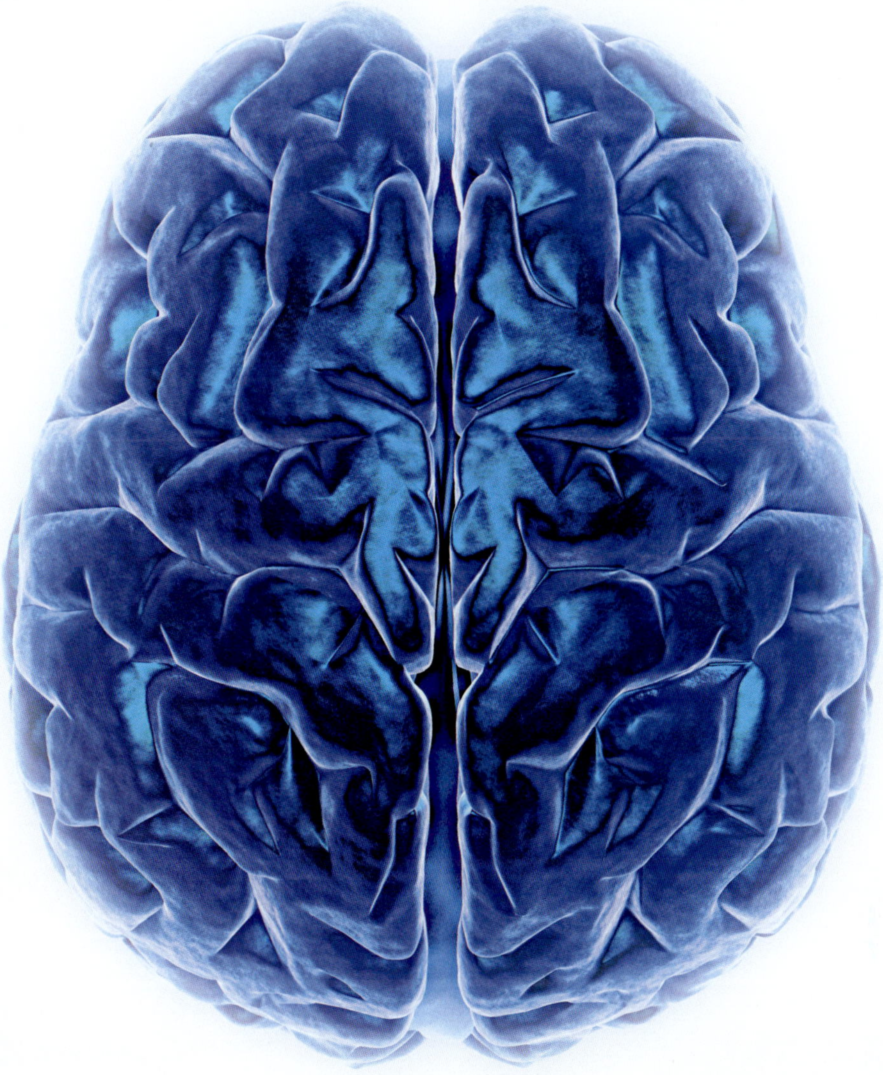

In psychology, déjà vu experiences are considered to be disruptions in brain function. Spiritualists believe them to be related to reincarnation.

Researchers question how anyone can know when and where they once lived during past lifetimes. Spiritualists believe that, in principal, everyone has the memory and knowledge of all their past lives stored in their subconscious. The only way to fully recall this knowledge is through past life regression, in which people see their other lives played out before them like a film. This can be somewhat frightening, though the fear is easily overcome. Déjà vu can therefore be regarded as nothing less than the reliving of a past life experience.

Three psychological explanations

The field of psychology, on the other hand, views these phenomena as pathological symptoms, for which it offers three possible explanations: (a) An emotional state has not yet been worked through, leading to a psychological defect that brings about irregular perceptions of new situations that require reorientation and adjustment. Déjà vu occurs as part of this transitional state. (b) A perceived situation triggers associations with repressed memories. The person does not want to remember them, but cannot suppress the memories. (c) A so-called familiarity illusion occurs, in which a situation is misperceived as part of a previous experience, despite the fact that no such experience has ever occurred outside of the mind itself.

Interpreting Dreams

A dream is an automatic, optically perceived experience occurring beyond the control of the consciousness during sleep. Dreams are considered the gateway to the subconscious, long thought to represent a state of mind common to mystics, poets, painters and musicians. Dreams are important; the inability to dream can lead to emotional disturbance. Human beings have always interpreted dreams, hoping to bring back information that can be applied to waking life.

The categorization of dreams

When the famous Austrian physician Sigmund Freud founded psychoanalysis at the end of the nineteenth century, he created a systematic science focused on the subconscious and emphasizing the fundamental role of dreams in the treatment of psychological problems and trauma. But Freud's is not the only theory of dreams. Other important psychologists to break ground in this field were C.G. Jung, Alfred Adler and Erich Fromm.

All dreams are not alike: these theorists differentiate between dreams that mask aggression, pursuit dreams, compensation dreams, daydreams, nightmares and wish fulfilment dreams. Regardless of the meaning hiding within the interior parade of images, this projection is always related to a particular state of mind. Jung was especially interested in the concept of the archetype, an ur-idea or image genetically shared by all people since the beginning of time, which can be passed on as a kind of collective inheritance. Archetypes are therefore part of a collective unconscious, revealing symbols that belong to all people in all times, commonly expressed in fairy tales, myths, religion and art.

All humans dream. Coherent optical images and feelings not under the control of the waking consciousness occur during sleep.

Since Sigmund Freud, dream interpretation is understood as an integral aspect of psychotherapy designed to cure neuroses, because dreams are expressions of the unconscious.

A legacy of ancient cultures

For a long time, the Western world has been convinced that a methodological approach to dream interpretation began in Europe with the development of modern psychoanalysis, but in reality, dream interpretation had long been considered a great art in civilizations as varied as Mesopotamia, Persia, Greece, Egypt, India, China, Tibet and the Native American cultures. People from every time and place have been fascinated by what the nocturnal dream world might symbolize. Dreams and their content were understood to be prophetic or clairvoyant. Cultures have always distinguished between dreams that foresee events and profane dreams that work through the personal trials of daily life. Dreams solve so many problems that they are a form of therapy in themselves, setting the course for physical and mental recovery by offering an individual the means for self-discovery and self-help.

Lucid dreaming

Modern dream research also covers the phenomenon of lucid dreaming. These are clear, transparent dreams in which the sleeping person is immediately aware that he or she is asleep. The sensation is like that of awakening fully conscious in the middle of a dream, raising the question of which is more genuine and true, the dream or the waking state. In their myths, native tribes in the jungles of Brazil long ago concluded that the illusion of the real world exists in the shadow of the reality of dreams, and they organize their lives accordingly.

What existed as long-accepted knowledge and an aspect of the secret teachings of shamans and sages has become an object of study for psychoanalysts in the West, where people now also realize that the soul speaks to us in our dreams. It is still difficult to unlock the secret language of dreams through purely scientific methods. As the so-called "primitive" world knows quite well, if we do not enter the dream world intuitively, it will forever remain an un-navigable labyrinth.

Sigmund Freud (1856–1939), the father of psychoanalysis, worked extensively in dream research.

Incorruptible Corpses

Some saints perform miracles long after their death by being spared the ravages of natural decomposition that normally befall the human remains of everyone who dies. Their bodies look just as they did at time of their deaths, despite never having been embalmed.

Saint Bernadette of Lourdes

Saint Bernadette died in 1879 at the age of 36. Her coffin was opened in 1908, and her corpse looked as though she had died just a short time before. The bluish veins in her forearms were lightly plumped and shiny. Her fingernails were intact, blushing a pale pink. In 1919, her coffin was opened once again, and the body was still intact. It looked almost the same as it had eleven years before. Coated with a film of wax, the body now lies in a shrine in the Chapel of Saint Bernadette in Nevers, France.

Other incorruptible saints

Saint Cuthbert of Lindisfarne, in northeast England, died in the year 687. In the sixteenth century, his corpse was still intact. His body had endured over 900 years completely unscathed!

In Poland, in 1922, the Soviet Red Army forced open the tomb of Saint Andreas Bobola, who had died in 1657. Those present were astonished to find that the body was perfectly preserved. His body had already been found intact in 1917, after which it was put on display so that the faithful could pray over it. Today, the saint's body lies in a church in Warsaw.

The bodies of individuals who had received the stigmata seem to have a tendency to be particularly well-preserved. Saint Catherine of Siena received the stigmata in 1375, but asked God to make the marks disappear and leave only the pain. Her prayer was answered, but, after her death in 1380, the stigmata appeared again under her still-intact skin. In 1430, the pope granted permission for her corpse to be exhumed – it was completely undecayed – and divided into relics. Four hundred years later, in 1855, the last pieces were divided, and even then, every small part remained in perfect condition.

The incorruptible Siberian lama

Hambo Lama Dashi Dorzho Itigilov, a Siberian Buddist leader, passed away in 1927 at the age of 75. Before he died he asked his assembled students to "visit and examine my body" after thirty years. Accordingly, his followers exhumed his body in 1957. They found him exactly as he was when he died: sitting in the lotus position with crossed legs. But because religious subjects were suppressed in the USSR during the 1950s, they buried the corpse again and spoke of it only within Buddhist circles.

In 2002, the young lama Bimba Dorzhiyev exhumed the corpse. He had located an old monk who had been present for the first exhumation in the 1950s and could guide them to where the body could be found.

Saint Bernadette of Lourdes died in 1879 at the age of 36. Forty years later in 1919, her body shows – as foretold – no sign of decay.

Dorzhiyev documented the event, along with two forensic scientists, a photographer and a dozen other witnesses. Itigilov's body was indeed fully intact, seventy-five years after his death. Today the body can be seen, still in the lotus position, in a Buddhist monastery in Ivolginsk. One reporter from the *New York Times* described the body as sitting on a simple table surrounded by candles and metal bowls filled with oil. It showed indisputable similarities to a photograph of the living lama taken in 1913. The limbs are flexible, the skin soft, the fingernails intact and the hair on his head still short.

"This is the greatest miracle of my life", said Hambo Lama Ayusheyev, who has been the spiritual leader of the monastery since 1995. "It shows that there are things over which time has no power. Many people simply do not see what is obvious, and when they do, they do not understand what they see." (13)

Saint Cuthbert from Lindisfarne in northeast England died in 687 AD. In the sixteenth century, his body was found unscathed in Durham Cathedral. The so-called Neville Screen has stood between the altar and Saint Cuthbert's tomb since 1380.

It remains an inexplicable puzzle why certain human corpses do not fall prey to the decaying process, but remain seemingly untouched over decades and even centuries.

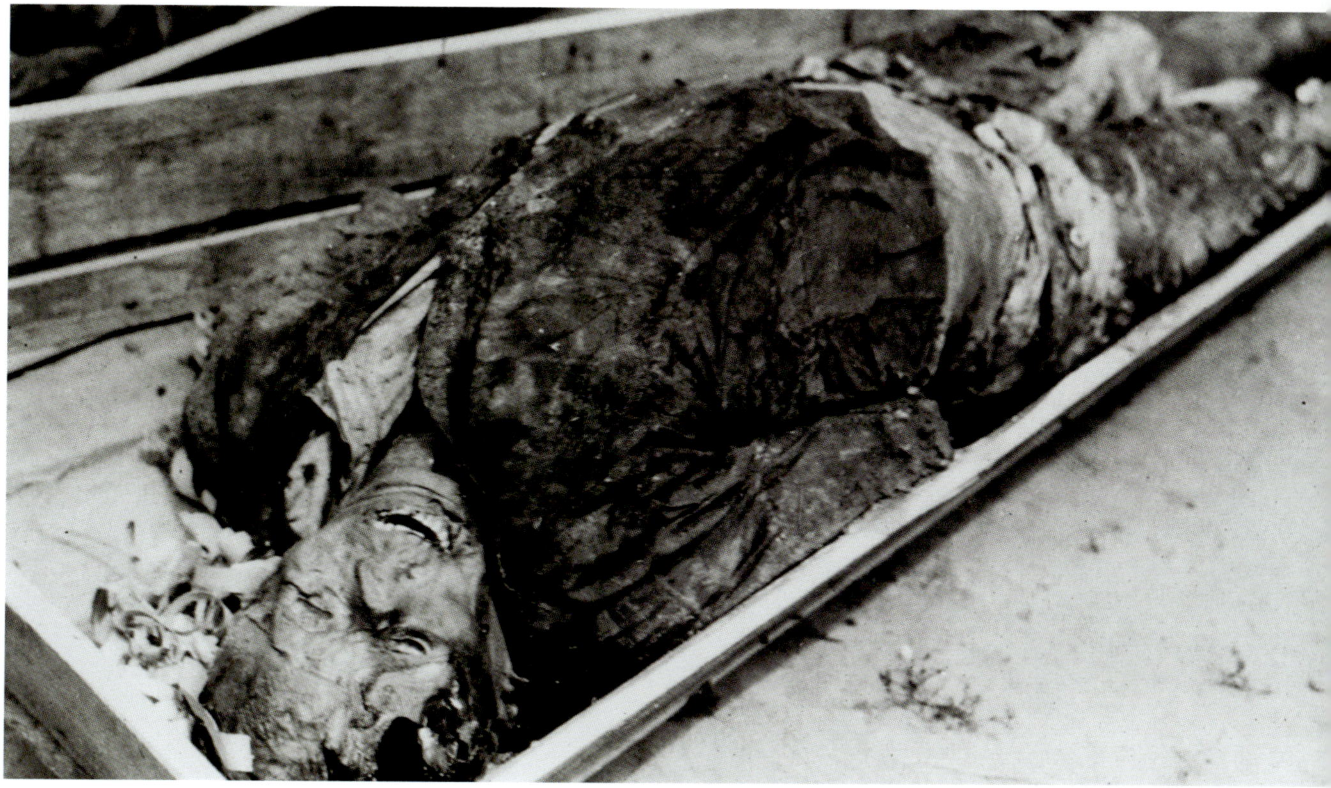

Strange Forces

The cosmos, the very universe that surrounds us all, was one of the first topics to fascinate students of the paranormal, the fantastic and the frontiers of science. Ever since people could think, they have asked whether we are alone in the universe. Do other cultures exist on distant planets? It is easy to see how this question formed one of the foundations of religion. Humanity's relationship with the cosmos, be it through catastrophic events or the mere fact of existence, has always deeply affected its religious development.

These days, many investigators view unusual phenomena and evidence of strange forces on the earth in light of recent research into UFOs. How is it possible, they ask, that the Dogon tribe in North African Mali has so much esoteric knowledge about the Dog Star, Sirius, including information that only recently became available to modern scientists? And what about those mysterious crop circles, found all over the world in increasingly complicated patterns? Other thinkers have tried to connect black holes with historically documented incidences of possible time travel. Was it once possible for people to travel through time? Many investigations in this area, of course, focus on the Bermuda Triangle, that region of the Earth where unexplained disappearances are most common. What strange forces are at work in this tropical place, where ships and aeroplanes suddenly disappear? Scientists have also investigated the mighty ground painting that stretches over 2.8 miles (4.5 km) of the Australian desert. Who was capable of creating this image of an Aborigine, one that can only be seen from a very great height?

The still unexplained, geometrically patterned crop circles can appear practically overnight. This is an aerial photograph of a particularly complex pattern cut into a wheat field.

Throughout the millennia, thousands of recorded sightings of unidentified flying objects have been connected with alien beings visiting Earth. The image above is a science fiction portrayal of a flying saucer over the former World Trade Center in New York City.

Unidentified Flying Objects

There are photographs of flying triangles and discs that have been sighted in every country in the world. There are also images of crop circles, reports of spaceship crashes and accounts of alien abductions. UFO enthusiasts and researchers can speak of thousands of unidentified apparitions in the sky, while the Internet vibrates with new reports of secret service and military cover-ups. What lies behind all of these accounts? Are we not the only ones in the universe? Is there intelligent life on other planets, and were "they" once here, or are they still?

Ancient Egyptian images of flying objects

While scholars have deciphered ancient Sanskrit texts that describe wagons flying across the heavens, and more than one Roman historian mentions flying shields, the most detailed ancient descriptions of unidentified flying objects stem from the Egyptians and were recorded during the reign of Pharaoh Thutmosis III (ca. 1483–1425 BC). The so-called Tulli Papyrus, for example, as translated by Donald J. Long in 1993, reads as follows: "In Year 22, third month, first day, in the sixth hour … it happened that the scribes were in the house of the life, when a circle of fire appeared in the sky. It had no head, but its mouth gave off a breath, that stank terribly. Its body was a rod long and a rod wide [1 rod = 170 feet, or 52 m]. It made no sound … now it came to pass that after three days this object appeared in greater numbers. They lit up the sky like the sun! They travelled to all four corners of the heavens … they rose high to the south and flew from there." (14)

Were these UFOs that the pharaoh saw flying across the sky nearly 3,500 years ago?

The sceptics

The pro-UFO lobby repeatedly offers evidence of UFO sightings, or even landings, on earth. According to officials, there is no proof for any of it. Conspiracy theorists are convinced that governments and their secret police forces have covered up or destroyed much of the evidence. Meanwhile, those claiming to have witnessed alien activity are increasingly the kind of people one would think could be trusted, including police officers, pilots and astronomers. In a 1991 study involving more than 300 reports of UFOs, the Society for the Scientific Investigation of Parasciences categorized the majority of sightings as optical illusions: an object like a weather balloon, for example, might be mistaken for an alien ship. The results also indicated that once a UFO sighting has been reported, additional ones cluster around it. Then, of course, there are the entrepreneurs who make money from UFOs. Films are produced as "proof", photographs of alien corpses are sold to the highest bidder, and sensational revelations, such as the discovery of secret CIA files, are written up in books. But how does this affect the alien sightings for which we do not have any alternative explanation? Did these really take place or not?

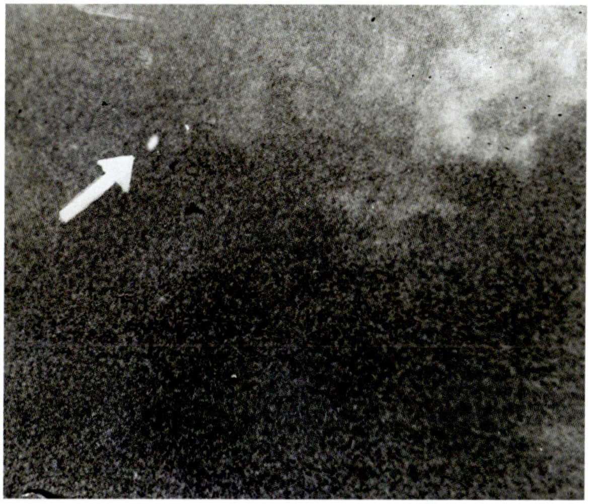

Photos claiming to show UFOs are common. Many photographic "proof" does not actually prove anything.

The A'le'inn is a bar and grill in the small town of Rachel, Nevada. Its UFO-themed décor has attracted a great number of visitors.

A Geiger counter is an instrument used to measure radioactivity.

A UFO lands in the Russian town of Voronezh

In 1989, the Russian news agency TASS issued the following press release:

"Soviet scientists have confirmed the landing of an unknown flying object in a park in the Russian city of Voronezh. They have identified the landing place and found traces of alien life forms ... Locals reported that the aliens visited the place at least three times, always after dark. They saw a large, glowing ball hovering over the park. According to eyewitnesses, a UFO landed, a door opened, and two or three human-like creatures and a small robot emerged. The aliens were 10 or even 13 feet tall (3 or 4 m), with very small heads, say witnesses. They took a walk near the ball or disk and disappeared back inside. Onlookers were overcome by feelings of fear and anxiety that lasted for several days."

Voronezh, a city of 800,000 inhabitants, lies some 300 miles (500 km) south of Moscow. After the first incident, large number of witnesses reported more than one landing, with more following. The landings pressed the grass and plants flat as if with a force field, an effect similar to that observed inside the mysterious crop circles.

Scientific investigation of the Russian incident

Professor Genrich Silanov, a physicist in the Laboratory for Spectrum Analysis of the Geophysical Institute of Voronezh, declared: "We discovered a circle some 65 feet (20 m) in diameter, with four imprẽssions about 1.5 to 2 inches (4–5 cm) deep, each with a diameter of 5.5 to 6.3 inches (14–16 cm), and also clearly recognizable, forming four corners of a rhombus. We collected two puzzling mineral samples. At first glance, these appeared to be a variety of black sandstone. But our mineralogical analysis showed them to be a substance not found anywhere on Earth."

The leader of the investigation, Ludmilla Marakov, said "The high levels of radioactivity measured here indicated that something out of the ordinary has taken place."

Another approach

In his 1967 book *Uninvited Visitors*, English UFO researcher Ivan T. Sanderson criticized the current preoccupation with UFOs as being too human-focused, leading us to think that anything that might come from outer space should be a replica of ourselves. For example, we talk about "people" from another planet. Author Donald Keyhole, among others, speaks of aliens as a dying race seeking a new place to live. Sanderson, in contrast, developed a theory in which UFOs are the product of an artificial intelligence (AI). Thus the inhabitants of UFOs are artificial life forms under the

On 23 December 1989, the Soviet botanist Valeri Dvuzhilny presented materials that supposedly had been left behind on Earth by aliens.

control of far superior intelligent machines. Humans and human-like creatures are not physically capable, he explains, of surviving in outer space. For this, artificial beings are needed, a new kind, either built using parts of our own DNA or purely mechanical.

On the cusp of a new civilization

Scientists working in the area of AI are convinced that we are standing on the cusp of a new civilization. They use the term "Singularity" to describe the moment when computers will be able to develop and program themselves to the point of developing a consciousness. Computer intelligence would then continue to develop at an extremely fast pace, leaving human intelligence far behind.

Whereas it took human intelligence millions of years to "break out" biologically, this time span bears no comparison to the speed of machine intelligence. We can think of this in terms of Moore's Law of 1965. Developed by Gorden E. Moore of the computer chip manufacturer Intel, the law states that the complexity of integrated circuits will double every twenty-four months. In 1971, the top integrated circuit held 2000 transistors; by the year 2000 the number was 42 million. As computer scientist and author Ray Kurzweil explained, the Singularity is near, and "the development will move so quickly that it will surpass our ability to imagine it. People won't notice it at first, because when it begins there will still be a recognizable version of the world in place. But the essence of what we call human intelligence will slowly dissolve. We will experience an intelligence that resembles the human variety, but which in fact towers high above it." (15)

Kurzweil believes that by the year 2040, we will be at the point where a domineering intelligent machine will rule the world, assuming, of course, that humankind survives long enough to make itself useful to this intelligence.

Aliens and their portrayal have always spurred on artistic fantasy. The English UFO scholar Ivan T. Sanderson criticizes these images as relying too much on the human form.

Intelligent Life in the Universe

Ever since we realized that the Earth is not the centre of the universe, that it moves around the sun and not the other way around, ever since the invention of the telescope led to the exploration and discovery of more and more of outer space, indeed, ever since we started to investigate the universe in the first place, we have wondered whether we are alone in its endless, ever-expanding vastness. There is much to suggest that we are not its only life form, and that intelligent life can be found on other planets.

A short calculation of probabilities

In the Milky Way galaxy alone there are 135 billion stars, all of which have one or more planets rotating around them. If one per cent of those that have an atmosphere, there are 13.5 billion such planets. If one per cent of those planets have water and simple life forms as well, then there are potentially 13.5 million stars that could have planets upon which life could develop as it did on Earth. If higher life forms developed only on an additional one per cent, we would still be talking about at least 135,000 planets where technology and civilization as we understand them are likely to exist. If a mere one per cent of these were more highly developed than ours, there could be 1350 planets with life forms superior to ourselves. The remaining potential 133,650 planets would fall into a different category entirely. We need to keep in mind that all of the above only refers to our own Milky Way galaxy, which is just one of many.

The meta-universe

Modern science assumes that our universe is not only one of many, but one of an infinite number of "many". It is therefore understood that, all things being equal, including how the universe came into being and the absolute number

Do aliens resemble humans, or are they beings that, if they exist at all, have nothing in common with our current ideas about life forms?

of other universes, the same mechanisms operative in our universe were also have been factors in the development of the others. This totality of universes is known as the meta-universe. While each universe is unique and at any given moment is living out its own history, it is only logical to assume that there are also many universes that have long since surpassed our stage of development, universes where what still lies in the future for us has already taken place. Life must have developed in those other universes, life in every form we are familiar with or can envision, including artificial life forms and different kinds of consciousness and intelligence bearing no resemblance to anything we can begin to imagine. We can, therefore, be fairly confident that a broad spectrum of potential life forms is out there, somewhere.

Data exchange between universes

The very nature of life, particularly of intelligent life, will lead it to improve itself, expand, investigate and seek out new places to live, or at least encourage their discovery. Life will always seek new paths. In our world, there are connections and interactions between otherwise completely distinct and separate elements.

This must be the way the different universes function within the meta-universe, all the more so since some are far ahead of others. It is therefore perfectly conceivable that some kind of data exchange has taken place. We cannot say what kind of information might have been involved because

On 25 July 1976 the space probe Viking 1 sent back images from the surface of Mars that included the famous "Martian Face". Parascientists see this as evidence of alien life on the planet.

it would have been processed and put to use long ago. Data is merely data if it is not linked with other data. Data becomes information only when it is part of a network. This suggests that since the dawning of time, life has crossed frontiers throughout the entire meta-universe.

Life, having forged its way through, will continue onward, expanding itself still further. In any case, it must be making its way through the meta-universe at an infinitely fast pace. Have we already been contacted? Are we being contacted? Will we be? In all probability, the answer is "yes".

ET – the most famous alien, from the 1982 film of the same name, directed by Steven Spielberg.

Crop Circles

The familiar crop circles are among the best-known unexplained phenomena in the world. Exceptionally complex patterns appear in fields practically overnight by means which no one has been able to satisfactorily explain. Accounts of mysterious crop circles go back hundreds of years. Some investigators have detected strong energy fields in the area, while others believe that UFOs and the aliens that are presumably inside them are responsible.

An aerial photograph of a crop circle discovered by a wheat farmer in Rockville, Colorado.

Crop circle season: early in the tear through summer

As early as 1880, the respected science journal *Nature* reported on a crop circle found in the English county of Surrey. Since 1978, they have become increasingly common, first in England and then in other places, attracting worldwide attention. England is still the preferred location, with 300 separate instances documented since 1991. Thousands more have been discovered elsewhere in the world, with their structure and layout becoming ever more complex.

Crop circles do not occur throughout the year. They have a regular season, starting early in the year and lasting throughout the summer, which is only natural given that this is the period when crops are standing in the fields. Noteworthy is the observation that the stalks within the circle are neither broken nor bent, but instead are bowed a few centimetres above the ground, which lets them continue to grow horizontally. No tracks are found leading into or out of a crop circle pattern, and the earth beneath is completely undisturbed.

Imitation crop circles

Strange things are observed inside the circles. Birds alter their flight path, cameras stop working, blinking lights appear in the sky, and batteries lose their charge. Investigators from many disciplines have looked at the phenomenon and come up with a number of theories. Some say the circles are insect damage, or result from red deer rolling around marking territory during courtship. Small, sudden tornadoes have been blamed, too. In recent years there have been a number of crop circle imitators, people who go into fields at night to create their own sensation. Specialists have no trouble telling the difference, though, because the imitations lack the complex structure and precision of the originals.

Comparable to the intervals of a musical scale

The American biophysicist William C. Levengood has observed the circles for years. He determined that the flexibility of the grain and its moisture level indicate that

it has been subjected to a strong pulse of heat, comparable to what happens inside a microwave oven. The increase in heat would have to take place in less than 30 seconds, he explains. The ground and stalks are covered in a glaze-like layer of iron oxide, an effect that only occurs with temperatures over 930 °F (500 °C). Strong energy fields measured inside the circles could have caused this. The mathematician Gerald Hawkins discovered that the relationship between the sizes of the multiple circles that are part of some patterns corresponds precisely to the ratio between the intervals on a musical scale. Both scientists see no sign of human intervention.

The stalks inside the mysterious circles are never bent, only laid over on their sides so that they can be straightened out again later without any damage to the grain. Crop circles always attract a crowd of onlookers.

This crop circle was discovered and photographed in England in the year 2000. The patterns have become increasingly complex in recent years.

Inhabitants of Other Planets

There is often a connection drawn between UFOs and crop circles. Many eyewitnesses have sighted UFOs or lights in the sky near places where crop circles are later found, and many of these have been documented photographically. The British author Benjamin Creme has concluded that, with the exception of the obvious forgeries, inhabitants of other planets are the ones responsible for the circles. As Creme has very plainly stated: "Those inside the UFOs visualize the pattern they want to create, then perfect the formation, adding a little extra here and there, by focusing their thoughts. Then they bring their vehicle down close to the surface of the field." (16)

The Sirius Mystery

The Dogon are an ancient people living in central Mali and northern Burkina Faso. They are simple savannah agriculturalists who also herd cattle and, most famously, are known for their metal and carved wood sculpture. The Dogon have extensive knowledge about Sirius, the brightest star in the firmament, including information of which even modern astronomers were completely unaware. Scientists have long been on the trail of the mystery. Were the Dogon visited by intelligent beings from the Dog Star, Sirius?

The Sirius Mystery by Robert K. G. Temple

"The evidence appears to be overwhelming that contact of this kind (a visit by beings from Sirius) could have taken place relatively recently – between 7000 and 1000 years ago. The information we have at hand can lead to no other conclusion." Thus wrote British author Robert K.G. Temple in 1976 in his book, *The Sirius Mystery*. (17).

There are inreasing indications, Temple writes, that the knowledge base of the Dogon is more than 5000 years old, and the ancient Egyptians already made use of it. The Dogon people, as their direct successors, inherited it from the Egyptians.

This photograph of the constellation Orion showing the brightly shining Sirius was taken in Flagstaff, Arizona in 1995.

The Dogon creation myth

The starting point for the Dogon creation myth is the star Digitaria, said to be a satellite of Sirius that rotates around it. Since the dawn of time, Digitaria has been pulsating with creative energy. As the smallest, but also the heaviest, of all the stars, it carries within it the seeds of all things, says the myth. Its movements on its own axis and in rotation around Sirius guarantee the continued existence of creative energy in the universe.

The subject of the myth is therefore not so much Sirius as its satellite, which taken together form a double star. What is mysterious regarding this Dogon tradition is that it is not possible to see the smaller companion star with the naked eye. Indeed, it was only in the late twentieth century that it could be seen by telescope, permitting us to differentiate between Sirius A and Sirus B today. According to the

Sirius in history
Sirius already had a special meaning in ancient Egypt, where it was worshipped as Sopdet (in Greek, Sothis). Many temples were constructed so that its light would fall on their altars. Sirius played an important role in everyday life as well as religion, and ancient Egypt's calendar was based on its rising. Much later, in the Middle Ages, Sirius served as a symbol and harbinger of rabies, which is why a dog, standing in for the Dog Star, is often present in medieval portrayals of pilgrims. Sirius guided early pilgrims following the road to the Holy Land, which is why the route was also called the Star Road. In the late 1990s, members of the Order of the Solar Temple committed mass suicide in the belief that they would be reborn on Sirius.

Dogon legend, a race of living beings called the Nommo came from this star system, which includes a known total of nine stars. They were similar to fish in appearance, coming to earth in a spindle-shaped ark. Many of the masks made by the Dogon are said to symbolize this event: with their geometric shape and obelisk-like outlines, they resemble a rocket-driven spaceship.

White dwarves

Sirius A is nearly twice the size of our sun, with a surface temperature twice as hot, causing it to radiate twenty-four times as much light. Sirius B, in contrast, is smaller than the

A medieval map of the constellation Orion with the Dog Star, Sirius, here portrayed literally as a dog because Sirius was considered the symbol and harbinger of rabies.

Were the Dogon, an ancient people living in central Mali and northern Burkina Faso, really visited by intelligent beings from the Dog Star, Sirius, giving them secret knowledge about the star?

earth, but so dense that one cubic metre of its matter weighs three million tons. Due to its high temperature and small size, it is categorized as a "white dwarf". White dwarves are relatively small stars near the end of their lives. They are in the process of collapsing in on themselves, greatly increasing their mass. Is the Dogon's knowledge so momentous as to suggest that alien intelligences visited this African people thousands of years ago? The central, unsolved problem remains how anyone could gain all this knowledge about a star not visible to the naked eye without any access to astronomical instruments and without any understanding of the movements and characteristics of heavenly bodies. As Walter Hain writes, while the Dogon are certainly an intelligent people, whether or not this comes from contact with alien intelligence is still open to question.

The Bermuda Triangle

The Bermuda Triangle is one of the greatest mysteries of the world. Numerous films and books have reported the mysterious incidents that have taken place in this notorious stretch of sea. For nearly a century, ships and aeroplanes have been disappearing without a trace there.

On December 5, 1945 five bombers took off from the naval base in Fort Lauderdale, Florida at 2 pm on a routine mission. They never returned.

The book by Charles Berlitz

The area between Florida, the Bermuda Islands and Puerto Rico has been known as the Bermuda Triangle ever since Charles Berlitz (1914–2003) wrote a book by that name in 1974. Berlitz proposed a number of theories explaining the mysterious, repeated disappearances of ships and aeroplanes in this area. In addition to his attempts at explanation, we also have a great many accounts from eyewitnesses and survivors of the incidents.

Individual cases

Between 1945 and 1975, thirty-seven aeroplanes, a weather balloon and forty-one ships were reported lost in the Bermuda Triangle. It is said that a nuclear submarine disappeared as well. A yacht was once found sailing through the sea with no crew. Not one of these incidents was accompanied by a distress call. Instead, there was sudden radio silence, after which everything disappeared. Eyewitnesses and survivors speak of multi-coloured mists, bubbling water, deafening silence or horrible noises, and instruments that stop working. If the vehicles are able to make it through the mist, their equipment starts to function again.

In one case, radio contact between a passenger airliner and the control tower was interrupted for ten minutes, during which time the aeroplane disappeared from the radar screen. After the landing the crew reported nothing out of the ordinary. They had not noticed the ten minutes without contact, but all their watches, and those of the passengers, were running ten minutes behind.

Theories and attempts at explanation

The following theories have been proposed:

- Aliens from Venus have built a base some 3000 feet (910 m) deep under the ocean, where pressure conditions correspond to those on their home planet. They use strong magnetic fields that cause matter to dematerialize.
- The lost continent of Atlantis lies under this part of the sea. Atlantis sank during an inundation that followed an ancient atomic war.

The Bermuda Triangle is misleadingly peaceful. Countless numbers of ships and aeroplanes have disappeared here without a trace.

• The laws of physics work differently here because of a disturbance in the time-space continuum. The objects that disappeared reappear in the future, in the past, in another part of the world or, alternately, can be found floating around the universe.

• The effects of the mysterious "Philadelphia Experiment" (see box, right) conducted by the US Navy in 1943 are responsible.

• Aliens have kidnapped people and taken objects back to their planet for study.

• Aliens from a desert planet come here to soak up water, inadvertently sucking up hapless ships and aeroplanes at the same time.

• A colony of unknown, human-like beings lives underwater here. They are responsible for all of these events.

• There is a kind of hole in the firmament directly over this area. This causes space to curve, pulling everything that passes beneath it out into space.

• Unknown, highly radioactive gases are emitted here from the centre of the earth, destroying ships and aeroplanes and inducing a trance-like state in people.

The sheer number of theories demonstrates just how much human interest this mysterious phenomenon attracts. Incidents are catalogued and theories devised, but no evidence as to the possible cause of these events has ever been found. Are there places in the world where the past, present and future exist parallel to each other? Researcher Ivan T. Sanderson says there are at least twelve such zones (see page 302). Only science, by increasing its efforts toward solving these mysterious cases, holds the answer.

The Philadelphia Experiment

In the 1940s the US Navy carried out the so-called Philadelphia Experiment. The goal was to make navy ships, together with their crew, invisible, thus permitting them to cross enemy lines unobserved. It was thought that Einstein's incomplete theory of unified fields might have a practical application in this area. Supposedly, the experiment involved the generation of a very strong electromagnetic field, which is said to have been successful. The image of the ship wavered and then completely dissolved from view. A short time later, the majority of the crew died, and the survivors suffered from incurable physical maladies. The political silence surrounding the experiment has made it impossible to confirm whether or not it really took place. Did the American military successfully create a magnetic field of this size?

A map of the Bermuda Triangle east of the Gulf of Mexico. It extends from the American coast south to Puerto Rico, then east to the Bermuda Islands that give it its name.

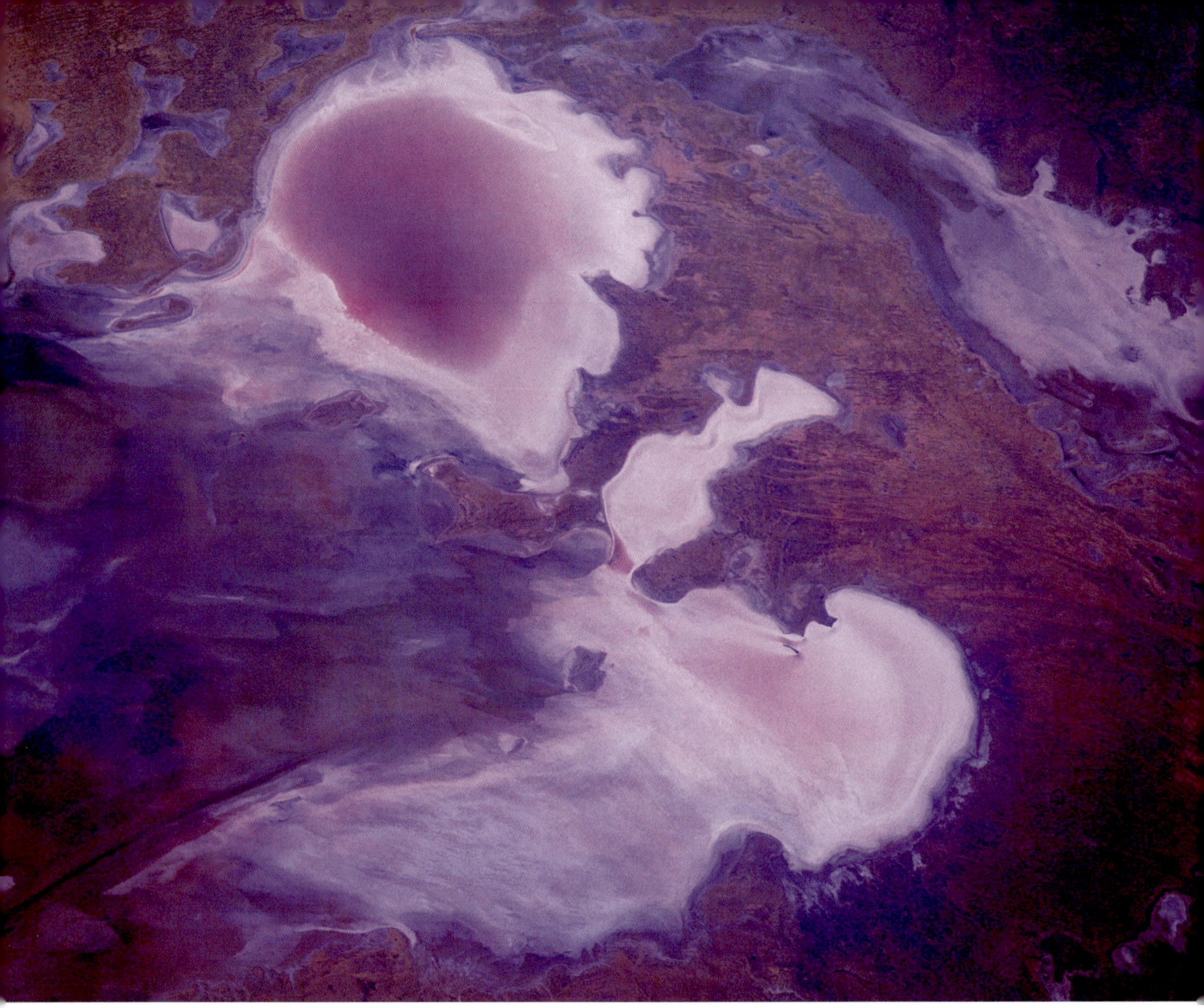

Lake Eyre, lying more than 50 feet (16 m) below sea level in the south Australian desert, is one of the largest salt lakes on earth.

The Picture of an Aborigine in the Australian Bush

Lake Eyre, one of the largest salt lakes in the world, is located in the desert of southwest Australia some 52 feet (16 m) below sea level. Depending on how the light falls, it can resemble a smooth field of snow in the middle of a desert. An enormous image of an Aborigine, 2.8 miles (4.5 km) long, was discovered here in 1998, an image that can only be made out from a height of over 3200 feet (1000 m). Thousands of aeroplanes must have flown over this spot. Why was it only discovered recently?

A FIGURE DRAWN WITH 20-FOOT-WIDE FURROWS

In 1998, a giant image of an Australian Aborigine was discovered north of Adelaide, near Lake Eyre. It was an easily recognizable, clearly drawn and perfectly proportioned figure measuring 2.8 miles (4.5 km) long with a circumference of 9.3 miles (15 km). It was discovered by Ray Goss, a businessman from a nearby city, who had received an anonymous fax telling him to go have a look.

Drawn, or, better said, excavated, the 20-foot- (6-m-) wide furrows forming the outline of the figure are barely recognizable at ground level. The image is simply too long and wide to be seen. However, from 3200 feet (1000 m) up in the air, it appears as a dark, rust-brown contour in the landscape. The dull beige desert soil provides perfect contrast. Goss described the figure as that of a man holding a spear in his hand.

The Australian government is planning to put a toxic waste dump and atomic fuel depot on Aboriginal land. It is thought that the image was created to stop this from taking place.

ALIENS AS AUTHORS OF THE IMAGE

Opinions as to the origins of this image vary widely. The mystery figure has attracted a lot of interest from the international media and speculation about its creator is rife. While some people think it was a prank by the local community to attract tourists to the region, others lean toward paranormal explanations, suggesting it could only be the work of extraterrestrials.

A THIRD THEORY

Atomic bomb tests were carried out by the British in this same south Australian desert between 1953 and 1963, leaving a large part of the land radioactive and many of its indigenous peoples permanently harmed. At that time, the Australian Aborigines, who were not yet recognized as legal citizens, were treated little better than animals. They received the right to social services in 1960 and, two years later, the right to vote, followed by full citizenship in 1967. Since then, the Aborigines have sued the government for 14 million Australian dollars for damages resulting from the atomic bomb testing.

Today, the Australian government is planning to install a toxic waste dump and atomic fuel depot on this land. A communiqué from the Aborigines states:

"You called our land Terra Nullius. But this is not an uninhabited wasteland suited only for mines and atomic waste depots. It is our homeland. The first wave of the invasion brought pastoral agriculture that turned us into refugees within our own land. We have succeeded, despite widespread genocide, in maintaining contact with our land. Today our land is threatened by the world's largest uranium mine, Roxby Downs, and by the planned atomic fuel depot at Billa Kalina, in the Lake Eyre Valley."

An increasingly strong suspicion forms that the image on the ground in the Australian desert was designed to achieve exactly what it has: to bring international attention to the area in order to draw attention to the government's intentions, which might possibly put a stop to the atomic fuel depot and stave off any further ravaging of the land and its people.

The alien theory, however, remains persistent. What the enormous image really means is still a mystery.

Australian police arrest a half-Aborigine woman at a demonstration in favour of land rights for indigenous peoples.

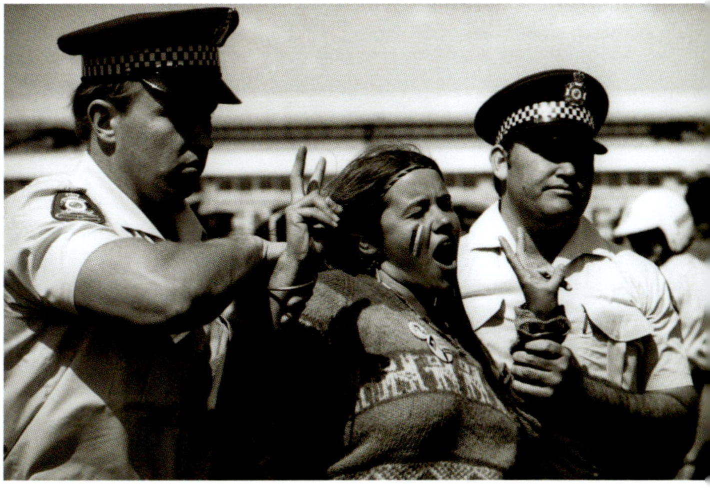

Time Travel

Throughout history there have been accounts of people who spontaneously disappear, only to reappear just as suddenly in a different place. Researchers speak of the different dimensions of time – past, present and future – existing next to each other as parallel universes. Holes in this space-time continuum serve as means of moving back and forth between different places and times. Is controlled time travel also possible? Could H.G. Well's dream of a time machine become reality?

Three cases of time travel

The soldier from Manila

In 1593, in Mexico City, a few soldiers noticed someone new on guard duty wearing a uniform completely different from theirs. When he was questioned, the guard responded that he was following orders and protecting the Governor's Palace in Manila. It had occurred to him that he was not, in fact, standing outside that palace, but orders being orders, he stayed on the job. Manila, however, lies some 11,000 miles (18,000 km) away from Mexico City. The interloper was declared mentally ill and imprisoned. Two months later, the news arrived from Manila that the governor had been assassinated on the very night the mysterious soldier had first popped up in Mexico. Officials in Manila had searched for him in vain, and his disappearance was thought to be related to the assassination. Since the soldier was Spanish, he had been able to communicate with the Mexican soldiers without any great difficulty, although they did remark on his peculiar accent.

The diplomat Benjamin Bathurst

In 1809 Benjamin Bathurst set off from Vienna on an important diplomatic mission to London. At a rest point along his journey he stepped behind his coach and was never seen again. The British blamed the French, claiming they had kidnapped him, but the French government swore that they had nothing to do with it. Mr. Bathurst had disappeared forever.

The 1985 film *Back to the Future*, directed by Robert Zemeckis, is one of the best-known films about time travel.

Time travel

Will it someday be possible to travel to the past or the future through black holes? The answer to this question is simple: time travel is easy; indeed, we already do it, though only in one direction. Philosophers have talked about the time continuum for millennia, comparing time to a river. The problem arises when we want to swim against the current or jump further forward downstream. The ideal is to enable travel through space and time in the desired direction at will. Naturally, this would open up new perspectives.

Insurmountable distances to faraway planets would not be a problem for an alien civilization that commanded time travel. Perhaps enormities like space and time are relative, and the boundaries between them not fixed. Who can say whether or not we will soon be able to travel back into the past to experience how our ancestors lived? Research has uncovered places where there are drawings of equipment and instruments that could not possibly have been known at the time they were made. Some hold aliens responsible, but it is equally possible these images were made by time travelers who journeyed from the present day back to the past to look in on early humankind.

In Montana, the judge August Peck disappeared in front of numerous witnesses while crossing an open field. Up to today no trace of him has ever been found.

Judge August Peck

In September 1880, Judge Augustus Peck from Gallatin, Montana, was visiting with his friend David Lang. Several witnesses were watching him walk across a field when he completely vanished. The people thought he had fallen into a hole, but neither the police nor the fire department could find any trace of him. To this day, no one knows the whereabouts of August Peck.

In 1593, a soldier was given the assignment of guarding the Governor's Palace in Manila, in the Philippines. He disappeared from his post, turning up in Mexico City at the same time.

Electromagnetic disturbances can cause a compass to malfunction – the needle spins back and forth wildly.

What is a solar mass unit?
Astronomical units are used to calculate, categorize and compare the size of heavenly bodies. Thus, while the Earth has been determined to weigh 5.977361×10^{24} kg, the sun, with a weight of 1.9891×10^{30} kg, is referred to as weighing 332,946 Earth masses. A figure of five solar masses, as in the discussion below, is therefore a seriously "astronomical" dimension.

Opposite page: The Tuareg are familiar with a region in the Sahara Desert that they refer to as the "Dunes of No Return". Strangers are warned and urged to avoid setting foot there; they are told they will never return.

Photograph below: German physicist Karl Schwarzschild (1873–1916) invented the term black hole to describe the final stage in the development of a star. As stars die, they collapse in on themselves due to gravity when their core processes shut down.

Twelve areas where travel between dimensions has been observed

In the course of his parascientific investigations, British author Ivan T. Sanderson (1911–1973) has identified twelve zones on Earth where the sudden disappearance of individuals without a trace has been reported; ten are located between 30 and 73 degrees longitude. One is the region of the Tuareg in the Sahara and includes what they have long called the "Dunes of No Return". As long as anyone can remember, strangers have been warned not to go there. Those who do, say the locals, find themselves lost, never to return. Researchers are aware that compasses do not work very well there, and electromagnetic disturbances have been identified.

Sanderson's studies led him to the theory that there are certain points around the world that one can step through and disappear. Some call these black holes, although they are unrelated to the black holes in astronomy. Ever since Einstein, scientists have understood that three-dimensional space and time cannot be considered separate, but instead function as a four-dimensional, space-time continuum. Quantum physicists are convinced that time moves both forward and backward. If science is able to help us decipher these mysterious phenomena, we will have an answer to the question of whether or not time travel is possible.

Black holes

The German physicist Karl Schwarzschild (1873–1916) invented the term "black hole" to describe the final stage in the life span of a star. As their core processes shut down, the stars collapse in on themselves due to the forces of gravity, creating what is referred to as a "gravitational collapse". Some stars that start out quite large will collapse in on themselves until they are very small, but with an extremely high mass. These are called white dwarves. Black holes are what results when neither light nor matter are emitted from a star, and a new space-time continuum is formed. The gravitational forces within a black hole are so enormous that space and time form a Singularity, a ring around a central hole, through which one can theoretically pass from one space and time field to another. Black holes are always the product of stars with an extremely high mass – the lower limit would be around five solar masses.

In addition to stellar black holes, primordial black holes have also been proposed. These have been in place since the birth of the universe and are absolutely enormous, with the mass of perhaps several million suns. They are said to be located at the centre of galaxies, nut there is still no proof that they exist. When a star implodes, time and space are change within the black hole, distorted by gravity and acceleration. Austrian mathematician Kurt Gödel (1906–1978) was convinced of the feasibility of boring a tunnel through time, if only one could adequately deform it first. Until the discovery of black holes, no one knew that this could happen. Theoretically, we are coming closer to this point every day.

Since 1986 mysterious signs and crosses of light have appeared all over the world. Their origin is unknown.

Light Signs and Crosses of Light

Since 1986, a mysterious phenomenon has been reported all over the world. Signs and crosses of light have appeared as if projected on facades, but also shimmering in the air like holograms. The appearances began in the USA, spreading to many other countries. With no identifiable source, a brightly lit cross or other shape suddenly appears from one moment to the next, visible even when the sun is shining, but never at night. No one has yet been able to identify the source of these mysterious lights.

Investigators from all countries are mystified

The light shapes in question will show up from one day to the next, without windows or panes nearby having been manipulated or replaced. After the first incidents in the USA, the phenomenon spread to Canada, Mexico, Germany, France, Slovenia, Australia, New Zealand and as far away as the Philippines. Eyewitnesses have related experiencing feelings of profound awe and peace when looking at the light signs and crosses. There is no plausible scientific hypothesis that proposes to explain them: investigators from all lands are mystified.

Possible explanations

Sceptics have suggested that the "signs" are simply reflections from a nearby windowpane. Speaking against this is that the form of a cross could only be created by horizontal and vertical framing, which itself would not reflect light. Panes can only reflect shapes in their own form: rectangles, squares and circles. In addition, the industrial production of glass produces a slightly wavy surface, and such glass almost never reflects a solid shape. Instead, it reflects diffusely on the wall, as anyone who has lived in a city has had the opportunity to observe. Finally – and this is the most amazing thing about the lights – most of them do not appear in urban areas; often there are no large facades nearby that could have caused a reflection. Physicists have pointed to double-glazing as the culprit. The vacuum between the two panes of glass creates curves that could project a cross. Against this theory is the fact that double-glazing does not typically contain a vacuum, but dry air. Not one of the many theories has succeeded in explaining the phenomena so far, in particular why it is that the lights get larger, as has been observed worldwide. Windowpanes in the affected area have not been replaced. The same ones have been in place for years without bringing about any comparable light effects. And while attempts at explanation fail, the phenomenon spreads ever further, leaving questions as to its origin unanswered.

Signs from aliens or of Christ's return

Currently, light circles and stars are particularly common in southern Germany. Shapes of light appear on facades in downtown Munich as if painted by a ghostly hand. Are these miracles, evidence of aliens, or simply another phenomenon for which scientists have no explanation? Some people, feeling that science has nothing more to contribute, have proposed that these lights are what UFOs really look like, signposts along the road to a new era. Many who have witnessed the light phenomenon report becoming particularly happy and hopeful about the future in its presence, for the cross is a symbol that Christ is near. Faithful Christians, in particular, see it as a sign of Christ's imminent return, convinced they have witnessed a genuine miracle.

In addition to the light crosses, hologram images in the same shape shimmer in the air. Scientists are mystified.

Light shapes on a facade in Berlin. They came from no identifiable source and are not, for example, reflections of windows across the way.

Ball Lightning

Among the many variations of lightning, such as ribbon lightning and sheet lightning, it is ball lightning that is associated with a large number of mysterious stories. Many investigators believe it is only an illusion, but numerous others claim to have witnessed its effects.

The creation of plasma balls in a Japanese laboratory

Lightning is an electrostatic discharge visible as an arc of light, which, although it lasts only a very short time, carries an extremely strong electric current measuring approximately 100,000 volts. Lightning can strike between clouds with different charges or between clouds and the earth. This is why people are advised not to take shelter under trees during a lightning storm, nor should they hide in caves or hold onto metal objects, for fear of being badly injured.

Ball lightning is a mysterious variant of lightning and experts repeatedly deny its existence. They explain it as an optical illusion in which the eyes play tricks. What people are really seeing, they say, is a reflection of normal lightning.

Japanese researchers believe that ball lightning is a kind of ball of plasma, but this theory is doubted because plasma balls climb like hot air balloons and ball lightning does not. The Russian physicist Pyotr Kapitsa thought that ball lightning was an electrostatic discharge taking place in the absence of electrodes, caused by static ultra-short waves of unknown origin, but which in any case form between the Earth and the clouds. New Zealand scientists John Abrahamson and James Dinniss believe that ball lightning is a loosely amalgamated, burning silicon substance created by forked lightning.

Ball lightning lasts up to thirty times longer than other kinds of lightning

According to eyewitnesses, the balls of light are approximately 8 inches (20 cm) in diameter and are seen in many different colours, with green, blue, yellow, orange and red being the most common. This information is drawn entirely from reports given by witnesses. There are almost no photographs of ball lightning and those that do exist are not usable, due to the nature of what is being photographed. Photos of light phenomena are very difficult to take and are rarely conclusive. Most could be pictures of almost anything, and are therefore not acceptable as proof. This makes it difficult to unveil the mystery of ball lightning.

Ball lightning lasts much longer than a normal lightning strike. The balls of lightning hold together for between 1 and 8 seconds, with the record reportedly being a flash that lasted 30 seconds. The bigger and brighter they are, the longer they last, and eyewitnesses claim that distinctly orange and blue balls last longer than those of other colours. Ball lightning can pass right through walls and windows

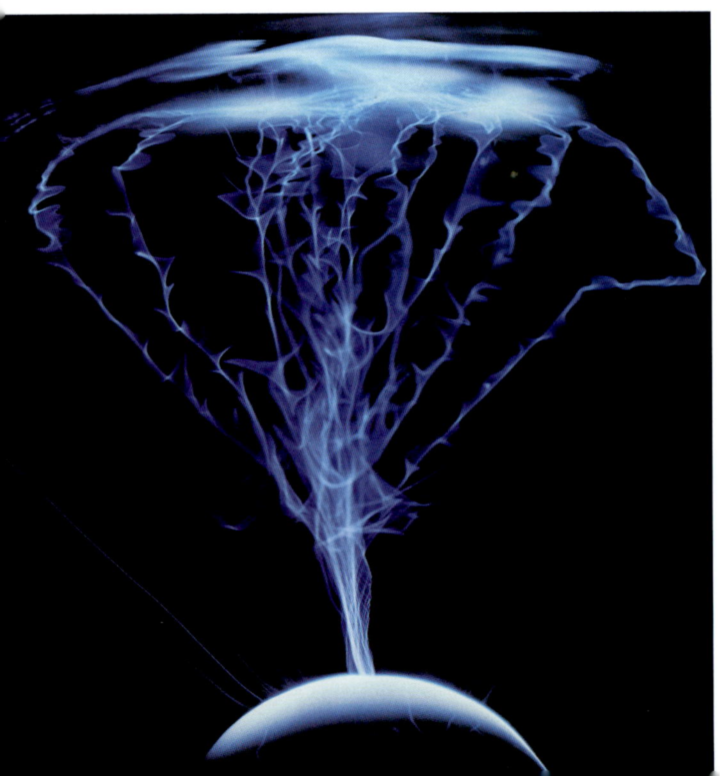

Japanese researchers believe that ball lightning is explained by plasma balls.

An eyewitness report from Brad Jagger

"When I was 9 years old, I was visiting Pittsburgh. In the hotel parking lot I suddenly saw a ball flying toward me that looked like a comet. It seemed to be about the size of a volleyball with a tail of light trailing off it. It came down and grazed my wrist and left a V-shaped burn. The strangest thing about the event was that I remember seeing the ball hit the blacktop and bounce back up into the air. It came down at about a 45 degree angle and bounced up at a 45 degree angle. I am now 36 years old and still have the scar on my wrist." (18)

without leaving any damage behind. They move relatively slowly, at a speed of perhaps 2.2 to 3.3 feet (2–3 m) per second, normally parallel to the ground, but now and then with an occasional jump.

Lightning discharges with enormous force over a city. Some experts believe that ball lightning is an optical illusion that, in reality, is just a reflection of normal lightning.

Energy like that of a glowworm

It was long assumed that ball lightning was exceedingly dangerous, leading to its being connected with phenomena like spontaneous combustion. But in reality, it represents no great danger. As some researchers put it, ball lightning has no more energy than a glowworm. There are even reports of witnesses who pushed a ball of lightning away from them with their bare hands with no ill effects.

Ball lightning has been observed all over the world in every time period. Many scientists do not doubt that it exists, but are still not able to explain it.

Many scientists believe that ball lightning holds energy comparable to that of a glowworm. This means that it is not anywhere near as dangerous as has long been thought.

The Tunguska Event

On 30 June 1908, at 7:14 a.m., an explosion of unimaginable force took place near the stony Tunguska River, a tributary of the Yenisei in Siberia. The explosion had the strength of a 10 to 15 megaton bomb, with some estimates even going as high as 50 megatons, which would be 1150 times as strong as the atomic bomb that was dropped on Hiroshima. One hundred years later, the Tunguska event is still one of the twentieth century's great unresolved puzzles.

A positive result of the meteorite strike

British astrophysicist Fred Hoyle explained the event as the result of a meteorite strike, but it was not until 1927 that an expedition managed to reach the rough terrain of the Tunguska River. They found a scene of utter destruction covering more than 1.5 square acres (6000 m^2) of obliterated forest. Entire herds of reindeer were annihilated and every living thing exterminated. It is thought that the meteorite broke apart in the atmosphere some 6 miles (10 km) above the site, which is why there is no impact crater. The pressure wave uprooted trees over an area of many miles, or the heat released burned them down. The bang of the explosion was as loud as 1000 thunderclaps. Witnesses from the settlement of Vanavara, about 40 miles (65 km) away, reported that it broke all their windows and doors. The pressure wave and glow were observed over 300 miles (500 km) away, and a woman in Huntingtonshire, England, observed the glow on the horizon shortly after midnight. According to Hoyle, on average at least one meteor storm per year passes near the Earth, and meteorite strikes are common. He sees catastrophes like this one as potentially responsible for many other unexplained phenomena on earth, such as the end of the Ice Age or the dinosaurs' extinction. This meteorite strike brought more than destruction; it also helped people. For example, the tremendous heat released turned the forest into a mass of glowing charcoal, which, where ores were present underneath the ground, set off a natural smelting process. The local nomadic tribes collected the melted copper and, because it was still soft, were able to work it in many useful ways.

This photograph taken on 13 February 1929 shows the overwhelming scale of the damage caused by the meteorite strike.

Cliffs on the shore of the Tunguska River in Siberia.

Other theories

Other eyewitnesses say they saw a long object glowing blue-white fall from the sky. A column of light 12 miles (20 km) high rose from the point of impact, topped by the familiar mushroom cloud. Dozens of hypotheses were proposed in the following years. German astrophysicist Wolfgang Kundt was of the opinion that this was a natural gas explosion following the release of perhaps ten million tons of natural gas from a fissure. Rising up into the upper atmosphere, the gas caught fire and exploded. Alternative explanations speak of the proximity of a very small black hole, the crash of an alien spaceship, the presence of antimatter, or the accidental detonation of a nuclear device by a UFO. Only a few hours after the Tunguska Event, a meteorite fell in a Ukrainian village near Kiev, lending strong support to Hoyles' theory. Meteorites tend to fall in clusters around the same time. Almost a hundred years after the mysterious event, with all the facts event well known, and after many years of investigation, there is still no final solution.

Similar incidents

An explosion similar to the one at Tunguska, though 100 times weaker, is thought to have taken place over the Amazon in 1930, as well as a comparable incident in North America during the 1960s. On 9 September 1979, there was an explosion over the South Atlantic that at the time was said to have been an atomic bomb test conducted jointly by Israel and South Africa. Known as the Vela Explosion after the Vela satellite that recorded it, it is still not at all clear that this was in fact an atomic bomb. The satellite could not confirm it as such due to an electrical malfunction. American researchers said it was a strike by a small meteorite. An atomic test, especially with Israeli involvement, could have led to some thorny political problems, suggesting that the American interpretation might be slightly one-sided.

Was a meteorite strike responsible for the catastrophe at Tunguska, which extinguished all life within an area of 1.5 square acres (6000 m^2)?

Rocca di Papa is a small village on Lake Alban in the Latium region about 15 miles (25 km) from Rome. There is a street here where gravity is reversed, so that cars roll "up" the mountains and water does not flow downhill.

Rocca di Papa

Rocca di Papa is a small village on Lake Alban in the Latium region of Italy, some 15 miles (25 km) from Rome. The location raises the question as to whether the laws of nature are universally valid, functioning the same way in all places and all times. Are there places in the world where the laws do not apply, where water flows up a mountain and gravity is reversed?

A bus with thirty passengers rolls up a mountain

A German pastor was eyewitness to the mysterious event in 1992: "Suddenly, the bus came to a halt along the Via dei Laghi while underway from Naples to Florence", he said, "where we had already heard that water could flow uphill. The bus driver stopped at the foot of the hill and put the bus into neutral. Slowly at first, then at normal speed, the excursion bus, with its thirty passengers, started to roll up the hill." A policeman and engineer were also on the bus, both confirming the incomprehensible. They swore there was no trick involved. Are there places in the world where gravity is reversed, where stones do not roll down the hill, but up? Where water flows down one side of the hill, and up the other side? How are we to make our way in an increasingly insecure world when even something as reliable as the phrase "what goes up, must come down" can be called into question? One can always calmly rely on another phrase, as scientists do in their realm of measurements and proofs, namely: "the exception proves the rule".

A stone falls from the ground, water flows up the mountain

Galileo Galilei (1564–1642), Johannes Kepler (1571–1630) and Isaac Newton (1643–1727) recognized and stated the law of gravity, considered the most secure law in the universe. Without it, our world would not exist: its individual parts would fall to pieces. The most constant of basic forces, gravity cannot be influenced by any other force or be reversed. At the same time, it is the most mysterious natural force. Although we sense it daily and its existence is proven in every way, there is still no mathematical theory describing it in a way comparable to all other natural forces. If gravity is reversed, however, if water flows and stones roll uphill, then the force that holds everything together is no longer guaranteed, shaking the basic foundations of the universe.

> *He who will only understand things that can be explained understands very little.*
>
> Marie von Ebner-Eschenbach (1830–1916)

These three photos illustrate an experiment in which a bottle is rolled up the mountain on the street in Rocca di Papa.

Only an optical illusion?

Arriving in the village of Rocca di Papa, one sees a long, straight section of the Via dei Laghi. At first the road declines gently, but then at the halfway point, where the road reaches its lowest point, it begins to ascend. This is where the mysterious section begins, where cars roll up the hill and water flows upward. The geologist Dr. Johannes Fiebag, when asked about this phenomenon, responded:

"If a level shows that what we have there is an upward gradient instead of a downward gradient, then this could be an optical illusion. If what we have is in fact an unexplained gravitational phenomenon, then naturally it would also affect the level. This makes it, in the end, difficult to decide. For the moment we are still confronted with a mystery." (19)

Author Eckard Etzold also explained the phenomenon, suggesting that the apparent anomaly in the gravitational field has a psychological rather than a physical cause. People saw water flow up hill because they believed they saw it. The optical illusion was created by peculiarities of the landscape. However, despite employing both classical and alternative investigative methods, he continued, we are not able to prove one way or the other whether this is an optical illusion or an unexplained phenomenon.

A space flight simulator can reproduce the weightlessness of outer space by reversing gravity. Objects float and do not fall down. Is it possible that there are a number of places on Earth where the law of gravity is reversed?

Sources

(1) Michell, John. *The View over Atlantis.* New York: Bantam, 1983.
(2) Wilhelm, Richard. *The Soul of China.* New York: Harcourt, Brace and Company, 1928.
(3) *San Pio de Pietrocina.* www.padrepio.catholicwebservices.com
(4) Richet, Charles. *Thirty Years of Psychical Research.* Translated by Stanley Debrath. Montana: Kessinger Publishing, 2003.
(5) Beers, Mark, Ed. *Merck Manual of Medical Information.* 2nd ed. New York: Pocket, 2003.
(6) Zaleski, Carol. *Otherworld Journeys: Accounts of Near-Death Experience in Medieval and Modern Times.* New York: Oxford University Press USA, 1987.
(7) Heuvelmans, Bernard. *On the Track of Unknown Animals.* London:
Kegen Paul, 1995.
(8) Raab, Wladislaw. *Unheimliche Begegnungen. Ein Forschungsbericht.* Munich, MG Verlag, 1997.
(9) Keel, John. *The Mothman Prophecies.* New York: Tor Books, 2002.
(10) http://nccam.nih.gov/news/2004/052704.htm
(11) Drossinakos, Christos. *Das Phänomen des Christos Drossinakos.* www.drossinakis.de
(12) *Joao de Deus.* www.staette-der-heilung.de
(13) *Wunder und Phänomenen.* www.diewunderseite.de
(14) Lars A. Fischinger. *Die Götter waren hier! Außerirdische Besucher durch die Jahrtausende.* Leipzig: Bohmeier Verlag, 2002.
(15) Kurzweil, Ray. *The Age of Spiritual Machines.* London: Penguin, 2000.
(16) Crème, Benjamin. *The Great Approach: A New Light and Life for Humanity.* Los Angeles: Share International, 2001.
(17) Temple, Robert K. G. *The Sirius Mystery.* Rochester, Vermont: Inner Traditions Press, 1987.
(18) Beatty, Bill. *Science Hobbyist.* www.amasci.com
(19) Fiebag, Johannes. *Rätsel der Menschheit.* Luxemburg, 1982; *Rätselhafte Vergangenheit.* Gütersloh, 1987; *Das Undenkbare denken. Vom Ursprung des Lebens bis zum Weltuntergang.* Gütersloh, 1987.

Borrmann, Norbert. *Vampirismus.* Munich: Diedrichs, 1999.
Borrmann, Norbert and Christiane. *Lexikon der Monster, Geister und Dämonen.* Cologne: Schwarzkopf und Schwarzkopf, 2001.
Brookesmith, Peter, ed. *When the Impossible Happens: Bizarre Events That Defy Science from Levitation to Spontaneous Human Combustion (The Unexplained).* New York: Harper Collins, 1986.
Charpak, Georges and Broch, Henri. *Debunked! ESP, Telekinesis, and Other Pseudoscience.* Baltimore: Johns Hopkins University Press, 2004.
Cotterell, Arthur. *The Encyclopedia of Mythology: Classical Celtic Norse.* London: Lorenz Books, 2000.
Cox, William. "Precognition: An Analysis." *Journal of the American Society for Psychical Research,* 50 (1956): 99–109.
Derlon, Pierre. *Secrets of the Gypsies.* New York: Ballantine Books, 1977.
Dessoir, Max. *Vom Jenseits der Seele.* Stuttgart: Enke, 1967.
Eisenbud, Jule. *The World of Ted Serios: "Thoughtographic" Studies of an Extraordinary Mind.* Jefferson, NC: McFarland and Company, 1989.
Fiebag, Johannes and Peter. *Zeichen am Himmel. Ufos und Marienerscheinungen.* Berlin: Ullstein, 1997.
Fiebag, Johannes. *Von Aliens entführt. Die 25 spektakulärsten Fälle seit Roswell.* Berlin: Ullstein, 1997.
Fiebag, Johannes. *Das UFO-Syndrom.* Munich: Droemer Knaur, 2001.
Fischinger, Lars A. *Begleiter aus dem Universum.* Lübeck: Bohmeier, 1999.
Frayling, Christopher. *Nightmare: The Birth of Horror.* London: BBC Books, 1996.
Gonzáles, José G. and David Heylen. *Criptozoologia: El enigma de los animales imposibles.* Madrid: EDAF, 2002.
Gööck, Roland. *Die letzten Rätsel dieser Welt.* Augsburg: Bertelsmann, 1994.
Hale, Gill. *Feng Shui.* New Castle, PA: Hermes 2001.
Horn, Roland M. *Gelöste und ungelöste Mysterien der Welt.* Munich: Dr. Bachmeier, 2000.
Horn, Roland M. *Rätselhafte und phantastische Formen des Lebens.* Lübeck: Bohmeier, 2002.
Hoyle, Fred. *Evolution from Space: A Theory of Cosmic Creationism.* New York: Simon and Schuster, 1984.
Jung-Stilling, Johann Heinrich. *Theorie der Geisterkunde.* Nördlingen, 1987.
Kardec, Allan. *Book on Mediums; Or, Guide for Mediums and Invocators.* York Beach, Maine: Weiser Books, 1989.
Kardec, Allan. *The Spirits' Book.* New York: Cosimo Press, 2006.
Messner, Reinhold. *My Quest for the Yeti: Confronting the Himalayas' Deepest Mystery.* London: St. Martin's Griffin, 2001.
Moody, Raymond. *Life After Life.* New York: Bantam, 1975.
Sanderson, Ivan T. *Uninvited Visitors.* Spearman, 1967.
Schreiber, Hermann and Georg. *Geheimbünde.* Augsberg: Bechtermünz Verlag, 1997.
Westwood, Jennifer, ed. *The Atlas Of Mysterious Places: The World's Unexplained Sacred Sites, Symbolic Landscapes, Ancient Cities And Lost Lands.* London: BCA, 1987.

Index

Picture credits

Archiv Christos Drossinakis: 263 (b.)

Archiv Reinhard Habeck: Dr. A. M. Juanéda-Calvier 76, 77 (t.); 79 (b.)

Archiv Ulrich Hellenbrand: 171

Berhorst, Robert (www.berhorst-net.de): 55 (r.)

Brachhausen, Robert (www.rolf-keppler.de): 311 (t.)

Corbis: 2/3 Bettmann, 4 Gianni Dagli Orti, 5 Greenhalf Photography, 6 Parapictures Archiv, 7 Dale O'Dell, 8 Bettmann, 10/11 Gianni Dagli Orti, 12/13 Jason Hawkes, 14 Danny Lehman, 15 Paul C. Pet/zefa (b.), 17 Klaus Hackenberg/zefa (t.), PNC/zefa (b.), 18 Kazuyoshi Nomachi, 19 Paul C. Pet/zefa (t.), Reuters (b.), 20 Randy Faris, 21 Gianni Dagli Orti (t.), Charles & Josette Lenars (b.), 22 Gianni Dagli Orti, 23 Archivo Iconografico, S.A. (t.), Angelo Hornak (b.), 24 Wolfgang Kaehler, 25 Hubert Stadler, 27 Bettmann (b.), 28 Lucidio Studio Inc., 29 Lucidio Studio Inc., 30 Paul Almasy, 31 David Reed (t.), Robert Holmes (b.), 32 Dave Bartruff, 33 Richard T. Nowitz (t.), Vanni Archive (b.), 34 José Fuste Raga/zefa, 35 Hans Georg Roth (t.), Gérard Degeorge (b.), 36 Chris Hellier, 37 Araldo de Luca (t.), Roger Wood (b.), 38 Adam Woolfitt, 39 Hugh Rooney/Eye Ubiquitous (t.), Adam Woolfitt (b.), 40 Adam Woolfitt, 41 John Wilkinson/ Ecoscene (t.), Adam Woolfitt (b.), 42 Roger Ressmeyer, 43 Stapleton Collection (l.), Hulton-Deutsch Collection (r.), 44 Adam Woolfitt, 45 Sandro Vannini, 46 Greenhalf Photography, 47 Sandro Vannini (t.), Cordaiy Photo Library Ltd. (b.), 48 Homer Sykes, 49 Adam Woolfitt (t.), Barry Lewis (b.), 50 Tim Hawkins/Eye Ubiquitous, 51 Greenhalf Photography (t.), Darryl Gill/Eye Ubiquitous (b.), 52 Adam Woolfitt, 53 Felix Zaska (t.), Philippe Giraud (b.), 54 Fridmar Damm/zefa, 55 Wolfgang Meier/zefa (t.), 56 Keren Su, 57 Richard T. Nowitz (t.), James L. Amos (b.), 58 Mark Laricchia, 59 Paul A. Souders, 60 Georgia Lowell, 61 Nevada Wier, 62 J. Balhi/Le Cherche-Midi/Corbis Sygma, 63 J. Balhi/Le Cherche-Midi/Corbis Sygma (t.), Dean Conger (b.), 64 William Manning, 65 Mimmo Jodice (t.), Paul C. Pet/zefa (b.), 66/67 Charles & Josette Lenars, 68 Bettmann, 69 Dave G. Houser/Post-Houserstock (t.), Kevin Schafer (b.), 70 Layne Kennedy (t.), Roman Soumar (b.), 71 Skyscan, 72 Charles & Josette Lenars, 73 Sophie Bassouls/Corbis Sygma (l.), Charles & Josette Lenars (r.), 74 Hulton-Deutsch Collection, 75 Angelo Hornak (l.), David Cumming/Eye Ubiquitous (r.), 84 Bettmann (t.), Terry Whittaker/Frank Lane Picture Agency (b.), 86 Buddy Mays, 87 Bob Krist (t.), Carl & Ann Purcell (b.), 88 Craig Lovell, 89 Bettmann (b.), 92/93 Greenhalf Photography, 94/95 Burstein Collection, 96 Ted Spiegel, 97 Mimmo Jodice (t.), Bettmann (b.), 98 Macduff Everton, 99 Third Eye Images (t.), Bettmann (b.), 100 Kevin Schafer, 101 Massimo Mastrorillo (t.), 102 Bettmann, 103 Bettmann (t.), Chris Hellier (b.), 104 Eliana Aponte/ Reuters, 105 Adam Woolfitt (t.), Staffan Widstrand (b.), 106 Chuck Keeler, Jr., 107 Bettmann (t.), Michael St. Maur Sheil (b.), 108 Hulton-Deutsch Collection, 109 Jonathan Hession/ Touchstone/Bureau L.A. Collections (t.), Richard T. Nowitz (b.), 110 Origlia Franco/ Corbis Sygma, 111 Elio Ciol (t.), Bettmann (b.), 112/113 Hulton-Deutsch Collection, 114 Stefano Bianchetti, 115 Bettmann (t.) (b/w-Stich), David Keaton (b.), 116 John C. Trever, Ph.D./ The Dead Sea Scroll Foundation, Inc., 117 Richard T. Nowitz (t.), Bettmann (b.), 118 Elio Ciol, 119 Brooklyn Museum of Art (t.), Dennis di Cicco (b.), 120 Bettmann, 121 Bettmann (t.), Inst. Optique/Zoko/Corbis Sygma (b.), 122 Inst. Optique/ Zoko/Corbis Sygma (t.), David Lees (b.), 123 Marco Torello/Grazia Neri/Corbis Sygma, 124 Brooklyn Museum of Art, 125 Lynsey Addario (l.), Bettmann (r.), 127 Paul C. Pet/zefa (b.), 128 Matthew Klein (b.), 130 Werner Forman, 131 Elio Ciol (t.), Christie's Images (b.), 132 Layne Kennedy, 133 Michael Nicholson (l.), Bettmann (r.), 134 Hulton-Deutsch Collection (l.), Francis G. Mayer (r.), 135 Christie's Images, 136 Orban Thierry/Corbis Sygma, 137 Reuters (t.), Damir Sagolj/Reuters (b.), 138 Bettmann (l.), Hulton-Deutsch Collection (r.), 139 Alessandro Bianchi/Reuters, 140 Brooklyn Museum of Art, 141 Brooklyn Museum of Art (t.), Mimmo Jodice (b.), 142 Magnus Johansson/ Reuters (t.), Fabian Cevallos/Corbis Sygma (b.), 143 Thierry Orban/Corbis Sygma, 144 Julio Donoso/Corbis Sygma, 145 Michael Boys (t.), Neri Grazia/Corbis Sygma (b.), 146 Bettmann, 147 Stefano Bianchetti (t.), Fine Art Photographic Library (b.), 148 Bettmann, 149 Reuters (t.), Gianni Dagli Orti (b.), 150/151 Bettmann, 152 Massimo Listri, 153 Stapleton Collection (t.), 154 Bettmann, 155 Bettmann, 156 Bettmann (l.), Corbis (r.), 159 Bettmann (t.), 160 Stapleton Collection, 161 Bettmann (t.), Bob Krist (b.), 162 Stapleton Collection, 163 Alberto Pizzoli/Corbis Sygma (t.), The Cover Story (b.), 164 Bettmann (t.), Sven Hagolani/zefa (b.), 165 Strauss/Curtis, 166 Theo Allofs/zefa, 167 Stapleton Collection (t.), Bettmann (b.), 168 Earl & Nazima Kowall (t.), Michael T. Sedam (b.), 169 Claudius/zefa, 170 Joson/zefa, 171 Jon Davies/Jim Reed Photography (t.), 172 Joson/zefa, 173 Aaron Horowitz (t.), Patrick Bennett (b.), 174 Michael & Patricia Fogden (t.), Fernando Camino/Cover (b.), 175 Underwood & Underwood, 176 Leonard de Selva, 177 Bettmann (t.), Jeff Vanuga (b.), 178 Paul Mounce, 179 Dave G. Houser/Post-Houserstock (t.), Bettmann (b.), 180 Bettmann, 181 Historical Picture Archive (t.), Austrian Archives (b.), 182 Keith Dannemiller, 183 Keith Dannemiller (t.), Bettmann (b.), 186/187 Bettmann, 188 Roy McMahon, 190 Bill Varie (t.), 193 Bettmann (b.), 194 Hulton-Deutsch Collection, 200 Bettmann, 201 Archivo Iconografico, S.A. (b.), 203 Bettmann (b.), 204 Bettmann, 208 Bettmann, 210 Bettmann, 211 Hulton-Deutsch Collection (t.), Bettmann (b.), 214 George B. Diebold (t.), Edward Holub (b.), 215 David Lees, 216 Lester Lefkowitz (b.), 217 Bettmann, 218 Sheldan Collins (t.), Elio Ciol (b.), 219 Hulton-Deutsch Collection, 220 Kapoor Baldev/ Sygma (t.), Reuters (b.), 221 Bettmann, 222 Bettmann (t.), Craig Lovell (b.), 223 William Findlay, 224 Earl & Nazima Kowall, 225 Roman Soumar, 226 Felix Ordonez/Reuters, 227 Anders Ryman (t.), Reuters (b.), 228/229 Bettmann, 230 Theo Allofs, 231 Tom Brakefield (t.), 232 Courtesy of Museum of M.D. Mallorca; Ramon Manent (t.), Ladislav Janicek/zefa (b.), 233 Corbis, 234 Buddy Mays, 235 Walter Geiersperger (t.), Stapleton Collection (b.), 236 Charles Philip Cangialosi, 237 Vo Trung Dung/Corbis Sygma (t.), Ralph White (b.), 238 Bettmann, 239 DK Limited (t.), Kevin Schafer (b.), 240 Bettmann, 241 Paul A. Souders (t.), Bettmann (b.), 242 Bettmann, 243 Bettmann (t.), Jason Burke/Eye Ubiquitous, 244 Peter Schouten/National Geographic Society/Reuters, 245 Kevin Schafer (b.), 246 Julie Houck (t.), Leonard de Selva (b.), 248 George D. Lepp, 249 Kevin Schafer (t.), Annie Griffiths Belt (b.), 250 Michael & Patricia Fogden, 251 W. Perry Conway (t.), Richard T. Nowitz (b.), 252 Guy Motil (l.), Darrell Gulin (r.), 253 Ron Watts, 254 Chris Mattison/Frank Lane Picture Agency, 255 Steve Bein (t.), Michael & Patricia Fogden (b.), 256/257 Dale O'Dell, 258/259 Alain Nogues/Corbis Sygma, 260 Ian Bradshaw,

261 Pallava Bagla (t.), Ron Boardman/Frank Lane Picture Agency (b.), 262 Hulton-Deutsch Collection, 263 Roger Ressmeyer (t.), 264 Bettmann, 265 Alain Nogues/ Corbis Sygma (t.), Nik Wheeler (b.), 267 Ragnar Schmuck/zefa (b.), 268 Lindsay Hebberd, 269 Christie's Images (t.), Paul Almasy (b.), 270 Reuters, 271 Chris Rainier (t.), Bettmann (b.), 272 Creasource (l.), Hulton-Deutsch Collection (r.), 273 Bettmann, 274 Chris Collins/zefa, 275 Phil Schermeister (t.), Summerfield Press (b.), 276 Cameron Heryet/MaXx Images Inc./zefa, 277 Frank Bodenmueller/zefa (t.), Robert Llewellyn (b.), 278 M. Thomsen/ zefa (t.), Ronald W. Weir/zefa (b.), 279 Matthias Kulka/zefa, 280 Turbo/zefa, 281 Jose Luis Pelaez, Inc. (t.), Corbis (b.), 282 Bettmann, 283 Angelo Hornak (t.), Corbis (b.), 284/285 Gideon Mendel, 286 G. Baden/zefa, 287 Bettmann (t.), Mark Peterson (b.), 288 Lester V. Bergman (t.), Bettmann (b.), 289 Thom Lang, 290 Envision, 291 Roger Ressmeyer/NASA (t.), Christian Simonpietri/Sygma (b.), 292 Paul Chinn/San Francisco Chronicle, 293 Reuters (t.), Christopher Cormack (b.), 294 Roger Ressmeyer, 295 Peter Adams/zefa (t.), Stapleton Collection (b.), 296 Bettmann (t.), Lawson Wood (b.), 298 Corbis, 299 Penny Tweedie, 300 Corbis Sygma, 301 Danny Lehman (t.), Paul Almasy (b.), 302 William Whitehurst (t.), 302/303 Aaron Horowitz (b.), 303 Jose Fuste Raga (t.), 306 Josh Westrich/zefa, 307 Rob Matheson (t.), Pat Jerrold/Papilio (b.), 308 Bettmann, 309 Wolfgang Kaehler (t.), Denis Scott (b.), 311 Jim Sugar (b.)

Dahmke-Schag, Petra (www.share-berlin.de): 304, 305

Fiebag/Dunkel: 16 (b.)

Fiebag/Eenboom: 81

Fischer-Leitl, Astrid: 101 (b.), 297

Habeck, Reinhard (www.reinhardhabeck.com): 78, 80, 82, 83, 85, 89 (t.)

Hausdorf, Hartwig: 77 (b.)

Ouvarov, Valerij/Hartwig Hausdorf: 90, 91

Parapictures Archiv: 184/185, 189, 190 (b.), 191, 192, 193 (r.), 195, 196, 197, 198, 199, 201 (t.), 202, 203 (t.), 205, 206, 207, 209, 212, 213, 216 (t.l., t.r.)

Ritter, Thomas (www.thomas-ritter-reisen.de): 26, 27 (t.)

Herbert Schöttl/SAFE – Schwitzerland. Arbeitsgemeinschaft für Freie Energie
(safeswiss.org): 314

Schorch, Robert M. / Hartwig Hausdorf: 15 t.

Stempell, Kyra: 128 (t.), 153 (b.), 157, 158, 159 (b.), 231, 245 (t.), 247

Tschirwa, Alexander (www.frankreich-experte.de): 126, 127 (t.), 129

Van de Weijgaert, Rien: 79 (t.)

Wiesli, Beatrix (www.lichtfluss.org): 266, 267 (t.)

This edition published by Parragon Books Ltd in 2014

Parragon Books Ltd
Chartist House
15–17 Trim Street
Bath BA1 1HA, UK
www.parragon.com

Copyright © Parragon Books Ltd 2007–2014

Original edition: ditter.projektagentur Gmbh
Project coordination and picture research: Irina Ditter-Hilkens
Authors: Herbert Genzmer and Ulrich Hellenbrand
Editing: Ulrike Kraus
Internal design: Claudio Martinez
Pack and cover design: Amy Child

English edition produced by: APE Int'l, Richmond, VA
Translation: Dr Maureen Basedow
Editing of English edition: Tammi Reichel

All rights reserved. No part of this publication may be reproduced, stored in a retrieval system or transmitted, in any form or by any means, electronic, mechanical, photocopying, recording or otherwise, without the prior permission of the copyright holder.

ISBN 978-1-4723-7511-7

Printed in China